Colonialism and the Jews in German History

Colonialism and the Jews in German History

From the Middle Ages to the Twentieth Century

Edited by
Stefan Vogt

BLOOMSBURY ACADEMIC
LONDON • NEW YORK • OXFORD • NEW DELHI • SYDNEY

BLOOMSBURY ACADEMIC
Bloomsbury Publishing Plc
50 Bedford Square, London, WC1B 3DP, UK
1385 Broadway, New York, NY 10018, USA
29 Earlsfort Terrace, Dublin 2, Ireland

BLOOMSBURY, BLOOMSBURY ACADEMIC and the Diana logo are trademarks of
Bloomsbury Publishing Plc

First published in Great Britain 2022
Paperback edition first published 2024

Copyright © Stefan Vogt, 2022

Stefan Vogt has asserted his right under the Copyright, Designs and Patents Act, 1988, to
be identified as Editor of this work.

Cover image: Deutsch-Ostafrika, Reise Bernhard Dernburg (© Bundesarchiv)

All rights reserved. No part of this publication may be reproduced or transmitted
in any form or by any means, electronic or mechanical, including photocopying,
recording, or any information storage or retrieval system, without prior
permission in writing from the publishers.

Bloomsbury Publishing Plc does not have any control over, or responsibility for, any
third-party websites referred to or in this book. All internet addresses given in
this book were correct at the time of going to press. The author and publisher regret
any inconvenience caused if addresses have changed or sites have ceased to
exist, but can accept no responsibility for any such changes.

Every effort has been made to trace copyright holders and to obtain their permissions
for the use of copyright material. The publisher apologizes for any errors or omissions
and would be grateful if notified of any corrections that should be incorporated
in future reprints or editions of this book.

A catalogue record for this book is available from the British Library.

A catalog record for this book is available from the Library of Congress.

ISBN: HB: 978-1-3501-5571-8
PB: 978-1-3503-1930-1
ePDF: 978-1-3501-5572-5
eBook: 978-1-3501-5573-2

Typeset by Deanta Global Publishing Services, Chennai, India

To find out more about our authors and books visit www.bloomsbury.com and
sign up for our newsletters.

Contents

List of figures	vii
List of contributors	viii
Acknowledgements	xiii

1   Introduction: Contextualizing German-Jewish history *Stefan Vogt*   1

Part I The precolonial era

2   Antisemitism and colonial racisms: Genealogical
perspectives *Claudia Bruns*   25

3   Sugar island Jews? Jewish colonialism and the rhetoric of 'civic
improvement' in eighteenth-century Germany *Jonathan M. Hess*   56

4   Racism, antisemitism and achievement: Christoph Meiners and his
theory of the nonequivalence of human beings *Felix Axster*   70

5   Boundary as barrier, boundary as bridge: Jewish and Christian
historiography on religious origins in nineteenth-century
Germany *Susannah Heschel*   89

Part II The colonial era

6   The role of antisemitism in German colonial racism *Ulrike Hamann*   113

7   From colonialism to antisemitism and back: Ideological
developments in the Alldeutsche Verband under the
Kaiserreich *Stefan Vogt*   134

8   'Our Dernburg' – 'The New Moses': The German Empire's 'Jewish'
colonial director and the satirical press *Axel Stähler*   156

9   A paradigm for repatriation projects: The African-American and
the Zionist examples and their interrelationship *Mark H. Gelber*   185

vi   *Contents*

Part III The postcolonial era

10 The predicaments of non-nationalist nationalism: The case of Hans
    Kohn, Robert Weltsch and Hannah Arendt *Christian Wiese*   209

11 Colonial revisionism and the Emin Pasha legend in Weimar
    and Nazi Germany *Christian S. Davis*   232

12 Trauma, privilege and adventure in transit: Jewish refugees in Iran
    and India *Atina Grossmann*   253

Bibliography   281
Index of names   302

Figures

2.1	Ebstorf world map, 1290–1300	28
2.2	The apocalyptic peoples 'Gog and Magog' in North-East Asia. Ebstorf world map, 1290–1300	30
2.3	The sons of Noah, Hartmann Schedel, Liber Chronicarum, 1493	39
2.4	Simon Marmion, *mappa mundi*, 1460	41
2.5	Hartmann Schedel, Liber Chronicarum, 1493	42
8.1	Max Slevogt, *Bernhard Dernburg*, 1904	159
8.2	Ludwig Stutz, 'Dernburgs Vortragserfolge', 1907	166
8.3	Hans Gabriel Jentzsch, 'Exzellenz Pascha Ben Dernburg in Neudeutschland', 1907	168
8.4	Ludwig Stutz, 'Die Heimkehr aus Ostafrika', 1907	172
8.5	Gustav Brandt, 'Talmudistischer Marine-Verwaltungs-Unterricht', 1909	175
9.1	Martin R. Delany, 1812–85	194
9.2	Ephraim Moses Lilien, Mose, 1908	199
12.1	Erika and Hasigro on motorcycle in desert, 1939	259
12.2	Erika birthday excursion to Ghan, Fars Province, 1940	260
12.3	Erika on donkey in desert, 1939	261
12.4	Pamphlet documenting meeting of Jewish Relief Association, 1945	269
12.5	From the pamphlet *Hello Chaps! This is BOMBAY*	271

Contributors

Felix Axster is a research associate at the Center for Research on Antisemitism (Technische Universität Berlin) and at the nationwide decentralized Research Institute Social Cohesion. His research interests include history and theory of antisemitism and racism, colonial history, history of labour, media history, and politics and culture of memory. His doctoral research focused on the significance of pictorial postcards for the genesis and circulation of colonial knowledge in the German Empire and its colonies. He is the author of *Koloniales Spektakel in 9 × 14: Bildpostkarten im Deutschen Kaisereich* (transcript, 2014) and, together with Nikolas Lelle, the co-editor of *Deutsche Arbeit: Kritische Perspektiven auf ein ideologisches Selbstbild* (Wallstein, 2018). Currently, he is working on the memory of the reunification and post-transition period, focusing on protests against the liquidation of former GDR enterprises.

Claudia Bruns is Professor for Historical Anthropology and Gender Studies at Humboldt University Berlin. Her research focuses on cultural history of Europe, racism and antisemitism, memory of the Holocaust, history of the body and sexuality, of European borders and boundaries, and postcolonial theory. Publications among others: *Europas Grenzdiskurse seit der Antike: Karten, Körper, Kollektive* (Böhlau, forthcoming), *Wissen – Transfer – Differenz. Transnationale und interdiskursive Verflechtungen von Rassismen ab 1700*, edited together with M. M. Hampf (Wallstein, 2018), Art. 'Rassismus', in *Gender & Wissen. Ein Handbuch der Gender-Theorien*, edited by Christina von Braun and Inge Stefan, 3rd edn (UTB, 2013), 'Politics of Eros: The German "Männerbund" – Discourse between Antifeminism and Anti-Semitism at the Beginning of the 20th Century', in *Masculinity, Senses, and Spirit in German, French and British Culture*, ed. Katherine Faull (Bucknell University Press, 2011).

Christian S. Davis is Associate Professor of History at James Madison University, where he teaches modern German, modern European and world history. He has a PhD from Rutgers University and is the author of *Colonialism, Antisemitism, and Germans of Jewish Descent in Imperial Germany* (University of Michigan Press, 2012). Chapters by Davis appeared in *Modern Antisemitisms in the Peripheries: Europe and Its Colonies 1880-1945* (New Academic Press, 2019) and

German Colonialism in a Global Age (Duke University Press, 2014). Additional work can be found in the *Journal of Colonialism and Colonial History* and *The Leo Baeck Institute Year Book*.

Mark H. Gelber is Professor Emeritus and former director of the Center for Austrian and German Studies at Ben-Gurion University of the Negev in Beer-Sheva, Israel. He has written, edited and co-edited nineteen books and authored some ninety academic essays, book chapters and scientific articles. He has been a visiting professor and honorary guest researcher in Germany, Austria, Belgium, Slovenia, New Zealand, China and the United States. His most recent books include *Jewish Aspects in Avant-Garde. Between Rebellion and Revelation* (co-edited with Sami Sjoberg, De Gruyter, 2017) and *Kafka after Kafka: Dialogical Engagement with His Writings from the Holocaust to Postmodernism* (co-edited with Iris Bruce, Camden House, 2019); Mark Gelber was elected to membership in the Deutsche Akademie für Sprache und Dichtung (Darmstadt) in 2001. In 2018 the Republic of Austria selected him to receive the Austrian Medal of Honor in Science and Art, First Class (Österreichisches Ehrenkreuz für Wissenschaft und Kunst, 1. Klasse). A Festschrift in honour of Mark Gelber, *Wegweiser und Grenzgänger. Studien zur deutsch-jüdischen Kultur- und Literaturgeschichte*, was published in 2018.

Atina Grossmann is Professor of History at the Cooper Union in New York City. She has held fellowships from the Davis Center at Princeton University, the Mandel Center of the United States Holocaust Memorial Museum, the American Academy Berlin, the German Marshall Fund, the American Council of Learned Societies and the National Endowment of the Humanities, as well as guest professorships at Humboldt University Berlin, Friedrich Schiller University Jena and University of Haifa. Relevant publications include *Jews, Germans, and Allies: Close Encounters in Occupied Germany* (Princeton University Press, 2007); *Wege in der Fremde: Deutsch-jüdische Begegnungsgeschichte zwischen New York, Berlin und Teheran* (Wallstein, 2012); and co-editor, *Shelter from the Holocaust: Rethinking Jewish Survival in the Soviet Union* (with Mark Edele and Sheila Fitzpatrick, Wayne State University Press, 2017), *The JDC at 100: A Century of Humanitarianism* (with Avinoam Patt, Linda G. Levi and Maud S. Mandel, Wayne State University Press, 2019) and *Unser Mut: Juden in Europa 1945–48* (with Kata Bohus and others, De Gruyter, 2020) as well as an article in a special issue on 'Confronting Hatred: Neo-Nazism, Antisemitism, and Holocaust Studies Today' in the *Journal of Holocaust Research* (2021). Her current research focuses on 'Trauma, Privilege, and Adventure: German Jewish Refugees in the Orient' as well as the entanglements of family memoir and historical scholarship.

Ulrike Hamann has written her PhD thesis in political sciences/postcolonial studies at Goethe University of Frankfurt am Main. As a fellow of the cluster of excellence 'Normative Orders' she studied and analysed the writings of resistance against German colonial racism during the colonial regime. Her dissertation was published as *Prekäre koloniale Ordnung: Rassistische Konjunkturen im Widerspruch. Deutsches Kolonialregime 1884–1914* (transcript, 2016). She was a postdoctoral researcher at the Berlin Institute of Migration and Integration studies (BIM) at Humboldt University. There she has led several research projects on migration, refugees and housing. She has published on racism, social cohesion and welcoming cultures, neighbourhood studies and super-diversity. She is currently director of the state agency 'Wohnraumversorgung Berlin'.

Susannah Heschel is the Eli M. Black Distinguished Professor and Chair of the Jewish Studies Program at Dartmouth College. She is the author of *Abraham Geiger and the Jewish Jesus, The Aryan Jesus: Christian Theologians and the Bible in Nazi Germany* (University of Chicago Press, 1998) and *Jüdischer Islam: Islam und jüdisch-deutsche Selbstbestimmung* (Matthes & Seitz, 2018), and she and Umar Ryad have just co-edited *The Muslim Reception of European Orientalism* (Routledge, 2018). She has also edited *Moral Grandeur and Spiritual Audacity: Essays of Abraham Joshua Heschel* (Farrar, Straus & Girpux, 2001). She is currently writing a book with Sarah Imhoff, *Jewish Studies and the Woman Question*. She is a Guggenheim Fellow and held fellowships at the National Humanities Center and the Wissenschaftskolleg zu Berlin. She has received four honorary degrees and held research grants from the Ford Foundation and the Carnegie Foundation.

Jonathan M. Hess (1965–2018) was Moses M. and Hannah L. Malkin Distinguished Professor of Jewish History and Culture at the University of North Carolina, where he also served as chair of the Department of Germanic and Slavic Languages and Literatures and director of the Center for Jewish Studies. His prize-winning monographs include *Germans, Jews and the Claims of Modernity* (Yale University Press, 2002), *Middlebrow Literature and the Making of German-Jewish Identity* (Stanford University Press, 2010) and *Deborah and Her Sisters: How One Nineteenth-Century Melodrama and a Host of Celebrated Actresses Put Judaism on the World Stage* (University of Pennsylvania Press, 2018). He was also the co-editor of two collected volumes and the author of numerous scholarly articles in anthologies and journals such as *Eighteenth-Century Studies, German Quarterly, Jewish Quarterly Review, Jewish Social Studies* and *New German Critique*.

Axel Stähler teaches North American Literature and Culture and Literary Theory at the University of Bern and is Honorary Professor of Comparative Literature at the University of Kent. His research interests include modern Jewish writing and intermediality. He has published widely on Anglophone Jewish literature, British Jewish writing, the Holocaust and the convergence of Zionist, racial and colonial discourses in early-twentieth-century German Jewish literature and culture. His most recent publications include *Zionism, the German Empire, and Africa* (De Gruyter, 2018), the award-winning *Edinburgh Companion to Modern Jewish Fiction* (co-edited with David Brauner, Edinburgh University Press, 2015), *Orientalism, Gender, and the Jews* (co-edited with Ulrike Brunotte and Anna-Dorothea Ludewig, De Gruyter, 2015), a special issue of *European Judaism* on *Writing Jews in Contemporary Britain* (co-edited with Sue Vice, 2014) and a monograph on the British Mandate for Palestine and literary constructions of Jewish postcoloniality in Anglophone Jewish writing, *Literarische Konstruktionen jüdischer Postkolonialität: Das britische Palästinamandat in der anglophonen jüdischen Literatur* (Winter, 2009). He is a Leverhulme Research Fellow, currently working on a book project on the representation of the destruction of Jerusalem in nineteenth-century European literature, art and music.

Stefan Vogt is *Wissenschaftlicher Mitarbeiter* and research coordinator at the Martin Buber Chair for Jewish Thought and Philosophy as well as a *Privatdozent* for Modern History at the History Department, both at Goethe University in Frankfurt am Main. He received his PhD in History from the Free University Berlin in 2004 and has previously worked at the University of Amsterdam, at New York University and at Ben-Gurion University of the Negev in Beer-Sheva. His main research areas are German-Jewish history, the history of nationalism and the history of colonialism. He is the author of two monographs, *Subalterne Positionierungen: Der deutsche Zionismus im Feld des Nationalismus in Deutschland, 1890-1933* (Wallstein, 2016) and *Nationaler Sozialismus und Soziale Demokratie: Die sozialdemokratische Junge Rechte 1918-1945* (Dietz, 2006), and of a number of articles on the history of Zionism, German-Jewish history and the history of nationalism and antisemitism. He is also the co-editor of the

xii *Contributors*

volume *Unacknowledged Kinships: Postcolonial Studies and the Historiography of Zionism* (forthcoming).

Christian Wiese holds the Martin Buber Chair for Jewish Thought and Philosophy and is Director of the Buber-Rosenzweig-Institute for Modern and Contemporary Jewish Intellectual and Cultural History at Goethe-University Frankfurt am Main. After receiving his PhD from Goethe-University Frankfurt am Main and his Habilitation from the University of Erfurt, he held guest professorships in Montreal, at Dartmouth College and in Dublin, before he became the director of the Centre for German-Jewish Studies at the University of Sussex (2007–10). He was also a guest professor at the University of Pennsylvania and the ETH Zürich. His main research fields are German-Jewish history, the history of Zionism, modern Jewish religious philosophy, the history of Jewish-Christian relations and the history of antisemitism. Among his many publications are *Challenging Colonial Discourse: Jewish Studies and Protestant Theology in Wilhelmine Germany* (Brill, 2005), *The Life and Thought of Hans Jonas: Jewish Dimensions* (Brandeis University Press, 2007) and *Denken in Zeiten der Gottesfinsternis. Essays zur jüdischen Religionsphilosophie und Ethik nach der Shoah* (Evangelische Verlagsanstalt, 2021). In 2019, he published an edition of the biblical writings of Martin Buber as part of the *Buber-Werkausgabe*.

Acknowledgements

This book is the result of a long conversation between its editor and its authors, as well as other scholars, which took place over the last several years. It emerged from a number of conference sessions at the Annual Conference of the German Studies Association between 2016 and 2019, as well as the workshop *Kolonialismus und Judentum in Deutschland* in Berlin in July 2018. In addition to the authors of the collection, the editor wishes to thank Christine Achinger, Doron Avraham, Ulrike Brunotte, Geoff Eley, Malina Emmerink, Kristin Kopp, Miriam Rürup and Andrew Zimmerman for their thoughtful and inspiring contributions to this conversation.

The conference sessions, as well as the resulting book, grew out of the research project *Der Kolonialismus und die Juden in Deutschland*, funded from 2015 to 2018 by the *Deutsche Forschungsgemeinschaft*. The volume has also been edited within the context of the interdisciplinary LOEWE research project 'Religious Positioning: Modalities und Constellations in Jewish, Christian, and Muslim Contexts' at the Goethe-University Frankfurt am Main and the Justus-Liebig University Gießen, funded by the Hessian Ministry of Science and Art. The Berlin workshop has been made possible by the generous support of the Selma Stern Center for Jewish Studies Berlin Brandenburg, which also hosted it, and the Moses Mendelssohn Center for European Jewish Studies in Potsdam. The editor wishes to thank these institutions for their generosity. At Bloomsbury Academics, the book project was supported from the beginning, and the book was expertly and most kindly convoyed from the first proposals all the way to the printing press, by Laura Reeves, Rhodri Mogford and their colleagues. Their collaboration was not only immensely helpful but also extremely enjoyable. The editor also wishes to thank the Leo Baeck Institute New York for giving permission to reprint Susannah Heschel's Leo Baeck Memorial Lecture as well as Getty Images for providing the cover photo. Last but not least, the editor wishes to express his gratitude to the tremendously professional language editors, Alissa Jones Nelson, Michal Kirschner and Talia Penslar.

We all owe much more than it is possible to express here to one person who was not able to contribute to the book: Jonathan M. Hess. As one of the pioneers of the research on the intersection of German Jewish and German colonial history, he was about to attend the Berlin workshop as keynote speaker when he suddenly and tragically passed away. It was also planned to include an original contribution by Jonathan Hess into this volume. The editor is most grateful to his widow, Beth S. Posner, for agreeing to include his pioneering essay *Sugar Island Jews* instead. This essay, which was written in 1998, represents not only the beginnings of the research in this field, but also of what utimately became Jonathan Hess's life work. The editor also wishes to thank Johns Hopkins University Press for granting the right to reprint the essay. This book is dedicated to the memory of Jonathan M. Hess.

1

Introduction

Contextualizing German-Jewish history

Stefan Vogt

For a long time, the study of Jewish history, and especially of German-Jewish history, has been living a rather solitary life. Across large swathes of the relevant scholarship, it has been separated from general history and from most of its constitutive segments. This is particularly true, and particularly persistent, with regard to the history of colonialism. Although in recent years German-Jewish history has increasingly been considered in connection with other aspects of German history, it is still almost completely segregated from colonial history. Not even the remarkable growth and conceptual development both fields have experienced in the last two decades have had any significant impact on this situation. Nor has the fact that the relations between Jewish and colonial histories are visible in many political constellations and debates, from conflicts in the Middle East to the re-emergence of antisemitism and racism in Europe, altered these circumstances. The isolation of German-Jewish history from colonial history, it seems, is a particularly stubborn variant of the long-standing tradition of isolating German-Jewish history from German history more generally.

Beginning with the *Wissenschaft des Judentums* in the nineteenth century – at a time when neither Jewish scholars nor Jewish topics were admitted to German universities, other than as arguments for Christian hegemony – Jewish history in Germany usually found itself outside or on the margins of established academic institutions. After Nazism had eliminated even these enclaves and expelled or murdered its exponents, Jewish history was practically absent from the post-war academic landscape in Germany. Early initiatives, such as the foundation of the *Germania Judaica* library in Cologne in 1959, originated outside the academy, and it would be almost twenty years before the first tiny institutes for Jewish studies were founded at West German universities. The first generation of scholars who have researched German-Jewish history since the late 1960s – most notably Monika Richarz, Reinhard Rürup and Steffi Jersch-Wenzel – remained an active but small group for three decades. In 1996, the Israeli historian Shulamit Volkov still characterized the situation as 'quite bleak'. She wrote: 'In fact, just as the proponents of the *Wissenschaft des Judentums* did not manage to pave their way into the academic establishment in nineteenth-century Germany, and had to be content with special, separate institutions, so too do the relevant institutions in present-day Germany function outside the mainstream academic world.'[1]

A similar isolation can be detected with regard to the topics and themes studied in the field of German-Jewish history. This is evident, for example, in the fact that many of the major synthesizing studies of German history either relegate Jewish history to a separate chapter or do not address it at all, apart from antisemitism and its consequences.[2] At least until the 1990s, Jewish history was treated as a marginal aspect of German history, in terms of both the amount of scholarly attention it received and its assigned location, which was clearly peripheral.[3] If Jews appeared at all, they were depicted as passive objects of German history – either of emancipation and integration or of antisemitism, exclusion and persecution. Jewish history was largely conceived as part of the history and prehistory of the Holocaust, at the same time when Holocaust studies and the study of antisemitism have themselves only begun to mature into significant topics among German historians.[4] Even the most benevolent scholars usually contented themselves with asking about Jews' 'contribution' to German history and culture, while failing to acknowledge that without Jews, this history and culture would not have emerged or existed in the first place. Jews as agents of German history (or even of Jewish history) were almost non-existent in the scholarly literature.

In the meantime, this situation has changed considerably. Jewish history – and Jewish studies more broadly – now have a stronger institutional basis, and a new generation of scholars of German-Jewish history has emerged.[5] Most of these scholars agree that German-Jewish history has to be seen and studied as an integral part of German history in general, and that Jews were active protagonists in modern German bourgeois society, including its emergence, development and conflicts. Both Jewish and non-Jewish cultures are considered dynamic fields, the borders of which are constantly negotiated and contested.[6] The idea of a Jewish 'contribution' to German history and culture has been replaced by what Steven Aschheim has called 'co-constitution' – that is, the understanding that Jews were actively involved in creating what became modern German society as well as in its developments and transformations.[7] Despite all this, however, true

Introduction

integration has not yet been achieved. Although Jews' co-constitutive role in German history and culture is widely acknowledged, Jewish history is still often disconnected from its various non- or not-only Jewish contexts. A particularly striking example of this is the relationship between Jewish history and the history of colonialism in Germany. Until very recently, these histories have been studied in almost complete isolation from one another.[8]

The reasons for this have as much to do with politics as with scholarship. The debate about the relationship between Jewish history and colonial history is fraught with political implications, many of which relate to the Arab–Israeli conflict. Many scholars of colonial history and postcolonial studies,[9] in their support for the Palestinian side in this conflict, have chosen to identify the Zionist movement and the state of Israel rather simplistically with colonialism.[10] From an opposite, no less simplistic perspective, the study of the relationship between Jewish history and colonial history, regardless of its outcome, is often equated with support for the 'Zionism is colonialism' thesis. This makes it difficult to investigate this relationship at all, as such endeavours are drawn into a conflict between two highly controversial positions.

Moreover, the attempt to contextualize German-Jewish history, especially if this context is the history of colonialism, easily gets mixed up in the debate about the singularity of the Holocaust. This is much more than just an academic debate. The fact that the National Socialist murder of the European Jews was unprecedented in scope and character was not readily accepted in the decades after the Second World War, certainly not in Germany. German acceptance of this fact was the result of a long political struggle, and it has often been called into question since – for example, in the *Historikerstreit* of the 1980s, in Martin Walser's 1998 speech in Paulskirche, in the debates about Germans as victims of the Second World War in the 2000s and most recently by members of the right-wing Alternative für Deutschland party.[11] Thus there is a great sensitivity regarding any tendency to relativize the significance of the Holocaust – and for good reason. However, this sometimes leads to a situation in which any approach which places the Holocaust in the context of a wider perspective provokes disapproval, defamation or even denunciation as antisemitic. Comparative genocide studies, for instance, or research on the continuities between the ideologies and practices of German colonialism on the one hand and Nazism on the other, often become the subject of heated debates. This also affects research on the relationship between German-Jewish history and colonial history more generally. As a result, such research is usually avoided, as scholars shun the unpleasant debates it might evoke.

To be sure, contextualizing German-Jewish history with respect to the history of colonialism is a difficult endeavour. It can easily lead to false conclusions, oversimplifications and the disappearance of particularities. For instance, some scholars have drawn direct lines from the Herero and Nama genocide – perpetrated by colonial Germany in what is today Namibia – to the Nazi Holocaust, thus characterizing the Holocaust as an enlarged version of a colonial atrocity.[12] In addition, antisemitism is often reduced to a mere variant of racism, which ignores both historic and systematic differences between the two ideologies. However, this must not lead us to the conclusion that it is inappropriate to look for continuities between colonialism and Nazism, or for connections between antisemitism and racism. Moreover, it should not prevent us from relating the experiences of German Jews to colonial structures more generally. This collection is based on the premise that it is wholly possible to contextualize German-Jewish history with respect to the history of colonialism in a careful and critical way which avoids these pitfalls and their normative implications. This is especially the case when one looks at empiric cases in which Jewish history and colonial history actually intersected – as the authors in this collection do – rather than discussing this question on a purely theoretical level or short-circuiting different historical periods. In this way, we can study these intersections without losing sight of the peculiarities of Jewish history and the singularity of the Holocaust. At the same time, it is important to break through the deadlock of rejected conversations and tabooed discourses which some of the self-appointed guardians of the singularity thesis try to impose. The goal of this collection is to show that contextualizing German-Jewish history with respect to the history of colonialism in no way minimizes the uniqueness of this history but is in fact the only way to truly appreciate its uniqueness, its significance and its far-reaching implications, which extend well beyond Jewish history itself.

Towards contextualization

Even though it is one of the least-recognized contexts in which German-Jewish history unfolded, colonialism is nevertheless one of the most important, for a number of reasons. The first and most obvious reason is temporal in nature: the peak of German colonialism, and of European colonialism in general, at the end of the nineteenth and beginning of the twentieth centuries coincided with both the zenith of Jewish presence in German society and culture and the transformation of antisemitism into a political force of the first order. Moreover, antisemitism and colonial racism intersect on several levels: in their ideological content – think of the racial semantics of modern antisemitism – in their respective genealogies and in their protagonists and representative organizations. In both the relationship between non-Jewish and Jewish Germans and that between Germans and their colonial 'Others', crucial questions of national identity and belonging were discussed and often decided to the detriment of both the Jews and the colonized. In fact, the Jews were often treated as an internal colonized group in some sense and were sometimes ostracized in similar ways and on similar grounds as non-European peoples in the colonies.[13]

German colonialism has only very belatedly received significant scholarly attention. For quite some time, it was considered an unimportant detail in both German history and colonial history.[14] This situation has changed dramatically. Particularly in the last twenty years, a wealth of research has been undertaken and published on almost all aspects of German colonialism.[15] Following a global trend, cultural-historical perspectives have dominated this research, addressing the biopolitical mechanisms of colonial rule, the role of colonial knowledge or colonialism's repercussions on German culture and society, among other topics. In addition, the scope of the field has expanded greatly – both chronologically, in that it now includes the prehistory of German colonialism in the eighteenth and nineteenth centuries as well as its afterlife following 1918, and geographically, in that it now encompasses territories where colonial penetration was informal or merely desired, such as the Middle East, Latin America and most significantly the European east. Many of these developments seem to invite the scholar to draw connections between German colonial history and German-Jewish history, yet very little has been done in this vein so far.[16]

Historians of German colonialism are not alone in this neglect. In other colonial histories, Jews have largely remained equally absent. In the introduction to their 2017 collection *Colonialism and the Jews*, Ethan Katz, Lisa Leff and Maud Mandel presented a convincing explanation for this: 'Colonial powers and anticolonial nationalists', they argue, 'and later, their historians and theorists relied heavily upon binaries to chart plans for the future and offer observations of the past and the present. The place of Jews in colonial history does not fit neatly into such dichotomous frameworks.'[17] Politically, economically and ideologically, Jews were often positioned either in-between or on both sides of the colonial divide, being at the same time victims and beneficiaries of colonial structures of domination, forms of exploitation and modes of inclusion and exclusion. They never collectively represented an imperialist power but rather suffered from various kinds of antisemitic disparagement, disenfranchisement or even persecution in their respective countries; yet at the same time, they were usually not placed at the bottom of colonial race hierarchies. Jews participated in colonial discourses and politics, but they were also subject to colonial oppression. As a group, but frequently also as individuals, they were part of both colonizing and colonized cultures.[18] This made it difficult to integrate them into the narratives of colonialism and decolonization.

In the years immediately following the Second World War, this difficulty seems to have been less of an obstacle to thinking about the connections between Jewish history – especially the history of the Holocaust – and colonial history. Thinkers such as Hannah Arendt, Aimé Césaire, Jean Améry and W. E. B. Du Bois felt that the Jewish experience was relevant to understanding the colonial condition and vice versa.[19] Even if their respective analyses did not always succeed in avoiding the problems mentioned earlier – Césaire, for instance, tended to equate the Holocaust with the crimes of colonialism rather than relating the two in a nuanced way – their work is nevertheless full of important impulses when it comes to thinking about Jewish and colonial histories as interconnected. In Holocaust studies, these impulses have only been picked up very recently, in what has become known as the discipline's 'colonial turn'. Scholars have begun to look into the dynamics of representations of the Holocaust in colonial and postcolonial settings, the relationship of the Holocaust to other genocides, the relevance of experience documenting and prosecuting Nazi crimes in relation to dealing with atrocities committed in colonial and postcolonial genocides, or the role colonial knowledge played in the establishment of the National Socialist racial state. They have also investigated the itineraries of Jewish refugees from Nazi Germany and Nazi-controlled Europe through colonial and semi-colonial spaces.

Within the historiography of German colonialism, however, Jewish history still appears almost exclusively as a question of whether there is a continuity between colonialism and the Holocaust. Since the early 2000s, historians such as Jürgen Zimmerer have argued that racist ideologies, orders and practices were developed and tested in the German colonies which the Nazis would later adopt and direct at the Jews.[20] In this case, the reference to the Holocaust helped to direct attention to colonial history – especially to the Herero and Nama genocide, which until that time had been practically ignored in both academic and public discourses. Moreover, these studies have established that certain aspects of the genocidal knowledge the Nazis used in their attempt to exterminate the Jews had originally been developed in the colonial context. However, it has also become clear that the road 'from Windhoek to Auschwitz' was a twisted one, with lots of turn-offs and intersections along the way. At times, research has too hastily straightened out this road. More importantly, these studies did not usually consider the possible intersections between colonial history and contemporaneous Jewish history, but rather postulated connections across different historical epochs, which were difficult if not impossible to prove. Nevertheless, these were important steps towards connecting Jewish history – or rather a significant part of it, namely the history of antisemitism and the Holocaust – with colonial history. While these attempts need to be critically re-examined, we should also follow them up with further steps, extending the contact zone in two directions: towards other aspects of colonial history, especially the history of colonialism in metropolitan society, and towards other facets of Jewish history, in which Jews feature not only as victims but also as active protagonists in politics, society and culture.

In scholarship on German-Jewish history, colonialism has been as absent as Jews have been in research on German colonial history. Whereas scholars working on British or French Jewish history have begun to see empire as a crucial framework for their research, thus initiating what is often called the 'imperial turn' in Jewish studies, this framework is still practically non-existent in the German case.[21] The authoritative work on German-Jewish history, for example, the four-volume *German-Jewish History in Modern Times*, makes no note of it.[22] This is true even though a small number of pioneering scholars, some of whom have also contributed to this volume, had already made this connection in the 1990s. Jonathan Hess, for instance, has shown that at the beginning of the nineteenth century, both adversaries and supporters of Jewish emancipation used colonial concepts in their argumentation.[23] Others have analysed the resistance of the *Wissenschaft des Judentums* to Protestant-Christian hegemony and have demonstrated that this struggle adhered to anti-colonial patterns.[24] In addition, scholars have made direct, if complex connections between German Orientalist scholarship, which was developed in no small degree by Jewish scholars, and the colonial projects and imaginations directed at the east.[25] Certain scholars of the history of German Zionism have shown that colonial ideologies and practices were important references for this form of Jewish self-understanding and self-empowerment.[26] Nevertheless, this has not yet amounted to a 'turn' of any kind. Instead, works that study the intersections of German-Jewish and German colonial history remain few and far between.

Only very recently have we seen signs that this situation might change. Again, a number of the authors in this volume are at the forefront of this development. In 2012, Christian Davis published the first monograph explicitly dedicated to the relationship between colonialism and the Jews in German history. In

8   *Colonialism and the Jews in German History*

this study, he looks at the intersections of the colonialist and the antisemitic movements in Wilhelmine Germany, as well as analysing two notable colonial politicians of Jewish descent: Paul Kayser and Bernhard Dernburg, the latter of whom was both the first German colonial secretary and the first head of a German government department who had Jewish ancestors.[27] A few years later, Ulrike Hamann published her study on German colonial racism, in which she analyses the mutual influence between this racism and contemporary German antisemitism for the first time.[28] Meanwhile, Ulrike Brunotte and others have produced two collected volumes which focus on the role of Orientalism in Jewish history, both with a strong emphasis on the German case.[29] The present volume picks up these initiatives and carries them forward. It is also the first to systematically collect studies on the relationship between German-Jewish and German colonial history covering the period from the Middle Ages to the twentieth century. It not only provides a representative, up-to-date picture of this emerging research area – thus complementing the similar, equally pioneering endeavour by Ethan Katz, Lisa Leff and Maud Mandel, which focuses on the British and French cases – but also adds to the existing scholarship and presents new, path-breaking research in this field.[30]

The need to contextualize

Scholarly initiatives to contextualize Jewish history have faced harsh rebukes from authors who fear that such contextualization will deflect scholarly and public attention from antisemitism, relativize the Holocaust and its historic significance and contest the space for remembering the persecution and murder of the Jews. While some of these authors argue on a purely polemical level, others have raised serious concerns. The historian Dan Diner is among those who have voiced a more profound critique of contextualizing approaches.[31] While he sees the need to engage with colonial history and the inhumanity of colonialism, and while he also concedes that it is important to remember these crimes and their victims, he nevertheless strictly rejects historical analysis that connects this with the history of antisemitism and the Holocaust in any way. He argues that the Holocaust followed a completely different logic than colonial violence, as it did not emerge as a consequence of enlightened rationalism, but constituted a fundamental break with it. 'Despite the absoluteness of colonial violence', Diner writes, 'the Holocaust, as pure annihilation, stands beyond war, conflict or hostility. Its violence is not intended to break the peoples' will, nor to enforce anything. Death through annihilation is essentially a death without reason.'[32] Therefore, he argues, universalizing the Holocaust in a way that enables its connection with other, particularly colonial or postcolonial genocides or violence would mean erasing its historic peculiarity. According to Diner and others, the Holocaust and colonialism must also be remembered separately, and there is no way to escape the fact that these memories compete with each other. Finally, in this view, the histories from which the Holocaust and the inhumanities of colonialism emerged are also separate histories. This means it would not make sense to study either the histories of antisemitism and racism or Jewish history and the history of colonialism together. There is a fear that contextualizing Jewish history will obliterate its uniqueness in favour of an unspecific history of minorities and violence.

There is good reason to consider Jewish history – and German-Jewish history in particular – as something unique, and the most salient reason is indeed the Holocaust. The Holocaust was a truly singular attempt to build an entire nation on, and to secure its position of undisputed global hegemony through, the complete extermination of a racially defined group. Even if one does not agree with Diner's thesis that the Holocaust represents a complete break with rationality, the lack of any rational purpose behind the murder of the Jews clearly stands out. Antisemitism also has unique features beyond its manifestation in the Holocaust: antisemitic ideology has the powerful potential to 'explain' practically everything, is capable of transforming a single delusional idea into a comprehensive *Weltanschauung* and is almost limitlessly flexible in its actual manifestations.[33] It works with a very specific set of tropes and semantics, which includes the idea of a Jewish world conspiracy or the inversion of the actual structures of hegemony into the notion that Jews would dominate – or even colonize – non-Jews. Thus antisemitism plays a very distinct, central role in the political and ideological structures of modern societies.[34] However, this cannot be an argument against contextualization. Neither antisemitism nor Jewish history emerged or exist in a historical vacuum. Jewish history may very well be unique, but it is not solitary.[35]

Moreover, there is no reason to assume that contextualization entails dissolving a phenomenon into its context. Rather, it means adding new factors to the interpretation of that phenomenon, thus making it even more unique, while at the same time realizing that this very uniqueness is the result not only of inherent qualities but also of this phenomenon's specific position within larger historical structures. It also entails understanding that the peculiarity of a specific history does not contradict the fact that this history is connected to other histories via numerous ties. For German-Jewish history, this is also the case with respect to the history of colonialism. Recent scholarship has shown that throughout the nineteenth and twentieth centuries, colonialism had an enormous influence on German politics and culture, even if the German colonial empire only lasted for about thirty years. As a major element of German history, it was of course also a major context for German-Jewish history. German Jews were active in various colonial contexts, such as the colonial movement, colonial economics and colonial politics, but also in anti-colonial discourses and practices. Given the social and cultural composition of the Jewish population in Germany, it would be extremely surprising if Jews had not been active in these ways. More importantly, however, colonialism affected the ways in which Jews saw themselves and their position in society, as well as the ways in which they were seen by non-Jewish members of that society. In addition, the position of Jewish people in German society was that of a colonized minority in several respects. For instance, scholarship on and representations of Jewish history had long been considered the domain of Christian theology, very similarly to the ways in which Europeans claimed authority over non-European histories and cultures.[36] Colonialist tropes figured prominently in non-Jewish discourses about Jews, whereas in colonialist discourses, antisemitic tropes were used to make racist discrimination seem plausible and legitimate.

This overlap of colonialist and antisemitic discourses suggests that contextualizing German-Jewish history with respect to the history of colonialism must go beyond recognizing that Jews co-constituted both colonial and anti-colonial ideologies and practices. In fact, there are genealogical and structural relationships between Jewish history and the history of colonialism which need to be explored in order to fully understand these histories. If colonialism is seen not merely as political rule over foreign territory but rather as the establishment of the hegemony of 'the West' over the rest of the world through political, economic and cultural means, in a process which reconfigured western societies as well, then this necessarily co-determined the Jews' position, both in the west and in the rest of the world. For example, colonialism was an important field in which the question of whether Jews belonged to the German nation was discussed, negotiated and contested. It was also the background against which Jews' 'whiteness' was either claimed or rejected. Conversely, if antisemitism played a constitutive role in the development of western modernity, then it must also have structurally affected colonialism. Moreover, the mutual applicability of elements of racist and antisemitic ideology to Jews and to colonial Others shows that these ideologies have developed not only in parallel but also in connection with each other. This is particularly obvious when we consider the period since the end of the nineteenth century, when antisemitism and racism became increasingly radicalized through various interrelated processes. At the same time, the colonial movement and colonial politics were also fields in which some Jews attempted to achieve and consolidate their acceptance into the German national collective at a time when such acceptance was still partly denied to them. Simultaneously, German colonialism could serve as a resource and a reference for German Zionists who prepared the ground for Jewish colonization in Palestine.[37]

Contextualizing German-Jewish history with respect to the history of colonialism not only deepens our understanding of Jewish history and the history of antisemitism; it is also a political necessity, as it can help to overcome the competition and at times outright hostility between struggles against antisemitism and against racism. Seeing German-Jewish history as related to and intertwined with colonial history could be the starting point for a joint effort to criticize, deconstruct and confront these ideologies together, in both their historic and their current manifestations. On an analytical level as well, German-Jewish history addresses fundamental political questions. Connecting it to the context of colonialism can show that the structures of inclusion and exclusion, of minority cultures and politics and of discrimination based on religion, culture or 'race' which characterized German-Jewish history are much more broadly significant than they would be if they affected only the relatively small Jewish segment of German society. Moreover, German-Jewish history – and Jewish history in general – can serve as a specific yet paradigmatic and influential case for the study of some of the most basic tensions and dynamics evident in modern society. This includes questions of identity and belonging, conflicts about equality and difference and the relationship between universalism and particularism.[38]

Contextualizing German-Jewish history, especially when this context is the history of colonialism, is a way of appreciating the full weight of this history while also enabling it to speak to today's social, cultural and political problems. To be sure, Jewish history is also relevant in its own right – not only due to the Holocaust but also to the pervasiveness and aggressiveness of anti-Jewish sentiments, ideologies and politics, and because Jews have played a co-constitutive role in the process of creating modern (and also pre-modern) societies. Nevertheless, this relevance is greatly enhanced when Jewish history is actively related to its historical and political contexts. The chapters in this

12   *Colonialism and the Jews in German History*

book set out to make the case for such an enlarged, enhanced perspective on German-Jewish history.

The chapters

The book is roughly organized in chronological order, beginning with a section on the precolonial era, followed by a section on the period of the German colonial empire and concluding with a section on the postcolonial period after the First World War. This reflects the growing consensus among scholars that colonialism affected German society not just during the roughly thirty years of formal colonial rule but over a much longer period, which began in early modern times (at the latest) and still endures today.[39] Claudia Bruns opens the first section with an inquiry into the historical intersections between anti-Judaism and antisemitism on the one hand, and colonial racism on the other, from the Middle Ages until the advent of the colonial era proper. She argues that anti-Judaic stereotypes developed in connection with other proto-racial discourses that were applied to Saracens, Turks, Mongols and other 'monstrous' people. With particular attention to colonial contact zones, she analyses the extent to which anti-Judaism became important in the formation of colonial racism and how colonial racism in turn became relevant to the transition from anti-Judaism to antisemitism. Felix Axster's chapter focuses on one specific author at the turn of the nineteenth century: the philosopher Christoph Meiners, who developed an influential theory of racial inequality which addressed the status of both Blacks and Jews. This theory, Axster argues, reacts simultaneously to the abolition of slavery and to the emancipation of the Jews during the French Revolution and introduces the concept of 'achievement' (*Leistung*) as a criterion of distinction between 'noble' and 'non-noble races'. In the last chapter in this section, Susannah Heschel explores how Protestant-Christian and Jewish scholarship in the nineteenth century viewed the relationship between these religions in different ways. Whereas Protestant theologians emphasized the dividing quality of the boundaries between Judaism and Christianity, proponents of the *Wissenschaft des Judentums* understood these boundaries as zones of transformation in which central elements of Judaism were retained. She shows that colonialism, and especially the relationship of Christianity and Judaism to Islam, played a crucial role in the development of these different perspectives.

This section also includes a reprint of a groundbreaking essay by the late Jonathan Hess. His 'Sugar Island Jews: Jewish Colonialism and the Rhetoric of

"Civic Improvement" in Eighteenth-Century Germany', which appeared in a literary studies journal in 1998, was one of the first to investigate the intersections between German-Jewish and German colonial history.[40] It analyses foundational texts on Jewish emancipation by Johann David Michaelis and Christian Wilhelm Dohm, who held contrary positions on this issue – Dohm being one of the most famous Christian advocates of emancipation and 'civic improvement' for the Jews, while Michaelis rejected this position. However, Hess argues that when one takes the colonial semantics and intentions of both authors into account, it becomes clear that their visions for Jews' place in German society were not so different after all. Both 'solve' the 'Jewish question' with a programme of colonial expansion: while Michaelis wants to send the German Jews to soon-to-be acquired 'sugar islands' in the Caribbean in order to put them to use as plantation workers, Dohm opts to employ Jews for the project of internal colonization in East Prussia. Hess had planned to contribute an original article to this collection; his untimely death prohibited him from doing so. Reprinting his first article on the relationship between German-Jewish and German colonial history, which basically laid the groundwork for the entire field, is not only intended to bring this important article to the attention of as many readers as possible but also to honour the great scholar who wrote it.

The second section of the book, which deals with the period in which the German Empire possessed its own colonies – that is, from the early 1880s until 1918 – begins with a chapter by Ulrike Hamann in which she investigates the ways in which antisemitism influenced the transformations of racist discourses during that period. Focusing on the lived experiences of those who were affected by the social and political practices resulting from theories of race, rather than on the theories themselves, the chapter investigates how different forms of racism (both discursive and practical) were informed, transformed and radicalized by antisemitism. To this end, she analyses the writings of Black intellectuals in Berlin and archival documents produced by an anti-segregation resistance movement and its opponents. In the subsequent chapter, Stefan Vogt also explores the relationship between racism and antisemitism – in this case, via the ideology and politics of the Pan-German League (Alldeutscher Verband). The League, which developed into one of the most important antisemitic organizations under the Kaiserreich, began life as a colonialist, imperialist pressure group. The chapter reassesses ideological developments in the Pan-German League, particularly the relationship between colonialism and antisemitism, from a perspective which relates both colonialism and antisemitism to the project of constructing national and *völkisch* identity. It shows that the shift in the

League's programmatic emphasis – from colonialism to antisemitism – was not a fundamental ideological transformation but rather a translation of existing ideas from one realm into another. This increasingly radical antisemitism did not replace colonialist ideology but rather expanded and complemented it, fitting all too well into the *völkisch* imperialism which the League had promoted from the very beginning.

While these two chapters follow a more structural approach, the third chapter in this section once again focuses on an individual case in which German-Jewish history and colonial history intersected. Axel Stähler explores the tense interrelation between Jewishness, Germanness and colonialism as it was negotiated in the imperial satirical press's engagement with the figure of the colonial director and later colonial secretary Bernhard Dernburg. The chapter traces Dernburg's representation in satirical magazines across the political spectrum in relation to both perceptions of the German colonial project and constructions of Dernburg's Jewishness. Stähler suggests that Dernburg's perceived Jewishness and his representation as an Oriental outsider were used to critique German colonialism, whereas pro-colonial voices frequently elided his Jewish descent. Finally, Mark Gelber's chapter is dedicated to the mutual perceptions of German-speaking Zionists and proponents of the African-American repatriation movement, most notably Martin Delany. In contrast and in addition to studies which emphasize the colonialist element in Zionist ideology and politics, Gelber suggests that we conceive of modern Zionism in Germany and Central Europe as a repatriation movement, introducing a new perspective on the contextualization of this specific element of German-Jewish history with regard to colonialism. He argues that while colonialism and repatriation are not necessarily mutually exclusive, they should be considered as separate projects with different objectives.

The third section of the book is devoted to Germany's postcolonial history – that is, the period after the First World War and the 1919 Treaty of Versailles, when Germany lost its colonial territories. It begins with Christian Wiese's analysis of anti-colonial notions in the writings of three eminent Jewish thinkers: Hans Kohn, Robert Weltsch, and Hannah Arendt. The chapter explores Kohn's and Arendt's critical reflections on Zionism and investigates the role their perceptions of colonialism played in these critiques. Wiese argues that in all three cases, the idealistic construction of a humanistic nationalism – including its anti-colonial elements – faced the dilemma of a historical crisis that was more powerful than the visions developed after 1918, and then again during and after the Second World War. Christian Davis's chapter examines Emin Pasha's presence in colonial debates in Weimar and Nazi Germany. Born to a Jewish family as Eduard Schnitzer, but known to his contemporaries by his adopted name, Emin Pasha emerged in the late nineteenth century as a hero of Imperial Germany's colonial movement. The chapter examines the positive remembrance of Emin Pasha after the German colonies were lost and the attempts made by the Nazi historian Walter Frank and others to undermine this memory. The reality of German-Jewish participation in the project of empire-building complicated the Nazi instrumentalization of the colonial past, as it appeared to contradict antisemitic stereotypes that painted Jews as unpatriotic and cowardly. Davis traces the emergence of a narrative concerning Jews and the lost colonies that made sense from a Nazi perspective, as it recognized the prominent involvement of men of Jewish descent in the old colonial order but cast Jewish participants as inauthentic German colonizers pursuing a form of colonialism informed by Jewish (rather than Aryan) racial instincts and practices.

In the final chapter, in both this section and the volume, Atina Grossmann adds yet another dimension to the relationship between German-Jewish and German colonial history – one that is encapsulated in her own parents' biography. Her chapter examines the intensely ambivalent and paradoxical experiences, sensibilities and emotions of bourgeois German Jews who found refuge in the 'Orient' of Iran and India after 1933. Drawing on archival sources, memoirs and letters, and an extensive collection of family correspondence and memorabilia from both Iran and India, including an almost daily exchange of letters between her mother in Tehran and her father in various British internment camps in India, Grossmann's chapter probes refugees' understandings of their own unstable position, the changing geopolitical situation and their efforts to come to terms with emerging revelations about the destruction of European Jewry. It shows that the intersection between German-Jewish and German colonial history is not simply an abstract concept but also an empirical fact that directly affected peoples' lives.

It is first and foremost on this empirical level that the chapters in this volume explore this important intersection. They provide the groundwork for a deeper, broader understanding of German-Jewish history and its location in the global histories of Germany and Europe more broadly.

Notes

1   Shulamit Volkov, 'Reflections on German-Jewish Historiography: A Dead End or a New Beginning?', *Leo Baeck Institute Yearbook* 41 (1996): 318. Michael Brenner notes that many of the historians of the first generation were trained by the émigré

scholar Adolf Leschnitzer, who taught as a *Honorarprofessor* – that is, a non-tenured adjunct professor – of Jewish history at the Free University of Berlin. See Michael Brenner, 'Orchideenfach, Modeerscheinung ode rein ganz normales Thema? Zur Vermittlung von jüdischer Geschichte und Kultur an deutschen Universitäten', in *Jüdische Geschichte: Alte Herausforderungen, neue Ansätze*, ed. Eli Bar-Chen and Anthony D. Kauders (München: Utz, 2013), 16.

2 See, for instance, Thomas Nipperdey, *Deutsche Geschichte 1800–1866: Bürgerwelt und starker Staat* (München: Beck, 1983); *Deutsche Geschichte 1866–1918, vol. 1: Arbeitswelt und Bürgergeist* (München: Beck, 1990); *Deutsche Geschichte 1866–1918, vol. 2: Machtstaat vor der Demokratie* (München: Beck, 1992); Hans-Ulrich Wehler, *Deutsche Gesellschaftsgeschichte*, 5 vols. (München: Beck 1987–2008); Heinrich August Winkler, *Der lange Weg nach Westen*, 2 vols. (München: Beck, 2000).

3 Similar observations have been made regarding other national Jewish histories. See, for example, David Feldman, *Englishmen and Jews: Social Relations and Political Culture, 1840–1914* (New Haven: Yale University Press, 1994), 1–17; Sylvie Anne Goldberg, 'On the Margins of French Historiography: Once Again, the History of the Jews', *Shofar* 14, no. 3 (1996): 47–62.

4 For the history of Holocaust studies in West Germany, see Nicolas Berg, *Der Holocaust und die westdeutschen Historiker: Erforschung und Erinnerung* (Göttingen: Wallstein, 2003); *Der Holocaust in der deutschsprachigen Geschichtswissenschaft: Bilanz und Perspektiven*, ed. Michael Brenner and Maximilian Strnad (Göttingen: Wallstein, 2012). On the history of research on antisemitism, see *Antisemitismusforschung in den Wissenschaften*, ed. Werner Bergmann and Mona Körte (Berlin: Metropol, 2004).

5 See, for instance, Stefanie Schüler-Springorum, *Die jüdische Minderheit in Königsberg/Preußen, 1871–1945* (Göttingen: Vandenhoeck & Ruprecht, 1996); Till van Rahden, *Juden und andere Breslauer: Die Beziehungen zwischen Juden, Protestanten und Katholiken in einer deutschen Großstadt von 1860 bis 1925* (Göttingen: Vandenhoeck & Ruprecht, 2000); Ulrich Sieg, *Jüdische Intellektuelle im Ersten Weltkrieg: Kriegserfahrungen, weltanschauliche Debatten und kulturelle Neuentwürfe* (Berlin: Akademie-Verlag, 2001); Simone Lässig, *Jüdische Wege ins Bürgertum: Kulturelles Kapital und sozialer Aufstieg im 19. Jahrhundert* (Göttingen: Vandenhoeck & Ruprecht, 2004); Uffa Jensen, *Gebildete Doppelgänger: Bürgerliche Juden und Protestanten im 19. Jahrhundert* (Göttingen: Vandenhoeck & Ruprecht, 2005); Mirjam Rürup, *Ehrensache: Jüdische Studentenverbindungen an deutschen Universitäten 1886–1937* (Göttingen: Wallstein, 2008); Stefan Vogt, *Subalterne Positionierungen: Der deutsche Zionismus im Feld des Nationalismus in Deutschland, 1890–1933* (Göttingen: Wallstein, 2016).

6 For a good discussion of this, see Samuel Moyn, 'German Jewry and the Question of Identity: Historiography and Theory', *Leo Baeck Institute Yearbook* 41 (1996): 291–308.

7 Steven E. Aschheim, 'German History and German Jewry: Boundaries, Junctions and Interdependence', *Leo Baeck Institute Yearbook* 43 (1998): 315–22.

8 Again, this is not unique to the German case. In the introduction to their recent collection, Ethan Katz, Lisa Leff and Maud Mandel have argued that in European history more generally, 'the subject of Jews and colonialism is hidden in plain sight, more polemicized or avoided than probed, let alone illuminated'. Ethan B. Katz, Lisa Moses Leff and Maud S. Mandel, 'Introduction: Engaging Colonial History and Jewish History', in *Colonialism and the Jews*, ed. Ethan B. Katz, Lisa Moses Leff, and Maud S. Mandel (Bloomington: Indiana University Press, 2017), 1. However, as I will argue further, the German case is particularly blatant.

9 For the academic field, I use the term 'postcolonial' without hyphen. If a hyphen is used, the term refers to the period after decolonization.

10 See, for instance, Ann Laura Stoler, 'By Colonial Design', *Pulse*, 10 September 2010, available online https://pulsemedia.org/2010/09/17/eminent-scholar-ann-stoler-endorses-boycott-of-israel/ (accessed 22 January 2021); Robert E. Young, *Postcolonialism: A Very Short Introduction* (Oxford: Oxford University Press, 2003), 14–16. This is not to say that Zionism is not entangled with colonialism at all. For a more nuanced and complex view of this relationship, see Derek J. Penslar, 'Is Zionism a Colonial Movement?', in *Colonialism and the Jews*, ed. Leff Katz and Mandel, 275–300; Stefan Vogt, 'Zionismus und Weltpolitik: Die Auseinandersetzung der deutschen Zionisten mit dem deutschen Imperialismus und Kolonialismus, 1890–1918', *Zeitschrift für Geschichtswissenschaft* 60 (2012): 596–617.

11 The literature on these debates is vast. See, for example, Ulrich Herbert, 'Der Historikerstreit: Politische, wissenschaftliche, biographische Aspekte', in *Zeitgeschichte als Streitgeschichte: Große Kontroversen seit 1945*, ed. Martin Sabrow, Ralph Jessen and Klaus Große Kracht (München: Beck, 2003); Micha Brumlik, Hajo Funke and Lars Rensmann, *Umkämpftes Vergessen: Walser-Debatte, Holocaust-Mahnmal und neuere deutsche Geschichtspolitik* (Berlin: Das Arabische Buch, 1999); *Germans as Victims: Remembering the Past in Contemporary Germany*, ed. Bill Niven (Houndmills: Palgrave Macmillan, 2006); Gerd Wiegel, *Die Zukunft der Vergangenheit: Konservativer Geschichtsdiskurs und kulturelle Hegemonie* (Köln: PappyRossa, 2001); *Themenheft Geschichtsrevisionismus und Antisemitismus: Wie die Rechten die Geschichte umdeuten*, ed. Bildungsstätte Anne Frank (Frankfurt am Main: Bildungsstätte Anne Frank, 2000).

12 See, for instance, Benjamin Madley, 'From Africa to Auschwitz: How German South West Africa Incubated Ideas and Methods Adopted and Developed by the Nazis in Eastern Europe', *European History Quarterly* 35 (2005): 429–64. It must be added, however, that the majority of scholars working in this field have a much more nuanced understanding of this continuity.

18   *Colonialism and the Jews in German History*

13   This has been recognized, for instance, by Stuart Hall, 'The West and the Rest: Discourse and Power', in *Formations of Modernity*, ed. Stuart Hall and Bram Gieben (Cambridge: Polity Press, 1992), 188.

14   Paradigmatic for this view is Lewis H. Gann, 'Marginal Colonialism: The German Case', in *Germans in the Tropics: Essays in German Colonial History*, ed. Arthur J. Knoll and Lewis H. Gann (New York: Greenwood Press, 1987), 1–38.

15   The literature on German colonial history is now vast. A good overview of the development of the field can be obtained via a number of groundbreaking collections that have appeared since the late 1990s. See *The Imperialist Imagination: German Colonialism and Its Legacies*, ed. Sara Friedrichsmeyer, Sara Lennox and Susanne Zantop (Ann Arbor: University of Michigan Press, 1998); *'Phantasiereiche': Der deutsche Kolonialismus aus kulturgeschichtlicher Perspektive*, ed. Birthe Kundrus (Frankfurt am Main: Campus, 2003); *Das Kaiserreich transnational: Deutschland in der Welt, 1871–1914*, ed. Jürgen Osterhammel and Sebastian Conrad (Göttingen: Vandenhoeck & Ruprecht, 2004); *Germany's Colonial Pasts*, ed. Eric Ames, Marcia Klotz, and Lora Wildenthal (Lincoln: University of Nebraska Press, 2005); *German Colonialism, Visual Culture, and Modern Memory*, ed. Volker M. Langbehn (New York: Routledge, 2010); *German Colonialism and National Identity*, ed. Michael Perraudin and Jürgen Zimmerer (New York: Routledge, 2011); *German Colonialism: Race, the Holocaust, and Postwar Germany*, ed. Volk M. Langbehn and Mohammad Salama (New York: Columbia University Press, 2011); *German Colonialism in a Global Age*, ed. Bradley Naranch and Geoff Eley (Durham: Duke University Press, 2014). For a relatively recent survey of the state of the field, see Ulrike Lindner, 'Neuere Kolonialgeschichte und Postcolonial Studies', *Docupedia Zeitgeschichte*, 15 April 2011, available online: http://docupedia.de/zg/lindner _neuere_kolonialgeschichte_v1_de_2011 (accessed 11 February 2021).

16   It is indicative that none of the major current reference works on German colonial history mentions Jews, Jewish history or antisemitism. See Horst Gründer, *Geschichte der Deutschen Kolonien*, 7th edn (Paderborn: Schöningh, 2018); Winfried Speitkamp, *Deutsche Kolonialgeschichte*, 3rd edn (Stuttgart: Reclam, 2014); Hartmut Pogge von Strandmann, *Imperialismus vom grünen Tisch: Deutsche Kolonialpolitik zwischen wirtschaftlicher Ausbeutung und 'zivilisatorischen' Bemühungen* (Berlin: Links, 2009).

17   Katz et al., 'Introduction', 11.

18   This is particularly obvious in the French colonies in North Africa, where Jews were culturally integrated into the indigenous societies and, at the same time, participated in French culture and education. See Sarah Abrevaya Stein, *Saharan Jews and the Fate of French Algeria* (Chicago: University of Chicago Press, 2014); Joshua Schreier, *Arabs of the Jewish Faith: The Civilizing Mission in Colonial Algeria* (New Brunswick: Rutgers University Press, 2010); Daniel J. Schroeter, *The Sultan's Jew: Morocco and the Sephardic World* (Stanford: Stanford University

Press, 2002). However, it also applies, at least to some degree, to Jews' positions in metropolitan societies. See, for instance, David Feldman, 'The British Empire and the Jews, c. 1900', *History Workshop Journal* 63 (2007): 70–89; Vogt, 'Zionismus und Weltpolitik'.

19 These and other intersections were the topic of two important studies: Michael Rothberg, *Multidirectional Memory: Remembering the Holocaust in the Age of Decolonization* (Stanford: Stanford University Press, 2009); Bryan Cheyette, *Diasporas of the Mind: Jewish and Postcolonial Writing and the Nightmare of History* (New Haven: Yale University Press, 2013).

20 See Jürgen Zimmerer, *Von Windhuk nach Auschwitz?* (Berlin: Lit, 2011), which collects his most important essays on the topic. For a critique of this thesis, see Robert Gerwarth and Stephan Malinowski, 'Der Holocaust als "kolonialer Genozid"?', *Geschichte und Gesellschaft* 33 (2007): 439–66.

21 For studies promoting the 'imperial turn' in British and French Jewish history, see, for example, Feldman, 'The British Empire and the Jews', in *'The Jew' in Late-Victorian and Edwardian Culture: Between the East End and East Africa*, ed. Eitan Bar Yosef and Nadia Valman (Basingstoke: Palgrave Macmillan, 2009); Ronald Schechter, *Obstinate Hebrews: Representations of Jews in France, 1715–1815* (Berkeley: University of California Press, 2003). See also Israel Bartal, *The Jews of Eastern Europe, 1872–1881* (Philadelphia: University of Philadelphia Press, 2005).

22 *German-Jewish History in Modern Times*, ed. Michael A. Meyer, 4 vols. (New York: Columbia University Press, 1996–98). See also, for instance, Shulamit Volkov, *Die Juden in Deutschland, 1780–1918*, 2nd edn (München: Oldenbourg, 2000). This is probably an echo of the belated scholarly engagement with German colonial history more generally.

23 Jonathan M. Hess, *Germans, Jews and the Claims of Modernity* (New Haven: Yale University Press, 2002).

24 Susannah Heschel, 'Revolt of the Colonized: Abraham Geiger's Wissenschaft des Judentums as a Challenge to Christian Hegemony in the Academy', *New German Critique* 77 (1999): 61–85; Christian Wiese, *Challenging Colonial Discourse: Jewish Studies and Protestant Theology in Wilhelmine Germany* (Leiden: Brill, 2005).

25 Suzanne Marchand, *German Orientalism in the Age of Empire* (Cambridge: Cambridge University Press, 2009); John M. Efron, 'Orientalism in the Jewish Historical Gaze', in *Orientalism and the Jews*, ed. Ivan Davidson Kalmar and Derek J. Penslar (Waltham: Brandeis University Press, 2005), 80–93; Sabine Mangold, *Eine 'Weltbürgerliche Wissenschaft': Deutsche Orientalistik im 19. Jahrhundert* (Stuttgart: Steiner, 2004); Achim Rohde, 'Der Innere Orient', *Die Welt des Islams* 45 (2005): 370–411.

26 For pioneering studies, see esp. Paul Mendes-Flohr, 'Fin-de-Siècle Orientalism, the Ostjuden and the Aesthetics of Jewish Self-Affirmation', *Studies in Contemporary Jewry* 1 (1984): 96–139; Derek J. Penslar, *Zionism and Technocracy: The Engineering*

of Jewish Settlement in Palestine, 1870–1918 (Bloomington: Indiana University Press, 1991). See also Etan Bloom, *Arthur Ruppin and the Production of Pre-Israeli Culture* (Leiden: Brill, 2011); Vogt, *Subalterne Positionierungen*; Axel Stähler, *Zionism, the German Empire, and Africa: Jewish Metamorphoses and the Colors of Difference* (Berlin: De Gruyter, 2019). There is a much stronger tradition of relating the history of non-European and especially Palestinian and Israeli Zionisms to the history of colonialism, although some of this scholarship tends to simply equate Zionism with colonialism.

27 Christian S. Davis, *Colonialism, Antisemitism, and Germans of Jewish Descent in Imperial Germany* (Ann Arbor: University of Michigan Press, 2012). Dernburg's father, the national liberal politician Friedrich Dernburg (1833–1911), had converted from Judaism to Protestantism; his mother, Luise Stahl, was a Protestant.

28 Ulrike Hamann, *Prekäre koloniale Ordnung: Rassistische Konjunkturen im Widerspruch. Deutsches Kolonialregime 1884–1914* (Bielefeld: transcript, 2016). See also Claudia Bruns, 'Antisemitism and Colonial Racism: Transnational and Interdiscursive Intersectionality', in *Racisms Made in Germany*, ed. Wulf D. Hund, Christian Koller and Moshe Zimmermann (Berlin: Lit Verlag, 2011), 99–121. An important recent collection analyses this conjunction on a transnational level: *Modern Antisemitism in the Peripheries: Europe and Its Colonies 1880–1945*, ed. Raul Cârstocea and Éva Kovács (Vienna: New Academic Press, 2019).

29 *Orientalism, Gender, and the Jews: Literary and Artistic Transformations of European National Discourses*, ed. Ulrike Brunotte, Anna-Dorothea Ludewig, and Axel Stähler (Berlin: De Gruyter, 2014); *Internal Outsiders – Imagined Orientals? Antisemitism, Colonialism and Modern Constructions of Jewish Identity*, ed. Ulrike Brunotte, Jürgen Mohn, and Christina Späti (Würzburg: Ergon, 2017).

30 See Katz et al., 'Introduction'.

31 See esp. Dan Diner, *Gegenläufige Gedächtnisse: Über Geltung und Wirkung des Holocaust* (Göttingen: Vandenhoeck & Ruprecht, 2007). See also, for example, Steven T. Katz, *The Holocaust and New World Slavery: A Comparative History*, 2 vols. (Cambridge: Cambridge University Press, 2019); Samuel Salzborn, *Globaler Antisemitismus: Eine Spurensuche in den Abgründen der Moderne*, 2nd edn (Weinheim: Beltz Juventa, 2020); Gerwarth and Malinowski, 'Der Holocaust als "kolonialerGenozid"?'.

32 Ibid., 81.

33 On these potentials with respect to antisemitism, see, for instance, *Das 'bewegliche' Vorurteil: Aspekte des internationalen Antisemitismus*, ed. Christina von Braun (Würzburg: Königshausen und Neumann, 2004); Samuel Salzborn, *Antisemitismus als negative Leitidee der Moderne: Sozialwissenschaftliche Theorien im Vergleich* (Frankfurt am Main: Campus, 2010).

34 Important contributions to the analysis of this role include Moishe Postone, 'Anti-Semitism and National Socialism: Notes on the German Reaction to "Holocaust"',

New German Critique 19 (1980): 97–115; Klaus Holz, *Nationaler Antisemitismus: Wissenssoziologie einer Weltanschauung* (Hamburg: Hamburger Edition, 2001).

35 Diner's thesis of an inevitable competition between the memory of the Holocaust and the memory of colonial violence has been challenged by Rothberg, *Multidirectional Memory*, who provides a number of counterexamples. For a good discussion of this controversy, see Felix Axster and Jana König, 'Nachwort: Multidirektionalität in Deutschland', in *Multidirektionale Erinnerung: Holocaustgedenken im Zeitalter der Dekolonisierung*, ed. Michael Rothberg (Berlin: Metropol, 2021), 361–79.

36 See Susannah Heschel, *Abraham Geiger and the Jewish Jesus* (Chicago: University of Chicago Press, 1998); Christian Wiese, 'Struggling for Normality: The Apologetics of Wissenschaft des Judentums as an Anti-colonial Intellectual Revolt against the Protestant Construction of Judaism', in *Towards Normality? Acculturation and Modern German Jewry*, ed. Rainer Liedtke and David Rechter (Tübingen: Mohr Siebeck, 2003), 77–101.

37 A particularly interesting example of both is Otto Warburg, who was president of the World Zionist Organization from 1911 to 1920 and at the same time an active member of the German colonial movement. See Stefan Vogt, 'Zwischen Togo und Tel Aviv: Otto Warburg als Jude und Zionist in der deutschen Kolonialbewegung', *Geschichte in Wissenschaft und Unterricht* 72 (2021): 416–30.

38 For an ambitious attempt to apply this to the colonial and postcolonial world, see Aamir Mufti, *Enlightenment in the Colonies: The Jewish Question and the Crisis of Postcolonial Critique* (Princeton: Princeton University Press, 2007).

39 The groundbreaking work on including the precolonial period in German colonial history is Susanne Zantop, *Colonial Fantasies: Conquest, Family, and Nation in Precolonial Germany, 1770–1870* (Durham: Duke University Press, 1997). For a good study of German postcolonial history, see Britta Schilling, *Postcolonial Germany: Memories of Empire in a Decolonized Nation* (New York: Oxford University Press, 2014).

40 Jonathan M. Hess, 'Sugar Island Jews? Jewish Colonialism and the Rhetoric of "Civic Improvement" in Eighteenth-Century Germany', *Eighteenth-Century Studies* 32 (1998): 92–100.

Part I

The precolonial era

2

Antisemitism and colonial racisms

Genealogical perspectives

Claudia Bruns

European racism since the eighteenth century has often been seen as taking two paradigmatic forms: that of colonial racism, which in the broadest sense can be traced back to the history of slavery and imperial expansion, and that of antisemitism and anti-Judaism, the roots of which are localized in the Christian Middle Ages. Colonial racism seemed to concentrate in western European imperial and maritime powers with a long history of slavery and colonialism, while central and eastern Europe were understood as the 'heartland' of antisemitism.[1] Although influential theorists of racism and antisemitism (e.g. W. E. B. Du Bois, Frantz Fanon, Hannah Arendt) pointed to relevant connections between the two fields of research, these different forms of racism have rarely been analysed in the same perspective since then.[2] Bryan Cheyette provides us with a key reason for this absence: 'disciplinary thinking of all kinds – from nationalism to identity politics to academic specialization' in the aftermath of the Second World War – has 'increasingly separated out these analogous histories' and provoked 'different narratives of cosmopolitanism'.[3] The separate development of Holocaust and postcolonial studies increased this split.[4]

However, if one takes into account that the emergence of modern racism was interwoven with the development of colonial power structures as well as with the long history of anti-Jewish resentment, then the different racisms cannot be regarded as separate phenomena.[5] Rather – beyond a mere comparison, and while affirming the distinctive characteristics of anti-Black, anti-Muslim and anti-Jewish racisms – structural entanglements, interrelationships and processes of translation between them have the potential to enrich our insights into the historical complexity of racisms.

In Germany, the question of the links between antisemitism and colonial racism initially focused on the interpretative framework of the Holocaust.[6] According to Jürgen Zimmerer, the colonial genocide was an 'important source of ideas' for the National Socialists' mass murder of European Jews, contributing significantly to such an 'ultimate breach of taboo'.[7] For Jeffrey Herf, on the other hand, 'radical antisemitism' should not be compared with the anti-Black racism of slavery, because the aims, the intentions and the structures in which perpetrators operated were completely different in each case: 'paranoid' will to destroy on the one hand, 'mere' will to exploit on the other.[8] From a postcolonial perspective, such a privileging of certain motives and state organizational structures was less convincing.[9] Not least those who saw themselves still affected by the consequences of imperial violence demanded that research on colonial racism should be better integrated into comparative genocide research.[10] Holocaust researchers, however, warned that the 'singularity' of National Socialist crimes should not be relativized.[11] The view that antisemitism is interconnected with other forms of racism is still highly disputed in the German public sphere.[12]

This contribution aims to broaden the historical perspective and to strengthen the finding that the development of different forms of colonial racisms was closely related to the anti-Jewish 'proto-racisms'[13] of the Middle Ages. A process of mutual layering and citation of various proto-racisms began even before colonial expansion into the 'New World'. Anti-Judaism, for example, was interwoven from the beginning with proto-racist stereotypes of other groups, such as 'Mongols', 'Goths', 'Huns', 'Saracens' or 'Turks'.

Including premodern forms of racialization in the analysis of the complex history of discursive entanglements between different racisms does not mean to deny significant historical chances, to argue teleologically, or to be unaware of different epistemic frameworks at work in different periods of time.[14] Indeed, the 'alterity' of the Middle Ages and the early modern period is highly significant when it comes to understanding premodern forms of racialization properly. Nevertheless, religion – the most important source of authority in the Middle Ages – not only functioned as an important marker of cultural difference but also produced ascriptions of psychophysical difference, which were essentialized into 'absolute difference' in a cluster of interconnected ways at particular moments in history. Which of these differences were selected for essentialization varied over the *longue durée* – they were sometimes projected onto bodies, physiognomy and somatic attributes in one place; onto cultural practices in another; and onto a 'multiplicity of interlocking discourses elsewhere'.[15] Nonetheless, premodern images and practices of essentialized difference had an enormous impact on the long 'history of race-ing' and should therefore be integrated into our current understanding of how closely interconnected anti-Judaism, antisemitism and colonial racisms really are. Keeping this in mind, we might wish to change our view of history from that of a linear temporality to that of 'a field of dynamic oscillations between ruptures and reinscriptions' and 'of multiple temporalities that are . . . coextant within a particular historical moment'.[16]

Nevertheless, colonial conquest and Christian missionary practices in the early modern period considerably increased the discursive entanglements between (proto-)racisms and significantly contributed to the transfer of elements of religiously based anti-Judaism into colonial racist discourses.[17] The reverse is also true, as I will argue in this chapter: colonial racism – especially in its anti-Black variant, but also in its Orientalizing as well as its primitivist forms – also introduced new logics of justification in the nineteenth century, which would become relevant for the transition from anti-Judaism to antisemitism. Of course, this article cannot address the multiplicity of different levels of racial interrelations at stake, but – by analysing selected iconic artefacts, events and texts – it aims to hint at some crucial (turning) points in the long history of interrelations between anti-Judaism, antisemitism and colonial racisms. In doing this, it concentrates on Christian perspectives on Jews, Muslims and other Others, and therefore also mainly analyses Christian sources, discourses and readings of theological historical texts.

Transforming medieval Jews into 'monstrous others'

People in the Middle Ages had three terms at their disposal to describe the stranger – barbarian, heathen (*paganus*) and monster (*monstra*) – each of which drew different social boundaries. The term 'barbarian' referred to the linguistic foreigner, 'pagan' referred to the religious other and 'monster' primarily referred to a level of physical difference, but also to sexually and religiously deviant practices.[18] A certain combination of physical and cultural markers of deviance, which developed in the discourse around the 'monster', supposedly condensed into a proto-racist discursive pattern that was incorporated into anti-Judaism. As I would like to show, certain proto-racisms circulated back and forth between those others identified as 'monstrous', who were sometimes called Mongols; sometimes Huns, Goths or Saracens; but gradually – and above all – Jews.

Medieval maps of the world, the *mappae mundi* (see Figure 2.1), provide a particularly striking source in which to observe the processes by which

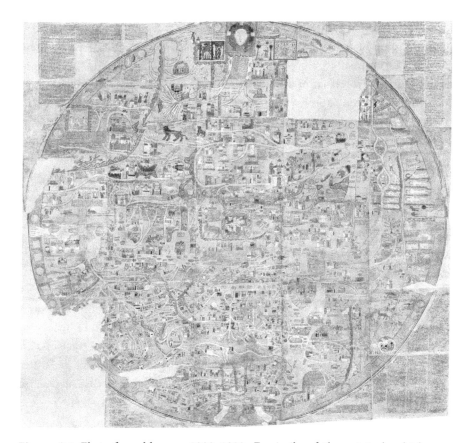

Figure 2.1 Ebstorf world map, 1290–1300. Facsimile of the original, which was destroyed in 1943. © Public Domain.

proto-racist patterns were superimposed and condensed, because such maps were used by Christian monks not so much to convey geographical orientation as to capture the entirety of their global knowledge in a structure of symbolic ordering.

The stranger the figure, the further away from the one's own (Christian) society it was placed on the map.[19] Thus in the *mappae mundi*, one frequently sees physically deformed, monstrous creatures located in border regions, locked in boxes (see the right-hand margin of Figure 2.1). Monsters were considered to be extreme creatures, those that deviated from the ideal of temperance and moderation, which was considered virtuous. They gave rise to theological questions, such as how they could be integrated into one's own *ordo* according to the rules of hermeneutics, whether they belonged to the *genus humanum* at all and whether or to what extent they were 'redeemable'.[20] These questions were later discussed in a similar way in relation to the inhabitants of the 'New World'. The existence of monstrous beings could either be read as a cautionary counter-image to the well-ordered creation, or it could indicate God's freedom to create whatever he wants.[21] Creation theology had a hard time simply excluding peripheral peoples. For Augustine, the *monstra* were part of the incomprehensible beauty of the universe and should therefore by no means be called 'ugly'.[22] He thus rejected Gnostic Manichaeism's dualistic image of God.[23] These theological controversies surrounding the status of the *monstra* are also reflected in their ambivalent depictions on world maps.

The Ebstorf world map, which was created in northern Germany around 1300, shows the apocalyptic peoples 'Gog and Magog' in the far north-east (*mappae mundi* were oriented to the east, therefore the north-east is located in the upper-left corner). The names 'Gog' and 'Magog' (Gog was initially said to stem 'from the land of Magog' and was later supplemented with a second people called 'Magog') are found in the Tanakh, in the Old Testament, in the Pseudepigrapha and the Qumran writings, in the targums and in other Jewish texts, in the New Testament, in the writings of the Church Fathers and in the Qur'an. In increasingly different but entangled ways, Gog and Magog constitute important figures in the eschatological settings and apocalyptic traditions of all three monotheistic religions.[24]

According to the prophecy of the Book of Ezekiel, God promises to bring back the scattered people of Israel to the land of their forefathers and unite them under the rule of King David. But, on a 'distant day', Gog, coming from the north and accompanied by various allies, will attack and plunder the land of Israel. This fierce invasion arouses the anger of God (or of the Messiah) who, finally, destroys the invader's armies and executes his judgments on them 'with plague and bloodshed'. Fire and brimstone fall from the sky, and the earth shakes (Ezek. 38-39). These 'wars of Gog and Magog', as the prophecy was called in later sources, are part of the assumption that the messianic age will be preceded by a period of great turmoil and suffering.[25] The belief in the messianic future was not a major issue in ancient rabbinic sources. Nevertheless, medieval and early modern Jewish writers developed the character of Gog and Magog 'in various nuanced ways' to represent antagonistic political entities that will play a leading role in the eschatological battles.[26]

Latin Christianity's hermeneutics of these eschatological events, although based on the Jewish tradition, became more starkly apocalyptic. They made Gog and Magog allies of 'Satan', the Antichrist, coming from the 'four corners of the earth' to fight against God in a gruesome final battle at the end of the millennium. This is described in the *Book of Revelation* (Rev. 20:7-8) – the so-called *Apocalypse of John*, the final book of the New Testament, which strongly stimulated the Christian eschatological imagination and can be understood as an allegory of the spiritual path and the struggle between good and evil. God would ultimately win this combat against the Antichrist, and the kingdom of God would dawn. Thus, the appearance of Gog and Magog was both feared and longed for because it was seen as a necessary part of humanity's final redemption.

This Christian version of the legend of Gog and Magog was further popularized when it was combined (at the latest around 700 CE, with the influential Revelations of Pseudo-Methodius) with the cycle of legends in the Epic of Alexander the Great, who is said to have locked up horrific peoples behind thick walls and depicted them as cannibals.[27] The Ebstorf map accordingly depicted Gog and Magog as man-eating *monstra* (see Figure 2.2): two of them sitting next to each other, naked, gleefully eating the limbs of a third person with light hair, who lies bleeding between them (see Figure 2.2).

As *monstra*, Gog and Magog were 'not only located on the border of the *ordo orbis*', as Marina Münkler points out, but temporally 'they constituted the border between the expulsion of the human race from earthly paradise to *eschaton*; spatially they marked the border of ecumenism in the north (as well as south and east); morally-theologically they constituted the boundary between the

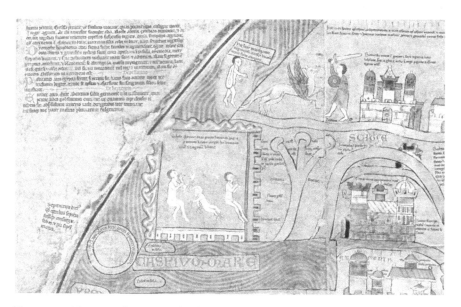

Figure 2.2 The apocalyptic peoples 'Gog and Magog' in North-East Asia. Detail of the Ebstorf world map, 1290–1300. Facsimile of the original. © Public Domain.

redeemable and the damnable; and anthropologically they designated the limits of the *genus humanum*.[28]

Although some influential theologians such as Augustine (354–430) refused to see the prophetical passages as a mirror of history and emphasized the symbolic significance of Gog and Magog as people 'led by the Devil', apocalyptic peoples soon served as a psychological projection for all those groups that were perceived as threatening and as not belonging to one's own group.[29] Early Christian scholars such as Eusebius (260/264–339/340) identified them with the Romans. Ambrose, the Bishop of Milan (339–397), linked Gog to the 'barbaric' peoples within Europe, such as the Goths, an association that can also be found in rabbinic texts.[30] Hieronymus (340–420) associated Gog and Magog historically with the Huns or Scythians (and eschatologically with the Antichrist).[31] Jews in the fourth century thought of Magog as the land of the ancient Teutons, the fierce enemies of Rome.

In the Middle Ages, the famous French exegete Rashi (Rabbi Shlomo Yitzhaki, 1040–1105), paradigmatic master of medieval rabbinic commentary, identified 'Christians (whom he designates "Esau," per established rabbinic tradition) as allies of Gog and Magog in the final eschatological battle against Israel'.[32] Rabbi David Kimchi (1160–1235) claimed that the names Gog and Magog referred to the Christians and the Turks, who at that time were perceived as the major threats to Jewish life and religion.[33] Even in the Tartar-Mongols, who unexpectedly invaded Europe around 1240, both Jews and Christians believed they recognized the peoples of 'Gog and Magog'.[34] After all, Christians and Jews had expected the arrival of the end times in that year and had been partly tormented and partly consoled by these apocalyptic expectations.[35] Christians soon began to assume that Jews were either in league with the Tartar-Mongols or were themselves behind the raids. Thus, the rumour circulated that Jews had secretly supported the invaders with armaments and wine.[36]

For their part, Jews assumed that the invading Mongols constituted the 'lost Tribes of Israel', who had come to 'liberate' the 'children of Israel from captivity' and Christian oppression.[37] Legend has it that those were the Ten of the Twelve Tribes of Israel that had been exiled from the Kingdom of Israel after its conquest by the Neo-Assyrian Empire *c.* 722 BCE.[38] The Ten Tribes traditionally played a role in Jewish apocalyptic thought, one that was 'almost identical to their function in the medieval Christian version of the dramatic events of the Last Days'.[39] The rabbinical sources that emerged after the destruction of the Second Temple were already expecting these strong warriors, led by the Messiah ben Joseph (Ephraim), to free Israel from the yoke of Edom – that is, Rome, which was later equated with Christianity.[40]

32   *Colonialism and the Jews in German History*

This connection between the apocalyptic peoples and the 'lost Jews', however, was also adopted by Christians (especially in Germany) and loaded with negative connotations – first and foremost in Petrus Comestor's (1100–78) influential *Historia scholastica*. The *Saxon chronicle* of Eike von Repgow from the early thirteenth century and the popular fictional travel account by John Mandeville also prove that the 'Ten lost Tribes of Israel' were identified with the 'enclosed peoples' of Gog and Magog as threatening Others.[41] In German literature, where the legend was more intensely anti-Jewish than elsewhere in medieval Christian Europe, the Ten Tribes were given a distinctive colouring.[42] Here the gradual fusion of the three legends – the stories of Gog and Magog, Alexander the Great and the Ten Tribes – gave rise to the powerful myth of the 'Red Jews': supposedly evil, savage, physically repulsive, 'unclean' pillagers who were waiting in the east for the Last Judgment and the arrival of the Antichrist to break out of their prisons and set out against Christianity.[43] Thus 'Gog and Magog' became ever more clearly associated with Judaism, which became the 'negatively charged antonym' of *christianitas*.[44] Some evidence from sources written by those who converted to Christianity in the sixteenth century indicates that Jews, for their part, later began to identify with the 'mighty Red Jews' and believed in the existence of a 'Jewish kingdom in the Caspian Mountains'. According to Rebekka Voß, the name 'Red Jews' even became a 'common expression for the Ten Tribes among the Jews of Central Europe', which also indicates that Jews were interacting dynamically with neighbouring cultures.[45]

Nonetheless, Latin Christendom's identification of Jews with the cannibalistic practices of end-times peoples also reflected the gradually deteriorating position of Jews in Christian-majority society. Every new wave of crusades to Palestine was accompanied by violent riots against Jews. But it was not until the Fourth Lateran Council (1215) that the church introduced momentous demarcations between Jews and Christians; from then on, Jews (and Muslims) were officially required to dress differently and to identify themselves by wearing badges, although this law was not enforced everywhere in the same way and actual practices varied. In the long run, the exclusion of Jews from guilds and from many professions was extraordinarily consequential for Jewish-Christian relations and led to numerous tensions. Around 1300, Jews were expelled from England and France. In 1348 and 1350, when the plague broke out in Europe, the Jewish populations in over two hundred German towns were murdered, often for poorly concealed economic or political reasons, in the wake of the widespread fear of the plague.[46] The pretexts for this were accusations of poisoning wells, desecrating the Host or 'Blood Libel' charges. Such charges asserted that Jews sought to obtain 'Christian blood' for religious or medical purposes, or even ate the hearts of murdered children on Passover.[47] In addition, stimulated by crusaders' reports on the 'secret rituals of the (Muslim) infidels', ritual cannibalism had become an integral part of anti-Jewish accusations since the 'Fulda case' in 1235.[48] It was in the aftermath of these developments that the Ebstorf world map was created, depicting the end-times peoples of Gog and Magog as anthropophagic – the same peoples whom legends and popular exegesis identified with the horrific 'enclosed Jews' (*iudei inclusi*). Even on Martin Waldseemüller's maps of America in 1507, 'enclosed Jews' can still be found behind high mountains in the far north-east. It was not until the 1580s that they disappeared from cartographic representations, together with Gog and Magog.

While *monstra* could initially be assigned a meaningful function in the Christian cosmos, the identification of the apocalyptic nations with Jews developed in parallel with their increasing repudiation and condemnation. Religious otherness was combined with an essential otherness and linked to spatial and social segregation. At the same time, the rather fluid chain of 'deviants', all of whom were fixed in a similar pattern of difference, formed a discursive fabric that was mutually authenticating and reinforcing.[49]

Transferring anti-Jewish stereotypes into the missionary-colonial context

The identification of Gog and Magog with the Jews at the edge of the world lived on in the minds of North American settlers for a long time and called up ideas of the Hebrew descendants of the First Nations.[50] The Scottish theologian John Major, who taught in Paris, wrote in 1510 that depictions of wild animals and *monstra* seen on Ptolemaic maps had now been proven by 'experience'. Even on a very practical level of colonial conquest, Columbus considered his overseas military operation a direct continuation of the violent expulsion of Jews from the Iberian Peninsula.[51] European Christian demonology, as Ella Shohat has noted, prefigured colonial racism and similar *conquista* practices across the Atlantic.[52]

Judaism soon served 'as a template to describe foreigners and define the nature of non-Christians' not only in medieval Europe but also in the colonies. This is amply illustrated by the Protestant missionary literature of the sixteenth and seventeenth centuries.[53] Although the Puritan settlers of New England identified strongly with 'Old Israel', they saw themselves simultaneously 'as the better Jews and the only true Christians'.[54] By traversing the 'condition of wilderness', they sought to attain spiritual purity and to create a 'second Eden'.[55] For them, First Nations peoples constituted a kind of mirror image: supposedly without religion of their own, they nevertheless stemmed from 'ancient Israel' and, as was often assumed, the 'Ten lost Tribes'.[56] In the settlers' millenarian theology, Native Americans consequently played an important role for the renewed dawning of the kingdom of God.

According to the legend of the Ten lost Tribes, Jews were supposed to appear in every corner of the world before the Messiah's second coming, and so Christians tended to see them everywhere and even invented them in the most remote regions in order to hasten the 'second coming'. Thus the French missionary Josef Lafitous Moeurs, for example, drew parallels between Jewish and ancient Greek religion and the religious system of the Iroquois. Even the colonization of the Pacific was accompanied by speculations about the 'long-lost Jewish tribes'. And as late as 1800, missionaries in China and India were still 'discovering' people with Israelite roots.[57] When the Puritans first began to settle in New England, they predominantly viewed Native Americans as 'noble savages' who needed to be led to the 'right path' of Christian faith. In their eyes, these Jewish tribes, 'lost in the wilderness', initially remained relatively innocent compared to contemporary European Jewry, since they had never known Christ and therefore could not be accused of having killed him.[58]

Nevertheless, this identification with the Ten lost Tribes had ambivalent implications for the 'American Indians'. Their philosemitic idealization could easily turn into fierce rejection, which again referred back to older anti-Jewish stereotypes. It was the Pequot War (1636–8) which ended the relatively peaceful coexistence between the Pequot people and the New England settlers.[59] As the expanded 'mission to the Indians' did not meet the Puritans' high expectations and social tensions within the settler community came to the fore, King Philip's War – also known as the Great Indian War – in 1675 led to the rise of the older proto-racist notion of the 'wild' and 'primitive' origins of the 'American Indians'.[60] Anti-Jewish stereotypes were increasingly projected onto the 'Indians', who from then on were more clearly identified with Gog and Magog as cruel, threatening, apocalyptic destroyers.[61] Thus the demonizing variant of the Ten lost Tribes theory rose to the surface once again.[62]

Similar lines of reasoning can be discerned in other colonized parts of the world, as Tudor Parfitt has demonstrated. For example, the supposedly negative characteristics of the Khoi Khoi (the so-called 'Hottentots'), whose status as members of the *genus humanum* was called into question, were also attributed to their alleged Jewish heritage.[63] In 1612, Patrick Copland claimed to have observed similarities between Khoi Khoi and Jewish rites,[64] an observation which the German South African scholar Peter Kolb (1675–1726) confirmed as late as 1700.[65] And the threatening military successes of the Maori in New Zealand were explained with reference to their supposedly Jewish ancestry and some striking similarities in trade practices and language, as Parfitt has shown.[66] The British missionaries, who mainly came from the lower middle class, were familiar with few texts apart from the Holy Scriptures or the ancient classics, which they used to decipher unknown territories and their inhabitants.[67] Accordingly, the biblical image of the Jew, however ambivalently interpreted, was often used to explain the appearance or behaviour of foreign or unfamiliar groups.[68] The 'invented identity of a *known* other' was imposed on unknown (colonized) peoples.[69] This way of seeing colonized people as 'Jewish' transferred deeply ambivalent character attributions from medieval and early modern religious contexts into the modern era, thus becoming an integral part of the colonial racialization process.

At the beginning of the nineteenth century, certain allegedly Jewish racial characteristics were still being derived from an assumed similarity between Jewish and colonized groups. The English schoolmaster and historian John Bigland (1750–1832), who summarized the common philosophical positions on the category of 'race' for a wider readership, described the case of an Englishman who, in his first contact with the Indian Kashmiris, was extremely surprised because to them they looked so similar to the Jews – so much so that he immediately believed he had been transferred to a 'nation of Jews'.[70] For Bigland, this case served as evidence that Jews could maintain their appearance (especially their fair skin) over long periods of time and despite reproductive links with native peoples. References to the colonial context therefore played an important role in the racialization of European Jews.

Conversely, anti-Jewish stereotypes in European Enlightenment circles were legitimized by resorting not only to religious arguments but also to colonial discourse. As the philosopher Voltaire informed his educated French readership in a 1764 encyclopaedia article, Jews had not only made 'human sacrifices' but had themselves been 'cannibals', similar to the 'Tentirytes' in Egypt, the 'Gascons', the 'Saguntines' and so-called 'savages' from the Mississippi region. But Jews were inferior even to these 'savages', because they offered 'human sacrifices (especially young women) without economic necessity'.[71]

The equation of Jews with 'savages' was associated with a division into 'good' past Jews and 'bad' present Jews.[72] In the eighteenth century, the colonized were located not only in other places but also in other eras. Thus, at the end of the nineteenth century, German colonialists such as Carl Peters, Karl Mauch and Leo Frobenius were able to use the idea of the 'noble Jew' of the past to valorize certain indigenous groups (who were to be won as allies), and at the same time to propagate the antisemitic version of the 'dirty, money-greedy Jew' of the present. Carl Peters wrote the following about a people group adjacent to Rhodesia:

> How absolutely Jewish is the type of this people! They have faces cut exactly like those of ancient Jews who live around Eden. And the way they wear their hair, the curls behind the ears, and the beard drawn out in single curls, gives them the appearance of Aden – or of Polish – Jews of the good old type.[73]

The description of Jews as 'noble savages' from a submerged, historic age correlated with the trend towards the valorization of 'young nations' and a 'cult of the primitive' within Europe.[74] Whereas the philosopher David Hume had placed the Barbarian Germanic tribes on the lowest level of the inner-European 'racial hierarchy', following Christoph Meiner's publications, Germans could regard themselves as the 'epitome of European civilization' precisely because of their 'primitive' powers.[75]

Intersections between anti-Jewish and anti-Muslim discourses

Similarly to the development of primitivist-colonial racism, the differentiation between Christians and Muslims in the Saracen period, which extended into the fourteenth century, developed from the outset on the basis of Christian perceptions of Jews.[76] First and foremost, the Byzantines, who were under pressure from Islamic invasions, contributed to the negative stereotyping of Muslims by spreading horror stories about them – not least because they expected this would improve their chances of receiving military support from Latin Christendom. Among these were a number of stereotypes borrowed from anti-Jewish ideas: from Muslims allegedly denying Christians access to the holy sites to reports of church desecration, rape and accusations of ritual infanticide and cannibalistic practices. Also in religious terms, there seemed to be some similarity to Judaism. For instance, some Crusade literature interpreted Muhammad's laws as a resurrection of the old Mosaic laws, and the Muslim reconquest of Jerusalem was perceived as a return to the 'old law' of the Jews.[77] Moreover, Christians assumed that the land of the Saracens had been settled by descendants of the Jewish Shem (one of Noah's sons) and that Muhammad had a Jewish mother. On the whole, therefore, one might say that Christian perceptions of Muslims were shaped not only by biblical concepts of Judaism but also by elements of Christian anti-Judaism.

It was during the Crusades that the Christian world first developed a greater interest in the independent study of Islam, knowledge of which had long been rather vague. While followers of the Muslim faith were initially still perceived as 'heretics', and thus as apostates in their own religious community, in the course of the armed conflicts they were increasingly labelled as 'infidels' and 'pagans', and thus further distanced from the faith. It was not until 1143 that Abbot Peter Venerabilis of Cluny made an effort to translate the Qur'an into Latin – a project which he commissioned in Toledo, Spain – though less with the aim of better understanding Islam than to be able to fight Islam more effectively. Nevertheless, the clearly defined boundaries between Christianity and Judaism remained the central issue for him: he described the 'licentious and blasphemous Jews' as 'far worse than the Saracens'.[78] Muslims were sometimes seen as being closer to recognizing the 'truth about Jesus' than the Jews were, since the Qur'an mentions Jesus respectfully several times; this led to the assumption, which was intensively discussed during the second half of the fifteenth century, that Muslims might more easily convert to Christianity than members of other faiths, especially Jews.[79] Nonetheless, in the early seventeenth century, Calvinist millenarianism professed the opposite assumption: that the Christian Book of Revelation included the Jews' conversion to Christianity, after which the Jews would fight against the Ottoman Empire in the Battle of Armageddon.[80] In 1146, however, when a special tax to finance the Second Crusade was under discussion, the French clergymen Rudolphe even said it was 'not possible to go to war against the Saracens as long as the Jews, the real enemies of Christ, are spared in our midst'. He demanded that one should 'first avenge he who was crucified against his enemies who live here in the midst of us' and only then 'fight the Turks'.[81]

In fact, Jews living in the Rhineland were attacked by marauding crusaders and farmers in the run up to the First Crusade in the spring of 1096. Subsequently, Muslims and Jews were jointly attacked not only in Palestine but also within Europe (from the Crusades to the expulsions from Iberia), which in its own way contributed to the formation of a similar, overlapping image of the 'Other' – even if this was not completely congruent.[82]

Canon law tended to lump Muslims together with Jews and put them under similar legal restrictions. While to some extent this led to a *modus vivendi* for those Muslims who lived within Christian societies, Christian culture also developed a very negative image of Muslims, which drew on the same apocalyptic biblical theology that described Jews as a nation of destroyers.[83] Pseudo-Methodius's *Apocalypse* – written in Syriac in the second half of the seventh century and translated into Latin in eighth-century France – which was widely distributed in western Europe, transformed the wild 'pagan hordes' who were assailing Christianity into the 'sons of Ishmael', by which he meant Muslim Arabs.[84] He described how they would conquer all Christian territories, massacring most of their inhabitants and reducing the rest to slavery. The influential Protestant reformer Martin Luther later also identified the apocalyptic people Gog and Magog with the Turks of his own day.[85] In a comment on his *Table-Talk* he relegated Muslims and Jews to the same level as Catholics.[86] Thus, it was not only 'colonialism that brought anti-Semitism and Islamophobia to the fore and linked the two', as Ethan B. Katz has claimed, drawing on the observations of Frederick Cooper and Ann Laura Stoler.[87]

Even before colonialism, proto-racist images of both Jews and Muslims circulated back and forth between Christian representations of the two groups. Christian perceptions of Muslims were not only shaped within a Jewish framework but also vice versa – characterizations of Muslims served to describe Jewish identity.[88] By the eighteenth century at the latest, anti-Muslim, orientalizing stereotypes were applied to the Jewish populations of Europe, whereas anti-Jewish stereotypes had previously been incorporated into Orientalisms.[89] Accordingly, in antisemitic discourses of the eighteenth and nineteenth centuries, European Jews – perceived as 'oriental' – were often considered sexually lascivious, incapable of forming a state, corrupt as well as tyrannical and oppressive of women. Such stereotypes were linked back to older Hellenistic images of the Persians, formed in the aftermath of the Persian Wars, and Enlightenment philosophers' images of the Ottoman Turks. Moreover, anti-Turkish discourse developed ethnographic topoi and patterns of classification which initially served to describe the Ottomans, but which – similarly to anti-Jewish topoi – were later transferred to the colonized population in the Americas as well.[90]

The formation of proto-racist differences between Noah's sons

Anti-Judaism developed not only in close relation to primitivist and anti-Muslim but also to emerging anti-Black racism. In this context, the story of the Old Testament patriarch Noah's three sons – Shem, Ham and Japheth – is revealing. According to biblical legend, Ham surprised his father when he fell asleep drunk and naked in his tent. Ham not only committed the sacrilege of not turning his gaze away from his father's exposed genitals but he also told his brothers about the embarrassing incident. As a result of this shameful act, Noah cursed Ham's descendants to be servants of the other two, who would have turned their eyes away from their father and covered his nakedness. This scene, which is described briefly and soberly in the Bible, took on heightened significance because Noah's three sons became the vectors through which moral qualities were linked with different religions, territorial configurations and ultimately also skin colours.[91] In the version that would eventually prevail, the eldest son Shem was associated with Judaism, the Orient or Asia; the middle son Japheth with Christianity as well as Europe; and the youngest son Ham with Islam, Africa or the south.

In this depiction in the 1493 *Nürnberger Weltchronik*, the theologically legitimized hierarchy among the sons is clearly shown (see Figure 2.3). The only good son is Japheth, on the right-hand side of the image, who turns away and covers his eyes so as not to see his father's nakedness. Ham wants to spread the embarrassing story and is portrayed with a gaunt face, a long beard and a sharp nose, which marked him not only as an unbeliever but potentially also as 'Jewish'.[92] While Ham's Blackness initially stood for his sinfulness, the symbolic meaning gradually became a physical one. But it was not until the early modern period that Ham's descendants were more explicitly identified as

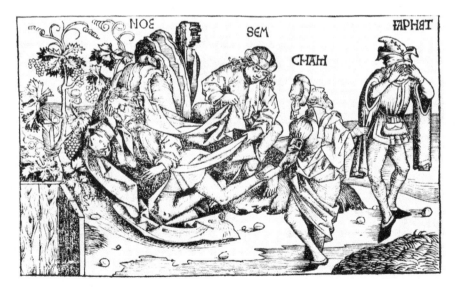

Figure 2.3 The sons of Noah, in the Nuremberg Chronicle (Liber Chronicarum) by Hartmann Schedel. Print manuscript of the German edition (Nuremberg: Anton Koberger, 1493), Folio XVI. © Public Domain.

40   *Colonialism and the Jews in German History*

people with Black skin, condemned to slavery by the weight of 'Noah's curse' – as it was called from the seventeenth century onward – thus providing biblical justification for the enslavement of millions of Africans. In opposition to Ham's increasing Blackness, the figure of Japheth became more and more explicitly white. At the same time, the Jewish Shem moved into a closer relationship with the Black Ham.[93]

To demonstrate these striking shifts, I would like to compare the depictions of Noah's sons in two late medieval maps. The colourful world map of 1460, attributed to Simon Marmion, shows Noah's sons in striking resemblance to each other – a similarity which is even reflected in the continental landscapes, which are amazingly similar in all three parts of the world (see Figure 2.4). Only Shem, who personifies Asia, is highlighted, his right hand raised and pointing upward, indicating the way to paradise or to God.

Noah's Ark can be seen on Mount Ararat behind him, symbolizing humankind's salvation after the flood. Japheth returns his gaze, looking up to him, indicating a special connection between the two in which Ham has no part, as he looks directly at the viewer. Ham represents the African continent and points with his left hand to a large city, which is supposed to represent Athens.[94]

On the world map in the illustrated *Nürnberger Weltchronik* by the physician and humanist Hartmann Schedel (1493), about thirty years later, we can see clear shifts (Figure 2.5). Marmion's map placed Japheth with Ham on the underside of the inhabited world, but in the course of the new convention of orientating maps towards the north, Japheth has been moved up and thus significantly upgraded. He stands on the same level as his older (also in the religious sense) brother Shem, whose covenant with God he has taken over. Japheth's special closeness to God is further emphasized by the fact that Jerusalem, placed in the middle of the world, is directly accessible to him (along a virtual line), while 'the way to salvation' is blocked for the other two brothers by several mountain ranges.

Shem and Japheth represent a kind of mirror for each other. Their gestures correspond, they look at each other – a relationship from which the third brother is excluded. Moreover, it is striking that the geographical space in which the end-times peoples of 'Gog and Magog' were traditionally shown enclosed behind high walls is on this map also separated from the rest of the world, contains no monsters, but is placed near Shem. It would not have been difficult for contemporaries to establish a connection between Shem and the *iudei inclusi*, as mediated by the symbolic order of the now 'natural' mountain borders. Moreover, Shem's physiognomy depicts very dark features. In this respect, not only is Ham devalued by his spatial placement at the lower edge of the image, but Shem is

Figure 2.4 Simon Marmion, *Mappa mundi* (1460). Jean Mansel, *La Fleur des Histoires: Valenciennes, manoscritto, penna, inchiostro e colori su pergamena* (Brussels: Bibliothèque Royale de Belgique, 1459–63), Ms. 9231, fol. 281v. © Bibliothèque Royale de Belgique.

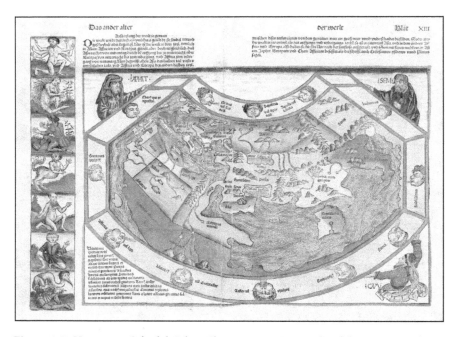

Figure 2.5 Hartmann Schedel, Liber Chronicarum. Facsimile of the German edition (Nuremberg: Anton Koberger, 1493, repr. Puchheim, 1970). Original format: 33 × 44 cm, 636 pages, with c. 1,800 woodcuts by Michael Wolgemut (1434–1519) and Wilhelm Pleydenwurff. Facsimile of the originals from the Melk and Metten monasteries. Austria: Melk Monastery Library. Folio XIII. © Melk Monastery Library.

also loaded with negative connotations and stylized as Japheth's apocalyptic, evil mirror. Moreover, Shem has moved to the same side as the sinful Ham; the latter is still below him but forms a vertical line with him, which can be read as a connecting line, if not a line of descent. This closer relationship between Shem and Ham is also depicted in Schedel's genealogical table of Noah's three sons, in which Shem's and Ham's descendants were interchangeable. Sometimes Ham and sometimes Shem was depicted with the stereotypical features of a 'Moor', as Benjamin Braude has shown.[95]

It was not until the period between 1400 and 1800 that a clear classification and hierarchy between the two was established. While Ham gradually descended into enslavement, the sons of Shem (and with him, Muslims and Turks) adopted the attributes of the monstrous ruler Nimrod, another of Ham's descendants. In addition, the three sons were now assigned different skin colours. In 1666, Georgius Hornius (1620–70) – a Palatine geographer, theologian and professor of history in Leiden, the Netherlands – declared that Ham's descendants were Black, Shem's yellow and Japheth's white, and that humanity should be divided into 'Japhetites', 'Semites' and 'Hamites'.[96] Shem's assumed proximity to or even identification with the Black Ham served to further degrade him.[97]

Interrelations between anti-Black racism and modern antisemitism

In the mid-eighteenth century, philosophers such as Voltaire took up the motif of the special closeness between 'Hamites' and 'Semites'. In his 1764 *Essai sur les Mœurs*, he claims that Jews are just as 'inferior' as Blacks.[98] According to Voltaire, they resemble each other in terms of their common sexual perversions; their unoriginal, plagiarized language; as well as in their particularly high capacity to transmit diseases.[99] In order to legitimize colonialism and slavery, anti-Black racism had consolidated to such an extent that it could now, in turn, serve as a model for a racializing anti-Judaism in Europe. Thus the figure of the Black in Voltaire's text becomes the model (*'comme nous voyons le Nègres'*) from which he derives his constructions of what is Jewish.

Shortly thereafter, by transferring ideas from anti-Black racism, Prussian Jews could be imagined as 'colonial subjects' who had to prove their right to exist and their 'usefulness' to the state through slave-like labour in (soon to be colonized) eastern Prussia or outside Europe. As Jonathan Hess worked out, between 1774 and 1819 alone, there were about forty proposals to exile the Jews overseas, on sugarcane plantations and in various colonial territories.[100]

In the mid-nineteenth century, European travellers still noted particular physiognomic similarities between Jews and people of colour, on the basis of which they speculated about a long-ago kinship. For example, the Polish liberal aristocrat and revolutionary Adam G. de Gurowski (1805–66), who took refuge in the United States in 1849, wrote that upon arrival in the United States, he considered 'every fair-skinned mulatto a Jew' because he was sufficiently familiar with 'their facial features' from Poland. Both had 'pale, clove-colored skin, thick lips, frizzy hair'. He therefore wondered whether these similarities had perhaps emerged from an early connection between Jews and Egyptians.[101] Certain patterns of observation, which this Polish liberal had brought from Europe to the United States, and which assigned Jews a certain physiognomy, allowed him to establish a connection between Blacks and Jews.

For their part, colonial racist stereotypes could also alter perceptions of German Jews. This process is illustrated by the example of Wilhelm Marr, a disappointed German liberal of the 1848 movement and the 'founding father' of German racial antisemitism, who underwent a kind of training in racism during his stay in America and, back in Bremen, transferred his newly gained insights from anti-Black racism to the Jewish minority in Germany.[102] Colonial and anti-Black racism played a prominent role in the transition from anti-Judaic arguments to antisemitic ones, which he was instrumental in promoting.[103] Over the course of the nineteenth century, anti-Black racist stereotypes were projected more and more explicitly onto the Jewish body and eventually attached to 'Jewish blood'.

This also led to discursive entanglements of anti-Black and primitivist racism, which had the effect of mutual authentication and reinforcement. According to the elitist French novelist Arthur de Gobineau's (1816–82) essay on the *Inequality of the Human Races*, Jews in prehistoric times were 'as stained by mixing with Black blood . . . as the Hamites'.[104] Therefore, 'the Israelites, . . . who were all . . . fashioned after a Black pattern . . ., consistently remained at the lowest level of civilization typical of the race'. Israelites, as a Black branch of the Jewish family tree, would have had a Black 'ancestral mother', lived in caves, been substantially weakened by mixing with Blacks and would have sunk to a 'more primitive level of culture', namely that of 'Bushmen' or Aboriginals (he tellingly referred to them as 'Australian Negroes'). They are therefore incapable of creative cultural achievement.[105] All people with 'Black blood', including certain Jewish groups, such as the 'Chorreans', would have to 'perish in the face of civilization', 'as many of the Natives of North America do today'.[106] Gobineau thus drew not only on elements of anti-Black racism but also on the primitivist-colonial topos of the 'dying races' in order to make a statement about Jews or to racialize them.[107] The idea of the 'dying races' already includes the 'extermination' of Jews, insofar as they were declared colonial subjects or 'savages' subject to annihilation.

In close association with Gobineau, it was left up to the antisemitic writer Houston Steward Chamberlain (1855–1927), whose ideas had an important influence on National Socialist ideology, to sum up the 'prevailing view' around 1900, according to which the 'Semite' was the 'most complete half-breed' one could imagine, namely as the 'fruit of a cross between Negroes and whites!'[108] What Gobineau had 'preached' fifty years ago, according to Chamberlain, became the orthodox opinion around 1900, as allegedly even the famous German historian Leopold von Ranke represented in his 'ethnology': 'The Semites belong among the half-mulatto intermediaries between whites and Blacks.'[109] Moreover, Chamberlain explicitly speculates whether this 'mixing' between Jews and Blacks might have had its origin in a liaison by which the biblical patriarch Noah fathered his son Shem – a view which easily carried older religious ideas over into modernity. In the turn from anti-Judaism to modern antisemitism, however, recourses to more recent colonial and anti-Black racisms are also clearly evident. The deepening of this identification of Jewishness with Blackness may be due not least to Germany's entry into the ranks of the colonial states. After all, sympathy for formerly enslaved Blacks in the United States during the Wilhelmine era of the German Empire diminished to the extent that Germans themselves were involved in colonial wars, slavery and exploitation.[110]

The assumed proximity of Jews to Blacks seemed to allow for the naturalization of invisible difference, a perspective which greatly benefited from the persuasive power and daily reproduced reality of the colonial project. According to Neil MacMaster, the figure of the 'Black' even served as the basic model of the inferior 'racial other', which was cited in anti-Jewish discourses for the purpose of racializing Jews.[111] The earlier historical cases we have discussed, however, also make it clear how important anti-Jewish stereotypes were for the development of colonial racist discourses.

Concluding reflections

In order to address the complex history of discursive entanglements between different racisms, it turned out to be helpful to take a genealogical view that transcends the horizon of the nineteenth and twentieth centuries as well as national borders. However, taking a historical and transnational perspective on these issues in no way entails relativizing specifically localizable responsibilities for the deadly consequences of racist discourses. On the contrary: in this expanded perspective, colonial racism and antisemitism cannot be played off against each other, but rather, in their relationship to one another, they prove to be varieties of a common, basic racist framework that has circulated between different places and spaces; has integrated certain topoi (such as *cannibalism*) but also abandoned them in favour of other powerful symbols (such as *Black blood*); and, despite all these changes, has continuously produced mutually reinforcing effects.

Despite this discursive entanglement, the various 'racial discourses' did not function in the same way in every respect or in every historical context. In the German Empire prior to 1900 (especially before the outbreak of the Herero and Nama uprisings in the colonies), for example, Black men were represented as childish servants and were thus portrayed as less threatening than male Jews, who played the role of dominant world rulers in the showcase of antisemitic conspiracy theories. The stereotype of deviant sexuality common to both racisms was also understood differently for Black than for Jewish men: Blacks were considered hyper-sexual and physically strong but not very intelligent; in contrast, Jews were hyper-intellectual but impotent, perverse and sickly. Yet these various racist discourses merged, inspired each other and introduced a racist pattern of perception in almost every part of the world. On the other hand, racism could also be mobilized to legitimize counter-discourses or alternative self-images – for example, in the figure of the 'Indian Jew' as the embodiment of a threatened but 'noble (wild) people' in legitimate need of protection or in the hope of redemption linked to the legend of the 'Ten lost Tribes of Israel'.

It is possible to identify alternating relationships between antisemitism and colonial racisms right down to the level of the politics of remembrance. For example, the American ABC series *Roots* (1977), which shattered all viewer records in the United States in the 1970s, depicted the history of enslavement through a Black family saga, which in turn provided the decisive impetus for the production of the American NBC series *Holocaust* (1978, first broadcast in 1979). The latter told the story of National Socialist persecution through the history of a European Jewish family and would become essential to Germany's confrontation of the Shoah.[112] The fact that this Jewish family was called 'Weiss' (*White*) of all things impressively shows that their story was told as a mirror image of the Black protagonists in *Roots*, while at the same time symbolically remaining within the racist Black-and-white colour scheme – although presumably in this case with the intention of attributing the privileged status of 'whiteness' to Jews.

How topical and necessary it is to reflect on such discursive entanglements between different racisms is further demonstrated by the virulent dispute over the structural similarities between anti-Muslim and antisemitic racisms in the present.[113] Whereas Jews were perceived as threatening 'Others' of the nation, Muslims, according to Matti Bunzl, today move into the position of the 'Others' of Europe.[114] Analogies between anti-Islamic and anti-Jewish discourses are also evident in the accusation that both religious communities are primarily loyal to their own religious duties and tend to mislead the (Christian) milieu.[115] Whereas Jews were perceived as representatives of modernity in the nineteenth century, Muslims today are considered backward and premodern, especially with regard to women's rights. Similarly to anti-Black and primitivist discourses, anti-Muslim racism is dominated by a pejorative view of Islam as the inferior representative of 'the Orient', which 'the West' has to 'civilize', while anti-Jewish hostility is fed by projections of 'too much rationality, wealth, and power'.[116] Yet similar infiltration fantasies as those we know from the history of antisemitism culminate today in the distorted image of an existentially threatening 'Islamization of Europe', which updates medieval and early modern apocalyptic images of the enemy developed in anti-Judaism as well as in propagandistic Crusade and Turkish war literature.[117] However, the complexity and long history of the interrelationships between different racisms only become apparent when, beyond mere comparison, the processes of mutual intertwining and transfer between them are brought into sharper focus. Such an 'entangled history of Othering'[118] might also serve as a starting point for cross-cultural alliances, a 'politics of recognition'[119] able to associate different forms of racism as closely connected.[120]

Translated by Alissa Jones Nelson.

Notes

1 Neil MacMaster, *Racism in Europe 1870–2000* (New York: Palgrave, 2001), 5; George L. Mosse, *Towards the Final Solution* (London: dent, 1978), 56, 70.

2 See Glynis Cousin and Robert Fine, 'A Common Cause: Reconnecting the Study of Racism and Antisemitism', *European Societies* 14 (2012): 166–85; Ethan B. Katz, 'An Imperial Entanglement: Anti-Semitism, Islamophobia, and Colonialism', *American Historical Review* 123 (2018): 1190.

3 Bryan Cheyette, *Diasporas of the Mind: Jewish and Postcolonial Writing and the Nightmare of History* (New Haven: Yale University Press, 2013), viii.

4 Cousin and Fine, 'A Common Cause', 175.

5 The interrelationships between different racisms currently constitute an emerging field of research. See, among others, Tudor Parfitt, *Hybrid Hate: Jews, Blacks, and the Question of Race* (New York: Oxford University Press, 2020), which appeared after this manuscript was completed; *Wissen – Transfer – Differenz. Transnationale und interdiskursive Verflechtungen von Rassismen ab 1700*, ed. Claudia Bruns and M. Michaela Hampf (Göttingen: Wallstein, 2018); *Antisemitism and Racism: Current Connections and Disconnections*, ed. Christine Achinger and Robert Fine (New York: Routledge, 2017).

6 Jürgen Zimmerer, 'Holocaust und Kolonialismus: Beitrag zur Archäologie des genozidalen Gedankens', *Zeitschrift für Geschichtswissenschaft* 51 (2003): 1118.

7 Ibid., 1119.

8 Jeffrey Herf, 'Comparative Perspectives on Anti-Semitism: Radical Anti-Semitism in the Holocaust and American White Racism', *Journal of Genocide Research* 9 (2007): 575–600.

9   See Dirk Moses, 'Conceptual Blockages and Definitional Dilemmas in the Racial Century: Genocide of Indigenous Peoples and the Holocaust', *Patterns of Prejudice* 36 (2002): 19.

10 See i.a. Dirk Moses, 'The Fate of Blacks and Jews: A Response to Jeffrey Herf', *Journal of Genocide Research* 10 (2008): 269–87. For an (ambivalent) assessment of the explanatory potential of the colonial paradigm, see the review article by Thomas Kühne, 'Colonialism and the Holocaust: Continuities, Causations, and Complexities', *Journal of Genocide Research* 15 (2013): 339–62.

11 See Daniel Levy and Natan Sznaider, *Erinnerungen im globalen Zeitalter: Der Holocaust* (Frankfurt am Main: Suhrkamp, 2001), 149; Steven Katz, *The Holocaust and Comparative History* (New York: Leo Baeck Institute, 1993); Kühne, 'Colonialism and the Holocaust'.

12 This can be seen, for example, in the controversy regarding the cancellation of Achille Mbembe's invitation to give a keynote lecture at the Ruhrtriennale art and music festival in 2020, which prompted a fierce discussion of antisemitism in the German media. See Irit Dekel and Esra Özyürek, 'What Do We Talk About When We Talk about Antisemitism in Germany?' *Journal of Genocide Research*, published online 4 December 2020, available online: https://doi.org/10.1080/14623528.2020.1847859 (accessed 3 March 2021). As Glynis Cousin and Robert Fine put it, the 'ghost of the Israel-Palestine' conflict also 'haunts the current separatism between racism and antisemitism'. Cousin and Fine, 'A Common Cause', 176.

13 Following Wulf D. Hund, Benjamin Isaac and Roxann Wheeler, one can speak of 'proto-racist constellations' in which certain physical features were tied to a set of fixed character traits among certain groups, which were thought to be unchangeable – this was already the case in antiquity. See Wulf D. Hund, *Rassismus* (Bielefeld: transcript, 2007), 13. The term 'proto-racism' thus refers not to a 'weaker form' of racism but rather to an older type of racism that existed before the anthropological concept of race was introduced as a result of European colonialism.

14 For a substantial criticism of efforts to trace the concept of racism back to premodern times, see Vanita Seht, 'The Origins of Racism: A Critique of the History of Ideas', *History and Theory* 59 (2020): 343–68.

15 See Geraldine Heng, *The Invention of Race in the European Middle Ages* (Cambridge: Cambridge University Press, 2018), 27.

16 Ibid., 21.

17 See Claudia Bruns and M. Michaela Hampf, eds., 'Transnationale Verflechtungen von Rassismen ab 1700: Versuch der Systematisierung eines Forschungsfelds', *Wissen – Transfer – Differenz*, 9–63.

18 Marina Münkler, *Erfahrung des Fremden: Die Beschreibung Ostasiens in den Augenzeugenberichten des 13. und 14. Jahrhunderts* (Berlin: Akademie Verlag, 2000), 206, 212.

19 Klaus E. Müller, *Der Krüppel: Ethnologia passionis humanae* (München: Beck, 1996), 148–84.

20 Around 1310, Pietro Abano established the head as the decisive criterion for determining the humanity of monsters. Marina Münkler, 'Monstra und mappae mundi: Die monströsen Völker des Erdrands auf mittelalterlichen Weltkarten', in *Text – Bild – Karte: Kartographien der Vormoderne*, ed. Jürg Glauser and Christian Kiening (Freiburg: Rombach, 2007), 149–74, here 166; see also Marina Münkler and Werner Röcke, 'Der ordo-Gedanke und die Hermeneutik des Fremden im Mittelalter: Die Auseinandersetzung mit den monströsen Völkern des Erdrandes', in *Die Herausforderung durch das Fremde*, ed. Herfried Münkler (Berlin: Akademie, 1998), 722.

21 Augustine, *The City of God*, Books 1–10, translated and with an introduction by William Babcock, ed. Boniface Ramsey (Hyde Park: New City Press, 2012), 8, 2.

22 Ibid.

23 Münkler and Röcke, 'Der ordo-Gedanke', 733, 735.

24 Andrew Gow, 'Gog and Magog on *Mappae mundi* and Early Printed World Maps: Orientalizing Ethnography in the Apocalyptic Tradition', *Journal of Early Modern History* 2 (1998): 61–88.

25 Meghan Beddingfield, 'Gog and Magog', in *Encyclopedia of the Bible and Its Reception*, ed. Constance M. Furey et al., vol. 10 (Berlin: De Gruyter, 2015), 504–18, here 506.

26 Ibid., 507. For the early modern period, see Rebekka Voß, *Disputed Messiahs: Jewish and Christian Messianism in the Ashkenazic World during the Reformation* (Detroit: Wayne State University Press, 2021).

27 Andrew R. Anderson, *Alexander's Gate, Gog and Magog, and the Enclosed Nations* (Cambridge: The Mediaeval Academy of America, 1932), chap. 2, esp. 49–50.

28 Münkler, 'Monstra und mappae mundi', 173.

29 Nicholas M. Railton, 'Gog and Magog: The History of a Symbol', *Evangelical Quarterly* 75 (2003): 23–43, here 34.

30 Beddingfield, 'Gog and Magog', 506.

31 Railton, 'Gog and Magog', 34.

32 Beddingfield, 'Gog and Magog', 509. Avraham Grossman, 'The Commentary of Rashi on Isaiah and the Jewish-Christian Debate', in *Studies in Medieval Jewish Intellectual and Social History*, ed. Elliot R. Wolfson, Lawrence H. Schiffman and David Engel (Leiden: Brill, 2012), 47–63, here 54.

33 Railton, 'Gog and Magog', 29.

34 Anna-Dorothee von den Brincken, 'Gog und Magog', in *Die Mongolen: Ein Volk sucht seine Geschichte. Begleitband zur Ausstellung 'Die Mongolen', Haus der Kunst München, 2. März bis 28. Mai 1989*, ed. Walther Heissig and Claudius C. Müller (Innsbruck: Pinguin, 1989), 28.

50   *Colonialism and the Jews in German History*

35 Israel Yuval, *Two Nations in Your Womb: Perceptions of Jews and Christians in Late Antiquity and the Middle Ages*, trans. Jonathan Chipman (Berkeley: University of California Press, 2006), 288–91.

36 Andrew Colin Gow, *The Red Jews. Antisemitism in an Apocalyptic Age, 1200–1600* (Leiden: Brill, 1995), 54, note 71. See the source in Sophia Menache, 'Tartars, Jews, Saracens and the Jewish-Mongol "Plot" of 1241', *History. The Journal of the Historical Association* 81 (1996): 319–42; Yuval, *Two Nations in Your Womb*, 284–5.

37 The Marbach Chronicle of 1222 attests that some Jews saw Genghis Khan as the Davidic Messiah who promised them deliverance from Christian enslavement. (Some also saw the Mongols as kin to the biblical magi).

38 See Zvi Ben-Dor Benite, *The Ten Lost Tribes: A World History* (Oxford: Oxford University Press, 2009).

39 Rebekka Voß, 'Entangled Stories: The *Red Jews* in Premodern Yiddish and German Apocalyptic Lore', *AJS Review* 36 (2012): 1–41, here 7.

40 Ibid.

41 *The Travels of Sir John Mandeville*, translated and introduced by Charles William Reuben Dutton Moseley (London: Penguin Books, 2005), 165–6; *Das Zeitbuch des Eike von Repgow in ursprünglich niederdeutscher Sprache und in früher lateinischer Übersetzung*, ed. Hans F. Massmann (Stuttgart: Litterarischer Verein, 1857), 68–9; Gow, *The Red Jews*, 50–1.

42 'Only here was a specific name given to the imaginary Jewish people of the apocalypse that has no parallel in other European languages.' Voß, 'Entangled Stories', 5.

43 Andrew Colin Gow, 'Kartenrand, Gesellschaftsrand, Geschichtsrand: Die legendären *judei clausi/inclusi* auf mittelalterlichen und frühneuzeitlichen Weltkarten', in *Fördern und Bewahren: Studien zur europäischen Kulturgeschichte der frühen Neuzeit. Festschrift anlässlich des zehnjährigen Bestehens der Dr. Günther Findel-Stiftung zur Förderung der Wissenschaften*, ed. Hedwig Schmidt-Glintzer (Wiesbaden: Harrassowitz, 1996), 141. For further details on the 'Red Jews', see Gow, *The Red Jews*.

44 Münkler, *Erfahrung des Fremden*, 212.

45 Voß, 'Entangled Stories', 6.

46 See the discussion of the different motivations for the massacres in Iris Ritzmann, 'Judenmord als Folge des "Schwarzen Todes": Ein medizinhistorischer Mythos?' *Medizin, Gesellschaft und Geschichte* 17 (1998): 123.

47 See Pope Innocent IV's 1247 papal bull to the bishops of France and Germany; repr. in Josef Kastein, *Eine Geschichte der Juden* (Wien: Löwith, 1935), 360.

48 While the Jews were occasionally accused of cannibalism in antiquity as well, Gavin Langmuir asserts that such accusations did not re-emerge until 1235. See

Gavin I. Langmuir, *Toward a Definition of Antisemitism* (Berkeley: University of California Press, 1996), 263–81.

49 Martin Przybilski, 'Jüdische Körper als Subjekte und Objekte des kulturellen Transfers in der Vormoderne', in *'Rasse' und Raum: Topologien zwischen Kolonial-, Geo- und Biopolitik: Geschichte, Kunst, Erinnerung*, ed. Claudia Bruns (Wiesbaden: Reichert, 2017), 62–3.

50 Ulrike Brunotte, '"The Jewes did Indianize; or the Indians doe Judaize": Philosemitismus und Antijudaismus als Medien kolonialen Transfers im Neuengland des 17. Jahrhunderts', in *Wissen – Transfer – Differenz*, ed. Bruns and Hampf, 235–7.

51 As Columbus noted in his *Journal*, written for the king of Spain: 'So after expelling the Jews from your dominions, your Highnesses, in the same month of January, ordered me to proceed [*sic*] with a sufficient armament to the said regions of India.' Cited in Cousin and Fine, 'A Common Cause', 167.

52 Ella Shohat, 'Taboo Memories and Diasporic Visions: Columbus, Palestine and the Arab-Jews', in *Performing Hybridity*, ed. May Joseph and Jennifer Natalya Fink (Minneapolis: University of Minneapolis Press, 1999), 136–7.

53 Ulrike Brunotte, 'From *Nehemia Americanus* to Indianized Jews: Pro- and Anti-Judaic Rhetoric in Seventeenth-Century New England', *Journal of Modern Jewish Studies* 15 (2016): 188–207, here 188.

54 Ibid.

55 Ibid., 192.

56 Ibid., 199.

57 To cite one example, C. T. E. Rhenius, who came to southern India with the English Church Missionary Society in 1813, noted that 'the Vishnu and Shiva sects and religious worship exhibit a strong likeness to the Jewish dispensation'. Quoted according to Tudor Parfitt, 'The Use of the Jew in Colonial Discourse', in *Orientalism and the Jews*, ed. Ivan Davidson Kalmar and Derek J. Penslar (Waltham: Brandeis University Press, 2005), 53.

58 Brunotte, 'From *Nehemia Americanus*', 199.

59 Ibid., 201.

60 Ibid.

61 Brunotte, 'The Jewes did Indianize', 245.

62 Brunotte, 'From *Nehemia Americanus*', 201.

63 See Parfitt, 'The Use of the Jew', 61.

64 Ibid.

65 Ibid., 67.

66 Ibid., 61.

67 Ibid., 55.

68 Ibid., 51.

69 Ibid., 67.

70 John Bigland, *An Historical Display of the Effects of Physical and Moral Causes on the Character and Circumstances of Nations: Including a Comparison of the Ancients and Moderns in Regard to Their Intellectual and Social State* (London: Longman & Company, 1996 [1816]), 72–3.

71 Francois Marie Arouet (de) Voltaire, 'Cannibals', in *The Works of Voltaire. A Contemporary Version*, trans. William F. Fleming, vol. IV (New York: E. R. DuMont, 1901), 5.

72 Parfitt, 'The Use of the Jew', 67.

73 Carl Peters, *The Eldorado of the Ancients* (New York: Negro University Press, 1969 [1902]), 72.

74 Claudia Bruns, 'Wilhelminische Bürger und "germanische Arier" im Spiegel des "Primitiven": Ambivalenzen einer Mimikry an die kolonialen "Anderen"', *Comparativ. Zeitschrift für Globalgeschichte und vergleichende Gesellschaftsforschung* 9, no. 5 (2009): 15–33, here 27–9.

75 Susanne Zantop, *Colonial Fantasies: Conquest, Family, and Nation in Precolonial Germany, 1770–1870* (Durham: Duke University Press, 1997), 81–90.

76 Suzanne Conklin Akbari, 'Placing the Jews in Late Medieval English Literature', in *Orientalism and the Jews*, ed. Kalmar and Penslar, 34.

77 More rarely, characterizations of Muslims also served to describe Jewish identity. See ibid., 36.

78 Quoted in Karl Heinrich Rengstorf and Siegfried v. Kortzfleisch, *Kirche und Synagoge. Handbuch zur Geschichte von Christen und Juden*, vol. 1 (Stuttgart: Klett-Kotta, 1968), 120–1.

79 Noel Malcom, *Useful Enemies: Islam and the Ottoman Empire in Western Political Thought, 1450–1750* (Oxford: Oxford University Press 2019), 42.

80 Ibid., 272.

81 Quoted in Béla Grunberger, Pierre Dessuant, and Max Looser, *Narzissmus, Christentum, Antisemitismus: Eine psychoanalytische Untersuchung* (Stuttgart: Klett-Cotta, 2000), 289.

82 Andrew Jotschky, 'Ethnic and Religious Categories in the Treatment of Jews and Muslims in the Crusader States', in *Antisemitism and Islamophobia in Europe*, ed. James Renton and Ben Gidley (London: Palgrave Macmillan, 2017), 25–49.

83 Ibid., 51.

84 Ibid.

85 Gow, *The Red Jews*, 6.

86 Luther portrayed Catholicism even as the greater of the two evils. Ibid., 91.

87 Katz, 'An Imperial Entanglement', 1192.

88 Conklin Akbari, 'Placing the Jews', 36.

89 Achim Rohde, 'Der Innere Orient: Orientalismus, Antisemitismus und Geschlecht im Deutschland des 18. bis 20. Jahrhunderts', *Die Welt des Islams* 45 (2005): 410;

see for different stages and forms of Orientalism: Lourens Minnema, 'Different Types of Orientalism and Corresponding Views of Jews and Judaism: A Historical Overview of Shifting perceptions and Stereotypes', *Antisemitism Studies* 4 (2020): 270–325.

90 See the summary in Almut Höfert, *Den Feind beschreiben: 'Türkengefahr' und europäisches Wissen über das Osmanische Reich 1450–1600* (Frankfurt am Main: Campus, 2003), 313–21.

91 Benjamin Braude, 'The Sons of Noah and the Construction of Ethnic and Geographical Identities in the Medieval and Early Modern Periods', *The William and Mary Quarterly* 54 (1997): 133.

92 See Ruth Mellinkoff, *Outcasts: Signs of Otherness in Northern European Art of the late Middle Ages* (Berkeley: University of California Press, 1993); Robert Bartlett, 'Illustrating Ethnicity in the Middle Ages', in *The Origins of Racism in the West*, ed. Miriam Eliav-Feldon, Benjamin H. Isaac, and Joseph Ziegler (Cambridge: Cambridge University Press, 2009), 137.

93 Augustine and Jerome even depicted Ham as representing Judaism, because Jews would have seen Christ naked on the cross. See Braude, 'The Sons of Noah', 133.

94 *Das Buch der Karten. Meilensteine der Kartographie aus drei Jahrtausenden*, ed. Peter Barber (Darmstadt: Primus Verlag, 2006), 72.

95 See the genealogical tables in Braude, 'The Sons of Noah', 122–4.

96 Michael J. Wintle, *The Image of Europe: Visualizing Europe in Cartography and Iconography throughout the Ages* (Cambridge: Cambridge University Press, 2009), 187; Martin W. Lewis and Kären Wigen, *The Myth of Continents. A Critique of Metageography* (Berkeley: University of California Press, 1997), 30, 218, notes 63–4.

97 Braude, 'The Sons of Noah', 140. This old connection between Sem and Ham took on a devastating new actuality in the context of the Rwandan genocide, as old (missionary) assumptions about a close relationship between Jewish and Tutsi peoples were circulated. See William F. S. Miles, 'Hamites and Hebrews: Problems in "Judaizing" the Rwandan Genocide', *Journal of Genocide Research* 2 (2000): 107–15.

98 'On les regardait du meme œil que nous voyons le Nègres, comme une espèce d'homes inférieure'; Francois Marie Arouet (de) Voltaire, 'Essai sur les mœurs et l'ésprit des nations', *Œuvres Complètes de Voltaire*, nouvelle édition, vol. 11 (Paris: Éditions Garnier Frères, 1878 [1761]), 223.

99 Thus the claim that Jews were more likely to be infected with leprosy than other peoples from warm climates had previously been associated with Blacks. See Peter Martin, *Schwarze Teufel, edle Mohren* (Hamburg: Hamburger Edition, 2001), 292.

100 Jonathan M. Hess, 'Sugar Island Jews? Jewish Colonialism and the Rhetoric of "Civic Improvement" in Eighteenth-Century Germany', *Eighteenth-Century Studies* 32 (1998): 92–100; see also Jacob Toury, 'Emanzipation und Judenkolonien in der

54   *Colonialism and the Jews in German History*

öffentlichen Meinung Deutschlands 1775–1819', *Jahrbuch des Instituts für deutsche Geschichte* 11 (1982): 17–53.

101 'On my arrival in this country I took every light-colored mulatto for a Jew. Could not these Jewish mulattoes have descended from some crossing between the Jews and the Egyptians at a time previous to the Exodus?' Adam de Gurowski, *America and Europe* (New York: D. Appleton & Co, 1857), 177.

102 Claudia Bruns, 'Towards a Transnational History of Racism: Interrelationships between Colonial Racism and German Anti-Semitism? The Example of Wilhelm Marr', in *Racism in the Modern World: Historical Perspectives on Cultural Transfer and Adaptation*, ed. Manfred Berg and Simon Wendt (New York: Berghahn, 2011), 122–39; Moshe Zimmermann, *Wilhelm Marr: The Patriarch of Anti-Semitism* (New York: Oxford University Press, 1986).

103 See Bruns, 'Towards a Transnational History of Racism', 122–39; Sander Gilman, 'Einführung', in *Rasse, Sexualität und Seuche: Stereotype aus der Innenwelt der westlichen Kultur* (Reinbek bei Hamburg: Rowohlt, 1992), 24–32.

104 Graf Arthur de Gobineau, *Die Ungleichheit der Menschenrassen* (Berlin: Kurt Wolff Verlag, 1935 [1853–1855]), 167.

105 Ibid., 205.

106 Ibid., 208.

107 See Norbert Finzsch, '"Der kupferfarbige Mensch [verträgt] die Verbreitung europäischer Civilisation nicht in seiner Nähe": Der Topos der *dyinggrace* in den USA, Australien und Deutschland', in *Wissen – Transfer – Differenz*, ed. Bruns and Hampf, 67–90.

108 Houston Stewart Chamberlain, *Die Grundlagen des 19. Jahrhunderts* (München: F. Bruckmann, 1899), 355, note 1.

109 Ibid.

110 See Heike Paul, 'Africa in America? Colonial Constructions of African Americans in German Writings about the USA, 1870–1914', in *Wissen – Transfer – Differenz*, ed. Bruns and Hampf, 184–97.

111 Neil MacMaster, '"Black Jew–White Negro". Anti-Semitism and the Construction of Cross-Racial Stereotypes', *Nationalism and Ethnic Politics* 6, no. 4 (2000): 66.

112 Christian Berndt, 'Auswirkungen der TV-Serie "Holocaust": Dieses Mitleid mit den Opfern war neu', *Deutschlandfunk Kultur* Zeitfragen, 23 January 2019, available online: https://www.deutschlandfunkkultur.de/auswirkungen-der-tv-serie -holocaust-dieses-mitleid-mit-den.976.de.html?dram:article_id=439092 (accessed 19 September 2020); see Levy and Sznaider, *Erinnerungen im globalen Zeitalter*, 131–4.

113 For two contrary positions, see Matthias Küntzel, '"Islamophobia" or "Truthophobia"? Berlin's Anti-Semitism Center is Going Astray', 2008, available online: http://www.matthiaskuentzel.de/contents/islamophobia-or-truthophobia (accessed 14 October 2010); *Islamfeindschaft und ihr Kontext: Dokumentation*

der Konferenz 'Feindbild Muslim – Feindbild Jude', ed. Wolfgang Benz (Berlin: Metropol, 2009). See also Julia Edthofer, 'Gegenläufige Perspektiven auf Antisemitismus und antimuslimischen Rassismus im post-nationalsozialistischen und postkolonialen Forschungskontext', *Österreichische Zeitschrift für Soziologie* 40 (2015): 189–207.

114 See, for example, Matti Bunzl, *Anti-Semitism and Islamophobia: Hatred Old and New in Europe* (Chicago: Prickly Paradigm Press, 2007). Ethan B. Katz described this position as the 'replacement theory': 'Muslims in contemporary Europe have become the "new Jews"', whereas he designates the longer-term historical relationship between antisemitism and Orientalism as the 'Orientalism school'. See Katz, 'An Imperial Entanglement', 1191.

115 Yasemin Shooman, 'Islamfeindlichkeit und Antisemitismus – Diskursive Analogien und Unterschiede', in *Antisemitismus: Ein gefährliches Erbe mit vielen Gesichtern*, ed. Milena Detzner and Ansgar Drücker (Düsseldorf: IDA, 2012), 25–7.

116 Birgit Rommelspacher, 'Was ist eigentlich Rassismus?' in *Rassismuskritik, vol. 1: Rassismustheorie und -forschung*, ed. Paul Mecherli and Claus Melter (Schwalbach: Wochenschau-Verlag, 2009), 26.

117 Almut Höfert, 'Das Gesetz des Teufels und Europas Spiegel: Das christlich-westeuropäische Islambild im Mittelalter und der Frühen Neuzeit', in *Orient- und Islambilder. Interdisziplinäre Beiträge zu Orientalismus und antimuslimischem Rassismus*, ed. Iman Attia (Münster: Unrast, 2007), 85–110.

118 Ari Joskowiez, *The Modernity of Others: Jewish Anti-Catholicism in Germany and France* (Stanford: Stanford University Press, 2013), 29.

119 Paul Berman, 'Reflections: The Other and the Almost the Same', *The New Yorker*, 28 February 1994, 61–6, here 66.

120 I would like to thank Alissa Jones Nelson for her careful translation of this chapter and Rainer Kampling for very helpful comments.

3

Sugar island Jews?

Jewish colonialism and the rhetoric of 'civic improvement' in eighteenth-century Germany

Jonathan M. Hess

In March 1782 Johann David Michaelis's *Orientalische und exegetische Bibliothek* (Oriental and Exegetical Library) published a rather strange contribution for a journal dealing with questions of biblical exegesis.[1] Written by Michaelis himself, a professor in Göttingen and author of the pre-eminent late eighteenth-century work on Mosaic law, this essay entered into a heated political debate, the discussion on Jewish emancipation that had been unleashed by Christian Wilhelm Dohm's 1781 book *Ueber die bürgerliche Verbesserung der Juden* (On the Civic Improvement of the Jews).[2] Dohm, claiming that the 'degenerate' character of the 'Jewish nation' was a product of political and historical circumstance, argued that it was the task of the state to rehabilitate the Jews and transform them into productive members of a non-Jewish body politic. In this context, Dohm proposed that the government lift economic and social restrictions, admit Jews to the military and move them away from trade and into the more 'productive' and more 'honorable' fields of agriculture and the crafts.[3] Michaelis, writing as the 'astute expert' on ancient Judaism whom Dohm had quoted to bolster his argument,[4] sought to use his professional expertise to correct Dohm and put an end to this debate on 'civic improvement':

> Do the laws of Moses contain anything that would make it impossible or difficult for the Jews to be completely naturalized and melt together with other peoples? One should nearly think so! Their intention is to preserve the Jews as a people separated from all other peoples, . . . and as long as the Jews retain the laws of Moses, as long as they for example do not dine with us . . . they will never melt together with us – like the Catholic and Lutheran, the German, Wend and Frenchman, who all live in a single state.[5]

Michaelis argues against granting Jews civil rights here by adopting Dohm's basic blueprint for political modernization. Like Dohm, Michaelis envisions a multiconfessional, multinational political order that would naturalize and melt together its subjects, an all-encompassing, all-assimilating state that he – like Dohm – conceives of as the antithesis of the perceived Jewish insistence on national particularity.[6] What distinguishes Michaelis from Dohm is thus not his antagonistic stance towards Jewish otherness but the conviction that this otherness cannot be eradicated, the assumption that Jews are as Jews intrinsically incapable of being turned into productive members of a non-Jewish state.

At this point, Michaelis goes beyond all questions of biblical exegesis. Rather than speaking as an expert on Mosaic law, he continues his argument by vaguely invoking the racial theories of his Göttingen colleagues, Christoph Meiners and Johann Friedrich Blumenbach. Michaelis does not follow Dohm and see the Jews simply as displaced persons, as 'unfortunate Asiatic refugees'.[7] Jews differ from Germans, Wends and Frenchmen, rather, because they are the 'unmixed race of a more southern people' that even in ten generations will not have the proper bodily strength to perform military service for a German state.[8] In this framework, what perpetuates Jewish national character is not just Mosaic law but an innate racial Jewishness inherited from the Jews' Asiatic climate of origin, an almost ineradicable physical difference that makes it impossible to assimilate the Jews into a non-Jewish state. Michaelis's insistence on racial incompatibility, however, does not lead him to reject Dohm's proposal that the Jews be made more useful to the state. Adopting Dohm's basic programme to move the Jews away from trade, Michaelis proposes his own solution to the Jewish question: 'Such a people can perhaps become useful to us in agriculture and manufacturing, if one manages them in the proper manner. They would become even more useful if we had sugar islands which from time to time could depopulate the European fatherland, sugar islands which, with the wealth they produce, nevertheless have an unhealthy climate.'[9] The ideal – if not the most practical – solution to the Jewish question, Michaelis argues, lies thus in colonial expansion, in relocating the southern Jewish race to a climate that would enable Jews to become economically productive. As a southern race of Asiatic refugees, the Jews need to be displaced once again, sent to a Caribbean climate analogous to their place of origin where they might become colonial subjects promoting the wealth of the European fatherland. Dohm's goal of Jewish economic integration, Michaelis implies, can only be achieved by political deportation, by a model of colonial expansion that puts the Jewish race into its proper place.

Given this logic, it has been customary to claim Michaelis as an important figure in the rise of secular antisemitism, thus reading his fantasy of colonial expansion as a secondary by-product of his racial Jew-hatred.[10] This sort of teleological reading, of course, has the problem of reducing Michaelis to a mere foreshadowing of nineteenth-century concepts of an alien Jewish race. It thus obscures the extent to which, in eighteenth-century Germany, as elsewhere in Europe, racial thinking and colonial fantasies tended to be discourses mutually implicated in each other.[11] Seeing Michaelis's colonial fantasy as motivated solely by racial antisemitism in any form, moreover, also deflects our attention from a more immediate issue: it obscures the way in which Michaelis's colonialist argument actually works entirely within the logic of Dohm's proposals for the civic improvement of the Jews. Dohm's plan for Jewish emancipation hinges on a similar model of colonial expansion, a vision of internal rather than external colonization. Prussia under Frederick the Great pursued an aggressive policy of internal colonization and managed population growth, subsidizing foreign colonists, primarily farmers and artisans, to settle in the country, particularly its eastern regions, and contribute to economic growth. By 1786, one-sixth of the Prussian population consisted of such colonists, a figure that surpassed that of all other European states.[12] Jews, of course, were never invited in as colonists, and the domestic Jewish population was closely controlled so as to be kept to a minimum. In the areas of West Prussia gained in the 1772 partition of Poland, in fact, four thousand Jews were removed from their homes in order to make room for foreign colonists.[13] Dohm, writing as a Prussian civil servant, opens his treatise by noting this apparent contradiction in Prussian colonial policy. Casting population growth as the 'final purpose' and 'most reliable barometer' of a state's general prosperity,[14] he insists that it hardly makes sense to continue the policy of limiting Jewish population and economic productivity while one expends large funds to attract foreign colonists. In this way, Dohm introduces his project as a challenge to Prussian colonial policy, offering up his proposals for the 'civic improvement' of the Jews as a substitute for the current practice of subsidizing foreign colonists.[15]

Clearly, Michaelis's racial thinking cannot be reconciled with Dohm's basic argument that civic improvement can rehabilitate and assimilate the degenerate Jewish nation. Michaelis's argument that Jewish difference cannot be eradicated openly contradicts Dohm. The colonial solution Michaelis offers to the Jewish question, however, does not ensue solely from incipient racial antisemitism; it also follows from the core of Dohm's argument for Jewish emancipation. Both Michaelis and Dohm solve the Jewish question with programmes of colonial expansion. Michaelis's fantasy of Jewish colonial subjects in the Caribbean is the perfect inversion of Dohm's plan for civic improvement, a scenario in which the unlikely situation of an overpopulation of the European fatherland would make it advisable to depopulate and use Jews as foreign colonists abroad. Michaelis's solution to the Jewish question thus blatantly inverts – and perverts – the logic of civic improvement, casting the Jews not as substitutes for foreign colonists on the domestic front but as domestic elements whose deportation abroad will promote the general prosperity of the fatherland.

Given this structural similarity between the visions of internal and external colonization at the root of the differences between Dohm and one of his most prominent opponents, it should not be surprising that proposals for Jewish colonial resettlement were not a rarity in the debates on Jewish civic improvement. Indeed, starting with an anonymous 1774 work that purported to have knowledge of a pre-Columbian Jewish colony on the Ohio river,[16] the topic of Jewish colonies was debated rather widely in the German press, with no fewer than forty proposals for Jewish resettlement published between 1774 and 1819.[17] Many of the authors interested in Jewish colonies implicitly follow Michaelis and propose overseas resettlement, in Botany Bay, Australia, in unnamed desolate coastal regions and in Palestine.[18] At the same time, however, many contributions recommend internal Jewish colonies in Prussia, typically agricultural settlements in desolate, previously uncultivated regions. The proposals for domestic colonies, moreover, rarely derive from the racial anti-Jewish prejudice that underwrites Michaelis's colonial project. Indeed, many of the proposals for Jewish colonies and *Judendörfer* (Jewish villages) come from proponents of 'civic improvement', from liberal-minded government officials[19] and, in one case, from the Prussian Jewish community itself.[20]

Some of these proposals did actually leave the drafting table. Indeed, from 1785 to 1789, Joseph II set up numerous agricultural Jewish colonies in Galicia and Bukovina, one of which had the name 'Neu-Jerusalem' (New Jerusalem). Of these Austrian Jewish settlements, none received the capital and technical support given to other foreign colonists, largely because the authorities feared Jews would use such funds to engage in trade; as a result, none of the Jewish colonies survived.[21] My interest here, however, lies not in the actual experience of Jewish colonies. In what remains of this paper, rather, I would like to reflect on the symbolic function of such colonial projects in the more general debates on Jewish emancipation. Rather than tracing the link between certain resettlement projects and the rise of racial antisemitism, I would like to focus on the role Jewish colonial proposals assume in arguments for granting the Jews civil rights, the ways in which separate Jewish colonies were viewed as ideal agents of rehabilitating the Jews and transforming them into productive subjects that might eventually melt together with others in a new political order. In their rhetorical construction of domestic Jews as potential foreign colonists, Jewish colonial proposals clearly tell us little about eighteenth-century Jewish history. They do, however, underscore a dynamic central to the position of the Jewish question in eighteenth-century German political discourse, an essential link between enlightenment visions of political modernization and fantasies of colonial expansion – internal and external.

I

Rather than trying to survey all the relevant literature on this question, I would like to explore the role that fantasies of colonial expansion play in arguments for Jewish civic improvement by concentrating on one particular text, attempting in this way to draw some provisional conclusions about the colonial politics of Jewish emancipation. The text in question, a 1783 'Schreiben eines deutschen Juden, an den Präsidenten des Kongresses der vereinigten Staaten von Amerika' (Letter of a German Jew, to the President of the Congress of the United States of America), is important not simply because it is perhaps one of the strangest proposals for Jewish colonies.[22] It was also published by Dohm himself in his capacity as co-editor of the *Deutsches Museum* (German Museum), one of the most prominent political periodicals of the 1780s and the journal in which he originally had planned to publish his project on the 'civic improvement' of the Jews.[23]

This letter, written by an unnamed Jew whom the poet Leopold Friedrich Günther von Gökingk had allegedly met on a trip, echoes much of Dohm's argumentation about political and economic restrictions contributing to the 'depravity' of Jewish national character. Rather than following Dohm and arguing for changes in the civil status of German Jews, however, this letter asks the president of the Continental Congress to allow two thousand Jewish families to immigrate to America and set up a Jewish colony there. This figure is quite astonishing if one considers that Prussia proper, for instance, counted only about sixteen hundred Jewish families at this time.[24] This letter, importantly, is not a plea for naturalization or citizenship.[25] Noting that the United States already 'tolerates' Jews, the author casts the German-Jewish immigrants as potential colonial subjects who, if granted the proper privileges, will help promote the wealth and prosperity of the United States:

Sugar Island Jews? 61

The peace treaty between the distinguished American states and England has led many of us to conclude, with great interest, that you now possess large stretches of practically uninhabited land. It may take more than a century for the inhabitants of the thirteen united provinces to increase to such an extent that they would be in a position to populate and cultivate the land they already possess (much like, for instance, the Duchy of Württemberg is populated and cultivated). Should these stretches of land lie desolate during these hundred years, or become a too large hunting ground for a few roaming savages [*herum streifende Wilde*]? . . . You have the legislative power in your hands, and we demand nothing more than to become subjects [*Unterthanen*] of the thirteen provinces. We will gladly contribute twice as much in taxes toward the good of these provinces if we only receive the permission and financial support to set up colonies and engage in agriculture, trade, arts and sciences.[26]

The vision of the United States that emerges from this letter looks uncannily similar to eighteenth-century Prussia. Now that the former colonies have thrown off the yoke of colonial rule, the thirteen provinces are perceived to be in a perfect position to engage in their own project of internal colonization, subsidizing foreign colonists to cultivate their 'practically uninhabited' land and help increase their population. In the newly independent thirteen provinces, moreover, the Native Americans occupy the same position occupied by Jews in Germany. The 'roaming savages', like the 'depraved' German Jews, live outside the logic of economic productivity and population growth. Like Prussia, then, the United States. pursues its current policy of internal colonization by displacing a domestic population which it deems utterly unassimilateable, a domestic population which cannot be the object of a programme of civic improvement.

The neat symmetry the letter constructs between Prussia and the United States is not just a result of its allegedly Jewish author's lack of sophistication in political matters. Blatantly undermining its claims to authenticity at all turns, the 'Letter of a German Jew, to the President of the Congress of the United States of America' clearly functions as a trope, on the level of both its alleged destination and its basic argument. In its fundamental gesture of casting German Jews as potential foreign colonists in the United States, the letter to the American president addresses itself less to the US government than to the German reading public. There is, incidentally, no record of this letter having been received by any branch of the US government, nor does there seem to have been any discussion in the Jewish community of these plans to relocate two thousand families to the United States.[27] When the letter was reprinted as a separate pamphlet in 1787, moreover, it was addressed to the 'American President O . . .' – an obvious

62 *Colonialism and the Jews in German History*

fabrication – and listed as being 'edited' by Moses Mendelssohn (who had died the year before and whose name it misspelled).[28] Using the 'American president' as a trope, this fictional correspondence thus performs for its German readers an inversion of the logic of Michaelis's colonial proposal. In constructing German Jews as desirable colonists for the United States, this letter has the opposite effect of Michaelis's argument against Dohm: it casts the Jews not as racial others that need to be deported but as valuable domestic resources the German states are in a position to lose to the United States.

The figurative use of the 'American president' is central to the way in which the letter introduces its argument for colonization. The *Deutsches Museum*, the journal that published the letter, appeared in Leipzig, in Saxony. Rather than reflecting on either its place of publication or its alleged destination, the letter opens by setting up a peculiar relationship between the American president and the King of Prussia. There are, it seems, very particular reasons why the letter constructs a vision of the United States that looks like Prussia:

Honorable Mr. President,

You will give me special forgiveness if I do not give you the proper title, since this is not known to me. You are the leader of a united state that has waged war with the most powerful monarchy in the world and has won even more than what it fought for. In this capacity alone, you would be justified to demand from every European court (and even more so from a Jew!) the title 'Your Supreme Highness' [*Durchlauchtigster*], a title you deserve more than many of our royalty . . . A man like yourself is certainly just as little concerned with complete forms of address as the King of Prussia, who has forbidden people to use his entire form of address, or even a tenth of it. Even if you were simply a well-honored lord [*wohledler Herr*] in the Dutch style, you would nevertheless not stop being a more important person for Europe than most members of the royal families [*Durchlauchtigkeiten*] of Germany; just as that great king would have shone forth above all the kings of Europe even if his grandfather had not assumed the throne.[29]

The war of independence has apparently won the former colonies much more than the right to govern themselves. Indeed, in winning a war waged against the most powerful monarchy in the world, the United States has gained an almost unprecedented international stature that makes it difficult for anyone, particularly the allegedly Jewish writer of this letter, to address its president by the proper title. In this context, importantly, the letter does not just compare the American president with Frederick the Great – a monarch, we are to think, who

Sugar Island Jews? 63

has similarly demonstrated his superiority over England. In arguing that the American president is superior to German royal families much in the same way as Frederick the Great shines forth above all the kings of Europe, the letter makes the United States seem like a version of Prussia in miniature, a microcosm of Prussia on the other side of the Atlantic.

In congratulating the president of the US congress on winning his war against England, then, this letter published in Saxony casts its alleged destination as a satellite of Prussia, a country that apparently deserves to be congratulated as the major European power. This letter, then, does much more than conflate Prussia and the United States – a strategy that in and of itself would hardly be unusual in political literature of the 1780s.[30] The letter to the American president casts its destination as a dislocated Prussian colony of sorts, a country much like Prussia but with no economic or political connection to the Prussian fatherland. What the former British colonies have won in their war of independence, it seems, is the right to be like Prussia. In this context, England's loss has become Prussia's gain. Given this symbolic appropriation of the United States as a displaced microcosm of Prussia, it becomes difficult to read this suggestion to send two thousand Jewish families to set up a Jewish colony as a simple proposal for overseas immigration. The letter to the American president targets Frederick the Great as much as it does the American authorities. In content, the letter clearly proposes an overseas Jewish colony. In its form as a letter to the 'American president,' however, it contributes to Prussia's own expansion and establishment as a great power, symbolically constructing Prussia as the premier European state with a satellite on the other side of the Atlantic. Jews, it seems, are not merely potential resources for population growth and economic expansion which the various German states may be in a position to lose to the United States. As potential foreign colonists – and as letter writers – they are also absolutely crucial to Prussia's own programme of internal and external expansion.

The 'Letter of a German Jew' does more than subvert its claims to authenticity and construct its alleged destination as a strategic trope. It also argues for an overseas Jewish colony according to a logic that, if one reads it solely on the level of explicit content, discreetly undermines itself as well. On the one hand implicitly following Dohm, the letter contends that the 'degenerate' character of the Jews needs to be overcome by a programme of civic improvement, by what it calls a 'revolution [*Revoluzion*] in our entire way of living and thinking'. The only way to achieve this revolution in Jewish moral character, however, is by a strange form of international cooperation between Germany and the overseas Prussian satellite:

The physical well-being of my brethren concerns me, Mr. Lord President [*hochgebiet. Hr. Präsid.*], but their moral well-being concerns me far more. It would be foolishness to want to improve their moral well-being in their present condition. On the contrary, the [Jewish] nation will only get worse and worse. The wise men of our country, who understand very well that this worsening will cause the Christians themselves to suffer along with us, desire a revolution [*Revoluzion*] in our entire way of living and thinking, a revolution that no one but you, gracious Mr. President [*gnädiger Hr. Präsident*], can bring about. We hope, therefore, that you might deign to present a petition on our behalf to your most praiseworthy Congress. Granting this petition would honor humanity as a whole.[31]

In this context, the interests of 'humanity as a whole' coincide rather conveniently with the interests of both Germany as a whole and the newly independent Prussian satellite. In subsidizing two thousand Jewish families to become its colonial subjects, the United States will not just be inviting in foreign colonists who will contribute to its growth and economic prosperity. By guaranteeing the physical conditions for the moral regeneration of the Jewish nation, the American president will also be saving the German states from the threat of general moral depravity their unreconstructed Jewish population is threatening to spread. With their degenerate moral character, the Jews pose a fundamental threat to the German bodies politic, a threat that can be best overcome, it seems, by a colony in the United States. In setting up a Jewish colony, the American president becomes the saviour of Germany, the man who upholds the moral purity of Christian Germany by removing and reforming its dangerous Jewish elements.

Read solely in terms of its explicit content, then, the 'Letter of a German Jew' begins to sound like a programme for regeneration via deportation. Indeed, given the threat of universal moral depravity the letter invokes, the interests of 'humanity as a whole' would be better served by a much more radical solution, by a colony of all German Jews that would allow the entire Jewish nation to undergo civic improvement. The solution implicit in the logic of the letter would certainly fulfil two of the objectives that guide Dohm's project of civic improvement, namely regenerating Jewish character and making the Jews more useful to the state. It would complete this project of civic improvement, however, in such a way as to deplete the German states of potential resources, in such a way as to depopulate Germany and contribute to the economic prosperity and population growth of a country that has no explicit link to the German states. Sending the entire German-Jewish population off to an overseas Prussian satellite would certainly protect the German states from the threat of moral degeneration. Yet it might also upset the balance of power between Prussia and its displaced microcosm, giving the United States a boost in economic productivity and population growth that might make Prussia look like its dislocated colony.

Given the implicit threat that mass Jewish immigration might enable the United States to prove itself superior not just to England but to Prussia as well, it becomes clear who the ideal person is to bring about the desired revolution: not the American president who is superior to all German royalty but that king who already 'shines forth over all the kings of Europe', a king a sixth of whose subjects already consisted of such foreign colonists. The logical solution to the problem the letter poses is not an overseas Jewish colony but a Prussian invitation to German Jews to set up a colony that would both produce the necessary 'revolution' in their 'entire way of living and thinking' and contribute to Prussian colonial expansion. Confronting its German readers with the possibility of a mass population loss to a country that it rhetorically – and only rhetorically – appropriates as a displaced microcosm of Prussia, the 'Letter of a German Jew' points towards an obvious alternative: the use of Jews to promote Prussian internal expansion. In inviting in Jews as foreign colonists, moreover, Prussia would not only be pursuing a politics of internal colonization. It would also be engaging, on a symbolic level, in a programme of external expansion, an attempt to capture those potential resources that might otherwise become the property of its overseas satellite. In this sense, emancipating the Jews would not merely act as a functional substitute for the practice of inviting in foreign colonists to settle Prussia. Civic improvement would also function as a symbolic substitute for a foreign colony.

II

The project of the civic improvement of the Jews, as Dohm introduces it, figures as an integral part of a much larger vision of political modernization, the construction of a political order that would 'weaken the exclusive principles' of all particular societies and associations and 'dissolve' them 'in the great harmony of the state'. 'Government', Dohm writes, 'realizes its great intention when the nobleman, the peasant, the scholar, the artisan, the Christian and the Jew are all, more than anything else, *citizens*'.[32] Using the term 'Jewish emancipation' in this context, of course, is a bit of misnomer, not to mention an anachronism.[33] For Dohm's goal is not to emancipate the Jews as Jews but to regenerate their

66 Colonialism and the Jews in German History

character, to transform them into individuals who would be useful to the state. Given this dynamic, it makes sense that scholarship on the Jewish question has typically stressed its relation to the rise of the nation state, a political order that, in Hannah Arendt's words, 'perverts equality from a political into a social concept' and thus fails to constitute a 'political organization in which otherwise unequal people have equal rights'.[34] It is, indeed, by precisely such a perversion of equality from a political into a social concept that Dohm constructs his ideal of universal citizenship, issuing a call for civic improvement that inscribes Jewish otherness as an impediment to political modernization.

The dynamic I have been tracing in this paper, however, points towards a somewhat different framework for studying the position of the Jewish question in eighteenth-century political discourse. Clearly, the proposals for the civic improvement of the Jews represent an important moment in envisioning a state that is grounded in both concepts of universal citizenship and the general process of national consolidation. The examples we have been considering, however, would seem to suggest that the process of integrating and assimilating Jews into a modern political order may involve much more than the consolidation of the nation state via assimilation and internal colonization. For as a process of assimilating foreign resources, Jewish emancipation here is conceived of as analogous to – and a symbolic substitute for – the process of external colonization; in the case of the Jewish question, the project of national consolidation is articulated on the basis of fantasies of external colonial expansion. In the late nineteenth century, once a unified Germany had overseas colonies, it was not uncommon to locate in Frederick the Great's policy of internal colonization an anticipation of later German colonialist undertakings.[35] The examples we have been considering are important, of course, not because they anticipate later forms of German colonial expansion but because they indicate the extent to which, in the case of the Jewish question, fantasies of external colonial expansion are already inscribed into the project of internal colonization. Michaelis's fantasy of sugar island Jews, in other words, may indeed announce the beginnings of racial antisemitism; his vision of Jews as colonial subjects may also mark, however, a central moment in the discourse that wants to emancipate the Jews and admit them to the body politic.

Notes

1   First published as: Jonathan M. Hess, 'Sugar Island Jews? Jewish Colonialism and the Rhetoric of 'Civic Improvement' in Eighteenth-Century Germany', *Eighteenth-*

Century Studies 32 (1998): 92–100. © 1998 American Society for Eighteenth-Century Studies. Reprinted with permission of Johns Hopkins University Press.

2 Michaelis, *Orientalische und exegetische Bibliothek* 19 (1782): 1–40. Dohm reprints Michaelis's essay in the second volume of *Ueber die bürgerliche Verbesserung der Juden*, published in 1783. I quote both Dohm and Michaelis according to the facsimile reprint of Christian Conrad Wilhelm Dohm, *Ueber die bürgerliche Verbesserung der Juden: 2 Teile in einem Band* (Hildesheim: Olms, 1973). All translations are my own.

3 On Dohm, see Jonathan M. Hess, 'Modernity, Violence and the Jewish Question: Christian Wilhelm Dohm and the Eradication of Jewish Alterity', in *Progrès et violence au XVIIIe siècle*, ed. Valérie Cossy and Deidre Dawson (Paris: Champion, 2001), 87–116.

4 Dohm, *Ueber die bürgerliche Verbesserung der Juden*, part 2, 19, 97n, 136–7.

5 Ibid., 40–1.

6 On Dohm's concept of the state, see Hess, 'Modernity, Violence and the Jewish Question'. Dohm solves this dilemma by calling for a reformulation of Mosaic law that would return it to its original greatness – a point of origin he identifies less with biblical Judaism than with the situation of diaspora Jewry under Roman rule.

7 Dohm, *Ueber die bürgerliche Verbesserung der Juden*, part 1, 8.

8 Ibid., part 2, 51. Although Michaelis's concept of a southern race fits in well with the racial thinking of his contemporaries, his implicit notion of an unadulterated, specifically Jewish race constitutive of Jewish national character does not; in this sense, the concept of a racial Jewish identity would seem to be Michaelis's own innovation. On eighteenth-century race theory in Germany, see Susanne Zantop, *Colonial Fantasies: Conquest, Family, and Nation in Precolonial Germany, 1770–1870* (Durham: Duke University Press, 1997), 66–80, also, more generally, Nicholas Hudson, 'From "Nation" to "Race": The Origins of Racial Classification in Eighteenth-Century Thought', *Eighteenth-Century Studies* 29 (1996): 247–64. I discuss the site of the Jewish body in emancipation proposals in 'Modernity, Violence and the Jewish Question'.

9 Dohm, *Ueber die bürgerliche Verbesserung der Juden*, part 2, 41.

10 See Anna-Ruth Löwenbrück, *Judenfeinschaft im Zeitalter der Aufklärung: Eine Studie zur Vorgeschichte des modernen Antisemitismus am Beispiel des Göttinger Theologen und Orientalisten Johann David Michaelis (1717–1791)* (Frankfurt am Main: Peter Lang, 1995), also Barbara Fischer, 'Residues of Otherness: On Jewish Emancipation during the Age of German Enlightenment', in *Insiders and Outsiders: Jewish and Gentile Culture in Germany and Austria*, ed. Dagmar C. G. Lorenz and Gabriele Weinberger (Detroit: Wayne State University Press, 1994), 30–8.

11 See Zantop, *Colonial Fantasies*, 66–80.

12 See here, for instance, W. O. Henderson, *Studies in the Economic Policy of Frederick the Great* (London: Frank Cass, 1963), 126, but also the chapter on 'Die preußische

Einwanderung und ländliche Kolonisation des 17. und 18. Jahrhunderts', in *Umrisse und Untersuchungen zur Verfassungs-, Verwaltungs-und Wirtschaftsgeschichte besonders des Preußischen Staates im 17. und 18. Jahrhundert*, ed. Gustav von Schmoller (Hildesheim: Olms, 1974).

13 Schmoller, *Umrisse und Untersuchungen*, 593.

14 Dohm, *Ueber die bürgerliche Verbesserung der Juden*, part 1, 1–6, here 6.

15 See ibid., 89–94.

16 *Gedanken eines Land-Geistlichen über eine an dem Ohio-Fluss in Amerika entdeckte Juden-Kolonie* (Frankfurt am Main, 1774), https://digital.slub-dresden.de/werkansicht/dlf/7925/3, quoted and discussed in Don Heinrich Tolzmann, 'The German Image of Cincinnati Before 1830', *Queen City Heritage* 42, no. 3 (1984): 31–8.

17 See Jacob Toury, 'Emanzipation und Judenkolonien in der öffentlichen Meinung Deutschlands (1775–1819)', *Jahrbuch des Instituts für deutsche Geschichte* 11 (1982): 17–53. Toury's indispensable article does not include Michaelis or the work quoted previously, nor does it reflect, more generally, on the extent to which the seemingly marginal colonial argument figures into the very formulation of the Jewish question in the late eighteenth century.

18 The best known of these texts is Karl Wilhelm Friedrich Grattenauer, *Über die physische und moralische Verbesserung der heutigen Juden* (Leipzig: Voß, 1791); see Toury, 'Emanzipation und Judenkolonien'.

19 See here, for instance, Friedrich von Schuckmann, 'Ueber Judenkolonien: An Herrn Geheimen-Rath Dohm', *Berlinische Monatsschrift* 5 (1785): 50–8.

20 The proposals of the Prussian Jewish community are discussed in Sucher B. Weinryb, *Der Kampf um die Berufsumschichtung: Ein Ausschnitt aus der Geschichte der Juden in Deutschland* (Berlin: Schocken, 1936), 14–17.

21 See Maurycy Lewin, '*Geschichte der Juden in Galizien unter Kaiser Joseph II. Ein Beitrag zur Geschichte der Juden in Oesterreich*', Phil. diss., University of Vienna, 1933, 80–104, also, more recently and less detailed, Josef Karniel, *Die Toleranzpolitik Kaiser Josephs II*, trans. Leo Koppel (Gerlingen: Bleicher, 1985), 469.

22 'Schreiben eines deutschen Juden, an den Präsidenten des Kongresses der vereinigten Staaten von Amerika', *Deutsches Museum* 1, no. 6 (1783): 558–66. See, for background, Hans Lamm, 'The So-Called "Letter of a German Jew to the President of the Congress of the United States of America" of 1783', *Publications of the American Jewish Historical Society* 37 (1947): 171–7.

23 In general, it should be noted, Dohm tended to be ambivalent on the question of internal Jewish colonies. At times, he argued against such proposals, claiming they would only reinforce Jewish difference (see Dohm, *Ueber die bürgerliche Verbesserung der Juden*, part 1, 115–6). At other points, however, he tended to be less critical, granting implicit consent to those who argued that civic improvement could best be achieved by creating separate Jewish colonies; in a 1782 essay 'Ueber

die Juden-Toleranz' (On the Tolerance of Jews), Dohm critiques various aspects of an anonymous proposal for Jewish colonies without ever questioning its basic idea. Both the anonymous essay and Dohm's response were published in *August Ludwig Schlözer's Briefwechsel meist historischen und politischen Inhalts* 10 (1782): 250–5, 279–83.

24 See Albert A. Bruer, *Geschichte der Juden in Preußen* (Frankfurt am Main: Campus, 1991), 84. These figures do not include the large numbers of Jews residing in the areas gained in the 1772 Polish partition.

25 Indeed, when the letter was published in 1783, the American Congress was still debating the 'General Assessment Bill for Support of Christian Denominations', a bill that would have declared Christianity a state religion. Moses Mendelssohn, who encouraged Dohm to write his book *Ueber die bürgerliche Verbesserung der Juden*, refers to this bill as a potential danger in the closing of his 1783 *Jerusalem*; see Moses Mendelssohn, 'Jerusalem, oder über religiöse Macht und Judentum', in *Gesammelte Schriften Jubiläumsausgabe*, ed. Fritz Bamberger et al., vol. 8 (Stuttgart: Frommann-Holzboog, 1971–91), 99–204.

26 'Schreiben eines deutschen Juden', 566.

27 See Lamm, 'The So-Called "Letter of a German Jew"', 173.

28 *Schreiben eines deutschen Juden an den amerikanischen Präsidenten O ...*, ed. Moses Mendelsohn [*sic*] (Frankfurt am Main and Leipzig, 1787).

29 'Schreiben eines deutschen Juden', 558–9.

30 On the role of strategic conflations of Prussian absolutism and American (or British) forms of representative governments in late eighteenth-century political discourse, see Jonathan M. Hess, *Reconstituting the Body Politic: Enlightenment, Public Culture and the Invention of Aesthetic Autonomy* (Detroit: Wayne State University Press, 1999).

31 'Schreiben eines deutschen Juden', 565–6.

32 Dohm, *Ueber die bürgerliche Verbesserung der Juden*, part 1, 26.

33 On the term 'Jewish emancipation', see Jacob Katz, 'The Term 'Jewish Emancipation': Its Origin and Historical Impact', in *Emancipation and Assimilation: Studies in Modern Jewish History* (Westmead: Gregg, 1972), 21–45.

34 Hannah Arendt, *The Origins of Totalitarianism* (New York: Harcourt Brace Jovanovich, 1973), 54, but also 290–302. On Jewish emancipation and the nation state, see, for instance, Reinhard Rürup, *Emanzipation und Antisemitismus: Studien zur Judenfrage der bürgerlichen Gesellschaft* (Göttingen: Vandenhoeck & Ruprecht, 1975).

35 See here, for instance, the chapter on 'Die preußische Einwanderung und ländliche Kolonisation des 17. und 18. Jahrhunderts' in Gustav von Schmoller's 1898 *Umrisse und Untersuchungen zur Verfassungs-, Verwaltungs-und Wirtschaftsgeschichte besonders des Preußischen Staates im 17. und 18. Jahrhundert*, quoted earlier, 562–6.

4

Racism, antisemitism and achievement

Christoph Meiners and his theory of the nonequivalence of human beings

Felix Axster

This chapter deals with the establishment of the scientific theory of race in Germany *c.* 1800.[1] More specifically, I will show that the Göttingen philosopher Christoph Meiners (1747–1810) developed his doctrine on the inequality of humans and 'human races', which took shape around the time of the French Revolution of 1789, with reference to the emancipation of the Jews and the movement to abolish slavery and the slave trade. Thus, one might argue pointedly that the genesis of the scientific theory of race was a reaction to the emancipatory struggles of both Jews and slaves. One might also argue that the interlinkage of antisemitism and racism is an inherent part of the scientific theory of race from its very beginnings. But what stands out above all is that Meiners establishes 'achievement' (*Leistung*) as a crucial criterion for distinguishing between groups. As demonstrated in this chapter, this criterion functions both to mark the difference between the Self and the Other and as a mechanism to link racism and antisemitism. Furthermore, it introduces a genuinely modern component to Meiners's sometimes seemingly old-fashioned rationale for the inequality thesis. Consequently, the question arises of whether – and to what extent – this criterion is a constitutive element of modern racism and whether racism is a constitutive element of the modern 'achievement-oriented society' (*Leistungsgesellschaft*).

In what follows, while the aspect of interlinkage will be emphasized, it might be useful to mention that my considerations are not detached from the ongoing and highly controversial debates about the relationship between antisemitism and racism. At least in Germany, intersectional or comparative approaches are sometimes accused of ignoring the specifics of antisemitism and of ultimately relativizing the Holocaust. This accusation is concurrent with the attempt to separate antisemitism and racism, and in turn overlooks the historical (and even contemporary) interlinkage, especially with regard to the genesis of the concept of race. In dealing with this genesis, I do not mean to imply that either antisemitism or racism can be reduced to this one aspect. On the contrary, my reconstruction of Meiners's argument will demonstrate that this interlinkage is in fact the coupling of two specific phenomena, each of which has its own history and involves its own stereotypes.

According to literary scholar Susanne Zantop, Christoph Meiners is a 'crucial link in the emergence of modern racism, and, particularly, modern *German* racism'.[2] Although he faced much criticism by contemporary thinkers and researchers such as Johann Friedrich Blumenbach and Georg Forster, his writings anticipated some of the significant myths of modern racism and antisemitism established in the nineteenth century, for example, the so-called *Germanenkult*, or the idea that Jews were to be seen as cultural unproductive.[3] It is therefore hardly surprising that the German racialist Ludwig Schemann, who was a leading member of *völkisch* and National Socialist circles from the Kaiserreich until his death in 1938, stated in his major work *Die Rasse in den Geisteswissenschaften* that Meiners was one of those who laid the foundation for a scientific understanding of race.[4] Even though Meiners has not gained that much attention within the field of critical research, his impact on racial thinking in the nineteenth and twentieth centuries must not be underestimated.

Interlinkages

In his 1790 essay 'Über die Natur der Afrikanischen Neger, und die davon abhangende Befreyung, oder Einschränkung der Schwarzen' ('On the Nature of African Negroes, and the Liberation, or Restriction, of Blacks That Follows Therefrom'), Meiners engages mainly with abolitionist positions, that is, the movement to abolish both slavery in the American colonies and the transatlantic slave trade. This movement became considerably more visible on the eve of the French Revolution, as witnessed by the founding of the Society for Effecting the Abolition of the Slave Trade in London in 1787 and the Society of the Friends of the Blacks in Paris the following year.[5] When he wrote his essay, Meiners could not have known anything about the slave uprising that erupted in Haiti in 1791 and led to the independence of the French colonial empire's most important colony.[6] He may, however, already have had a sense that the progressive ideals of the

Enlightenment, and more particularly the attempt to implement them during the French Revolution, would have a global impact. As we will see further, in this context he was also thinking of the emancipation of the Jews.[7]

The essay opens with a critical stocktaking of the Enlightenment. Initially, Meiners seems to take a sympathetic and empathetic stance. For example, in the very first paragraph he writes:

> So it is no wonder that in the very age during which peoples and estates that had been abused for too long rose up against their tyrants, held them to a terrible reckoning, and loudly reclaimed their offended and near-forgotten rights, the most famous authors of all nations should forma league, as it were, striving to elevate, in our part of the world, the Jews, and in the New World, the Negroes, from out of the condition of contempt and servitude into which both had been cast.[8]

Yet shortly thereafter, Meiners invites us to consider the following: 'The awakening love of liberty degenerated into an attack on noblemen and the aristocracy, and the hatred of oppression became a feverish enthusiasm for an equality of all estates and peoples that is as impossible as it would be unjust.'[9] Finally, he categorically states:

> And as little as subjects will ever be given rights and freedoms equal to those of their rulers, children's rights and freedoms equal to those of adults, women's rights and freedoms equal to those of men, servants' rights and freedoms equal to those of their masters, lazy and ignorant people's rights and freedoms equal to those of active and educated people, declared villains' rights and freedoms equal to those of blameless or meritorious citizens, so little will Jews and Negroes, as long as they remain Jews and Negroes, be able to obtain the same privileges and freedoms as the Christians and white people among whom they live or whom they obey.[10]

Meiners's attitude to the multifaceted political and social developments he was confronted with around 1790 was clearly an ambiguous one. This ambiguity is expressed in his distinction between genuine and false or harmful Enlightenment.[11] Accordingly, Meiners's work is characterized, on the one hand, by 'unbroken optimism about progress' and an 'Enlightenment or pedagogical tendency'.[12] On the other hand, he also insisted on the necessity and legitimacy of an estate-based order and struggled 'for the preservation of the *ancien régime*'.[13] Moreover, the quoted passages show that Meiners referred to the suppression and deprivation of rights of both Jews and slaves. In this context, it is striking that he invokes various power relations – between children and adults, women and men, servants and their employers – to render more plausible the notion of a 'natural order' that needs to be immunized against the Enlightenment postulate of freedom and equality – which, in Meiners' view, has been taken too far. As will be shown, the invocation of these power relations is significant because it functions as a framework with which the distinctions between 'white persons' and 'Blacks' on the one hand and between Christians and Jews on the other hand can be made evident, or at all articulable and comprehensible.

It should be noted at this point that in the article under discussion here, Meiners was mainly concerned with demonstrating that the system of slavery was legitimate in principle, even if he did speak out in favour of improving this system. In the spirit of the so-called 'civilizing mission', he argued that European slave traders and slave holders had no right to wantonly mistreat their slaves, and that it was their duty to teach the slaves to work, 'such as to improve these people and make them happier than they would be if they were left to their own devices'.[14] The question concerning the status of the Jews, in turn, only comes up as a footnote of sorts. It is nevertheless revealing how Meiners interweaves this question with considerations on the 'nature' of the slaves. To comprehend this, it is necessary to reconstruct Meiners's sometimes confusing train of thought. At one point he states: 'In contrast to this claim concerning the natural equality of all persons are the unanimous testimonies of all travelers who have described to us the wild, barbaric, and semi-cultivated peoples of other parts of the world'.[15] While this quotation is also to be understood in the context of Meiners's efforts to delegitimize the abolitionist movement, he mentions Europe a bit later. He first notes: 'In no other part of the world was or did man become as beautiful, strong, active, courageous, and sensitive to the fortune and misfortune of others, and as rich in terms of the arts, sciences, and virtues, as in Europe'.[16] He then argues that the diversity of persons and peoples is less pronounced in Europe than in other parts of the world, and that 'experience' shows that certain properties – both good and bad – reproduce themselves in 'certain lineages' (*gewissen Geschlechtern*) such that there has developed, 'from earliest times', a 'distinction between noble and non-noble lineages'.[17] Thus, Meiners posits a relationship between what cultural studies theorist Claudia Bruns calls the 'old estates order and the racially organized colonial order'.[18] Furthermore, he more or less implicitly posits a relationship between 'non-noble lineages' and Jews. This becomes clear when he points out that the 'non-Slavic European peoples would never have been able to grant the Jews privileges equal to their own, or to consider them equal to themselves'.[19]

What emerges here is the subtle establishment of specific but intertwined forms of differentiation: on the one hand, between Europe and other parts of the world or between European cultivation and non-European barbarism, and on the other hand, between 'noble and non-noble lineages' within Europe. While suggesting that the Jews belong to the 'non-noble lineages' of Europe, Meiners creates a mirror relation of sorts between colonialist/racist and intra-European religious distinctions. In other words, Meiners's reference to colonial discourse – the 'testimonies of all travelers' – is framed by reflections about the old estates order and the position of Jews therein. Emphasizing the differences within this order – the 'distinction between noble and non-noble lineages', that is, among others, the distinction between non-Jews and Jews, which was made 'from earliest times' – might thus serve to lend historical depth to colonial forms of othering or to merely rationalize them. At the same time, the reference to colonial discourse serves as a framework intended to render a specific distinction between Jews and 'non-Slavic European peoples' more plausible. This corresponds with Meiners's remark that it would 'never have occurred' to Europeans to 'draw similar distinctions between themselves and colonists of other nations of the same origin'.[20] Once again, this is a reference to colonialism or – to quote Claudia Bruns again – a 'reference to racial homogeneity within the group of white colonial rulers'.[21] Since this reference is meant to naturalize the assumed homogeneity of 'non-Slavic European peoples' and therefore to emphasize the inferior status of Jews, it demonstrates that a colonialist-racist mode of differentiation is brought to bear upon antisemitic forms of othering. Finally, it should be noted that Meiners's argumentation, while explicitly linking colonial or anti-Black racism and antisemitism, is implicitly structured by anti-Slavic racism.

To sum up the first part of my analysis, Meiners tends to link two experiences, taking experience as evidence. The colonial experience, which he claims has shown that persons are of unequal constitution and of unequal value, serves for him as a framework by which to justify the inferiority of the Jews. In this context, a colonial 'process of racializing the Jewish population' emerges.[22] By contrast, the intra-European experience, which Meiners claims has led from 'earliest times' to the distinction between 'noble and non-noble lineages', serves to historically anchor the colonial system of categories. Thus, the way he links the discourse of race to the questions concerning the status of the Jews suggests that the exclusion of the Jews for centuries contributed to the discourse of racial inequality. In this sense, one could perhaps speak of a 'Judaization' of colonial subjects.

Achievement (*Leistung*)

Like other theories of race, Meiners's theory of race, which he developed in numerous publications, is characterized by a peculiar tension.[23] On the one hand, he constantly refers to nature; accordingly, he presents the claim that the 'essence' of collectives – whether they are races, peoples, tribes or nations – can be identified and described.[24] On the other hand, Meiners conceives of nature as a dynamic point of reference. The world of race is far from static; Meiners notes numerous hybridizations and transformations, such as degeneration and uglification on the one hand and refinement, perfection and beautification on the other. Consequently, while Meiners's analytic approach to human life and the history of humanity, concisely expounded in his 1785 book *Grundriß der Geschichte der Menschheit* (*Outline of the History of Humanity*), starts from the premise that everything and everyone can be deduced or traced back to two primal races (the 'Caucasian' and the 'Mongolian'),[25] he is also forced to admit the following: 'The number of races that may arise, and have in part already arisen through displacement of peoples into various parts of the world and climate zones is too large to be determined.'[26]

A similar observation can be made regarding the elaborate system of categories that structures the process of racial differentiation, attribution and valuation. Here too, there is a tension, namely between biological/somatic criteria used to distinguish between groups (such as stature, obesity, skin colour, beard and hair growth and head shape) on the one hand and cultural/ethical criteria (including lifestyle, empathy, beauty/ugliness and virtuousness) on the other hand. This particular combination clearly allows an especially comprehensive and fine-tuned account of human life. At the same time, according to the deconstructive reading of media theorist Christine Hanke, one can discern a '"desperate" search for evidence' that reveals the basic vacuity of the signifier 'race'.[27]

The aspect I am mainly concerned with here is that of the criterion 'achievement' (*Leistung*) used to distinguish between groups. In the first part of my analysis, I already suggested that Meiners considers activity (*Tätigkeit*) a specific characteristic of Europeans. In the context of listing various virtually analogous power relations, Meiners also points out the dichotomy of active versus lazy and/or non-diligent races. This dichotomy is concisely expressed in one sentence that constitutes a summary of Meiners's considerations on the theme of equality and inequality. Meiners begins his summary by arguing that it is unjust to have inequality among equals; however, he continues, it is equally unjust to declare persons equal 'whom nature or other insuperable causes have rendered unequal'.[28] Meiners speaks of a 'sacred law of nature', according to which 'it is given and provided [*geleistet*] to every one as much as he himself can give and achieve [*leisten*]'. His conclusion is as follows: 'So those who give less and achieve less than others cannot without injustice demand as much as they can'.[29]

The historian Nina Verheyen has recently drawn attention to the semantic shift that the topos of achievement has undergone during the past 200 years. At present (and this has already been the case for several decades), the term 'achievement-oriented society' (*Leistungsgesellschaft*) is a common self-description, mainly of western capitalist societies, implying increases in economic productivity, as well as the link between professional position, social status and individual performance. Yet in the bourgeois discourse on virtue *c.* 1800, the predominant connotation was a different one, namely 'the appreciation of sociability and family life'.[30] Moreover, the interpretation of the notion of achievement that was common *c.* 1800 not only has little to do with today's 'optimization-obsessed, productivity- and efficiency-oriented understanding', but also provides 'inspiration for the exact opposite' – *Leistung* meant gathering and doing something for others, a 'joyous activity oriented towards reciprocity'.[31]

The deployment of the concept of achievement within the framework of Meiners's theory of race is at odds with Verheyen's findings.[32] At this point, it seems useful to refer to another article by Meiners, which was published in two parts in 1791, that is, one year after the essay on slavery and abolitionism. There Meiners attempts to outline the characteristic of Germanness or – to quote the title – the 'Natur der Germanischen und übrigen Celtischen Völker' ('Nature of the German and Other Celtic Peoples'). As Meiners makes clear at the outset, the essay is an 'investigation of the . . . noblest race of men'.[33] Meiners deduces this attribute not just from such features as physical size, strength, courageousness, beauty, fair skin, blonde hair and blue eyes but also from the circumstance that the 'Celtic peoples . . . [considered] obesity and paunchiness a condition meriting punishment, as it was seen to lead to men and youths losing their strength and being rendered less capable to stand manly work and hardship'.[34] Elsewhere, Meiners speaks of 'activity . . . as a distinctly German . . . characteristic'.[35] Finally, he distinguishes between Germans and Italians, attributing to the latter an 'insuperable torpor' which, he claims, leads Italians 'to endure heat and cold, hunger and thirst, rather than to engage in strenuous work'.[36]

As these quotations clarify, in Meiners view, achievement (*Leistung*) is associated with activity, proficiency, diligence, exertion, discomfort and work. Moreover, achievement emerges as the central criterion for determining the value of persons and human collectives. This is the case, for example, when

Meiners notes that the 'strongest, greatest, most beautiful, and most courageous nations are also the most ingenious and inventive', and when he concludes that '[the] spiritual gifts of nations can only be judged according to the proportion of what they have *achieved* in the whole period of their existence'.[37] In this sense, it can be said that – to return to the Nina Verheyen's argument – the modern meaning of achievement is very much already present in Meiners's reflections and considerations, namely as a 'lens or template by which to view the world, establish hierarchies between people, and domesticate people'.[38]

Global division of labour

Immanuel Wallerstein, the sociologist and world system theorist, pointed out the link between the development of the achievement paradigm (as evident in the notion of the 'achievement-oriented society'), the emergence of bourgeois society and the function of modern racism. The egalitarian content of bourgeois society, which according to Wallerstein is mainly manifested in the universalism of the claim to freedom and equality, is to a significant extent shaped by the idea of achievement and the notion 'that privilege earned by merit is somehow more acceptable, morally and politically, to most people than privilege earned by inheritance'.[39] As for racism, it causes the '"ethnicization" of the workforce'.[40] Precisely because the continuously expanding system of capital accumulation depends on the integration of labour power and is simultaneously constrained to minimize production costs (which include the cost of labour power), racism (like sexism) is required as a 'magic formula' of sorts, capable of bringing about 'an ethnicized but productive workforce'.[41] This could be summed up as follows: In contrast to the estates-based order, which is structured by origin and lineage, the principle of achievement is potentially egalitarian. However, racism introduces the logic of origin and lineage into the achievement-oriented society, attributing different degrees of achievement and achievement potential to various specifically defined collectives.

As noted earlier, in his essay on abolitionism, Meiners is mainly concerned with demonstrating the legitimacy of slavery. Accordingly, he has in mind a system characterized by a global division of labour. On the one hand, he diagnoses a 'revulsion against all serious and persistent work' among slaves (or Africans in general). On the other hand, he also argues that these persons can learn 'all manner of manual tasks that require no real design, no artistic eye, very easily'.[42] Because of this 'capacity to learn manual tasks', he continues, slaves

78   *Colonialism and the Jews in German History*

can be 'used for all manner of domestic chores and common handicrafts'.[43] In this sense, according to Meiners, this is an issue of 'rendering them useful' and augmenting 'their powers and their predispositions for the good'.[44] Elsewhere he claims that Africans were 'rescued from death by the slave trade, and forced to engage in useful work against their will', thereby becoming 'not just happier and improved persons in a different part of the world, but also instruments of other people's prosperity'.[45] As suggested earlier, for Meiners, this constitutes the ethical value of slavery. He conceives of slavery as an educational project for the benefit not only of Europe but humanity as a whole.[46] The fact that Meiners takes the possibility of the slaves' destruction through work into account and the way in which he does this is remarkable. He calculates that if '100,000 more slaves would perish than were born' on the plantations, this would demonstrate that the slave trade and slave labour are 'ruinous to the black race of humans, but not that they are detrimental to the human race in its entirety'.[47]

But what about the Jews? What is Meiners's assessment of their capacity for work and achievement? First and foremost, it should be made clear that Meiners regards the Jews as one of the 'oriental peoples' (*morgenländische Völker*), which in his model are located between the 'races' he describes as Caucasian (white) and Mongolian (Black).[48] Meiners deploys what could be considered classic Orientalist ascriptions and stereotypes, and which he obtains mainly from travel reports.[49] In other words, one can discern what historian Achim Rohde calls 'overlaps between Orientalist and antisemitic discourses' or a 'type of inwardly directed Orientalism', rendering it apparent once again that the putative racial otherness of the Jews is postulated within the framework of colonialist/racist modes of differentiation.[50] This can also be seen with regard to the topos of achievement and/or with regard to the dichotomy of torpor versus laziness on the one hand and activity versus diligence on the other, which also plays a significant role in this context: 'The Orientals . . . are far less lively and restless than we are.'[51] Elsewhere, Meiners assesses the ability of the 'Orientals' to work, and in doing so makes reference to the transatlantic slave trade and/or slave labour. The 'Orientals', he argues, are 'incomparably slower than Europeans in their work and undertakings, and almost require such stimulants to work' as were deployed on American plantations.[52] It is also telling that Meiners discerns a lack of sensory refinement and creative power, leading, in his view, to an inability to 'appreciate beauty in works of art, . . . to develop original works of art, or even . . . to imitate the works of European artists'.[53]

Meiners does credit the 'Orientals' with 'certain skills, artifices, and manual capacities that are unique to them, and which can be regarded in a certain way as the artistic instincts of these peoples, or as the natural fruits of their particular disposition.[54] He goes on to speak mainly of craftsmanship (of which he claims, however, that as opposed to its European counterpart, it is characterized mainly by poor organization), as well as of artistry, trickery and science. With regard to science, he explicitly mentions the Jews, claiming that they – like Arabs, Persians and the upper castes of Hindu society – have appropriated 'the scientific knowledge of Europeans'. Thus, Meiners acknowledges a certain affinity for science but qualifies this by adding that '[even] in the sciences, the Orientals have always tended to learn what others invented rather than make important inventions of their own'. In any case, Meiners considers the Jews to be among the 'great peoples of the Orient'.[55] One reason he is interested in them is that, in his view, the long-standing presence of Jews in Europe is what makes the question of assimilation urgent. Accordingly, Meiners states that 'the Jews have indisputably been Europeanized in some respects, especially with respect to industriousness and activity'.[56] At this point it becomes clear that Meiners was influenced by the idea of acclimatization, which established a connection between climatic influences and the essence and changeability of collectives such as races or peoples.[57] Thus, climate has to be seen as a further factor regarding his system of racial categorization and differentiation. Nevertheless, according to Meiners, the question that arises is 'whether the errors the Jews have been accused of by all European nations for many centuries result from their condition or are manifestations of their ancestral nature'.[58] Moreover, he adds, one needs to ask whether the Jews 'will be willing and able to fulfill all duties of useful citizens or whether it would be better to advise them to build a new Jerusalem for themselves in their old fatherland'.[59]

In the passage quoted, Meiners refers to unspecified 'apologies that have been written for the Jewish nation'.[60] The question of whether Jewish 'errors' ought to be traced back to their circumstances or their 'nature' and the formulation 'useful citizens' are clearly reminiscent of the 1781 book *Ueber die bürgerliche Verbesserung der Juden* (*On the Civic Improvement of the Jews*) by Christian Wilhelm Dohm. According to historian Reinhard Rürup, this book, which 'decisively shaped the debate on emancipation for decades', is characterized by a fundamental ambiguity.[61] On the one hand, in the words of literary scholar Stephan Braese, it is 'a document that has initiated the process of emancipation within German-speaking countries like no other'.[62] On the other hand, it helped prepare 'ideologemes and arguments . . . that would soon enter the arsenal of modern antisemitism'.[63]

The starting point of Dohm's argument is a 'mercantilist utilitarianism' that linked emancipation to the 'revenue interest of the state that is organized according to mercantilistic principles'.[64] Accordingly, in his preface Dohm already states that his work is motivated by the idea of making Jews 'more beneficial members of civil society' and 'more useful to our states'.[65] He goes on to repeatedly speak of diligence, which seems to act as a kind of admission ticket to civil or bourgeois society and its form of state organization: 'To our established states every citizen must be welcome who observes the laws and increases the wealth of the state by his diligence'.[66] In making this claim, Dohm is guided by the notion of a correlation between a state's prosperity and the growth of its population such that the state 'must strengthen itself by increasing population', in Michel Foucault's words.[67] In any case, in his preface, Dohm certifies that Jews have been put into an 'oppressive condition' by 'prejudices of the darkest centuries'. Jews, he writes, have only become 'corrupt as people and citizens because they have been denied the rights of both'. One of the central prerequisites of the programme of 'civic improvement' is the assumption that Jews have 'developed their character because of the employment prescribed for them'.[68] Consequently, Dohm demands freedom of trade and free choice of profession for Jews, but with the qualification that access to commerce as a classically Jewish line of business be made more difficult and, in return, agriculture and acceptance into the arts and sciences be promoted.[69]

Dohm and Meiners are at opposite ends of the political spectrum. After all, Dohm argues in favour of emancipation, whereas Meiners seems to have rejected it. And while Dohm attributes the Jews' 'oppressive condition' mostly to restrictions regarding their choice and practice of various professions and to the social conditions they therefore lived under, Meiners refers to the 'ancestral nature' of 'Orientals'. In a certain sense, the essay 'Ueber die Natur der morgenländischen Völker' ('On the Nature of the Oriental Peoples') can be understood as a response to Dohm, although Jews are only mentioned in passing. Be that as it may, Meiners postulates that his essay contains 'some data for a decisive answer to the question' concerning the effect of the environment/social situation on the one hand and nature/essence on the other.[70] And he makes it clear that Jews 'are still more similar to the peoples with whom they share the same origin . . . than to the nations among whom they have been transplanted'.[71] At the end of the text, he notes the following: 'If the Jews had as much courage as the ancient Greeks, or Saxons, or Norsemen, they would long have considered snatching the promised land from the hands of those few miserable robbers that have remained in the Palestine they have abandoned'.[72]

Despite the political differences, however, there is also a striking degree of overlap between the two authors. This is particularly true of the central role that the factors of diligence, beneficence, usefulness and achievement play in their respective schools of thought. While, as explained earlier, these factors act as a ticket to civic or bourgeois society and the modern state for Dohm, Meiners sees them as testifying to the value (or lack thereof) of particular 'races'. Either way, they serve as criteria for (non-)affiliation and define the boundaries between inclusion and exclusion. This also has an impact on the access to or deprivation of rights. Once again, both authors differ on the exclusive character of rights. Whereas Dohm considers the possibility of granting equal rights to Jews, Meiners defends the idea of a different legal status based on 'experience' and/or nature and/or race. Nevertheless, in both approaches, the access to rights is bound to certain conditions. This means that one must earn rights and legal status as an equal citizen. There are different ways of earning rights; Dohm, for example, refers to obeying laws. But the main criterion in both Meiners and Dohm's considerations is achievement. Thus, the entitlement to participation corresponds to the assumed ability (or inability) to achieve. Furthermore, achievement becomes the central criterion for measuring the value of people. Stephan Braese writes that, by linking the emancipation of the Jews to their 'economic and political utilization', Dohm helped 'prepare the ground for "modernized" anti-Jewish attitudes'. Meiners can be viewed as an actor who further builds on Dohm's preparations only a few years later.[73]

Conclusion

Christoph Meiners played a crucial role in the formation process of modern *German* racism. In this context, one important aspect is the faith in progress inherent in Meiners's thinking, particularly evident in the notion 'that human nature gradually increases in visible and invisible excellence from the Oriental to the Slavic, and from the Slavic to the Celtic peoples'. As for the nationalist dimension of Meiners's theory of race, it is part of a vision of progress, which almost inevitably leads to the Germans' domination of the world:

> It cannot be denied . . . that in no Celtic nation are all the virtues of human nature developed to a higher degree than in the Germans. By these preponderant advantages the noble German nation became the conqueror, or founder, and master of all other peoples; and through the nations descending from, or ruled by, the Germans, Europe became, and will continue to become more and more the master of all other parts of the world.[74]

Meiners attributes the European domination of the world, and the German domination of Europe, primarily to the factor of achievement, a factor which also mediates between the static and dynamic dimensions of his world view. This means that the capability for a specific achievement and the willingness to achieve constitute both the image of oneself and of the other. More precisely, they constitute the opposition between the self-image and the images of various others. It is assumed, for example, that Germans are particularly capable of performing in science and art. In contrast, Jews and Africans are presumed not to have this ability. However, Meiners makes some distinctions here: As an 'Oriental people', Jews are capable of appropriating and imitating German-European knowledge, as well as works of science and art; nevertheless, they are presumed not to be capable of independently performing in these areas. Africans, on the other hand, are only suitable as slaves for manual labour in households or on plantations.

Here, Meiners separates manual labour from intellectual work, which he regards as not having the same value. On the one hand, Meiners attributes the willingness and ability to perform to a certain position on the scale of 'human nature'. On the other hand, he allows for the possibility of development and change. Thus, his ideas about slavery and the global division of labour are based on the conviction that Africans have a fundamental disgust for labour per se. Nevertheless, he admits that they can be educated to work – for their own benefit as well – albeit only as manual labourers. In a similar vein, Meiners concedes that Jews have Europeanized themselves, at least in some respects. Even if Meiners does not explicitly mention this here, it is reasonable to assume that he attributes the partial disposition of Jews to science and art to the process of Europeanization. Nevertheless, this disposition is never as strong and as authentic as that of non-Jews. In any case, the idea of being able to educate other people to achieve through work runs through Meiners's oeuvre.

This idea also underpins Dohm's vision of Jewish emancipation. Even more than Meiners's, Dohm spells out the promise of equality in bourgeois society. And by defining diligence, or rather the willingness and ability to perform as a central criterion for belonging to this society, he conditions this promise on meeting the bourgeois demands for achievement. Maybe Dohm's plans for occupational restructuring (from trade to agriculture and art/science) already hint at the separation between the sphere of production and the sphere of circulation that was to be so momentous for the further development of antisemitism.[75] In any case, in Dohm's work, the bourgeois ideal of achievement also functions as a norm that organizes the inclusion or exclusion of others, in this case, the Jews.

And even if inclusion is intended here, Dohm provides the basis for potential exclusion due to alleged economic uselessness or unproductivity.

Unlike Dohm, Meiners can hardly be characterized as a proponent of the principles of bourgeois society. However, the reference to achievement signals a certain bourgeois element in his theory of inequality and inequivalence. He thus postulates inferior status for both Africans and Jews compared to that of Germans and Europeans. This means that antisemitism and colonial racism intersect in Meiners's work precisely in his reference to achievement as a criterion for the value of human beings. And yet, this does not mean that antisemitism and colonial racism merge into one single ideology. This is illustrated by the fact that Meiners does not identify the differences between noble and non-noble races within Europe with the differences between Europeans and colonized peoples, even if he posits a connection between the two, and by the fact that these differences emerge from independent archives of knowledge ('testimonies of all travelers' as well as traditional knowledge 'from earliest times'). On the other hand, Meiners's considerations on the status of Jews seem to aim at the exclusion from modern European societies, whereas Africans/slaves were to be integrated into global value chains through forced labour on plantations (with mass mortality accepted).

This difference should be stressed. If the emergence and development of modern racism is linked to the history of slavery and to the establishment of the global division of labour, as it is in Meiners' thinking, then it becomes clear that antisemitism follows a different logic. For Meiners, and unlike Dohm, Jews were not to integrate into the global value chain (maybe this explains why Jews and antisemitism only play a subordinate role in his thinking). To the contrary, regarding the history of antisemitism in the nineteenth century, Jews were seen as the embodiment of capitalist modernity, whereby antisemitic propaganda took the form of an authoritarian revolt against capitalist distortions. This holds true for the topos of 'German work', which began to gain prominence half a century after Meiners's death.[76] This topos is based on the idea that the Germans had developed a special work ethic, which could be distinguished from a supposedly Jewish one. In this context, the idea of an opposition between the common good ('German work') and self-interest ('Jewish work') emerges. And while 'German work' is seen as authentic and organic, 'Jewish work' is associated with alienation and profit maximization. Even if Meiners's antisemitic image of the Jewish other is not yet a very developed one, the corresponding self-image is already clearly apparent in his work. It is based on the idea that achievement is the result of a specific racial disposition, and that it is directed to the benefit of a racially defined collective. In this self-image, 'race' and achievement are merged in a thoroughly modern connection. It is no coincidence that in this context, Jews are specifically regarded by Meiners as one of the peoples who are not fully capable of achieving and are viewed as the main enemies of German work half a century later. Accordingly, it seems appropriate to refer to Meiners's reflections on the status of Jews as antisemitism, notwithstanding the well-known fact that the term only developed in the 1870s.[77] Meiners's case indicates that the ideology of achievement was a constitutive element in the genesis of modern scientific racism and antisemitism, and that this racism and antisemitism was, in turn, constitutive for the emergence of modern achievement-oriented society.

Translated by Max Henninger.

Notes

1 For a general account of the genesis of the scientific theory of race in the eighteenth century, see Sarah Reimann, *Die Entstehung des wissenschaftlichen Rassismus im 18. Jahrhundert* (Stuttgart: Franz Steiner Verlag, 2017).

2 Susanne Zantop, *Colonial Fantasies. Conquest, Family, and Nation in Precolonial Germany, 1770–1870* (Durham: Duke University Press, 1997), 82.

3 See Frank Schäfer, 'Nachwort', in Christoph Meiners, *Ueber die Natur der Afrikanischen Neger, und die davon abhangende Befreyung oder Einschränkung der Schwarzen*, ed. Frank Schäfer (Hannover: Matthias Wehrhahn Verlag, 2000), 65–78.

4 See Ludwig Schemann, *Die Rasse in den Geisteswissenschaften. Studien zur Geschichte des Rassengedankens. Band III: Die Rassenfragen im Schrifttum der Neuzeit* (München and Berlin: J.F. Lehmanns Verlag, 1943) 273 and 19.

5 See Robin Blackburn, *The Overthrow of Colonial Slavery 1776–1848* (London: Verso, 1988); Adam Hochschild, *Bury the Chains. Prophets and Rebels in the Fight to Free an Empire's Slaves* (Boston: Houghton Mifflin, 2005).

6 See Susan Buck-Morss, *Hegel, Haiti, and Universal History* (Pittsburgh: University of Pittsburgh Press, 2009); Michel-Rolph Trouillot, *Silencing the Past. Power and the Production of History* (Boston: Beacon Press, 1995).

7 For a general account of the status of Jews and the people of colour in the discourse of the Enlightenment, see Gudrun Hentges, *Schattenseiten der Aufklärung. Die Darstellung von Juden und 'Wilden' in philosophischen Schriften des 18. und 19. Jahrhunderts* (Schwalbach: Wochenschau Verlag, 1999). See also Andreas Pečar and Damien Tricoire, *Falsche Freunde. War die Aufklärung wirklich die Geburtsstunde der Moderne?* (Frankfurt a. M.: Campus Verlag, 2015), especially 83–151.

Racism, Antisemitism and Achievement

8 Meiners, *Natur der Afrikanischen Neger*, 5.

9 Ibid.

10 Ibid., 6.

11 See Friedrich Lotter, 'Christoph Meiners und die Lehre von der unterschiedlichen Wertigkeit der Menschenrassen', in *Geschichtswissenschaft in Göttingen. Eine Vorlesungsreihe*, ed. Hartmut Boockmann and Hermann Wellenreuther, (Göttingen: Vandenhoeck & Ruprecht, 1987), 30–75, here 44.

12 Ibid., 44 and 43.

13 Schäfer, 'Nachwort', 75.

14 Meiners, *Natur der Afrikanischen Neger*, 18. See also Felix Axster, 'Arbeit an der "Erziehung zur Arbeit", oder: die Figur des deutschen Kolonisators', in *'Deutsche Arbeit'. Kritische Perspektiven auf ein ideologisches Weltbild*, ed. Felix Axster and Nikolas Lelle (Göttingen: Wallstein Verlag, 2018), 226–51; *Zivilisierungsmissionen. Imperiale Weltverbesserung seit dem 18. Jahrhundert*, ed. Boris Barth and Jürgen Osterhammel (Konstanz: Universitätsverlag Konstanz, 2005); Anton Markmiller, *'Die Erziehung des Negers zur Arbeit'. Wie die koloniale Pädagogik afrikanische Gesellschaften in die Abhängigkeit führte* (Berlin: Dietrich Reimer Verlag, 1995).

15 Meiners, *Natur der Afrikanischen Neger*, 10.

16 Ibid., 11–12.

17 Ibid., 18.

18 Claudia Bruns, 'Antisemitism and Colonial Racism. Transnational and Interdiscursive Intersectionality', in *Racisms Made in Germany*, ed. Wulf D. Hund, Christian Koller and Moshe Zimmermann (Berlin: Lit Verlag, 2011), 99–121, here 104.

19 Meiners, *Natur der Afrikanischen Neger*, 18.

20 Ibid., 19.

21 Bruns, 'Antisemitism and Colonial Racism', 104.

22 Ibid.

23 Meiners wrote extensively. The 1885 edition of the biographical publication *Allgemeine Deutsche Biographie* speaks of the 'remarkable, indeed staggering volume of his literary achievements'. Carl von Prantl, 'Meiners, Christoph', in *Allgemeine Deutsche Biographie 1885*, available online: https://www.deutsche-biographie.de/sfz59983.html (accessed 12 February 2020). According to Lotter, Meiners published 44 monographs, some of them in several volumes, and more than 180 essays. See Lotter, 'Meiners und die Lehre', 36. Zantop, *Colonial Fantasies*, in particular 81–97, engages extensively with Meiners's theory of race. For a general account of theories of race and their inherent tensions, see Robert J. C. Young, *Colonial Desire. Hybridity in Theory, Culture and Race* (London: Routledge, 1995).

24 Nature is not only referred to in the title of the essay on slavery and abolitionism but also in the titles of other works, such as *Ueber die Natur der Germanischen und übrigen Celtischen Völker* ('On the Nature of the Germanic and Other Celtic

Peoples') or *Ueber die Natur der morgenländischen Völker* ('On the Nature of the Oriental Peoples'). I return to these other texts later.

25 See Christoph Meiners, *Grundriß der Geschichte der Menschheit* (Lemgo: Verlag der Meyerschen Buchhandlung, 1785).

26 Meiners, *Natur der Afrikanischen Neger*, 15.

27 Christine Hanke, 'Zwischen Evidenz und Leere. Zur Konstitution von "Rasse" im physisch-anthropologischen Diskurs um 1900', in *Der Gesellschaftskörper. Zur Neuordnung von Kultur und Geschlecht um 1900*, ed. Christine Hanke, Hannelore Bublitz and Andrea Seier (Frankfurt a. M.: Campus Verlag, 2000), 179–235, here 181.

28 Meiners, *Natur der Afrikanischen Neger*, 6.

29 Ibid.

30 Nina Verheyen, *Die Erfindung der Leistung* (München: Hanser Berlin, 2018), 20.

31 Ibid.

32 Lars Distelhorst, 'Die Glühbirne und der Möbelpacker. Über den Begriff der "Leistung" als leere Abstraktion', in *Zonen der Selbstoptimierung. Berichte aus der Leistungsgesellschaft*, ed. Felix Klopotek and Peter Scheiffele (Berlin: Matthes & Seitz Berlin, 2016), 38–52, here 39, notes the following: 'The principle of achievement [*Leistung*] always comes into play when it is a matter of comparing human beings and classifying their activities in accordance with hierarchical value systems that determine who shall receive which part of the cake.' See also Lars Distelhorst, *Leistung. Das Endstadium der Ideologie* (Bielefeld: Transcript Verlag, 2014).

33 Christoph Meiners, 'Ueber die Natur der Germanischen und übrigen Celtischen Völker', *Göttingisches Historisches Magazin* 8 (1791): 1–48, here 1.

34 Ibid., 7.

35 Ibid., 20.

36 Christoph Meiners, 'Zweyte Abhandlung über die Natur der Germanischen und übrigen Celtischen Völker', *Göttingisches Historisches Magazin* 8 (1791): 67–124, here 122.

37 Ibid., 73 (emphasis mine).

38 Verheyen, *Die Erfindung der Leistung*, 16.

39 Immanuel Wallerstein, 'The Ideological Tensions of Capitalism. Universalism versus Racism and Sexism', in *Race, Nation, Class. Ambiguous Identities*, ed. Immanuel Wallerstein and Etienne Balibar (London and New York: Verso, 1991), 29–36, here 32.

40 Ibid., 33.

41 Ibid., 33, 35.

42 Meiners, *Natur der Afrikanischen Neger*, 32, 40.

43 Ibid., 40.

44 Ibid., 9, 10.

45 Christoph Meiners, 'Historische Nachrichten über die wahre Beschaffenheit des Sclaven-Handels und der Knechtschaft der Neger in West-Indien', *Göttingisches*

Racism, Antisemitism and Achievement   87

Historisches Magazin 6 (1790): 645–79, here 649; Christoph Meiners, 'Fortgesetzte Betrachtungen über den Sclavenhandel, und die Freylassung der Neger', *Göttingisches Historisches Magazin*, 2 (1793): 1–58, here 56.

46 In one passage, Meiners explicates his notion of a global division of labour in some detail. Without slaves, 'no sugar plantations could be maintained, as neither Americans nor Europeans are able to endure the hard labor associated with planting and growing sugar cane, and with extracting sugar cane juice'. Without slaves, 'most coffee, sugar, rice, and tobacco plantations would also perish'. Thus, it is 'only [slaves] who provide us with sugar' and 'other precious commodities from the New World, and who provide many millions of white and nobler people with the livelihood and the prosperity associated with the production, shipping, and sale of these products, not to mention the immense sum of pleasant sensations caused by consumption of these American products'. Christoph Meiners, 'Ueber die Rechtmässigkeit des Negern-Handels', *Göttingisches Historisches Magazin* 2 (1788): 398–416, here 409.

47 Ibid.

48 See Christoph Meiners, 'Ueber die Natur der morgenländischen Völker', *Göttingisches Historisches Magazin* 7 (1790): 385–455.

49 On Orientalism as discourse or relation of domination, see Edward Said, *Orientalism* (New York: Vintage Books, 1979).

50 Achim Rohde, 'Der innere Orient. Orientalismus, Antisemitismus und Geschlecht im Deutschland des 18. bis 20. Jahrhunderts', *Die Welt des Islams* 45 (2005): 370–411, here 410.

51 Meiners, 'Natur der morgenländischen Völker', 404.

52 Ibid., 417.

53 Ibid., 426.

54 Ibid., 430.

55 Ibid., 432.

56 Ibid., 454.

57 See Iris Borowy, 'Akklimatisierung. Die Umformung europäischer Landschaft als Projekt im Dienst von Wirtschaft und Wissenschaft, 1850–1900', *Themenportal Europäische Geschichte*, 2009, available online: https://www.europa.clio-online.de/ essay/id/fdae-1493 (accessed 12 February 2020).

58 Ibid.

59 Meiners, 'Natur der morgenländischen Völker', 454. Meiners announces he will be publishing an investigation devoted specifically to answering these questions, though no such investigation was in fact ever published. See Lotter, 'Meiners und die Lehre', 55.

60 Meiners, 'Natur der morgenländischen Völker', 454.

61 Reinhard Rürup, 'Emanzipation und Krise – Zur Geschichte der "Judenfrage" in Deutschland vor 1890', in *Juden im Wilhelminischen Deutschland 1890–1914*, ed. Werner E. Mosse (Tübingen: J.C.B. Mohr, 1976), 1–56, here 5.

62 Stephan Braese, 'Kommentar zu Christian Wilhelm Dohm', in *Theorien über Judenhass – eine Denkgeschichte. Kommentierte Quellenedition (1781-1931)*, ed. Birgit Erdle and Werner Konitzer (Frankfurt a. M.: Campus Verlag, 2015), 35–43, here 43.

63 Ibid.

64 Ibid., 38.

65 Christian Wilhelm Dohm, *Ueber die bürgerliche Verbesserung der Juden* (Berlin and Stettin: Friedrich Nicolai, 1781), n. p. ('Vorerinnerung').

66 Ibid., 86.

67 Michel Foucault, *The Birth of Biopolitics: Lectures at the Collège de France, 1978–79* (Basingstoke: Palgrave Macmillan, 2008), 5.

68 Dohm, *Ueber die bürgerliche Verbesserung der Juden*, n. p. ('Vorerinnerung').

69 See ibid., 110–27. On the topos of civic improvement in general, see Nicolas Berg, '"Weg vom Kaufmannsstande! Zurück zur Urproduktion!" Produktivitätsforderungen an Juden im 19. und frühen 20. Jahrhundert', in *Das nennen Sie Arbeit? Der Produktivitätsdiskurs und seine Ausschlüsse*, ed. Nicole Colin and Franziska Schößler (Heidelberg: Synchron Publishers, 2013), 29–51; Shulamit Volkov, 'Die Verbürgerlichung der Juden in Deutschland als Paradigma', in *Jüdisches Leben und Antisemitismus im 19. und 20. Jahrhundert. Zehn Essays* (München: C.H. Beck, 1990), 111–30.

70 Meiners, 'Natur der morgenländischen Völker', 454.

71 Ibid.

72 Ibid., 455.

73 Braese, 'Kommentar', 35.

74 Meiners, 'Zweyte Abhandlung über die Natur der Germanischen Völker', 120–1.

75 This separation implies that the sphere of circulation is defined as the negative, exploitative and abstract part of capitalism, whereas the sphere of production was designated positive, creative and concrete. By associating them with the sphere of circulation, the anti-capitalist impulse is redirected against the Jews, who are seen as personifications of circulation, exploitation and general abstractness. See Moishe Postone, 'Anti-Semitism and National Socialism: Notes on the German Reaction to "Holocaust"', *New German Critique* 19 (1980): 97–115.

76 See Axster and Lelle, *'Deutsche Arbeit'*; Holger Schatz and Andrea Woeldike, *Freiheit und Wahn deutscher Arbeit. Zur historischen Aktualität einer folgenreichen antisemitischen Projektion* (Münster: Unrast Verlag, 2001).

77 See Rainer Erb and Werner Bergmann, *Die Nachtseite der Judenemanzipation. Der Widerstand gegen die Integration der Juden in Deutschland 1780-1860* (Berlin: Metropol, 1989).

5

Boundary as barrier, boundary as bridge

Jewish and Christian historiography on religious origins in nineteenth-century Germany

Susannah Heschel

The scholars who created the *Wissenschaft des Judentums* had expansive horizons.[1] Not only were they historians of Jews and philologists of Jewish texts, they also initiated the modern scholarly study of Islam and disputed the fundamental assumptions of scholarship on Christian origins. Emerging from traditional religious educations in classical rabbinic texts, they entered German universities and became critics of the scholarly methods they encountered. Far from seeking assimilation, they sought to overturn the standard narratives of western civilization by placing Judaism, not Christianity or Hellenic culture, as its foundation. Creating a new type of Jew and Jewish discourse – that of the scholarly public intellectual – they became cultural critics, not unlike Arab counterparts of the era whose interest in European *Wissenschaft* produced comparable responses. Arab scholars, like Jewish scholars, formulated critical analyses of European scholarship, such as Aḥmad Fāris al-Shidyāq (Lebanon, 1804–86), Rifāʿa Rāfiʿ al-Ṭahṭāwī (Egypt, 1801–73), Francis b. Fatḥ Allāh Marrāsh (Syria, 1836–86) and Muḥammad ʿAbduh (Egypt, 1849–1905).[2]

German scholarship of the nineteenth century, I will argue, reflected colonialist concerns, particularly when we examine the arguments put forward regarding relations and influences among the three monotheistic religions. Debates among Jews, Arabs and Christians over the interpretation of classical texts – rabbinic, New Testament, Qurʾanic – reflected the ongoing struggle of Jewish and Arab scholars for recognition in a European academic theatre dominated by Christians. Both politically and theologically, Jews and Arabs were not simply assimilating into German society but revolting against their colonized status under Christian hegemony in Europe and against Christian supersessionist theology. Jews insisted that Christianity was an unoriginal offshoot of Judaism; Arabs argued that Christians could barely read the Arabic texts they claimed to be analysing.[3] In the structure of their historical argumentation that placed Judaism as the religion that gave birth to both Christianity and Islam, Jewish historians were not simply revolting against their colonialized status but attempting to supplant Christian theological imperialism with Judaism through philological means. Arab scholars were creating a *nahda*, an Arab renaissance, that would display superiority to the European Christian culture that had for too long presented itself as the height of civilization. Christian scholars, well aware of the challenges, redoubled their efforts to demonstrate Christianity's superiority with orientalist motifs directed against both Jews and Arabs. There are, in other words, imperialist elements at the heart of the scholarly arguments.[4]

Colonialism is intimate. Fantasies, anxieties, mimicry, hybridities, projections and introjections abound, and the boundaries that are supposed to be impermeable quickly become porous. Most historians of Germany conventionally claim that German imperialism only began in the latter nineteenth century, with arms sales to the Ottoman Empire, investment in the Baghdad Railways, construction of roads, hospitals, and factories in Palestine and the acquisition of lands in Africa, culminating in the Berlin conference convened by German chancellor Otto von Bismarck in 1884–5 to regulate European colonization in Africa. Historians of Poland, on the other hand, speak of Prussia's acquisition of a piece of Poland during the partitions of the 1770s as 'colonialism'. In classic colonial terms, Poland was to be 'Germanized', while Prussia was to be protected against any possible 'Polonization'.

Moreover, Susanne Zantop has pointed to widespread German nationalist and orientalist fantasies of colonialism that already flourished, she argued, in the eighteenth century, before Germany became a colonizing power. Those fantasies did not occur in a vacuum but in response to Prussia's acquisition of large numbers of Polish Catholics and Jews by Protestant Prussia during the partitions of Poland – its initial venture as a colonial power. Indeed, historians of Poland refer to Prussia's acquisitions of Polish territory and populations during the three partitions as 'colonization'.[5] Efforts to 'Germanize' the new Polish Catholic population within Prussia were undertaken, and yet even in the mid-nineteenth century the Prussian government was still worrying that the Poles had a 'longing to break away . . . [and] cannot be won by any concessions'.[6] Even after the unification of Germany, the once-Polish territory was not yet viewed as reliably Germanized. Bismarck and the chancellors that followed him undertook the typical measures of colonizing powers in the realms of education, language, religion, culture and so forth, all with the aim, as Antony Polonsky writes, 'at encouraging German colonization' despite 'bitter opposition from the Poles'.[7] Regulating Prussian Poland meant a project of Germanizing the Poles without permitting them to Polonize the Germans; Polish assimilation into Germany had to occur without altering the nature of the majority culture. As boundaries opened, barriers were erected; this was an internal colonization that further stimulated concern over establishing cultural, religious and ethnic boundaries.

Robert Liberles has noted that precisely when Prussia began to gain a population of Catholic and Jewish Poles in the 1770s, debates were kindled over the so-called 'Jewish Question'.[8] Christian Dohm published *Über die bürgerliche Verbesserung der Juden* in 1781, and ten years later similar language was invoked on behalf of women's rights by Theodor von Hippel in his pamphlet, *Über die bürgerliche Verbesserung der Weiber* (1792). Those debates over Jews continued unabated, as did broader discussions over women's equality and over the absorption of minorities, as Aamir Mufti has noted.[9]

Arabs were not positioned in the precisely same way in Europe as were Jews, and my purpose is not to draw equivalencies but rather to call attention to certain striking parallels. As Lital Levy has demonstrated, the Arab *nahda* bore similarities to the Jewish *Haskalah*. In addition, Arab and Jewish scholars had similar critiques of European Christian philology; as topics of Christian investigation, both sought to reverse the gaze with their evaluations of the Christian world; both sought some degree of assimilation into Europe yet also desired distinctiveness, illustrating the ambivalence characteristic of colonial mimicry. Jews were orientalized in ambivalent terms by Europeans, at times rejecting those images and at other times embracing them. Jews were called 'German speaking Orientals' by the historian Heinrich von Treitschke, '*orientalische Fremdlinge*' by the publicist Wilhelm Marr and '*Wüstenvolk und Wandervolk*' by the economist Werner Sombart.[10] Jews were gendered female – or, rather, the image of the 'beautiful Jewess' functioned as a marker of borderlines and as a placeholder for hybrid knowledge, as Ulrike Brunotte writes, in the debates over 'whether the Jewish religious minority could be integrated as equal to the Christian majority and how the Jews assimilated as citizens in the modern nation-states'.[11] Jews and Arabs were further united as 'the enemy', that which must be extruded, to enable the production of the modern, Christian, European 'West'. I am not going to pursue the Jewish-Arab parallels extensively in this article but point to elements that deserve further consideration.

What occurred in the political realm in the late eighteenth century in Prussia continued during the course of the nineteenth century, with periodic

92 *Colonialism and the Jews in German History*

outbursts of concern over Catholics and Jews, their membership in the German nation, loyalties to the German state and potential 'contamination' of German society. After a chunk of Poland was acquired by Prussia, political anxieties over boundaries began to be reflected in German literature, as Kristin Kopp has demonstrated.[12] Poland became Germany's imagined 'wild east', to be tamed of their sensual and barbaric qualities while Germany presented itself as a *Kulturvolk* and a colonizing empire to its European imperial neighbours. The anxiety was of 'reverse diffusion', of Poles and Polishness moving westward into Germany.[13]

How were concerns with boundaries reflected in the theological writings in Germany? Since both Protestants and Jews were engaged in a redefinition of the origins, essences and historical fates of their respective religions, their theological models may have produced the cultural tools necessary for political conquest and control. They certainly made an impact on the self-understanding of Jews and Christians over the significance and historical influence of their respective religions. Yet each side viewed the boundaries differently. Christian scholars established barriers by limiting the degree of Jewish influence they were willing to acknowledge in both early Christianity and early Islam, whereas Jewish scholars sought to create bridges, emphasizing the extent to which Judaism infiltrated the New Testament and the Qur'an.

Christian scholarship: Boundary as barrier

Some of the finest German scholars of early Christianity were faculty members or students of the Tübingen School, which flourished from the 1830s to the 1860s.[14] Its guiding figure was Ferdinand Christian Baur, professor of theology at the University of Tübingen, a towering intellect whose analysis of the first two centuries of Christianity became wildly influential well into the twenty-first century, and who was also a significant interpreter of Hegel and Schelling. Perhaps the best known and most radical of his students was David Friedrich Strauss, whose 1835 *Life of Jesus* brought Tübingen School methods to a devastating analysis of the Gospels and New Testament scholarship, causing a scandal throughout Europe and bringing an end to Strauss's academic career. Nonetheless, the philological methods and modes of historicist analysis developed by the Tübingen School were profoundly influential within Protestant theology and were also adapted by scholars in other fields.[15]

Baur developed an architectonic of early Christianity that spoke of a tension within the first two centuries between what he termed Jewish Christianity and

Gentile Christianity. The term 'Jewish Christianity' was a modern invention, developed as a category for the many diverse groups labelled as 'heretical' by the Church Fathers who claimed to find some sort of Jewish practices or ideas or ethnicity in each group; these heretical groups are known from pseudepigraphical or heresiological texts. The term 'Jewish Christianity' does not appear in ancient texts but became prominent in German theological discourse with the Tübingen School; Baur made the term central to the historiography of Christian origins. He and his colleagues used the term to identify pseudonymous texts of antiquity that seemed to them neither obviously Christian nor Jewish, such as the Pseudo-Clementines. More important, Baur and his followers claimed that individual New Testament passages reflected either Jewish Christianity or Gentile Christianity, two opposing tendencies that sparked conflicting religious and political tendencies until their resolution at the end of the second century with the emergence of the Church.

Defining the 'Jewish Christians' of antiquity was hotly debated during the nineteenth century: were they ethnic Jews who had joined the Jesus movement? Christians who practised circumcision? People with a 'Jewish' legalistic way of thinking? Most important, the term functioned as a border crossing, indicating when and in what ways Jews turned into Christians and what elements of Judaism they brought with them. Who were Jewish Christians? For Baur, the term signified those who believed Jesus was the messiah but who retained aspects of Jewish law (particularly, circumcision) and were opposed to Pauline theology.[16] A more Lutheran definition comes from Albert Schwegler, another member of the Tübingen School, who argued that Jewish Christianity failed to recognize 'the basic difference between Christianity and Judaism, between law and gospel'.[17]

But what marked the 'Jewishness' of Jewish Christianity? While German-Jewish thinkers were identifying lofty theological ideas of ethics and monotheism as Jewish, Protestants defined Jewishness in ethnic and cultural terms, or in religious terms opposite to Christianity (law, not gospel), and sought to minimize Judaism's influence on the Church and to distinguish between Old Testament teachings and Jewish Christian beliefs. Karl Reinhard Köstlin distinguished between Jewish Christianity and Ebionitism: the former recognized the originality of Jesus' religious consciousness, even trying to harmonize it with some minimal observance of Jewish law, whereas the Ebionites failed to recognize that a new element had appeared with Jesus, seeing his teachings solely within the framework of Judaism.[18] Apparently he believed that the more committed one was to Judaism, the less able one was to recognize the novelty of Jesus. Adolph Schliemann defined Jewish Christians as Christians who had once been Jews and retained a Jewish perspective,[19] while Albrecht Ritschl distinguished between Old Testament influences that were Christianity's legitimate inheritance and Jewish Christian sects whose views ultimately exerted no significant influence on the emerging Church. By the turn of the century, as James Paget writes, the great historian and liberal Protestant theologian Adolf von Harnack concluded that 'Christianity's claim to be the fulfillment of the Old Testament promises did not in any sense align it with Judaism and thus with Jewish Christianity'.[20]

The debate over Jewish Christianity spilled into the scholarly analyses of Islamic origins, bringing some of the Christian and Jewish theological commitments to bear on early Islam. Jewish scholars, starting with Abraham Geiger in 1833, were actively demonstrating the parallels between the Qur'an and rabbinic literature, arguing for a Jewish context of Islamic origins. Harnack, however, suggested that Islam, in accepting prophecy but rejecting Trinitarianism, must have developed out of a gnostic Jewish Christianity that he considered superior to the abstruse Trinitarianism of medieval Christianity and closer to Protestantism, but not to Judaism. 'Islam is a transformation on Arab soil of a Jewish religion which itself had been transformed by gnostic Jewish Christianity'.[21]

Harnack saw the influence on Islam transmitted via the Jewish Christians of southern Mesopotamia, Elkasites.[22] The Qur'an mentions 'Jews, Sabians and Christians', leading some scholars to argue that Sabians were Jewish Christians.[23] Daniel Chwolson identified the Sabians with both Elkasites and Mandaeans, Arabian offshoots of the Jewish Christian Ebionites. Thus, while Jewish influences within earliest Christianity were said to have been purged by the end of the second century, they reappeared as major influences on early Islam. The argument functions to deny Jewish influence on Christianity and sees Islam arising within a Christian heretical group that was never fully eradicated. Claiming Islam's emergence from Christian heretics is a medieval Christian argument clothed in modern scholarly apparatus that has had a long life. Hans-Joachim Schoeps, in a widely read study of Jewish Christians originally published in 1949, argued that although Jewish Christianity disappeared within Christianity by the third or fourth century, it was preserved in Islam to this day.[24] More recently, Francis de Blois has suggested that there may have been an outpost in Mecca of Nazoraean Jewish Christians who conveyed Pauline teachings to Muhammad – or that Muhammad may have learned those teachings in Syria from contact with Melkite or Jacobite Christians.[25] The rabbinic texts and contexts outlined by Jewish scholars are displaced by Jewish Christianity, a phenomenon known only through the textual sources of its enemies, the Church Fathers. Leopold Zunz once remarked that German scholars were more adept at Mongolian than Hebrew. Judaism's motherhood had been simply eradicated.

Jewish scholars participated in those debates but analysed the Jewish Christian 'heretical' groups not in terms of their orientation to Jesus and early Christianity but towards early Judaism. Thus, Geiger adapted Baur's architectonic for his study of ancient Judaism, arguing that it was dominated by the conflicting tendencies of liberal Pharisees and conservative Sadducees. Countering the Tübingen School's understanding of Jewish Christianity, Geiger claimed that the milieu of an ancient text can 'first be able to be determined when the Jewish Christian sects are considered more carefully according to the perspectives outlined earlier, in so far, namely, as their adherents come more from Sadducean or from Pharisaic circles'.[26] Ebionites, he argued, maintained closer connections to the Pharisees and were not antagonistic towards the rabbis. If the text is to be called Jewish Christian, its position reflects not an opposition to Judaism but a Sadducean dissension from Pharisaic Jewish beliefs and commitments.

Historians are never unaffected by the politics of their day, though the particulars may not be apparent until much later. The idea that Jewish Christians in antiquity infiltrated and distorted early Christianity and may have created Islam reflected contemporary German concerns regarding the influences and impurities that might be entering Prussia, whether from Poles or Jews, and the need to preserve a pure Christianity or a pure Germany. The historiographical arguments of the Tübingen School mirrored the anxieties of colonialism: how to rule over another people, viewed as inferior, without being affected by them. In the writings of the Protestant historians, the second century became an allegory for the nineteenth century: boundaries had to be fixed, and whatever managed to get through would have to be quickly transformed, with Jewish Christians turned into (real) Christians by purifying them of their Jewishness, a task that was not entirely successful, they argued. Hence all the more reason that the Catholic church, which had been infiltrated by Jewish elements in the second century, had to be 'purified' by the Protestant Reformation. Judaism was historical detritus that Christianity had to expel in order to flourish. The political parallels are obvious: charges that Jews were contaminating Germany were rife, and Christian concerns to protect against Judaism ranged from Harnack's call for eliminating the Old Testament to dejudaization of the New Testament and hymnal carried out during the Third Reich.[27]

Jewish scholars who sought to demonstrate the crucial need for historians to gain knowledge of Judaism and Hebrew sources were not simply revolting against Christian hegemony; they were also attempting to supplant it. Protestant scholars presented early Christianity as a movement of reform, purging itself of Jewish accretions, and Geiger defined Pharisaism in similar language, as a movement of reform promoting a democratic, progressive and liberal version of Judaism. Indeed, Geiger used the very language of the Protestant Reformation, writing that the Pharisees were calling for the 'priesthood of all believers'. He wrote, 'To all is given the inheritance, the kingdom, the priesthood and its power of sanctification.' ('*Allen ist gegeben das Erbe, das Königreich, das Priestertum und die Heiligung.*')[28]

A maternity crisis

Religions are born, not revealed by God and not invented by humans, according to the imagination of the nineteenth century, and being born raises the question of maternity: just what religious beliefs and cultural traditions gave birth to these various religions? That Judaism is the mother religion, while Christianity and Islam are its daughters emerged as a cliché of Jewish scholarship during the nineteenth and twentieth centuries; as recently as 1995 the medieval historian Anna Sapir Abulafia wrote with confidence: 'Any consideration about relations between Judaism and Christianity must begin with an obvious point. Christianity is a daughter religion of Judaism and as such it draws much of its validity from the very sources that Jews have always claimed as their own.'[29]

Until very recently, Christian theologians objected to the metaphor. The German Protestant theologian Gustav Volkmar, whose work was part of the Tübingen School, wrote in 1857 that 'the Judaism that formed the religious background to Jesus and Christianity was not the Pharisaic Judaism dominant during the Second Temple era' but the 'virgin womb of the God of Judaism'.[30] God's virginity, unlike Mary's, means that Christianity has no older sibling; it is God's only child – God did not give birth to Judaism. He may be the God worshipped by Judaism, but He is not the creator of Judaism. Historicism be damned: Christianity was born of God, and whatever may have been derived from Judaism (which was not the offspring of God) was superseded. Christianity is the first-born son of the virgin; Christianity, in this view, is Christ himself.

The anxiety of origins reflected in the metaphor of God's virgin womb carried both theological and political implications. Theologians of Christianity wanted to demonstrate its distinctiveness and originality and stressed the boundaries between the religions, which Jewish scholars denied, striving instead to prove

Judaism's centrality to western civilization by insisting on the derivative nature of Christianity and Islam, erasing boundaries but also establishing a unidirectional flow of influence. A greater problem, as the historian Israel Yuval has pointed out, is that the favoured Jewish metaphor of mother-daughter erases the possibility of Christian influence on Judaism; more properly, he writes, historians should recognize that 'both are daughter religions of biblical Judaism'.[31]

Scholars of modern German literature have called attention to the role played by the 'beautiful Jewess' as a 'marker of borderlines and as a placeholder for hybrid knowledge'.[32] For Jewish writers, by contrast, Jewish women were imagined with greater ambivalence, linked to expressions of nostalgia for an earlier era but also vilified as agents of assimilation, conversion and abandonment of Jewish tradition and identity. In Christian theological writings, the Hebrew Bible often functions as a beautiful Jewess: the Hebrew Bible is the mediating figure between ancient Near East paganism and civilized Christianity; as a border text, it is liminal, fully belonging to neither Judaism nor Christianity. It is intriguing but also marked with some ambivalence: does the Hebrew Bible prefigure and authenticate Christianity or does it spoil the originality of the New Testament? After all, the Hebrew Bible contains both the soaring poetry of the psalms and the vulgar carnality of Leviticus. Its plasticity evoked affirmation and even philosemitism from theologically conservative Christians and condescension and even antisemitism from the *Kulturprotestanten*. At the hands of German Protestants and their historical-critical methods, 'the Hebrew Bible underwent a tripartite process of transformation: it was historicized; the Hebrew language was given a poetological quality; and, last but not least, the book was orientalized'.[33]

The beautiful Jewess, Andrea Polaschegg writes, is presented as a prisoner or victim of a patriarchal Jewish father and his religion. Christian depictions of the Hebrew Bible, too, imply it is a prisoner or victim at the hands of the Jews and their Levitical, legalistic religion, Jews who are unable to grasp the spiritually transcendent, ethical teachings of the Hebrew Bible fulfilled in Christianity. Trapped by Judaism, the Hebrew Bible awaits redemption by Christianity, reflecting the master narrative of colonialism: the 'brown woman who has to be saved by white men from their brown, patriarchal oppressors'.[34] In this way, the Hebrew Bible takes on the ambivalent qualities of the Beautiful Jewess who 'represents the ethos of enlightened tolerance and feminine tenderness, but she is also described as possessing a dangerously foreign beauty'.[35] Similarly, the Hebrew Bible is depicted not only as the poetic beauty of the Psalms but also as containing foreign, bizarre and even dangerous elements of tribal violence.

Wissenschaft des Judentums

The *Wissenschaft des Judentums* is recognized, in the words of Nils Römer, as 'one of the major spiritual and intellectual responses to the crisis of modernity and as an instrument in the struggle for emancipation'.[36] In its effort to uncover documents about Jewish life and write narratives about the long span of Jewish history, the *Wissenschaft des Judentums* provided an important source of Jewish identity. Writing about Leopold Zunz's important essay of 1818, *Etwas über die rabbinische Literatur*, considered a founding document of the *Wissenschaft des Judentums*, Amos Bitzan writes that its agenda is more philosophical than historical, oriented to an 'ideal of character formation'.[37] While it produced narratives about Jewish experience, the *Wissenschaft des Judentums* was also an effort to reconceive the role of Jews and Judaism in western civilization. Indeed, the end of Jewish political autonomy and the resulting Jewish diaspora signalled not an end to Jewish history but, in the words of Isaac Markus Jost (1793–1860), author of one of the first multivolume narratives of Jewish history, the 'dawnglow of the Jewish religion', the 'heralds of a new creation' and 'blessings ... soon received by all receptive peoples'.[38] The study of history was also transformative for the historian; in 1833, a young Abraham Geiger wrote to another pioneering Jewish scholar, Leopold Zunz (1794–1886), that in becoming scholars 'we became men and wanted manly fare, we wanted *Wissenschaft*'.[39]

Noted nineteenth-century German historians such as Leopold von Ranke and Heinrich von Treitschke described past German conquests of lands and peoples to indicate and celebrate the scope of German imperial power. The *Wissenschaft des Judentums* began by painting a broad scope of Jewish intellectual power: Zunz's essay, *Etwas über die rabbinische Literatur*, presents the wide range of Jewish literature, extending far beyond religious texts and codes of law to include all sorts of Jewish expression over the centuries. Ultimately, the goal was not simply the reconstruction of the Jewish past, for Zunz, but the reorientation of historical scholarship to recognize the extent of Jewish influence on western history; he wrote: 'The extraordinary influence which the religious knowledge of the Hebrew exercised on the nations of Christianity and Islam lent their national literature a universal significance. ... This literature supersedes that of any other pre-Christian nation, and thus constitutes for the history of mankind and its spiritual development noteworthy monuments and reliable sources'.[40]

Geiger's own discovery of *Wissenschaft*'s manliness came with his study of the Qur'an and his demonstration of the extent to which rabbinic ideas, practices and texts had penetrated Muhammad's beliefs, the text of the Qur'an and early Islamic religious practices. For example, Geiger recognized Mishnah Sanhedrin 4:5, that saving one life is equivalent to saving the whole world, within Qur'an Sura 5:32. The mockery of Noah's Ark, in Sura 11:40, corresponds to Midrash Tanhuma and the Qur'an's assertion that 'the waters of the flood were hot' (Sura 11:42, Talmud Bavli Zevachim 113b, Talmud Bavli Sanhedrin 108a).[41] Noah, Geiger writes, appears in the Qur'an as a figure who admonishes sinners, following similar representations in rabbinic literature, 'and serves Muhammad's ends perfectly, as Noah in this way is a type of himself'.[42] Geiger also suggests that Muhammad rejected a Talmudic statement (Talmud Bavli Sanhedrin 104) that the son cleanses the father, but the father does not cleanse the son. Instead, Muhammad, according to Geiger, reinterpreted the statement in the Qur'an so that ancestors grant merit to their descendants, 'zehut avot', implying that Muhammad constructed Abraham as a prototype of himself: a public preacher who won converts, was a model of piety, established a monotheistic religion, believed he was given messages from God and so forth.[43] Muhammad knew and made extensive use of rabbinic literature, but he shaped it for his own political purposes.

Two decades after his study of the Qur'an, Geiger turned to the New Testament, arguing that Jesus's teachings were neither a break with Judaism nor anything new; Jesus was one of the liberal, progressive Pharisees of his era who sought to democratize Jewish religious practice and detach it from priestly control. However, Paul betrayed Jesus's message by mixing it with pagan philosophy. The outcome was Christianity, a religion about Jesus, rather than the faith of Jesus, which was Judaism. By contrast, Geiger viewed Islam more favourably, as the religion that insisted on strict monotheism, rejected anthropomorphism, upheld religious tolerance and maintained an ethical religious law. While Christianity was carried in the womb of Judaism, Islam was not only born of Judaism but also suckled and nurtured by it, Geiger claimed. In his view, Christianity was the daughter who strayed, whereas Islam was the daughter who adhered to the mother. Most important: neither Christianity nor Islam, Geiger insisted, was a new religion; both were simply a 'manifestation of Judaism'.[44]

Geiger's contemporary, the historian Heinrich Graetz, disagreed; Christianity was born, in his presentation, from marginalized groups of ignorant Galilean Jews who were easily duped into apocalyptic fantasies brought to them by Jesus, whom Graetz identified not as a Pharisee but as one of the Essenes, a marginal group at best. By contrast, Islam, Graetz wrote, was 'nursed at its [Judaism's] breast. It was aroused by Judaism to bring into the world a new form of religion with political foundations . . . and it exerted an enormous influence on the shape and development of Jewish history.'[45]

Purifying religion

The Jewish effort to claim itself as progenitor of Islam and Christianity continued during the course of the nineteenth century. Geiger's comparison of the Qur'an with rabbinic texts launched a long tradition of German-Jewish scholarship that explored those parallels, by figures such as Hartwig Hirschfeld, Israel Schapiro, Eugen Mittwoch, Isaac Gastfreund and Heinrich Speyer, among others.[46] In 1840, Ludwig Ullmann, who had studied at the same time as Geiger at the University of Bonn, translated the Qur'an into German, while Albin de Biberstein translated the Qur'an into French. In 1857 the first Hebrew translation appeared, rendered by Hermann Reckendorff. Rabbinical students at the seminars in Berlin, Breslau and Budapest, as well as at the *yeshiva* in Würzburg, studied Arabic. The myth of the 'Golden Age' of Muslim Spain was developed, along with the claim that Islam was the religion of tolerance, in contrast to Christianity. The image of a tolerant Islam, in contrast to an intolerant Christianity, was popular at the time; Heinrich Heine's 1823 play, *Almansor*, was among several literary works of the era depicting a romantic, welcoming Muslim Spanish culture that serves as a model for an enlightened religion necessary to the modern world.[47] Moreover, one of the most prominent German-Jewish scholars of Islam, Gustav Weil, viewed Islam as the Enlightenment religion par excellence: 'A Judaism without the many ritual and ceremonial laws, which, according to Muhammad's declaration, even Christ had been called to abolish, or a Christianity without the Trinity, crucifixion, and salvation connected therewith – this was the creed which, in the early period of his mission, Muhammad preached with unfeigned enthusiasm.'[48]

Not all Jewish thinkers agreed, of course. Ludwig Philippson, Heinrich Graetz and Franz Rosenzweig are three German-Jewish thinkers whose view of Islam was less than enthusiastic, but who were also not scholars of Arabic.[49] While continuing to demonstrate the influence of Judaism on Islam, Graetz used that influence as proof of Islam's lack of originality. Thus, Graetz wrote in his eleven-volume *Geschichte der Juden*, published between 1853 and 1878, that 'the best that the Qur'an contains, is borrowed from the Bible or the Talmud' (*Das Beste, was der Koran enthält, ist der Bibel oder dem Talmud entlehnt*).[50] Graetz, who for so long was antagonistic to Geiger (though reconciled in later years, as Michael Meyer has demonstrated), pointed to parallels between Islam and Judaism but drew very different conclusions.[51] The Islamic declaration that 'there is no God but Allah' was taken from Judaism, Graetz wrote, and Muhammad's subsequent addition, 'and Muhammad is his prophet' was simply a reflection of his 'arrogance'.[52] While Geiger understood Muhammad as a genuine religious believer, Graetz wrote that Muhammad 'first conceived [his religious teachings] when suffering from epilepsy, and he communicated them to his friends, pretending they were revealed to him by the angel Gabriel'.[53]

What did Islam ultimately offer to Jews? Graetz at times contradicts himself. He wrote of the glorious era of Muslim Spain that led to a flourishing of Jewish culture, but he also wrote that Islam became Judaism's 'second enemy'.[54] Muhammad himself, Graetz writes, 'hated the Jews in his innermost heart' and 'exchanged the attitude of a humble prophet for that of a fanatical tyrant'.[55] Ultimately, Graetz writes, 'fanaticism, together with the love of war and conquest, had already taken possession of the Arabians, and they accepted the Qur'an as a whole, alike its revolting features and the truths borrowed from Judaism, as the unquestionable word of God. Judaism had reared a second unnatural child'.[56]

Graetz held even more cantankerous views of Christianity, claiming it was the first and most dangerous enemy of the Jews. Nearly every section of the *History of the Jews* opens with an account of Jewish persecutions and suffering at the hands, primarily, of Christians. That lachrymose account of Jewish history makes Graetz's depiction of Christian origins a kind of historiographical theodicy.

In Graetz's depiction, Jesus was an earnest, gentle, moral figure who emerged within the Essene community, which had attempted to hasten the messianic era through an ascetic lifestyle. The fervour of Jesus's preaching, he argues, was attractive primarily to Galilean Jews, who were ignorant, superstitious, primitive simpletons susceptible to apocalyptic fantasies, charlatans and false messiahs. Jesus called himself the 'Son of God' and the 'Son of Man', terms Graetz claims were derived from the Essenes, and Jesus claimed to have power over demons and Satan. Graetz's Jesus encouraged moral righteousness, and he did not attempt to reform Judaism, nor did he object to the sacrificial system, but he was of little interest to the well-educated Jews of Judea, who were immersed in scholarly study of Torah. For Graetz, as for Geiger, Christianity began with Paul, who synthesized Jewish monotheism with paganism, producing a religion attractive to Greek and Roman pagans as well as Hellenized Jews.

Geiger's scholarship portrayed large historical expanses that included Christianity and Islam, at least in their earliest, formative periods, within the rubrics of Judaism. His argument erases religious boundaries and implies an imperialist nature to Judaism, on the theological level. Both Jesus and Muhammad are educated, cultivated, genuinely religious figures who exemplify the best of Judaism's liberal teachings and demonstrate what Jews have to offer to society, including contemporary Germany. Graetz, by contrast, depicts Jesus as a marginal figure, appealing to the ignorant masses that are easily swayed by apocalyptic and mystical enthusiasms, while Muhammad is a crafty politician who used religion to further his own interests. For Graetz, both Jesus and Muhammad, and the Galilean Jews in general, may represent the pious, poor, uneducated Poles who lack German language, Bildung and Kultur; Evan Goldstein points to the parallel drawn by Friedrich Nietzsche in *The Antichrist*, written in 1888, between the early Christians of the New Testament and Polish Jews: 'Neither has a pleasant smell.'[57]

Parallels with the *nahda*

As Lital Levy points out, both the *nahda* and the *Haskalah* define themselves with metaphors of awakening, light and progress, always emphasizing the centrality of Europe.[58] The focus of both was on revival of language, culture and identity. Primary was a linguistic renewal of the Arabic of pre-Islamic poetry and Hebrew of the Bible, respectively. They focused on creating wide networks, printing, and translating, and a politics of nationalism that would bring cultural revival. Neither wanted a break with tradition; as Tarek el-Ariss writes, the *nahda* was 'a discovery not only of Europe but also of the Arab past and of Russia and India.'[59] Both Jews and Arabs also redefined religion, rejecting clerical power, doctrine and the absoluteness of religious law; instead, Judaism and Islam were to be morally edifying, rational, flexible, tolerant, open to scientific thought and assisting adherents in their entry into modernity and society. The *nahda*, it should be added, included Jewish participants; one of them, Shimon Moyal, published an Arabic-language introduction to the Talmud.[60] Jewish and Arab struggles were similar: inner conflicts of self-definition, transculturation, authenticity and modernity.[61] Reports by Arabs of their travels to learn the methods of European scholarship and of Jews who entered German universities in the 1830s have a similar tone; the critique of European scholars of Arabic by Ahmad Faris al-Shidyaq (Libanon, 1804–1886) in his book, *Leg over Leg*, and the report of Rifa' Tahtawi in his book, *An Iman in Paris*, echoed Geiger's critique of Christian scholars of Hebrew.

Conclusion

Movements of religious reform share similar motifs of wanting to cleanse, purify, liberalize and return to a pristine point of origin. While such a return to origins often calls forth a longing for an imaginary moment of Christian onset, the rise of liberal theology and historicism complicated the theological wish. By the mid-nineteenth century, Protestants scholars defined the project of theology as the historical reconstruction of Christian origins, but that reconstruction involved recognition that Christianity emerged not ex nihilo, as a singular, pristine religion, but within Judaism. From its moment of onset, Christianity had to undertake an effort at self-definition, cleaning itself of whatever Jewish accretions it wanted to reject, in order to emerge through a process of purification.

Scholars of the *Wissenschaft des Judentums* were similarly concerned with purging Judaism and Jewish identity – *Wissenschaft* (scholarship) was to replace *Wissen* (knowledge), as Zunz put it – and were also searching for a guiding leitmotif, whether a unified course of Jewish history, such as Graetz produced, or an undercurrent of liberalism as Geiger claimed for Pharisaism, or an identification of a presumed 'essence' of Judaism with Enlightenment religion, as claimed by Weil, Hermann Cohen, Baeck and many others. Yet for the Jews, the point of origin of Judaism was not enmeshed in a different religion. Studies of the ancient Near East did not begin until late in the nineteenth century, and the Babel-Bibel controversy was larded with anti-Jewish, if not antisemitic motifs. For Jews, insisting on the autochthony of Judaism was essential and served as a Jewish counterpart to Christian theological supersessionism. Comparisons of biblical religion with Babylonian or Egyptian religious ideas or practices were dismissed by Jewish theologians as superficial or used as opportunities to insist that biblical religion had rebelled against the paganism, idolatry and immorality of the surrounding environment. 'Paganism' was an artificial construct that became a crucial rhetorical device in defending Jewish autochthony and uniqueness.

The 'philological uncanny' that Geiger, Weil, Graetz and so many other Jewish scholars experienced when discovering Jewish phrases, ideas and practices within the Qur'an and the New Testament brought them pleasure, satisfaction and even a kind of compensation for their loss of Orthodox religious faith. Having departed from the absolutism of Jewish Orthodoxy and rejected divine dictation of the words of Torah, they could instead experience satisfaction by demonstrating the historical impact of Judaism on other religions, garnering for Judaism the title of mother religion. The politics of the era of Jewish emancipation thus became, textually conceived, not simply an emancipation from Judaism, nor an emancipation from the restrictions of the European nation states, but rather an imagined transformation of western history into a theological empire of Judaism and its influences. A certain solace for the loss of religious belief could be established, but the danger became a new kind of imperialist historicism that, at times, failed to recognize the distinctive agency and subjectivity of Islam as well as of Christianity. Glimmers of a shift might be found in some of the concluding moments of that great German-Jewish *Wissenschaft*. At the turn of the century, Israel Friedlaender broke the confines of Islam as a rational religion and began studying Shiism and even arguing for its influence on false messianic movements within Judaism.[62] Josef Horovitz, writing in the early years of the twentieth century, and Heinrich Speyer, writing in the 1930s, hint in their work at an understanding of the Qur'an not simply as a receptacle of Jewish ideas but as an interpreter of the Bible and Midrash, a point that the Qur'an scholar Angelika Neuwirth has recently revived in her intertextual studies of the Qur'an.[63]

On the Christian side, Jewish interventions did not spark greater Christian sympathy for Judaism. The effort to construct boundaries aroused an anxiety in Protestant theology over the historicist claim that, contextualized within first-century Judaism, Jesus said nothing new or original. The rebuttal came not in historicist form but by evoking racial theory, which arose to academic respectability during the course of the nineteenth century. Jesus may have repeated Jewish teachings, but spiritually he was unique – so claimed Theodor Keim, Daniel Schenkel and Karl von Hase, in the 1860s and 1870s, among others. Finally, at the turn of the century, his uniqueness was allegedly rooted in his racial distinction: he was an Aryan. The appalling antisemitic activities of the so-called Institut zur Erforschung und Beseitigung des jüdischen Einflusses auf das deutsche kirchliche Leben (Institute for the Study and Elimination of Jewish Influence on German church Life), founded in 1939, should be neither ignored nor dismissed as a marginal phenomenon because it fulfilled a long unspoken Christian wish: to rid itself of the shame at having originated from Judaism.[64]

Within Christianity, there is some victory. Geiger's understanding of Jesus as a Pharisee is by now standard in New Testament textbooks, and he continues to be credited by scholars of Islam as having founded their field. The end of the empires and the difficult processes of decolonization left religious thought with new challenges, from fundamentalists, Jewish, Christian and Muslim, wanting a return to origins and turning a blind eye to everything in between, and from liberals who seem at times to have forgotten the distinctive message of their religion, making the sermons of rabbis and pastors sound nearly identical, as Uriel Tal pointed out.[65] Most important, if colonialism was now to be repudiated, so was supersessionism. In 1965, the Roman Catholic church's declaration, *Nostra Aetate*, rejected supersessionism, and in 1980 the Church of the Rhineland declared it would no longer missionize Jews.

The situation today is all the more remarkable for some of its differences. Moshe Rosman questions whether Jewish history can be written without geographic boundaries; the study of Jews and colonialism has emerged as a key project; Jewish history today is increasingly written in a less explicitly lachrymose tone.[66] The 'Third Quest' of the historical Jesus that has emerged in recent decades includes a more historical-critical approach to the rabbinic sources and greater attention to other Jewish material from the late Second Temple period (e.g. the Dead Sea Scrolls, Josephus and Philo, the Pseudepigrapha, archaeological remains). In an echo of Geiger's arguments, Daniel Boyarin, in *The Jewish Gospels*, portrays both Jesus and the Gospel authors as Jews engaged in intra-Pharisaic debate, but Boyarin goes further, arguing that Jesus fulfilled Jewish messianic expectations, which he claims included anticipation of a suffering messiah, and that Trinitarian doctrines find their impetus in an ancient Jewish belief in a duality of divinity.[67] Scholarship on Islam is gradually coming to recognize that by focusing on the earliest Islamic texts, and defining Sharia as the central principle of Islam, Orientalism created a narrow definition of an 'authentic' Islam so that subsequent, broader cultural and theological developments within Islam came to be described as deviant or marginal. Because Orientalists were governed by the principle that 'the original is the authentic', Robert Wisnovsky argues that they reified Islam based on texts of the so-called classical period of 700–1050.[68] That narrow set of texts created a distorted historical paradigm, and in his recent book Shahab Ahmed urges scholars to 'conceptualize Islam in expansive, capacious, and contradictory terms'.[69]

Jewish thinkers, such as my father Abraham Joshua Heschel, could now speak in positive terms of both Christianity and Islam without disparaging their unique message, or discrediting them because of their negative views of Judaism. Anxieties remain, but boundaries are no longer sites of contention. Islamic Studies has moved beyond the classical period, and now the influences of Christianity and Islam on Judaism are being investigated by Gideon Libson and Israel Yuval, among many others.[70] The foundation came out of the great German-Jewish scholarly tradition of the *Wissenschaft des Judentums*, among so many others. To them we owe our gratitude and admiration.[71]

Notes

1 First published as Leo Baeck Memorial Lecture 59, published by the Leo Baeck Institute New York and Berlin. Reprinted with permission.

2 Susannah Heschel, *Jüdischer Islam: Jüdisch-Deutsch Selbstbestimmung und der Islam* (Berlin: Mathes und Seitz, 2017).

3 Susannah Heschel, 'German-Jewish Scholarship on Islam as a Tool of De-Orientalization', *New German Critique* 117 (2012): 91–117.

4 I discuss this at greater length elsewhere. See my article, 'The Rise of Imperialism and the German Jewish Engagement in Islamic Studies', in *Colonialism and the Jews*, ed. Maud Mandel, Lisa Leff and Ethan Katz (Bloomington: Indiana University Press, 2016), 54–80.

5 Antony Polonsky, *The Jews in Poland and Russia*, vol. 2 (Oxford: The Littman Library of Jewish Civilization, 2010), 150.

6 Ibid., 147.

7 Ibid., 150.

8 Robert Liberles, 'From Toleration to Verbesserung: German and English Debates on the Jews in the Eighteenth Century', *Central European Quarterly* 22 (1989): 3–32.

9 Aamir Mufti, *Enlightenment in the Colony: The Jewish Question and the Crisis of Postcolonial Culture* (Princeton: Princeton University Press, 2007).

10 Axel Stähler, 'Orientalist Strategies of Dissociation in a German "Jewish" Novel: Das neue Jerusalem (1905) and Its Context', *Forum for Modern Language Studies* 45 (2009): 51–89.

11 Ulrike Brunotte, 'The Beautiful Jewess as Borderline Figure in Europe's Internal Colonialism: Some Remarks on the Intertwining of Orientalism and Antisemitism', *ReOrient* 4 (2019): 166–80, here 167.

12 Kristin Kopp, *Germany's Wild East: Constructing Poland as Colonial Space* (Ann Arbor: University of Michigan Press, 2012).

13 Ibid., 120.

14 There are several excellent studies of the Tübingen School: Horton Harris, *The Tübingen School* (Oxford: Clarendon Press, 1975); Peter Hodgson, *The Formation of Historical Theology: A Study of Ferdinand Christian Baur* (New York: Harper and Row, 1966); Johannes Zachhuber, *Theology as Science in Nineteenth-Century Germany* (Oxford: Oxford University Press, 2013); James Carleton Paget, 'The Definition of the Terms Jewish Christian and Jewish Christianity in the History of Research', in *Jewish Believers in Jesus*, ed. Oskar Skarsaune and Reidar Hvalvik (Peabody: Hendrickson, 2007), 22–52; also; see my book, *Abraham Geiger and the Jewish Jesus*, for a discussion of Geiger's application of Tübingen School methods to his study of early Judaism. See also Peter C. Hodgson, 'F.C. Baur's Interpretation of Christianity's Relationship to Judaism', in *Is There a Judeo-Christian Tradition? A European Perspective*, ed. Emmanuel Nathan and Anya Topolski (Berlin: De Gruyter, 2016), 31–52.

15 Susannah Heschel, 'Abraham Geiger and the Emergence of Jewish Philislamism', in *'Im vollen Licht der Geschichte': Die Wissenschaft des Judentums und die Anfänge der kritischen Koranforschung*, ed. Dirk Hartwig, Walter Homolka, Michael J. Marx and Angelika Neuwirth (Würzburg: Ergon Verlag, 2008), 65–86.

16 Paget, 'The Definition of the Terms', 31.

17 Ibid., 32.

Boundary as Barrier, Boundary as Bridge   107

18 Karl Reinhold Köstlin, 'Zur Geschichte des Urchristenthums', *Theologische Jahrbücher* (1850): 1–62; 235–302; cited by Harris, *The Tübingen School*, 219.

19 Paget, 'The Definition of the Terms', 33.

20 Ibid., 36.

21 Adolf von Harnack, 'Der Islam', in *Lehrbuch der Dogmengeschichte*, vol. 2 (Tübingen: Mohr, 1909), 529–38, here 537.

22 Ibid.

23 Qur'an 2:62; 5:69; 22:17.

24 Hans-Joachim Schoeps, *Das Judenchristentum: Untersuchungen über Gruppenbildungen und Parteikämpfe in der frühen Christenheit* (Bern: Francke, 1964).

25 Francois de Blois, 'Nasrani and Hanif: Studies on the Religious Vocabulary of Christianity and of Islam', *Bulletin of the School of Oriental and African Studies* 65 (2002): 1–30.

26 Abraham Geiger, 'Apokryphen zweiter Ordnung', *Jüdische Zeitschrift für Wissenschaft und Leben* 7 (1869): 135.

27 Susannah Heschel, *The Aryan Jesus: Christian Theologians and the Bible in Nazi Germany* (Princeton: Princeton University Press, 2008).

28 Abraham Geiger, *Urschrift und Übersetzungen der Bibel in ihrer Abhängigkeit* (Breslau: J. Hainauer, 1857), 223. This particular statement of Geiger's gained widespread attention. Critics who opposed his interpretation of Pharisaism as a liberalization, in contrast to the Sadducees, argued that 2 Maccabees 2:17 describes not Pharisaism but Israel's position vis-à-vis the heathen world. See Johann Wilhelm Hanne, 'Die Pharisäer und Sadducäer als politische Parteien', *Zeitschrift für wissenschaftliche Theologie* 10 (1867): 239–63.

29 Anna Sapir Abulafia, *Christians and Jews in the Twelfth-Century Renaissance* (London: Routledge, 1995), 63; cited by Israel Yuval, *Two Nations in Your Womb: Perceptions of Jews and Christians in Late Antiquity and the Middle Ages*, trans. Jonathan Chipman (Berkeley: University of California Press, 2006), 26.

30 Gustav Volkmar, *Die Religion Jesu und ihre erste Entwicklung nach dem gegenwaertigen Stande der Wissenschaft* (Leipzig: F.A. Brockhaus, 1857), 33, 37. Quoted in Susannah Heschel, *Abraham Geiger and the Jewish Jesus* (Chicago: University of Chicago Press, 1998), 161.

31 Yuval, *Two Nations in Your Womb*, 27.

32 Brunotte, 'The Beautiful Jewess', 167.

33 Andrea Polaschegg, *Der andere Orientalismus: Regeln deutsch-morgenländischer Imagination im 19. Jahrhundert* (Berlin: de Gruyter, 2005), 166, as cited by Brunotte, 'The Beautiful Jewess', 171.

34 Gayatri Spivak, 'Can the Subaltern Speak?', in *Colonial Discourse and Post-Colonial Theory: A Reader*, ed. Patrick Williams and Laura Chrisman (New York: Columbia University Press, 1994), 66–111.

35 Brunotte, 'The Beautiful Jewess', 174.

36 Nils Römer, *Jewish Scholarship and Culture in Nineteenth-Century Germany: Between History and Faith* (Madison: University of Wisconsin Press, 2005), 3.

37 Amos Bitzan, 'Leopold Zunz and the Meanings of Wissenschaft', *Journal of the History of Ideas* 78 (2017): 235.

38 I.M. Jost; cited by Michael Brenner, *Prophets of the Past: Interpreters of Jewish History*, trans. Steven Rendall (Princeton: Princeton University Press, 2010), 39.

39 Letter to Zunz, 13 October 1833; in Ludwig Geiger, 'Aus Leopold Zunz' Nachlass', *Zeitschrift für die Geschichte der Juden in Deutschland* 5 (1892): 223–68, here 248.

40 'Leopold Zunz', in *Brockhaus Konversations-Lexicon*, vol. 7, 531; cited by Ismar Schorsch, *Leopold Zunz: Creativity in Adversity* (Philadelphia: University of Pennsylvania Press, 2016), 79.

41 Abraham Geiger, *Was hat Muhammad aus dem Judenthume aufgenommen?* (Bonn: F. Baaden, 1833), 86.

42 Ibid., 85.

43 Ibid., 98–9.

44 Abraham Geiger, 'Review of Aloys Sprenger, Das Leben und die Lehre des Mohammad', *Jüdische Zeitschrift für Wissenschaft und Leben* 2 (1863): 185–91, here 186.

45 Heinrich Graetz, *Geschichte der Juden: Von den ältesten Zeiten bis auf die Gegenwart*, vol. 5: Geschichte der Juden vom Abschluß des Talmuds (500) bis zum Aufblühen der jüdisch-spanischen Kultur (1027), 4th edn (1861; Leipzig: Leiner, 1909), 118.

46 Isaac Gastfreund, *Mohammed nach Talmud und Midrasch*, 3 vols. (Berlin: Geschel, 1875–80); Hartwig Hirschfeld, *Jüdische Elemente im Koran: Ein Beitrag zur Koranforschung* (Berlin, 1878); Israel Schapiro, *Die haggadischen Elemente im erzählenden Teil des Korans* (Leipzig: Fock, 1907); Heinrich Speyer, *Die biblischen Erzählungen im Qoran* (Gräfenhainichen: Schulze, 1931); Eugen Mittwoch, *Zur Entstehungsgeschichte des islamischen Gebets und Kultus* (Berlin: Reimer, 1913).

47 See, for example, the study by Jonathan Skolnik, *Jewish Pasts, German Fictions: History, Memory, and Minority Culture in Germany, 1824–1955* (Stanford: Stanford University Press, 2014).

48 Gustav Weil, *The Bible, the Qur'an, and the Talmud* (London: Longman, Brown, Green, and Longmans, 1846), ix.

49 For an excellent examination of the views of Islam in the writings of Ludwig Philippson and Heinrich Graetz, see Klaus Herrmann, 'Das Bild des Islam im Reformjudentum des 19. und 20. Jahrhunderts', in *Orient als Grenzbereich? Rabbinisches und ausserrabbinisches Judentum*, ed. Annelies Kuyt and Gerold Necker (Wiesbaden: Harrasowitz, 2007), 217–47. For the best analysis of Franz Rosenzweig's views of Islam, see Robert Erlewine, *Judaism and the West: From Hermann Cohen to Joseph Soloveitchik* (Bloomington: Indiana University Press, 2016), 52–77.

50 Graetz, *Geschichte der Juden*, vol. 5, 102.

51 Michael A. Meyer, 'From Combat to Convergence: The Relationship between Heinrich Graetz and Abraham Geiger', in *Reappraisals and New Studies of the Modern Jewish Experience: Essays in Honor of Robert M. Seltzer*, ed. Brian M. Smollett and Christian Wiese (Leiden: Brill, 2015), 145–61.

52 Graetz, *Geschichte der Juden*, vol. 5, 101.

53 Ibid., 71.

54 Ibid., 118.

55 Ibid., 76.

56 Ibid., 84.

57 Personal communication from Evan Goldstein, 3 November 2016. Nietzsche's remark appears in the opening paragraph of chapter six of *The Antichrist*.

58 Lital Levy, 'The Nahda and the Haskalah: A Comparative Reading of "Revival" and "Reform"', *Middle Eastern Literatures* 16 (2013): 300–16.

59 Tarek el-Aris, 'Introduction', in *The Arab Renaissance: A Bilingual Anthology of the Nahda* (New York: Modern Language Association, 2018), xv–xxx, here xxv.

60 Levy, 'The Nahda and the Haskalah', 307.

61 Ibid.

62 Israel Friedlaender, 'Shiitic Elements in Jewish Sectarianism', *Jewish Quarterly Review*, new series 2 (1912): 481–516.

63 Gudrun Jäger, 'Josef Horovitz – Ein jüdischer Islamwissenschaftler an der Universität Frankfurt und der Hebrew University of Jerusalem', in *Im vollen Licht der Geschichte*, 117–30; Heinrich Speyer, *Von den biblischen Erzählungen im Qoran* (Berlin: Akademie für die Wissenschaft des Judentums, 1924); Angelika Neuwirth, 'Qur'anic Studies and Philology: Qur'anic Textual Politics of Staging, Penetrating, and Finally Eclipsing Biblical Tradition', in *Qur'anic Studies Today*, ed. Angelika Neuwirth and Michael A. Sells (New York: Routledge, 2016), 178–206; Angelika Neuwirth, *Der Koran als Text der Spätantike: Ein europäischer Zugang* (Berlin: Verlag der Weltreligionen, 2010); Angelika Neuwirth, *The Qur'an in Context* (Leiden: Brill, 2011).

64 Heschel, *The Aryan Jesus*.

65 Uriel Tal, *Christians and Jews in Germany: Religion, Politics, and Ideology in the Second Reich, 1870–1914*, trans. Noah Jacobs (Ithaca: Cornell University Press, 1975).

66 Moshe Rosman, 'Jewish History across Borders', in *Rethinking European Jewish History*, ed. Jeremy Cohen and Moshe Rosman (Portland: Litman Library of Jewish Civilization, 2009), 15–29; Katz, Leff and Mandel, *Colonialism and the Jews*.

67 Daniel Boyarin, *The Jewish Gospel: The Story of the Jewish Christ* (New York: New Press, 2012).

68 Robert Wisnovsky, 'Islam', in M. W. F. Stone and Robert Wisnovsky, 'Philosophy and Theology', in *The Cambridge History of Medieval Philosophy*, vol. 2, ed. Robert Parnau (Cambridge: Cambridge University Press, 2010), 687–706.

69 Shahab Ahmed, *What Is Islam: The Importance of Being Islamic* (Princeton: Princeton University Press, 2015), 83.

70 Gideon Libson, *Jewish and Islamic Law: A Comparative Study of Custom during the Geonic Period* (Cambridge: Harvard University Press, 2003); Yuval, *Two Nations in Your Womb*.

71 My thanks to my wonderful colleagues whose conversations helped me formulate this article – in particular, Evan Goldstein, Jeremiah Riemer, Tomoko Masuzawa, Micha Brumlik, Christina von Braun, Richard Cogley, Joseph B. Tyson, Michael Meyer and most of all Robert Erlewine, my good friend and interlocutor. I also want to thank the three postdoctoral fellows in Jewish Studies at Dartmouth in the summer of 2016 for many stimulating discussions: Malgorzata Maksymiak, Sebastian Musch and Anna-Dorothea Ludewig.

Part II

The colonial era

6

The role of antisemitism in German colonial racism

Ulrike Hamann

After the German Empire began its programme of colonialist expansionism in the late nineteenth century, increasing numbers of Black people of various class and geographical backgrounds came to live in German towns and cities.[1] Until then, *white* Germans had had little lived experience of excluding or otherwise discriminating against Black people in everyday life, although they were relatively well versed in theories of 'race' and 'racial(ized) distinctions'. Such ideas, while not yet hegemonic or necessarily enshrined in law, had been propagated throughout Europe at least since the mid-seventeenth century. Furthermore, *white non-Jewish* Germans had long been familiar with an analogous ideological discourse, namely antisemitism. This discourse had been in use all over Europe for many centuries, in combination with antisemitic laws and practices, to justify the ostracism and systemic degradation of Jewish people. I argue that the antisemitism that was rife in the German Empire from its inception in 1871 exerted a major influence on the ways in which anti-Black racism was theoretically framed, both within Germany and later in the racially segregated, hierarchical administration of the newly acquired colonies. Extrapolating backwards from Hannah Arendt's thesis that colonial racism prepared German society for the Holocaust, I argue that the specific form of antisemitism present in the young German Empire laid the ideological groundwork for its biopolitical colonial regime. Moreover, the eliminationist element in antisemitic ideology made it possible to consider the relationship between *whiteness* and Blackness a matter of life and death.[2] I thus demonstrate that it was precisely because few people at the time had any personal experience with hierarchical power relations between Black and *white* people that the authorities knowingly chose to draw on the mechanisms of antisemitic discrimination already well established in Germany and to translate them into racist practices in the colonial regime.

114 *Colonialism and the Jews in German History*

By way of introduction, in the first section of this chapter, I present two case studies that illustrate the close entanglement of antisemitism and racism in this period. In the first case study, I draw on the writings of Mary Church Terrell and W. E. B. Du Bois, two African-American intellectuals who each spent some years during the late nineteenth century living in Berlin, the heart of the German Empire. In the second, I juxtapose these writers' experiences in Berlin with records of a resistance movement that rose up against German colonial power some thirty years later in Douala, Cameroon, around 1910. There Africans explicitly fought against the imposition of racial segregation, as well as the displacement and expropriation it entailed. Against this backdrop, in the second section I discuss the shifting relationship of racism and antisemitism from around the time of the 1884–5 Berlin Conference to the outbreak of the First World War in 1914. In the third section, I examine the role antisemitism played in constructing (colonial) anti-Black racism. Taking my cue from what has come to be known as the subaltern perspective, I analyse the racist system of colonialism in light not only of the records of the *white* ruling powers and the broader *white* population who benefitted from upholding it but also of those on whom it inflicted violent discrimination or even death; it is only through this analysis that we can understand the racism encountered by Church Terrell, Du Bois and the resistance movement in Douala in relation to the virulent antisemitism then active in Germany and elsewhere. This methodical approach implies that I will not verify whether the Black writers I quote were wrong or right about the structures of the racism they give witness to, nor do I say that the incidences they recall were representative for the kind of racism that most Black people encountered in this period. My interest lays in the strategies against anti-Black racism that were developed by these specific witnesses. I therefore take their writings as a lens for analysing the forms of racism they encountered. I use this method in order to prioritize the perspective of those who were attacked by racism because this perspective has been made invisible by many historical accounts.

Antisemitism as a transatlantic referential system

In the late nineteenth century, two young African Americans who would later play outstanding roles in the struggle for African-American civil rights in the United States studied in Berlin. Mary Church Terrell (1863–1954) and W. E. B. Du Bois (1868–1963) both arrived in Germany with family memories of the plantation regime of slavery. Yet they were members of the first generation raised with the promise of equal civil rights, a promise they defended tirelessly but did not see fulfilled in their lifetimes. Acutely aware of the precarity of their civil rights, they nonetheless challenged the 'colour line' (i.e. the codes of segregation) as well as racist social and political practices in their writings. The young Mary Church spent the years 1889 to 1890 in Berlin, where she studied languages. She wrote about her experiences in her autobiography and kept a journal, some unpublished entries from which are now held in archives.[3] W. E. B. Du Bois studied at Berlin University – later known as Humboldt University of Berlin – from 1892 to 1894 in the process of earning his PhD from Harvard University. He recorded his memories of this period in two autobiographical works as well as in unpublished notes held in various archives.[4] These documents have been analysed for this chapter.

By analysing their insights into racist practices in Germany at that time, I found remarkable references to antisemitism within the personal memories of these two intellectuals. Mary Church Terrell recounted several instances in which antisemitism was used by *white* Americans as a system of reference to explain racist practices to *white non-Jewish* Germans. At one point while she was living in a German guesthouse, two *white* Americans demanded that the host not allow Church Terrell to live in the same house as themselves. Because the host did not understand the grounds on which they claimed a difference between themselves and Church Terrell, the two *white* Americans gave her a lecture on racist practices, trying to identify a difference. In order to do so, they referred to a German practice of exclusion: antisemitism.[5] Church Terrell quoted her host, who could not 'see' a difference, in her autobiography: 'But the medical students told me I was greatly mistaken and declared that just as Jews are ostracized in Germany, so Negroes are socially ostracized all over the United States.'[6]

Evidently the two *white* Americans had had occasion prior to this encounter to observe similarities between contemporary German and American segregation practices. When the host tried to understand their demand in the light of her own (racist) concept of a racial hierarchy based on skin colour – 'She is not black. She is no darker than Frau General von Wenckstern, a Spaniard'[7] – the *white* Americans explained to her the American way of identifying 'race', which does not depend on skin colour: 'But she is classed a Negro in the United States, whether she is black or not. . . . If an individual has only a single drop of African blood in his veins, . . . white people in the United States consider him a Negro.'[8] As the one-drop rule was apparently not well known in Germany at this point,[9] Church Terrell was able to reframe the discussion: she chose to speak of the

116   *Colonialism and the Jews in German History*

social structures brought about by abolitionism and their impact on her life in the United States:

> I told Fräulein von Finck that I had attended school with white Americans all my life, that I had graduated from a high school, an academy, and a first-class college conducted by white Americans for white and black students alike. . . . I explained also that the discrimination against colored people in hotels, theaters, and schools, which had been so graphically described by the medical students, was practically confined to one section of the United States.[10]

By introducing the desegregation of both institutions and public life as evidence of the new norm in all but 'one section of the United States', Church Terrell managed to refute the 'African blood' discourse. Her aim in this act of resistance was clearly to delegitimize racism by depicting its principles and practices as abnormal. To be sure, racist practices have also been present or even dominant in the north, in contrast to what Church Terrell explained to her *white* host. Nevertheless, she used her narrative as an alternative truth against the racist narrative of the *white* Americans. Accordingly, the host refused to comply with the *white* Americans' request and did not ask Church Terrell to vacate the premises.

Another moment in Church Terrell's life illustrates how solidarity may emerge when antisemitism and anti-Black racism are brought into conversation with one another, even when the relationship between these two referential systems is lost in translation. Church Terrell had met a young German woman whom she liked but whose antisemitic sentiments caused her grave concern and made an actual friendship impossible. She thereupon used the absence of a colour line in German society to question the validity of her friend's antisemitism.

> After [my German friend] had criticized and ridiculed the Jews one day, I said 'Fräulein, I am a member of a race whose faults and mistakes are exaggerated by its enemies . . . just as you are exaggerating those of the Jews, and if you should come to the United States, many would make out as bad a case against us as you have made against the Jews. . . . There are good and bad in all races, and the Jews are no exceptions to a general rule.' But my young German friend did not understand this at all. She was sure I was exaggerating the facts. She could not believe that any human being could object to another solely on account of the color of his skin. If a race had all the vices and defects which she insisted were characteristic of the Jew, she could understand why people would not want to come into close contact with such a group, but for the life of her she could not comprehend why anybody would object to another human being because he happened to be a few shades darker than himself. It is always difficult for

one prejudice-ridden human being to understand why his brother should be obsessed by a prejudice which differs from his own.[11]

Church Terrell's observation on different forms of prejudice suggests that it is not possible to translate perfectly between systems of reference. Her acquaintance's antisemitism could not easily be mapped onto anti-Black racism, and the German antisemite could not understand Americans' investment in identifying people in terms of skin colour. Church Terrell first published this account in the United States in the 1940s, when it presumably caused much irritation. It demonstrated the inherent contradictions and absurdities of two ideological categories, the effects of which (segregation, ostracism, etc.) were perhaps similar, and yet the markers of which did not easily carry over – that is, they were clearly *culturally specific* to one society but not to the other. While skin colour served as a fundamental marker of race in the United States, the German antisemite declared it incidental. Even though the colour line seems not yet to have been much of an issue in Germany, *white non-Jewish* Germans did use insidious stereotypes and myths to ostracize a section of the population and marked it as 'the Other'. The targets in this case were Jewish Germans.[12]

Du Bois also describes witnessing practices in Germany that were similar to racist practices in the United States but directed to persons that were anticipated as Jewish. In an interview in 1960, he said:

> Once [between 1892 and 1894] I was with a German boy who looked Jewish and had very curly hair. We were out somewhere, at a dance or something of that sort, and I saw something which I immediately read as racial prejudice. He said, 'Oh no, you don't understand – the trouble is, they think that I'm a Jew.' As if I were not able to recognize racial prejudice when I see it![13]

Here Du Bois recalls the irritation he felt on seeing a familiar practice aimed at a different minority group. He points out that his own experience equipped him to read a particular practice as a discriminatory racist attack on himself. His German companion, on the other hand, read this same practice as an example of antisemitism directed at him personally ('They think that I'm a Jew'). Since the practice, which is not described in further detail in the interview, leads each of them to recognize and refer to a familiar referential system – the racism of the colour line in the case of the African American and the antisemitism of the German Empire around 1900 in the case of the German – we can deduce that both ideologies relied on similar practices. This could create Black–Jewish alliances and solidarity, at least on the personal level.[14]

Antisemitism's role in radicalizing public opinion on racial theories

The problem of the twentieth century is the problem of the color line.
—W. E. B. Du Bois, *The Souls of Black Folk*, 1886

Guided by this famous quotation from one of Du Bois's most significant works, I now explore a second case study from almost a quarter century later, towards the end of Germany's colonial period. It concerns racist policies in the German colony of Cameroon and demonstrates that the colour line (i.e. racialized segregation) was integral to colonial governance. In the process, I also examine another racist trope relying on antisemitism deployed by colonial officials who were trying to quell resistance in the colonies.

One major source of information here are the written records of the concerted resistance which the people of Douala and their spokesman, Rudolf Duala Manga Bell, mounted against the proposed imposition of colour-line segregation in the major port city of Douala from 1910 to 1914.[15] These records, which are now available for consultation in the colonial archives, consist in part of the published minutes of Reichstag proceedings.[16] The German government had signed a Protectorate Treaty with Cameroon following the Berlin Conference of 1884–5. In 1910, the government presented a master plan for Doula – an 'urban redevelopment scheme' – the aim of which was to prevent malaria, but only among the *white* population.[17] Accordingly the city was to be divided into a Black zone and a *white* zone, which would be further segregated by establishing a one-square-kilometre vacant zone between them. For hundreds of years, local and European merchants in Douala had lived and worked side by side, on an equal footing.[18] However, the German government now planned to evict the mixed population of several inner-city districts situated directly on the waterfront (Bonanjo, Bonapriso, Bonaduma, Akwa and Deido) and reserve these for *whites* only. This would involve the forced removal of 25,000 people from *c.* 900 hectares of land, on which stood 1,000 buildings. Most of the buildings in the vacant zone would be razed. Furthermore, the plan envisaged the expropriation and (meagre) compensation of any urban dweller whom the German government identified as Black. These citizens would have to move into new districts, which were to be built on former swamps in the city's hinterland. Their existing houses and land were to become German government property. The government estimated the cost of this 'urban development scheme' at 5.6 million Deutschmarks.

Long-established communities in Douala organized various forms of resistance against this scheme. Aside from petitions directed at the local colonial government and acts of civil disobedience to prevent evictions, their resistance also spread to the colonial metropolis – Berlin – where the German Reichstag would decide on the budget for the scheme.[19] They managed to have several petitions introduced in the Reichstag and thereby won the support of both Social Democratic Party politicians and certain Jewish German attorneys, whose Jewishness was often mentioned prominently in the press, as we will see further. These petitions were partly successful, as the scheme in Douala was repeatedly delayed for several months. In 1914, however, the local colonial administration seized on the outbreak of the First World War as a pretext to put the leaders of the resistance on trial; they were executed the very next day. Consequently, the Doualan resistance lent its support to the British troops, and the German military was soon forced to retreat from the city.

This conflict between the German government and the people of Douala can be interpreted from several perspectives. As I have argued elsewhere, the main axes of any conflict in this colonial context were, firstly, the Germans who adamantly asserted their position in a hierarchical order underpinned by dubious discourse on supposed racial distinctions and, secondly, the Doualans who persistently asserted their equality as signatories of the original Protectorate Treaty and hence the legitimacy of their claims to control over their property and equal rights before the law.[20] For example, while German politicians and medical 'experts' sought to justify their demand for Black and *white* segregation on the grounds of 'racial hygiene' – which was necessary, they alleged, because mosquitos transferred 'blood parasites' from Black bodies to *white* 'guardians of civilization' – the Doualans fundamentally questioned the need for segregation and were committed to creating hygienic conditions for all: a city that would be sanitary and thus healthy for each of its inhabitants.[21]

Since the Doualan resistance was proving effective, German media coverage of the situation took on an increasingly inflammatory tone. Things reached fever pitch when Colonial Secretary Wilhelm Solf used an antisemitic metaphor to delegitimize the resistance. Contesting the Doualans' 1914 petition, he spoke very plainly of their perceived intent:

> They want to use this surplus value created by the work of the white race [the supposed increase in property values due to the Europeans' presence, U. H.] to line their own pockets, to live off of it. *The whites are supposed to be the bees, while they themselves want to live a carefree life as drones.* Since they cannot persuade the Reichstag by stating their true intent, they make *false claims* that are

120   *Colonialism and the Jews in German History*

> calculated to excite *pity*. But such claims make an impression only on those who lack first-hand knowledge of the natives and of conditions in the Protectorate, and therefore are not in a position to assess their accuracy.[22]

This analogy had a significant impact on the tone of reports in the media and marked a turning point in the struggle. To understand why Solf used this particular image, we must examine the overall impact – and specifically the antisemitic efficacy – of his bees and drones metaphor.

Shifting interrelations between antisemitism and racism: The 'parasitic drone' metaphor

The cultural historian Eva Johach posits that the 'lazy drone' metaphor was commonly used in Europe by the late eighteenth century to indicate a 'parasitic' position in society (mainly of the aristocracy). The idealized bee metaphor persisted until the late nineteenth century, when it was increasingly supplanted by the concept of an organic society, although not before briefly gaining a new lease on life in relation to biopolitical issues.[23]

In 1895 the former German chancellor Otto von Bismarck used this metaphor in a speech to the right-wing Bund der Landwirte (German Agrarian League), describing parliamentarians as 'lazy drones' in striking contrast to 'productive' agriculturalists: 'We must stand together against the drones who govern us while producing nothing but laws, and plenty of them at that.'[24] While Bismarck did not directly identify the legislature as 'Jewish', the historian Hans-Ulrich Wehler remarks that Bismarck generally employed antisemitic sentiment 'unscrupulously . . . for his electoral purposes'.[25] One can therefore assume that in this speech as well, the metaphor was intended to evoke antisemitic connotations.

His analogy certainly must have resonated with the antisemitic persuasion of the Agrarian League.[26] At that time, the league was one of two major German professional associations that were aggressively antisemitic in tone.[27] Like many artisans, tradespeople, employees, students and anti-modern, 'culturally pessimistic' intellectuals organized in other contemporary organizations at the turn of the twentieth century, league members regarded themselves as 'modernization's losers'.[28] The league had been attempting to exclude Jewish members since the early 1890s.[29] Against this sociopolitical backdrop, Bismarck could reasonably expect that his statement would be taken up and interpreted as antisemitic. The natural scientific observations widely disseminated in popular publications on agriculture and forestry, as well as in contemporary school textbooks and the general press – for example, the idea that certain insects or typically 'parasitic' organisms pose a threat to other plants and animals – were frequently used to advance a politically biased world view, drawing analogies to human social behaviour and political relationships. In her book *Schädlinge* (Parasites), the historian and biologist Sarah Jansen offers a very convincing analysis of this parasite discourse.[30] Two paradigms are fused here: firstly, each individual has to be useful to the collective (or broader society); and secondly, the 'anti-social' behaviour of any individual (or group) ostensibly reaping the benefits of society without making any positive contributions poses a threat, both to this collective and to its individual members. In describing his political opponents – the Doualans – as drones, Colonial Secretary Solf aimed to evoke precisely this fusion of the 'lazy' and 'parasitic' tropes. In the next section, I analyse the clearly antisemitic implications of this drone metaphor in greater depth.

Politische Bilderbogen, an antisemitic pictorial broadsheet, took up the drone metaphor in 1898; the twenty-fifth issue opens with an explicitly antisemitic cartoon under the title 'Bees and Drones'.[31] This issue comprised a poster depicting German society as a beehive, with Bismarck at the centre. Whatever the bees did, they were accompanied by drones who robbed them. All the bees and drones had human faces. The drones were caricatures with stereotypically antisemitic features and were labelled with words such as 'usury' or 'Jewish regime' for added emphasis. The text on the back of the poster outlined the 'the drone-like nature of the Jews' and spoke positively of Bismarck, who – so the anonymous authors claim – encouraged the German people to launch an 'anti-drone liberation struggle'.[32]

In the nineteenth century, particularly after the German Empire completed the legal emancipation of the Jews in 1871, cultural assimilation progressively erased visual markers of difference, such as attire and hairstyle.[33] As the cultural theorist Christina von Braun has argued, antisemitic cartoons were a reaction to those missing markers. The fact that this genre proliferated in the late nineteenth century attests to a common desire to render Jews 'Others' in the face of their legal equality.[34] As we saw in Mary Church Terrell's account of her time in Berlin, caricatures produce specific forms of hatred, which are directed at real persons and intended to racialize human relationships. Insect metaphors were especially popular in antisemitic circles as a means of illustrating the alleged social and political relationships between Jews and non-Jews. As the historian Julia Schäfer has shown in her analysis of the Austrian magazine *Kikeriki* around 1918, antisemites in German-speaking countries identified with insects they believed

122   *Colonialism and the Jews in German History*

to be very industrious (ants, bees) and regarded threatening insects (bedbugs, lice, locusts) as symbols of parasitism.[35] Thus antisemites characterized Jews as parasites who lived off of others and thereby 'upset the balance of society', as the sociologist Klaus Holz has noted. The parasite stereotype was a political effort to demonize the Jews in biological terms, ultimately rendering them incommensurably different and dangerous.[36]

In their coverage of the Doualan resistance, many conservative newspapers – particularly those which shared the views of the nationalist Alldeutscher Verband (Pan-German League) – took up Solf's bees and drones metaphor with reference to the German colonial power and its African subjects.[37] The influential Alldeutscher Verband was a hotbed of discourses on eugenic 'racial hygiene' rooted in social Darwinism. Founded in 1891 to defend 'German trade interests', it became increasingly notorious for its antisemitic propaganda from 1912 onwards.[38]

Under the title 'Drohnenanwälte' (Drone Attorneys), the *Deutsche Zeitung* added a significant element to the ongoing coverage of the Douala question. This article attacked the Doualans' German attorney, Bodo Halpert, and identified him as Jewish. It was one of several articles in the 7 May 1914 issue which sought to delegitimize the protest against evictions in Doula by framing it not as local landowners' reasonable response to the German colonial government's imminent expropriation of their land and property but rather as a calculated means of speculation – that is, of making a profit on their property now that the 'bee' colonizers' hard work had (allegedly) increased its value.[39] The extent to which newspaper articles used the drone and bee metaphor in this context demonstrates its efficacy in rousing outrage and turning public opinion against the Doualans' legitimate concerns. Evoking the colonized people's 'parasitic' relationship to the colonizers provided a link to an already virulent antisemitic imaginary, projecting its full force onto opponents whom anti-Black racism had already rendered deeply suspect.

Yet how was it possible to apply an explicitly antisemitic metaphor to the portrayal of African colonial subjects? This strategy of double-stereotyping a colonial political opponent is notable in that it entangles two different kinds of ideology. The fact that many newspapers found it necessary to supplement the comprehensive arsenal of racist imagery available in 1914 with an explicitly antisemitic metaphor suggests that the latter's potency was greater than that of colonial racism at the time. Could it be that colonial anti-Black racism had already exhausted its capacity to explain colonial conflict? In the next section, I analyse the ways in which the antisemitic construction of a parasitic relationship between colonized and colonizer shifted colonial power dynamics. This final section offers a few concluding remarks on antisemitism's role in and repercussions for *white* German public perceptions of colonial governance and power relationships.

Antisemitism's role in constructing colonial anti-Black racism

While several studies have addressed the image of the 'Black Jew' and related discursive processes of Othering that racialize Jewish people as non-*white*, there appears to be no literature on the reverse manoeuvre.[40] I argue that the latter process constitutes an example of the potential Theodor W. Adorno had in mind when he called antisemitism a '"mobile" prejudice'.[41] The Adorno research group convened at the University of California, Berkeley, in the 1940s to research the psychological grounds for prejudice.[42] They found that antisemitism was an extremely elastic phenomenon that had 'little to do with the qualities of those against whom it is directed'.[43] This 'relative independence from the object' was evidently also at work in Colonial Secretary Solf's statement, in which he projected an antisemitic trope onto people who could not be linked to Judaism, either religiously or historically.[44] As Adorno wrote: 'The transference of unconscious fear to the particular object, however, the latter being of a secondary nature only, always maintains an aspect of accidentalness. Thus, as soon as other factors interfere, the aggression may be deflected, at least in part, from the Jews and to another group, preferably one of still greater social distance.'[45]

The relative flexibility of a 'traveling' trope – one that can be transposed from one object to another – is manifest in the constantly changing forms and functions of antisemitic stereotypes in each historically or culturally specific context, as the political sociologist Eva-Maria Ziege has noted.[46] In their surveys of the *white* middle class in the United States in the 1940s, Adorno and his colleagues found a strong correlation between anti-Black racism and antisemitism. This kind of objectification was characterized by a 'free-floating aggressiveness'.[47] Christina von Braun has observed that antisemitism renders 'the Jew' a signifier that puts non-Jews into a 'collective state of excitement'.[48] To achieve this effect, stereotypes must meet two paradoxical criteria: on the one hand, they should be familiar enough to connect directly with the unconscious mind; and on the other, they should not 'be open to deconstruction'.[49] The image of drones exploiting bees seems to fulfil both of these criteria. The metaphor's long history means it very likely spoke directly to the unconscious. Moreover, as

124   *Colonialism and the Jews in German History*

an alleged biological fact, it seemed relatively plausible and could not easily be disproved.

Obviously this image had the potential to incite aggression, inasmuch as it led those who imagined themselves part of an exclusively *white* German collective to feel exploited and mistreated by their drone counterparts. This was precisely the effect the colonial secretary had in mind when he directed the aggressive force of this antisemitic stereotype at the Doualans. But which kinds of images are liable to cause aggression? Which figures and tropes have such an effect? And if such figures and tropes can travel, then what makes them specifically antisemitic?

Along with antisemitic stereotypes, Adorno analysed the notion of 'unmediated and irrational power relationships'.[50] He noted that political omnipotence and economic power are commonly ascribed to 'the Jews'. In Solf's speech, both attributes are irrational. Lack of productivity as a synonym for a parasitism that had the potential to damage the notional collective was a common theme in the antisemitic discourse of the period, as was the premise that any such parasite must be eliminated in order to ensure the collective organism's survival. Thus the so-called 'crime' of laziness, which criminal law can neither prove nor disprove, becomes a capital crime – one legitimately punishable by death.

Yet even double-stereotyping and its subsequent media echo were no guarantee of the government's success in this matter. Another element was required. The Reichstag Petition Commission approved the segregation project in Douala on 9 May 1914, only after Solf had presented a telegram dispatched by the deputy governor of Cameroon the previous day.[51] This telegram alleged that the activist leader and spokesman Duala Manga Bell had secretly made contact with the British colonial power and had called on allied Cameroonian groups upcountry to surrender to Britain. Therefore Bell was charged with high treason and arrested. Ngoso Din, the unofficial Doualan ambassador to Berlin, was also arrested. In one fell swoop, the teetering colonial administration had regained complete control. The previously reluctant budget commission finally granted funds for the segregation project. Representatives of the resistance movement were quickly imprisoned. By highlighting the alleged menace to the balance of power in Cameroon, the German government cemented its power there: this was a political coup.

According to Adorno, antisemitism fulfils individuals' need for 'effortless "orientation" in a cold, alienated, and largely incomprehensible world'.[52] I have shown that the German colonial government invoked antisemitic stereotypes when accusing the Doualans of exercising power over something to which the government itself had explicitly laid claim. As Christina von Braun writes, such stereotyping is usually rooted in 'inverted projections' of a political power's own 'culpability'.[53] By casting blame on the Jews, the inverted antisemitic projection externalizes feelings of guilt. This creates a discrepancy between the relative social weakness of Jewish citizens and their imagined omnipotence.[54]

In depicting Jews and Africans as parasites, and both non-Jews in Germany and Germans in Cameroon as victims, the bees and drones metaphor concealed the actual political and economic power of the latter two. By reinforcing the Germans' sense of belonging to a (exclusive) collective, this image of the nation victimized by the colonized Other provoked myriad prejudices. This deeply rooted antisemitic stereotype exercised power over the German unconscious because it addressed 'unresolved problems', such as the impossibility of clearly defining national belonging.[55] Furthermore, the rise in social inequality brought about by an increasingly capitalized society complicated the colonial government's exercise of power. Political dissatisfaction was recast in an antisemitic portrayal of 'the Jews' as the behind-the-scenes puppeteers of bourgeois capitalist society.[56] In this context, social and economic change gave rise to all kinds of fear. Antisemitism was used to intensify these emotions.[57] Such an exceptional emotional state provoked not only a 'complete reversal between victim and murderer' but also a discrepancy between the Jewish people's alleged culpability and the verdict against them.[58] As Adorno noted, the widespread antisemitic assertion of the Jews' 'fraudulent character' could lead directly to the desire to eliminate all Jews.

This apparent mismatch between allegation, affect and legal framework led the antisemite to 'pursue his hatred beyond any limit and thus to prove to himself and to others that he *must* be right'.[59] This psychic overreaction reverses the burden of proof: precisely because the anger is so massive, there must be some basis for it. The use of the antisemitic drone metaphor, both in Solf's 'memorandum' and in the press, shows that this exceptional emotional state could be employed for political purposes by drawing on the psychological function of antisemitism. The German public hatred of the Doualans was disproportionate to their alleged 'crime', which was their attempt to use democratic means to defend themselves against expropriation and displacement.[60]

Solf's use of the bees and drones metaphor was surely intentional. He was clearly fishing for support among antisemitic groups that had just failed in their attempt to have Jewish Germans' civic equality revoked. He used the familiar antisemitic trope to increase public anger and frustration, which culminated in a hatred of 'political opponents' whom racism had already devalued. The fact that colonial subjects had the same rights as German citizens stoked fears of a loss of colonial power, and hence of personal standing, which led to the aforementioned exceptional emotional state. At the very moment the drone metaphor triggered an unconscious association with the antisemitic fear of a supposedly omnipotent, parasitic opponent, this exceptional emotional state transformed into hatred. Such hatred stems from the diffuse feeling that a political opponent is a threat to one's biopolitical life.

In the Doualan case, the opponent appeared to be threatening the German collective (i.e. the 'industrious bees'). This called for a powerful political reaction. The irrational fears surrounding a threat to collective life kindled a readiness for extreme violence beyond all legal proportionality. This willingness to kill was framed as a natural response to victimization. In this biologized reading of society, any aggression seeking a target necessarily perceives the Other as an absolute threat. Racist stereotypes had already rendered the Doualan resistance incommensurably different, and antisemitic stereotypes further generated a specific hatred that legitimized murder as the biopolitical regime's only possible logical response.

On 8 August 1914, Rudolf Duala Manga Bell and Ngoso Din were put on trial for high treason at the Douala district court. They were sentenced to death, with no right to appeal. Other Doualan representatives immediately raised objections with Karl Ebermaier, the governor of Cameroon, as did the Catholic bishop of Cameroon and both the Basel and the Baptist missions there. The latter sent a message saying that the Doualans would move voluntarily if the verdict was overturned. Ebermaier nevertheless confirmed the verdict, and the following day, 9 August 1914, the two representatives of the resistance movement were executed in the courtyard of the police station. Throughout the entire city, women and children wailed loudly at that moment.[61]

This travesty of justice was a matter of political expediency. The high treason charge was based on testimony that Duala Manga and other political representatives had held talks regarding a transfer to a British Mandate. As I have shown elsewhere, however, these considerations had long since been made public and were also justified: the Doualans no longer felt bound by the Protectorate Treaty, since the Germans had contravened its terms.[62] The Douala district colonial government used the outbreak of the First World War to justify a rapid trial and executed not only Duala Manga Bell and Ngoso Din but also around two hundred other activists later that month. Of these activists, the only names recorded are Ludwig Mpundo Akwa, Martin-Paul Samba, Mandola von Groß Batanga, A. Tokozo, J. Din, M. Mulobi, John Ekwe, Eb. Manga and H. Etoa.[63]

In an inverted projection of colonial guilt, a biological metaphor was used to cast the victims of this judicial crime as perpetrators who posed a threat to German society. A dangerous liaison of racism and antisemitism was used to incite collective emotions, simultaneously legitimizing the devaluation of their lives and portraying those same lives as a threat. In the biopolitical logic of this scenario, the colonial power had no choice but to kill any political opponent found 'guilty' of high treason. To date, no German government has ever acknowledged this judicial murder.[64]

Conclusion: Antisemitism's role in colonial racism

In the light of the aforementioned case studies, each of which points to the entangled interrelations between antisemitism and anti-Black racism, we can draw a number of conclusions. When the German Empire began its colonial project in the late nineteenth century, antisemitism offered *white non-Jewish* Germans a model framework for understanding racism. Antisemitic practices of attacking and excluding certain people could be used to explain to *white non-Jewish* Germans how anti-Black racism functioned in the United States. Conversely, as the accounts of Mary Church Terrell and W. E. B. Du Bois have shown, those confronted with anti-Black racism could identify antisemitism through the lens of discriminatory practices in Germany and could act in solidarity with those exposed to it. Furthermore, the cases of the two African Americans visiting Berlin at the moment at which the city rose to the status of a colonial metropolis suggest that antisemitism was much more common there, both in theory and in practice, than anti-Black racism at the time. Antisemitism could thus serve as a point of reference with a dual function: *white* Americans could use it to explain exclusionary practices to *white* Germans, while Black Americans could use it to identify potential attackers and to make a case against discrimination in both societies.

Following almost thirty years of German colonial power, however, and especially after the 1904 genocide of the Herero and Nama people in German South-West Africa (present-day Namibia), anti-Black racial theory was no longer absent in Germany. Racial distinctions had been used extensively to justify colonial rule. Nevertheless, at the moment when colonized subjects began objecting to the logic of the racialized discourse through which the segregation of Black and *white* people was to be enforced, the colonial state deployed antisemitism as an additional weapon in its anti-Black arsenal. The use of antisemitic discourses in the political campaign against Black people's claims to equality points to the fact that at this point in the colonial conflict, such discourses could (re)legitimize racism and expand its impact. These discourses were already thriving in the colonial metropolis and could therefore render colonial power structures more palatable to the German public. The exact same kind of eliminatory racial theory – as evident in the biologization of political affairs and the Herero and Nama genocide – culminated in a form of racism in which the death of the Other became the necessary basis for one's own life. This racism was linked to antisemitic stereotypes for a political purpose. In their formations and functions, both antisemitism and anti-Black racism remained mobile and adaptable; in terms of both tropes and targets, they could be applied to different contexts. However, this did not prevent those who were affected by antisemitism and anti-Black racism from emphatically laying claim to equality.

Drawing inter alia on sources from the period between 1890 and 1914, I have illustrated that antisemitism was deeply rooted in Germany at the time and played a particular role in politicizing colonial and anti-Black racism. In the early years of the German Empire, it served as a point of reference in transposing German practices of racial discrimination to other contexts. In the later years of the German Empire, antisemitism had acquired an eliminatory dimension – at least in the German imagination. This notional power struggle between Jews and non-Jews had become a notional competition for vital resources, ergo a life-or-death struggle. This imaginary, in which Germans were the victims and therefore had the right to use extreme violence to 'defend' themselves against life-threatening forces, was projected onto (*non-Jewish*) colonized Black people. Thus antisemitism – which, as Adorno and his colleagues have shown, had little connection to actual Jewish people in the first place – was used as a mobile concept to provoke a climate that would legitimate the execution of urban resistance movement activists in colonial Cameroon.

Since the colonized were striving for political equality, it was not only colonial policy that encountered a crisis of legitimacy. The biopolitical colonial regime had come to rely on racism as a form of government since at least 1910. It was precisely as this type of racism had begun to reach its epistemic limits that the colonized Doualans resisted the German colonizers. In this situation, when racism was well established as both an ideology and a policy and was challenged by resistance on the part of the colonized, antisemitism fulfilled a specific role.

The antisemitic imaginary, which conjured an imbalance in colonial power relations and portrayed Germans as victims, enabled the transformation of colonial anti-Black racism into a discourse that legitimized colonial crimes.

Notes

1   Throughout this contribution, the terms 'Black' and 'white' will not be used merely as descriptive colour markers. On the contrary, these categories are loaded with racism's long history and have been used to construct the concept of race. In order to highlight this, I mark the terms with different typographic styles. 'Black' as a political category will be rendered with a capital B based on the Black Power Movement's practice of reframing the construct through struggle. On the other hand, I will place 'white' in lowercase italic letters to mark the constructed nature of the category, which is linked to the aggregate system of Whiteness and its assumption of privileges.

2   See Foucault's notion of the origin of biopower in Michel Foucault, 'Vorlesung vom 17. März 1976 (Von der Geburt der Bio-Macht, Bio-Macht und Rassismus)', in *In Verteidigung der Gesellschaft: Vorlesungen am Collège de France 1975–76* (Frankfurt am Main: Suhrkamp, 1999), 276–305.

3   Mary Church Terrell, *A Colored Woman in a White World* (Amherst: Humanity Books, 2005). The relevant archives are at the Library of Congress, Washington, DC, Manuscript Division.

4   W. E. B. Du Bois, *Darkwater: Voices from within the Veil. Autobiography* (New York: Harcourt, Brace and Company, 1920); W. E. B. Du Bois, *The Autobiography of W.E.B. Du Bois: A Soliloquy on Viewing My Life from the Last Decade of Its First Century*, ed. Herbert Aptheker (New York: International Publishers, 1968); the unpublished documents are taken from the archives at the University of Massachusetts, Special Collections & University Archives Du Bois Papers: Microfilm and Print Editions.

5   In contrast, the historian Reinhard Rürup demonstrates that many colleges and hotels in the United States did not accept Jewish students or guests. See Reinhard Rürup, 'Antisemitismus und moderne Gesellschaft. Antijüdisches Denken und antijüdische Agitation im 19. und frühen 20. Jahrhundert', in *Das 'bewegliche' Vorurteil: Aspekte des internationalen Antisemitismus*, ed. Christina von Braun and Eva-Maria Ziege (Würzburg: Königshausen & Neumann, 2004), 81–100, here 94.

6   Church Terrell, *A Colored Woman*, 120.

7   Ibid.

8   Ibid.

9   Many of the southern states in the United States adopted the so called 'one-drop-rule' as a law in the first decade of the twentieth century after Church Terrell's

130   *Colonialism and the Jews in German History*

stay in Berlin. The fact that she mentions the 'one-drop-rule' when she recalls this episode in her autobiography from 1940 could mean that this idea was already present in the racist discourse in the United States at the end of nineteenth century. Alternatively, Terrell might have misremembered some of the specifics of her conversation with Fräulein von Finck. For the racist laws of that time see *States' Laws on Race and Color*, ed. Pauli Murray (Athens: University of Georgia Press, 1997).

10 Ibid., 121.

11 Ibid., 124.

12 At this time, German antisemitism was already increasingly dominated by the discourse of race, even though religious stereotypes were still present.

13 W. E. B. Du Bois in William Ingersoll, 'The Reminiscences of W.E.B. Bu Bois. Oral History Interview', Columbia University New York, Oral History Research Office, W.E.B. Du Bois Papers (Microfilm Edition), reel 88, 116.

14 There has been a debate in the United States about whether Du Bois displayed antisemitic views in some of his early writings. Space limitations do not allow a discussion of this here, except to say that the earlier quotes do show his awareness of the effects of antisemitism. On the debate, see Benjamin Sevitch, 'W. E. B. Du Bois and Jews: A Lifetime of Opposing Anti-Semitism', *The Journal of African American History* 87 (2002): 323–37.

15 See Ulrike Hamann, *Prekäre koloniale Ordnung: Rassistische Konjunkturen im Widerspruch. Deutsches Kolonialregime 1884–1914* (Bielefeld: transcript, 2016), 219–346.

16 Minutes of all parliamentary debates were kept. See *Stenographische Berichte über die Verhandlungen des Reichstags* (Berlin: Norddeutsche Buchdruckerei, 1871–1939). Records of the *Reichskolonialamt* (Colonial Administration) are held at the *Bundesarchiv* (Federal Archive) in Berlin-Lichterfelde (henceforth BAB).

17 For further analysis of this matter, see Manuela Bauche, *Medizin und Herrschaft: Malariabekämpfung in Kamerun, Ostafrika und Ostfriesland 1890–1919* (Frankfurt am Main: Campus, 2017); and Hamann, *Prekäre koloniale Ordnung*.

18 Regarding the history and complexity of Doualan society prior to the colonial regime, see Engelbert Mveng and D. Beling-Nkoumba, *Manuel d'Histoire du Cameroun* (Yaoundé: Centre d'édition et de production de manuels et d'auxiliaires de l'enseignement, 1978); Stefanie Michels, 'Schutzherrschaft revisited: Kolonialismus aus afrikanischer Perspektive', in *Die Vielfalt normativer Ordnungen: Konflikte und Dynamik in historischer und ethnologischer Perspektive*, ed. Andreas Fahrmeir and Anette Imhausen (Frankfurt am Main: Campus, 2013), 243–74; *Middlemen of the Cameroons Rivers: The Duala and their Hinterland, c. 1600–c. 1960*, ed. Ralph A. Austen and Jonathan Derrick (Cambridge: Cambridge University Press, 1999); Albert Wirz, *Vom Sklavenhandel zum kolonialen Handel: Wirtschaftsräume*

The Role of Antisemitism   131

und Wirtschaftsformen in Kamerun vor 1914 (Zurich: Atlantis-Verlag, 1972); also E. S. D. Fomin and Victor Julius Ngoh, *Slave Settlements in the Banyang Country, 1800–1950* (Buea: University of Buea Publications, 1998); Ugo Nwokeji and David Eltis, 'Characteristics of Captives Leaving the Cameroons for the Americas, 1822–37', *The Journal of African History* 43 (2002): 191–210.

19 Duala Manga Bell, Rudolf et al. 'An seine Exzellenz den Herrn kaiserlichen Gouverneur Dr. Ebermaier z. Zt. in Duala', 21 November 1912, BAB, R 1001/4427. 144–7; Chiefs of Duala, 'Brief an den Deutschen Reichstag vom 15. Januar 1913', BAB, R 1001/4428; Chiefs of Duala, 'Beschwerde gegen den Enteignungsbeschluss des Kaiserlichen Bezirksamts Duala vom 15. Januar 1913. Schreiben an das Kaiserliche Gouvernement Buea durch das Kaiserliche Bezirksamt Duala vom 20. Februar 1913', BAB, R 1001/4428.

20 See Hamann, *Prekäre koloniale Ordnung*, 247–53.

21 Hans Ziemann, 'Die Notwendigkeit einer Entfernung der Eingeborenen aus der Nähe der Europäer in Duala', 28 May 1910, BAB, R 1001/4427, 10–11, here 11.

22 Wilhelm Heinrich Solf, 'Denkschrift über die Enteignung und Verlegung der Eingeborenen in Duala (Kamerun)', 1 May 1914, *Verhandlungen des Reichstags. XIII. Legislaturperiode. I. Session, vol. 305: Anlagen zu den Stenographischen Berichten. Nr. 1547 bis 1703* (Berlin: Sittenfeld, 1914), 3269–388 (Solfdenkschrift), here 3302. Emphasis in the original, authors translation. For the petition, see Bodo Halpert, 'Petition gegen die Zwangsenteignung des Duala-Volkes. Anlage 27 der Solfdenkschrift, 1914/03', BAB, R 1001/4429/1.

23 Eva Johach, 'Der Bienenstaat: Geschichte eines politisch-moralischen Exempels', in *Politische Zoologie*, ed. Anne von der Heiden and Joseph Vogl (Zürich: diaphanes, 2007), 219–33, here 227–30.

24 Otto von Bismarck, 'Ansprache an die Abordnung des Bundes der Landwirte, June 9, 1895', in *Bismarck. Die gesammelten Werke. Reden. Dreizehnter Band 1885 bis 1897* (Berlin: Otto Stollberg Verlag, 1930), 609–12, here 611. My translation.

25 Hans-Ulrich Wehler, *Das Deutsche Kaiserreich, 1871–1918* (Göttingen: Vandenhoeck & Ruprecht, 1994), 133. My translation.

26 Hans-Jürgen Puhle, *Agrarische Interessenpolitik und preußischer Konservativismus im wilhelminischen Reich, 1892–1914* (Hannover: Verlag für Literatur und Zeitgeschehen, 1966), 133. See also Peter G. Pulzer, *Die Entstehung des politischen Antisemitismus in Deutschland und Österreich 1867 bis 1914* (Göttingen: Vandenhoeck & Ruprecht, 2004); Shulamit Volkov, 'Antisemitism as Cultural Code: Reflections on the History and Historiography of Antisemitism in Imperial Germany', *Leo Baeck Institute Yearbook* 23 (1978): 25–46.

27 The other association openly propagating antisemitism was the *Deutschnationale Handlungsgehilfenverband* (German National Association of Commercial Employees). See Thomas Gräfe, *Antisemitismus in Gesellschaft und Karikatur*

132   *Colonialism and the Jews in German History*

des Kaiserreichs: Glöß' Politische Bilderbogen 1892–1901 (Norderstedt: Books on Demand, 2005), 42.

28   Ibid., 15.

29   Rürup, 'Antisemitismus und moderne Gesellschaft', 88.

30   Sarah Jansen, *'Schädlinge': Geschichte eines wissenschaftlichen und politischen Konstrukts, 1840–1920* (Frankfurt am Main: Campus, 2003).

31   *Bienen und Drohnen: Politischer Bilderbogen*, no. 25 (Dresden: Verlag der Druckerei Glöß, 1898). See also Gräfe, *Antisemitismus in Gesellschaft*.

32   *Bienen und Drohnen*.

33   The German title of the law, which was originally issued for the *Norddeutsche Bund* in 1869 and adopted into the constitution of the German Empire in 1871, is 'Gesetz, betreffend die Gleichberechtigung der Konfessionen in bürgerlicher und staatsbürgerlicher Beziehung'.

34   Christina von Braun, 'Und der Feind ist Fleisch geworden: Der rassistische Antisemitismus', in *Der ewige Judenhass: Christlicher Antijudaismus, Deutschnationale Judenfeindlichkeit, Rassistischer Antisemitismus*, ed. Christina von Braun and Ludger Heid (Berlin: Philo, 2000), 149–213, here 187.

35   Julia Schäfer, *Vermessen – gezeichnet – verlacht: Judenbilder in populären Zeitschriften 1918–1933* (Frankfurt am Main: Campus, 2005), 433.

36   Klaus Holz, 'Die antisemitische Konstruktion des "Dritten" und die nationale Ordnung der Welt', in *Das 'bewegliche' Vorurteil*, ed. von Braun and Ziege, 60, 59.

37   *Norddeutsche Allgemeine Zeitung*, 4 May 1914; 'Des Reichstags schwarze Schützlinge', *Deutsche Zeitung*, 5 May 1914; 'Die Duala und der blamierte Reichstag', *Leipziger Neuesten Nachrichten*, 7 May 1914. Even the liberal *Berliner Tageblatt* uses the metaphor: 'Die Duala-Denkschrift. Schwarze 'Millionenbauern'', *Berliner Tageblatt*, 5 May 1914.

38   Gräfe, *Antisemitismus in Gesellschaft*, 43–4. See also Stefan Breuer, *Die Völkischen in Deutschland* (Darmstadt: Wissenschaftliche Buchgesellschaft, 2008).

39   'Drohnenanwälte', *Deutsche Zeitung*, 7 May 1914, BAB, R 1001/4432. See also *Leipziger Neueste Nachrichten*, 7 May 1914, BAB, R 1001/4432.

40   On the image of the 'Black Jew', see Birgit Haehnel, '"The Black Jew": An Afterimage of German Colonialism', in *German Colonialism, Visual Culture, and Modern Memory*, ed. Volker Langbehn (New York: Routledge, 2010), 239–59; *The 'Black Jew': Germans, Nazis, and Nature's Other Creatures*, ed. Herbert Louis Heinig (Bloomington: Author House, 2004); Sander L. Gilman, *On Blackness without Blacks: Essays on the Image of the Black in Germany* (Boston: G. K. Hall, 1982).

41   Theodor W. Adorno, 'Prejudice in the Interview Material', in *The Authoritarian Personality*, ed. Theodor W. Adorno, Betty Ruth Aron, Else Frenkel-Brunswik, Daniel J. Levinson, et al. (New York: Harper & Brothers, 1950), 605–53, here 610. This and the following quotations from *The Authoritarian Personality* are taken

The Role of Antisemitism   133

from the online edition: https://soth.alexanderstreet.com/cgi-bin/SOTH/hub.py
?type=document_details&browse=all&sourceid=S10019210&sortorder=docid
(accessed 27 March 2020).

42   The University of California commissioned the research. Besides Adorno, Else
     Frenkel-Brunswik, Daniel L. Levinson and R. Nevitt Sanford were involved in
     devising and conducting the so-called 'Studies in Prejudice' and thereby worked
     with psychoanalytical approaches and surveys. Begun before the overthrow of
     National Socialism, the research project was motivated mainly by antisemitism in
     Germany but also focused on antisemitism in the United States. The research results
     were first published in 1950 under the title *The Authoritarian Personality*.

43   Adorno, 'Prejudice in the Interview Material', 607.

44   See ibid., 608.

45   Ibid., 609.

46   Eva-Maria Ziege, 'Vorwort', in *Das 'bewegliche' Vorurteil*, ed. von Braun and Ziege,
     8.

47   Adorno, 'Prejudice in the Interview Material', 611.

48   Christina von Braun, 'Einführung', in *Das ,bewegliche' Vorurteil*, ed. von Braun and
     Ziege, 18.

49   Ibid., 19. My translation.

50   Adorno, 'Prejudice in the Interview Material', 632.

51   Adolf Rüger, 'Die Duala und die Kolonialmacht 1884–1914: Eine Studie über die
     historischen Wurzeln des afrikanischen Antikolonialismus', in *Kamerun unter
     deutscher Kolonialherrschaft*, ed. Helmuth Stoecker (Berlin: VEB Deutscher Verlag
     der Wissenschaften, 1968), 240–1.

52   Adorno, 'Prejudice in the Interview Material', 608.

53   Von Braun, 'Einführung', 11–12.

54   See Adorno, 'Prejudice in the Interview Material', 613.

55   Von Braun, 'Einführung', 19.

56   See Rürup, 'Antisemitismus und moderne Gesellschaft', 85.

57   See Von Braun, 'Und der Feind ist Fleisch geworden', 178.

58   See Adorno, 'Prejudice in the Interview Material', 630.

59   Ibid., 633.

60   See Gräfe, *Antisemitismus und Gesellschaft*, 37.

61   Rüger, 'Die Duala und die Kolonialmacht', 252.

62   Hamann, *Prekäre koloniale Ordnung*, 288.

63   Paulette Reed-Anderson, *Rewriting the Footnotes: Berlin und die afrikanische
     Diaspora* (Berlin: Die Ausländerbeauftragte des Senats von Berlin, 2000), 37.

64   See Christian Bommarius, *Der gute Deutsche: Die Ermordung Manga Bells in
     Kamerun 1914* (Berlin: Berenberg Verlag, 2015).

7

From colonialism to antisemitism and back

Ideological developments in the Alldeutsche Verband under the Kaiserreich

Stefan Vogt

The Alldeutsche Verband (Pan-German League) is one of the best-researched nationalist organizations of the Kaiserreich and the Weimar Republic – and for good reason.[1] The League was both the paradigmatic example of the radicalization of *völkisch* nationalism at the turn of the twentieth century and one of its main agents. There are also important ideological and organizational continuities between the Alldeutsche Verband and National Socialism.[2] With regard to the League's ideological development, most of the existing research paints a fairly coherent picture. It is claimed that, between its foundation in 1891 and the First World War, the Alldeutsche Verband gradually embraced antisemitism and distanced itself from its initial advocacy of colonialism and *Weltpolitik*.[3] This picture is quite accurate in a certain respect. Antisemitism did not become an official part of the League's platform until the Bamberg Declaration of February 1919, which stated that 'the Jews are an alien (*volksfremd*) element of the population' and called for the containment of 'Jewish influence'.[4] Only in 1924 were Jews officially excluded from membership in the Alldeutsche Verband.[5] Beginning in the early years of the twentieth century, and especially after the First World War, antisemitism did indeed move to the centre of pan-German ideology.

However, if we look at the Alldeutsche Verband from a perspective that understands colonialism as more than overseas expansionism and systematically relates both colonialism and antisemitism to the project of constructing national and *völkisch* identity, the picture changes significantly. From this perspective, the shift in the League's programmatic emphasis – from colonialism to antisemitism – was not a fundamental ideological transformation but rather a transposition of

From *Colonialism to Antisemitism and Back* 135

already existing ideas from one realm into another. A careful examination of the League's official and unofficial documents reveals that antisemitism was already central to its ideology in its early years, while colonial expansionism remained so at least until the end of the Kaiserreich. These were not two separate sets of ideologies, agendas and politics, but rather elements of a *völkisch* conception of the German nation which frequently intersected, often overlapped and at times even coincided. Both colonialism and antisemitism were in fact constitutive and intimately connected elements of the evolving pan-German ideology. They were thus not identical but certainly compatible. This entanglement also has implications for the relationship between colonialism, racism and antisemitism more generally.

Pan-German imperialism

The event that initially triggered the establishment of the Alldeutsche Verband was a genuinely colonialist issue: the signing of the Heligoland-Zanzibar Treaty in June 1890, in which Germany ceded control over parts of East Africa to Britain. Moreover, the establishment of the League was closely related to other colonialist initiatives of the 1880s, such as the founding of the Deutsche Kolonialgesellschaft (German Colonial Society) in 1887, which involved a great number of activists who later became pan-Germans. The Deutsche Kolonialgesellschaft was the product of the merger of two slightly older colonialist organizations, the Deutsche Kolonialverein (German Colonial Association) and the Gesellschaft für Deutsche Kolonisation (Society for German Colonization). Radical nationalist, *völkisch* and antisemitic ideas were particularly prominent in the latter, which was led by Carl Peters.[6] Peters had also initiated the *Erste allgemeine deutsche Kongress zur Förderung überseeischer Interessen* (First General Congress for the Promotion of Overseas Interests) in September 1886, a large gathering for representatives of nationalist pressure groups as well as prominent businessmen and scientists, who discussed issues of colonial politics, emigration and German culture abroad.[7] As a result of this congress, the Allgemeine Deutsche Verband zur Vertretung deutsch-nationaler Interessen (General German League for the Promotion of German National Interests) was founded; though relatively short-lived, this organization was in many ways a direct precursor of the Alldeutsche Verband and even provided the inspiration for its name.[8] The founding proclamation of the Alldeutsche Verband stated that the goal of the organization was to enable the Germans 'to belong to a master people (*Herrenvolk*) which actively takes its share of the world and does not seek to receive it by the grace or goodwill of another nation'.[9] The first chairman of the Alldeutsche Verband, Karl von der Heydt, was simultaneously chairman of the Deutsch-Ostafrikanische Gesellschaft (German East-African Society), another of Carl Peters's creations, which had implemented German colonial rule in what is today Tanzania. Calls to expand Germany's overseas territories and to challenge Britain's hegemony in various parts of the non-European world were a constant feature of early pan-German publications and propaganda.[10] There is no doubt that the Alldeutsche Verband was part and parcel of the colonial movement of the time, albeit a particularly radical part.

At the same time, and again from its inception, the Alldeutsche Verband vigorously called for German hegemony – and indeed colonization – in central and eastern Europe.[11] Pan-German authors developed expansion, domination and settlement schemes that were intended not only to bring most ethnic Germans under a greater German nation state but also to offer an alternative to Germans who might otherwise emigrate to North America, to provide the agricultural basis for sustaining an ever-growing German population and to secure the political and economic hegemony of the German Empire on the European continent.[12] In addition, the Alldeutsche Verband was very much occupied with the project of 'inner colonization' in eastern Prussia and the struggle with national minorities within Germany, especially the Poles. This topic also filled the pages of the *Alldeutsche Blätter*, the official publication of the League, and the minutes of the League's conventions from the very beginning.[13] The Germanization of the eastern parts of the existing German Empire, as well as of those territories beyond the empire's eastern borders that were envisioned as parts of a future Greater Germany, was considered vital to the existence of the German *Volk*. Thus continental imperialism was already a key element of pan-German ideology in the late 1880s and early 1890s. It remained so as long as the Alldeutsche Verband existed.

Just as the League never gave up its preoccupation with central and eastern Europe, so overseas colonialism also remained central to its ideology and politics. This included plans to further expand the German colonial empire. This position became most obvious in the second Moroccan crisis in 1911, during which the Alldeutsche Verband tirelessly campaigned for an aggressive policy that would supposedly lead to the creation of a new German colony in western Africa. The League printed more than 50,000 copies of Heinrich Claß's brochure *West-Marokko deutsch!* (West Morocco Must Be German!), distributed most of them for free and organized more than forty public meetings on this issue.[14]

Developing and expanding the existing German colonies, especially German South-West Africa, remained an important cause as well. For example, a lot of pan-German ink was spilled over ways to deal with the Herero and Nama revolts and the racist reorganization of the colony. Pan-Germans argued that the revolts had been caused by the Germans' lack of race consciousness and that any further trouble should be contained by means of intensified settlement, radical racial segregation and the relentless subjugation of the Africans – up to the point of annihilation, if necessary.[15] In southern Africa as well, the Alldeutsche Verband hoped to expand German territorial domination. Authors such as Max Robert Gerstenhauer fantasized about including the Boer republics in the German sphere of control, claiming that the Boers were actually part of the German national community.[16] Gerstenhauer also dreamt that in the long run, the German and Dutch colonies could be consolidated into a 'united upper and lower German colonial empire, India–Polynesia'.[17] More generally, a notion of 'Weltpolitik', which included reaching beyond the European continent, remained a positive reference point in pan-German statements throughout the period of the Kaiserreich.[18] Pan-Germans repeatedly emphasized that Germany was competing with Britain, Russia, France and the United States for world-power status.[19]

In an important essay, Dennis Sweeney has shown that overseas and continental imperialism not only always existed side by side in pan-German ideology, but that they were in fact systematically intertwined.[20] From the outset, he argues, the pan-Germans aimed to create 'a greater German empire via two interrelated means: an aggressive colonial policy overseas and the formation of a German-dominated sphere of influence in central and eastern Europe'.[21] The envisioned empire consisted of several zones of graded domination that included both European and non-European spaces.[22] Thus the transformation that took place after the turn of the century was not a shift from 'Weltpolitik' to 'Kontinentalpolitik' but the reframing of pan-German ideology in terms of biological racism and a dynamic understanding of imperial space. Imperialism was no longer confined to political control over territory outside the nation's borders but included ideas about economically and racially reconstructing this space according to the needs of the German Volk. In this process, the pan-German imperialist reference system became more global, not less so. It adapted to the demands of the globalizing capitalist economy and developed bio-racial concepts of social engineering which were applied to populations both within and outside Europe.

In this sense, eastern Europe and Africa belonged to a common, if variegated and structured space which imperialists sought to penetrate. When pan-

Germans spoke about German 'colonialism' in eastern Europe, they meant this quite literally.[23] This is why Ernst Hasse, in his 1905 treatise *Die Besiedlung des deutschen Volksbodens* (The Settlement of German National Soil), could begin his conclusions about reorganizing eastern Europe with a statement that would otherwise seem misplaced: 'The German Empire is a colonial empire.'[24] He was referring to colonization in the east, including inner colonization in eastern Prussia, but he intentionally located these endeavours within the framework of imperialism. Like overseas colonialism, continental imperialism was also essential to thwarting other nations' and empires' competing efforts to expand both politically and economically. Imperialist penetration and colonial restructuring of both continental Europe and the extra-European world were considered necessary steps towards the completion of the nation-building process, thus ensuring the future existence of the German *Volk*.

According to the pan-Germans, this process required the German Empire to attain and maintain the status of a world power. Or as one famous pan-German put it: 'We have to understand that Germany's unification would constitute a youthful escapade which the nation undertook in its old days, and from which it should have refrained due to its costliness, if this was intended to be the concluding rather than the starting point of the struggle for German world-power status.'[25] For Max Weber, the author of these words, as well as for other pan-Germans, it was clear that territorial expansion and the creation of German *Lebensraum*, the fight against foreign elements within the nation and on its borders and successful global competition with other great powers for resources, markets and control of infrastructures were the ingredients necessary to achieve this status. The alternative was not only the ultimate failure of the German nation-building project but also – and more dramatically – the decline of the German *Volk*. Both continental and overseas colonialism were thus essential preconditions which would enable the German *Volk* to exist and to thrive. For many pan-Germans, this was also precisely the reason for attacking the Jews.

Antisemitism and *Kontinentalpolitik*

It is of course important to note that under the Kaiserreich, antisemitism was not part of the Alldeutsche Verband's official program. Until at least the early 1900s, the League also had Jewish members, although it is impossible to determine how many.[26] Attempts on the local level to exclude Jews, as happened in Hamburg or Berlin, remained unsuccessful.[27] Nevertheless, it seems problematic to conclude that the Alldeutsche Verband was not initially an antisemitic organization.[28] While it is true that not all of its members were antisemites, many of them were, and even in the early years the League was a meeting point for antisemitic activists, authors and politicians. Prominent examples include Max Liebermann von Sonnenberg, Wilhelm Lattmann, Max Robert Gerstenhauer and Theodor Fritsch. Particularly among the organization's leadership, antisemitism was the rule rather than the exception. Ernst Hasse, who led the League from 1893 until 1908, was a case in point, and his successor, Heinrich Claß, even more so.[29] Although Hasse, Claß and other leaders were anxious not to present their antisemitic views as the League's official position, they certainly did not try to hide them. Hasse, for instance, who was also a member of the Reichstag for the Nationalliberale Partei (National Liberal Party), declared in a parliamentary debate in 1895 that it would be necessary to consider 'the Jewish question from the standpoint of a legitimate national egoism'.[30] For him, this meant reducing the number of Jews living in Germany by means of population policy and also limiting their alleged influence. In this demand, Hasse clearly excluded the Jews from the German nation. In private conversation and correspondence, his antisemitism was even more explicit.[31] Similar notions can be found among other leading pan-Germans, such as Eduard von Liebert and Paul Samassa.[32] Moreover, the League's leadership made no effort to curb its members' antisemitic activities outside the organization.[33] Instead, Hasse made it clear that the official caution in this respect was purely strategic – a strategy which suggests that many contemporaries did in fact consider the League antisemitic.[34]

For pan-German antisemites, Jews were a problem because they saw them as one of the various foreign forces threatening to undermine Germany's status as a world power and eventually to destroy the German *Volk*. According to the pan-Germans, they did so primarily either as eastern European immigrants or as internationally minded capitalists.[35] The first of these two incarnations was evoked, for instance, in the aforementioned Reichstag debate of March 1895, in which three bills intended to close the German borders to immigrants were discussed.[36] Two of them – put forward by members of the right-wing Deutschkonservative Partei (German Conservative Party) and the antisemitic Deutschsoziale Partei (German Social Party), respectively – were exclusively directed at Jews. The bill suggested by Hasse and his colleague Traugott-Herrmann von Arnim-Muskau, the vice president of the Alldeutsche Verband, did not mention Jews explicitly but spoke more generally of 'making the naturalization of foreigners more difficult'.[37] However, the debate made it clear that also this bill was to curb immigration from the east, especially Jewish immigration. This was necessary, Hasse explained, due to the high percentage of 'racial aliens' already living among the German population. For Hasse, these 'racial aliens' included not only new immigrants but also all the approximately 560,000 Jews living in Germany. He considered their presence a 'disadvantage for the Reich and for its consistent national development', and he argued that an increase in the number of such 'aliens' immigrating to Germany would cause severe damage 'because they affect the composition of the population most negatively'. Most of these immigrants, Hasse added, were either Slavs or Jews and were therefore 'nationally inferior'. This was also the grounds on which antisemitism was justified: 'In my eyes,' Hasse declared in the Reichstag session, 'the antisemitic movement is the manifestation of the so-called nativism (*Nativismus*) which we always find when a self-conscious nation (*Volkstum*) is flooded by fragments of alien peoples (*Völker*) and defends itself against the national and economic damage which results from this.'[38]

This 'nativism', of course, was nothing more than a euphemistic term for racism. Jews were subsumed under the category of inferior eastern European 'races' who had to be kept out of Germany. Hasse thus presented Jews and Slavs as a common threat to the German nation, and his antisemitism in this case was a form of racism. This was a prominent motive in many pan-German statements.[39] One pan-German activist said it was 'impossible to separate the Polish question from the Jewish question'.[40] To be sure, most pan-Germans still considered the struggle against '*Polentum*', as well as against Czechs and Hungarians in Austria, more urgent than fighting the Jews.[41] Nevertheless, Jews were also targeted, and the territory in the east which was to be included in the envisioned Greater Germany was meant to be as free of Jews as possible. At times, Jews from the east, Slavs, Africans and Asians were all lumped together and presumed to constitute one big threat to the German nation. 'Because we want to remain Germans,' wrote H. Wendland in the *Alldeutsche Blätter*, 'and because we want to prevent damage to our political, social, military, and economic capabilities, we object to admitting Jewish and Slavic immigrants from the east, to enlisting black or yellow workers, to our fellow countrymen overseas mixing with the natives.'[42] The pan-Germans clearly identified eastern European Jews as colonial Others, and pushing them back was part of the pan-German colonial project in the east.

Antisemitism and *Weltpolitik*

This was not the only version of antisemitism in the Alldeutsche Verband's ideology, however. Another form took aim at the alleged subversion of the

From Colonialism to Antisemitism and Back   141

German nation by the forces of international capital, which was associated with Jews. Antisemitism was related to colonialism in this case as well, but it was more than just a variety of racism. The appointment of Bernhard Dernburg – a banker who, as a Protestant with Jewish ancestry, was widely considered a Jew – as director of the colonial department of the Foreign Office and subsequently the first colonial secretary was met with considerable scepticism on the part of the pan-Germans.[43] While they had to admit that Dernburg gave fresh impetus to the colonial cause, they criticized what they perceived as his overemphasis on the 'commercial' aspects of colonialism and his neglect of the 'national' aspects.[44] Eventually the pan-Germans openly accused Dernburg of promoting the interests of big capital and working against the settlers and planters. Under Dernburg, they lamented, colonial decisions were made 'five minutes away from his office, in the big banking houses of Behrenstraße.'[45] Pan-German attacks on the influence of 'international big capital' and the 'abuse of concessions in the German *Schutzgebiete*' also singled out other Jews or persons they considered Jewish. These attacks were replete with antisemitic stereotypes: international big capital was nationally unreliable, and its Jewish representatives could easily morph from Germans into Englishmen; it promoted speculation, had the potential to initiate another 'founder's crash' and more 'stock exchange mischief' (*Gründer- und Börsen-Unfug*) and followed secret strategies to receive profitable concessions; and its agents were obsessed with profit and ruthlessly pursued their personal economic interests at the expense of the national community.[46] This was perceived as a threat to the nation because it would obstruct settlement activities in the German colonies and interfere with German economic interests around the world.

According to the pan-Germans, certain Jews were also undermining the German nation by promoting an overly benevolent policy towards the indigenous populations in the colonies. They accused Dernburg of 'excessive humanitarianism' and of failing to uphold an adequate 'racial position.'[47] A particularly popular target in this case was Ernst Vohsen, a leading representative of the German Colonial Society. Vohsen, who came from a Jewish family but was not religious himself, had worked for the Deutsch-Ostafrikanische Gesellschaft in the German colony of East Africa before he returned to Germany to assume multiple leading positions in the colonial movement. As a staunch supporter of colonialism as such, one who never questioned the legitimacy of German colonial rule or European superiority, Vohsen nevertheless advocated a relatively moderate policy towards the Africans and spoke out against particularly blatant instances of exploitation and violence.[48] He believed it was possible to elevate the

142 *Colonialism and the Jews in German History*

Africans to a position from which they could become associates (*Mitarbeiter*) of the Europeans and gradually achieve equality.[49] Although this was still a profoundly colonialist notion, it nevertheless distinguished Vohsen from many other German colonialists, who insisted on the Africans' complete and permanent submission to the Germans' '*Herrenstandpunkt*' (their position as undisputed masters). In this spirit, Vohsen also published German translations of the works of the African-American civil rights activist Booker T. Washington with his own Dietrich Reimer Verlag.[50]

On this basis, pan-Germans such as Max Robert Gerstenhauer claimed that Vohsen was subverting German race consciousness and national identity.[51] In 1905, Gerstenhauer launched a full-scale attack on Vohsen, which initially targeted him as one of the directors of the Siedlungsgesellschaft für Deutsch-Südwestafrika (Settlement Company for German South-West Africa), claiming that he had obstructed settlement efforts by driving up the prices of land and cattle. Simultaneously, Gerstenhauer also sought to undermine Vohsen's position as a leader of the German Colonial Society. Gerstenhauer's attack contained a number of antisemitic stereotypes, such as accusations of financial speculation and of pursuing individual goals at the expense of the common national good. Moreover, he claimed that Vohsen had undermined German rule in the colony by weakening the settlers and calling for the Schutztruppe to be reduced, thus facilitated the Herero uprising the previous year. This charge was embedded in the more general allegation that Vohsen's attitude towards the indigenous populations of the colonies was much too sympathetic. Obviously in the pan-German universe, antisemitic stereotypes of Jews as agents of internationalism, anti-nationalism and global capitalism could be combined with the idea that Jews were inappropriately close to the non-European 'races'. Once again, this resonated with the view that Jews were close to Poles and other Slavic peoples. Thus Jews were associated with what the pan-Germans considered inferior, colonized (or soon-to-be-colonized) peoples, both in eastern Europe and in Africa, and at the same time construed as representatives of a particularly powerful, threatening aspect of capitalist modernity.

The allegation that Jews were too 'friendly' towards the Blacks explicitly linked elements of antisemitism and colonial racism. Pan-Germans imagined that Jews and Blacks were colluding against the interests – and indeed the existence – of the German nation. They assigned these two groups different roles in this plot, according to their roles in the colonial economy. Whereas Blacks refused to produce the wealth necessary for the German nation to compete in the global market, Jews helped Blacks to avoid work and simultaneously sold out the colonies to Germany's enemies. Similarly, pan-Germans thought that Jews and Poles were colluding to undermine the racial make-up of the German nation. In all of these incarnations, antisemitism constituted part of the pan-German idea of an endangered German *Volk* which needed to achieve world-power status in order to survive. Thus it was never an alternative to colonialism but always complemented it. This is not to say that pan-German antisemitism did not change over time. In addition to being attuned to different imperialist spaces, it was also increasingly merged with biological racism and therefore radicalized. In this respect as well, it became more closely tied to colonial racism. Nevertheless, the compatibility of these two ideologies in itself was nothing new. This becomes quite clear when Ernst Hasse's antisemitism is compared to that of Heinrich Claß.

Transformations of pan-German antisemitism

Hasse was by no means a 'moderate' antisemite. Not only was he convinced that Jews were a separate race, and that of all the white races, they were 'most distant' from the Aryans, that is, the least white among the Whites. He also claimed that Jewish emancipation and Jewish immigration from the east obstructed the German nation-building process, adding that the long-established German Jews might pose an even greater danger than the new immigrants because they had accumulated wealth and power.[52] In his 1905 book *Das Deutsche Reich als Nationalstaat* (The German State as a Nation-State), he also employed the classic antisemitic technique of using fabricated or decontextualized quotations of Jews to articulate viciously anti-Jewish views without formally adopting them. He quoted a 'Jewish student Schwerenz' who supposedly stated that 'Jews are the typical representatives of the International' and are 'responsible for social turmoil'; he cited Theodor Herzl saying that Jews do not want to remain 'parasites in foreign lands'; and he recounted at length an interview which Max Nordau allegedly gave to the antisemitic French journal *La libre parole*, in which Nordau had supposedly described the Sixth Zionist Congress delegates' reaction to the Uganda proposal: 'These unfortunate ones,' the quote reads, 'numbering 178, begun to wallow on the ground, with bloodshot eyes, twisted faces, foam on their lips, in awful spasms.'[53] In a similar way, using a German national icon as a proxy, Hasse quoted the Prussian general Helmuth von Moltke, who had written that the Jews 'are directed by unknown leaders to pursue common goals', and that they would 'form a state within the state'.[54] Not only did he collect some

144 *Colonialism and the Jews in German History*

of the most common antisemitic stereotypes, such as the Jews' 'internationalism' or their alleged attempts to create secret clusters of Jewish power within their 'host societies', he also evoked clearly colonial racist ideas when he quoted Nordau describing the Zionist congress as resembling the western stereotype of a voodoo ceremony.

At the same time, however, Hasse conceded that German Jews could become Germans – in contrast to those immigrating from the east – provided they were willing to give up their religion and their customs and to speak German exclusively. Nevertheless, they should refrain from aspiring to take up influential positions in German culture and society. In Hasse's view, absorbing the Jews into the German *Volk* also required keeping their number small and eventually reducing it. These goals were thwarted by the process of Jewish emancipation and by the immigration of eastern European Jews. Without emancipation and immigration, he argued, 'Jews would have simply become extinct in Germany or would rightly have vanished into the German *Volk*'.[55] The solution Hasse proposed was to prohibit any further Jewish immigration, but this measure was in fact directed against the German Jews as well. If the border was closed, he argued, 'their number would greatly dwindle within a few generations. They would not and could not play a leading role in literature, art, and politics any more. They would no longer be able to threaten our race.'[56] Hasse had also called for this in the Reichstag debate in 1895. Preventing Jewish immigration, he declared, was necessary to 'protect the purity and particularity of our mother nation'.[57]

It is important to note that Hasse submitted this bill not only as the chairman of the Alldeutsche Verband but also as a member of the National Liberal Party and their Reichstag faction. It is therefore no coincidence that he advocated a Treitschke type of antisemitism. Heinrich von Treitschke, himself a former Reichstag delegate of the same party, had famously contended in his article 'Unsere Aussichten' that masses of Jewish peddlers from the east were about to flood Germany and to destroy the newly established nation state. In his view, what made these immigrants truly dangerous was that 'their children and grandchildren will one day dominate Germany's stock markets and newspapers'. Treitschke ostensibly conceded that he would merely demand that the Jews become Germans, but in practice this meant they had to disappear. At the same time, he listed a great number of quite hideous crimes which the Jews – especially those already living in Germany – had allegedly committed against the Germans, resulting in the notorious conclusion that 'the Jews are our misfortune!'[58] In a similar fashion, Ernst Hasse nominally offered the Jews

From *Colonialism to Antisemitism and Back* 145

a solution, but his solution in fact required them to perish. He seemed to direct his antisemitism at eastern European Jews, but he identified these 'Ostjuden' and their influence among German Jewry as well. Moreover, while he appeared to define 'the Jews' in a non-essentialist way which allowed for conversion and assimilation, he simultaneously introduced racial categories which already suggested much more radical 'solutions' to the 'Jewish question'. For Hasse, as for Treitschke, a more radical antisemitism which would preclude assimilation through cultural liquidation was impeded by his political affiliation to National Liberalism and by related strategic considerations. Both men also still lacked a comprehensive theory and an elaborate vocabulary through which to conceive of the Jews in strictly bio-racial terms. Yet the elements of a more radical antisemitism, from defining the Jews as essentially different to calling for their removal from the national community, were already present and ready to be unleashed.

It took a character like Heinrich Claß to actualize these potentials. Claß, who was one of Treitschke's students, developed his antisemitism most explicitly in his so-called *Kaiserbuch*, published in 1912.[59] For Claß, assimilation was not only a practical but also a theoretical impossibility. What mattered to him was not religion, national affiliation or personal conviction but race. 'As a consequence of the principles of his nature', he declared, 'the Jew is in all his deeds a Jew'.[60] His definition of who should be considered a Jew was based on ancestry, not on confession, language or culture. Everyone who had belonged to a Jewish community in 1871, along with all of their descendants, should be considered Jewish.[61] For lack of any applicable anthropological data or functional biological classifications, Claß had to refer to religion as a starting point, just as the Nazis did in the Nuremberg Laws. Yet for Claß, it did not matter whether a person was still a member of a Jewish community or whether he or she was religious. The principle was therefore clearly racial, not religious. 'The race is the source of the dangers', he wrote, and 'religion is nothing but an emanation of race'.[62] In Claß's view, Jews personified the polar opposite of the idealistic, creative Germans, pursuing only materialist goals as 'the people born for money-lending and intermediate trade, whose instinct and intellect is focused on acquisition'.[63] Thus having accumulated economic power, they had come to dominate German cultural and political life and constituted the reason for its disintegration and decline. To counter what he perceived as an existential threat to the German *Volk*, Claß suggested not only closing the borders to Jewish immigrants but also expelling all Jews who were not German citizens. Those who were German citizens would be subjected to an 'alien law' (*Fremdenrecht*), which would

146   *Colonialism and the Jews in German History*

exclude them from the right to vote, from holding public office, from a number of professions and from the right to own land.[64]

In many ways, Claß drew the conclusions which Hasse had not dared to draw. He moulded his convictions about the Jews' character and misdeeds into a coherent racist theory, and he made concrete suggestions on how to remove the Jews from the German nation. Conceptually, however, this was a radicalization of earlier pan-German antisemitism rather than a completely new invention. The removal of 'Jewish influences' on the German nation was now envisioned in physical and biological rather than cultural terms. At the same time, the Pan-German League became more and more outspoken in its opposition to the politics of the Wilhelminian state, which removed strategic impediments to such radical 'solutions'.[65] In parallel with the radicalization and racialization of pan-German imperialism, antisemitism also took on more sharply defined racial features, which in turn produced more radical and more outspoken antisemitic policies.[66] Nevertheless, the ideological basis for this dated back to the very beginning of the organization. Already for Hasse, Jews represented a biological threat which had to be confronted with demographic policies. The development of race theory and its widespread dissemination within the Alldeutsche Verband, along with practical experiences of racial policy in the colonies, provided ideological fodder for the radicalization of antisemitism and imperialism – a process for which the interfaces had long been in place.

Conclusion

The bio-racial radicalization of the Alldeutsche Verband's ideology, which began at the turn of the twentieth century and accelerated in the second decade of that century, affected both pan-German imperialism and pan-German antisemitism. In both cases, this was a development of existing pan-German ideological convictions, not a fundamental reorientation. Thus racial antisemitism did not replace colonialism as the core of pan-German ideology. Rather, antisemitism and colonialism were both considered necessary means to secure the existence of the German *Volk*. Together, as Ernst Hasse put it, they would keep the German *Volk* 'free of foreign influence, foreign dictation, and foreign extortion' and would produce the internal and external 'elbow room' (*Ellenbogenraum*) necessary for the *Volk* to unite, thrive and survive.[67] Antisemitism and colonialism were thus complementary elements of pan-German ideology. Moreover, pan-German antisemitism was often directly connected to colonial concepts and imaginations in one way or another. Jews were subsumed under the to-be-colonized peoples in the east, associated with foreign imperialist interests or accused of being too close to the Africans. Accordingly, until the end of the Kaiserreich, and beyond, colonialism and antisemitism were constitutive, interrelated elements of the Alldeutsche Verband's *völkisch* imperialist ideology.

With regard to the relationship between colonialism, racism and antisemitism in general, this suggests that while it would be wrong to simply subsume antisemitism under the category of racism, it is certainly necessary to consider both ideologies in conjunction, as well as in connection with colonialism and imperialism. Antisemitism could and indeed did work with notions which were developed in the colonial context. This was most obvious with regard to the category of race, but it was also the case when it came to population policy or concepts of global competition, for instance. Anti-Jewish racism could be and indeed was linked to anti-Polish, anti-Slavic and even anti-Black racism. At the same time, antisemitism also had ideological concepts at its disposal which were not available to anti-Polish or anti-Black racism. This included the idea that Jews were behind powerful, international economic or cultural forces. In addition, Jews and Blacks could be assigned different roles in a common plot, as was the case when Jews were accused of supporting African insubordination or even the revolts in the colonies. Antisemites associated Jews with 'despicable' colonized peoples as well as with 'evil' anti-German colonizers and even managed to connect these notions.

Therefore, antisemitism and colonial racism should not be seen as alternative or mutually exclusive ideologies but rather as complementary ideological formations. The Alldeutsche Verband is a prime example of this. It provides a unique historical setting in which colonialism and antisemitism intersected on a daily basis and over a substantial period of time. This also suggests that Jewish history more generally should be linked to the context of histories of colonialism and racism. This argument in no way denies the specific, indeed singular quality of Jewish history. Rather, it strongly suggests to explore these peculiarities within their larger contexts, as well as to consider the impact of Jewish history and the history of antisemitism on the histories of racism and colonialism. As an antisemitic organization, the Alldeutsche Verband was an important element in German-Jewish history; as a colonialist organization, it played a crucial role in its imperial and racist historical context. Analysing this organization thus provides immediate insight into the ways in which these histories were bound together. It can also help us find ways to study German-Jewish history and German colonial

148   *Colonialism and the Jews in German History*

history together, without losing sight of their particular origins, features and consequences.

Notes

1 Monographical studies of the Alldeutsche Verband include Alfred Kruck, *Geschichte des Alldeutschen Verbandes 1890–1939* (Wiesbaden: Steiner, 1954); Roger Chickering, *We Men Who Feel Most German: A Cultural Study of the Pan-German League, 1886–1914* (Boston: Allen & Unwin, 1984); Rainer Hering, *Konstruierte Nation: Der Alldeutsche Verband 1890 bis 1939* (Hamburg: Christians, 2003); Michael Peters, *Der Alldeutsche Verband am Vorabend des Ersten Weltkrieges (1908–1914): Ein Beitrag zur Geschichte des völkischen Nationalismus im spätwilhelminischen Deutschland*, 2nd edn (Frankfurt am Main: Lang, 1996). Biographical studies include: Johannes Leicht, *Heinrich Claß 1868–1953: Die politische Biographie eines Alldeutschen* (Paderborn: Schöningh, 2012); Stefan Frech, *Wegbereiter Hitlers? Theodor Reismann-Grone. Ein völkischer Nationalist (1863–1949)* (Paderborn: Schöningh, 2009). Of course the Alldeutsche Verband also appears prominently in most general studies of German nationalism, antisemitism and radical-right politics. See, for instance, Peter Walkenhorst, *Nation – Rasse – Volk: Radikaler Nationalismus im Deutschen Kaiserreich 1890–1914* (Göttingen: Vandenhoeck & Ruprecht, 2007).

2 On the history of the Alldeutsche Verband in the Weimar Republic and its continuities with Nazism, see Barry A. Jackisch, *The Pan-German League and Radical Nationalist Politics in Interwar Germany, 1918–1939* (Farnham: Ashgate, 2012); Uta Jungcurt, *Alldeutscher Extremismus in der Weimarer Republik: Denken und Handeln einer einflussreichen bürgerlichen Minderheit* (Berlin: De Gruyter Oldenbourg, 2016).

3 See Hering, *Konstruierte Nation*, 187–219; Chickering, *We Men Who Feel Most German*, 230–52.

4 'Erklärung des Alldeutschen Verbandes (Bamberger Erklärung)', Bundesarchiv Berlin (henceforth BAB), R 8048/123. However, by 1917 antisemitism had already been made a quasi-official position in a great number of articles in the League's papers, especially in the newly acquired *Deutsche Zeitung*. See, for instance, Konstantin von Gebsattel [Heinrich Claß], 'Alldeutsch – vielleicht alljüdisch?' *Deutsche Zeitung*, 18 June 1917, 1–2; Georg Fritz, 'Deutschtum und Judentum', *Deutsche Zeitung*, 28 June 1917, 1–2; Konstantin von Gebsattel, 'Das "Ferment der Dekomposition"', *Deutsche Zeitung*, 15 October 1918, 1–2. See also 'Protokoll der Sitzung der Hauptleitung und des Geschäftsführenden Ausschusses am 19. und 20.Oktober 1918 in Berlin', BAB, R 8048/121. In its meeting in September 1918,

the Geschäftsführende Ausschuss established a committee on the 'Jewish Question', which resulted in the foundation of the 'Deutschvölkische Schutz- und Trutzbund' (German Völkisch Federation for Protection and Defiance) as an antisemitic frontline organization. See 'Protokoll der Sitzung des Geschäftsführenden Ausschusses am 13. September 1918 in Hannover', BAB, R 8048/120. On the *Deutschvölkische Schutz- und Trutzbund*, see Uwe Lohalm, *Völkischer Radikalismus: Die Geschichte des Deutschvölkischen Schutz- und Trutz-Bundes 1919–1923* (Hamburg: Leibniz, 1970).

5 'Satzung des Alldeutschen Verbandes vom März 1925', BAB, R 8048/4.

6 The German Colonial Society is a remarkably understudied organization. There are only two monographs on the society, both of which are unpublished dissertations written in the mid-1960s: Richard V. Pierard, 'The German Colonial Society, 1882–1914', PhD diss., University of Iowa, Iowa City, 1964; Klaus Klauß, 'Die Deutsche Kolonialgesellschaft und die deutsche Kolonialpolitik von den Anfängen bis 1895', PhD diss., Humboldt Universität Berlin, Ostberlin, 1966. In addition, a master's thesis on the colonial movement in the Rhineland was published in the early 1990s: Ulrich Soénius, *Koloniale Begeisterung im Rheinland während des Kaiserreichs* (Köln: Selbstverlag, 1992). On Peters, see Arne Perras, *Carl Peters and German Imperialism, 1856–1918: A Political Biography* (Oxford: Oxford University Press, 2004).

7 'Aufruf zum ersten allgemeinen deutschen Kongreß zur Förderung überseeischer Interessen', BAB, R 8048/1, 5–7; 'Bericht über die Verhandlungen des Allgemeinen Deutschen Kongresses', *Kolonialpolitische Korrespondenz* 2 (1886): 265–75.

8 See Perras, *Carl Peters*, 86–99.

9 'Deutschland wach' auf!' *Frankfurter Zeitung*, 27 June 1890 (3rd morning edition), 4. All translations are mine.

10 See, for example, G. K., 'Deutschlands Weltstellung und der Weiterbau am deutschen Nationalstaat', *Alldeutsche Blätter*, 7 January 1894, 5–7; A. L., 'Zur kolonialen Sache', *Alldeutsche Blätter*, 18 March 1894, 56; 'Unsere Kolonialpolitik', *Alldeutsche Blätter*, 18 November 1894, 198–9; 'Deutschlands Interessen im Orient', *Alldeutsche Blätter*, 8 December 1894, 221–2; Ernst Hasse, 'Europäische oder Weltpolitik?', *Alldeutsche Blätter*, 11 June 1899, 193–4; Ernst Hasse, *Deutsche Weltpolitik (Flugschriften des Alldeutschen Verbandes, Nr. 5* (München: Lehmann, 1897). See also the series by M. G., 'Der Kampf der Buren gegen England – ein Kampf ums Deutschtum', *Alldeutsche Blätter*, 16 August to 8 November 1896.

11 There is a growing body of literature which analyses German eastward expansionism in terms of colonialism. See, for instance, David Blackbourn, *The Conquest of Nature: Water, Landscape, and the Making of Modern Germany* (London: Cape, 2006); *Germans, Poland, and Colonial Expansion to the East: 1850 Through the Present*, ed. Robert L. Nelson (Basingstoke: Macmillan, 2009);

150   *Colonialism and the Jews in German History*

Kristin Kopp, *Germany's Wild East: Constructing Poland as Colonial Space* (Ann Arbor: University of Michigan Press, 2012).

12 See Ernst Hasse, *Großdeutschland und Mitteleuropa um das Jahr 1950: Von einem Alldeutschen*, 2nd edn (Berlin: Thormann und Goetsch, 1895); Robert Gerstenhauer, 'Die Begründung Großdeutschlands durch die Besiedelung von Neusaß. Eine nationalpolitische Zukunftsbetrachtung', *Alldeutsche Blätter*, 12 June 1898, 121–3 and 19 June 1898, 126–7.

13 See 'Der deutsche Staat als Polonisator', *Alldeutsche Blätter*, 15 April 1894, 65–6; Fritz Bley, 'Alldeutscher Verbandstag in Hamburg', *Alldeutsche Blätter*, 10 September 1899, 297–307; P. B., 'Die deutsche Ansiedlungspolitik in den Ostmarken', *Alldeutsche Blätter*, 14 April 1906, 117–20. A major proponent of inner colonization within the Alldeutsche Verband was Alfred Hugenberg, who also wrote his dissertation on this topic. See Alfred Hugenberg, *Innere Colonisation im Nordwesten Deutschlands* (Strassburg: Trübner, 1891).

14 Leicht, *Heinrich Claß*, 141–6. See Heinrich Claß, *West-Marokko deutsch!* (München: Lehmann, 1911). Claß and the Alldeutsche Verband had already campaigned for this goal during the first Moroccan crisis between 1904 and 1906. See Heinrich Claß, *Die Besitzergreifung West-Marokkos, der Anfang und die Voraussetzung praktischer Weltpolitik* (Leipzig: no publisher, 1904); Heinrich Claß, *Marokko verloren? Ein Mahnruf in letzter Stunde* (München: Lehmann, 1904).

15 Conrad Rust, 'Grundzüge einer südwestafrikanischen Zukunftspolitik', *Alldeutsche Blätter*, 19 March 1904, 95–6; 'Verbandstag in Lübeck', *Alldeutsche Blätter*, 4 June 1904, 189–99; Adolf Fick, 'Regierungsweisheit und Rassebewusstsein', *Alldeutsche Blätter*, 10 December 1904, 425–6; 'Das Rassenproblem in Deutsch-Südwestafrika', *Alldeutsche Blätter*, 31 March 1906, 102–4.

16 See M. G. 'Der Kampf der Buren gegen England'; Gerstenhauer, 'Die Begründung Großdeutschlands'.

17 M. G. 'Der Kampf der Buren', 214. Gerstenhauer believed this could also include the 'Belgian–Flemish Congo'.

18 See, for example, M. G. 'Der Kampf der Buren', 214; Ernst Hasse, *Deutsche Weltpolitik* (München: Lehmann, 1897); Hasse, 'Europäische oder Weltpolitik'; Paul Samassa, 'Ziele und Wege deutscher Weltpolitik', *Alldeutsche Blätter*, 6 April 1901, 165–7, 13 April 1901, 177–9, 20 April 1901, 189–92; Ernst Hasse, *Weltpolitik, Imperialismus und Kolonialpolitik* (München, Lehmann: 1908); Claß, *West-Marokko deutsch*, 6; Felix Hänsch, 'Mittelafrika und Bagdadbahn', *Alldeutsche Blätter*, 21 June 1913, 201–2.

19 See Geoff Eley, 'Empire by Land or Sea? Germany's Imperial Imaginary, 1840–1945', in *German Colonialism in a Global Age*, ed. Bradley Naranch and Geoff Eley (Durham: Duke University Press, 2014), 19–45, especially 26–33.

From Colonialism to Antisemitism and Back 151

20 Dennis Sweeney, 'Pan-German Conceptions of Colonial Empire', in *German Colonialism in a Global Age*, 265–82.

21 Ibid., 268.

22 Paradigmatic for this was the concept developed in Hasse, *Großdeutschland und Mitteleuropa*. See also Daniel Fryman (Heinrich Claß), *Wenn ich der Kaiser wär': Politische Wahrheiten und Notwendigkeiten*, 4th edn (Leipzig: Dieterich, 1913), 136–88 (first published 1912).

23 See, for example, Hasse, *Großdeutschland und Mitteleuropa*, 19–42; Otto Hötzsch, 'Paul de Lagarde in seiner alldeutschen Bedeutung', *Alldeutsche Blätter*, 15 February 1902, 57, and 22 February 1902, 66–7.

24 Ernst Hasse, *Die Besiedelung des deutschen Volksbodens* (München: Lehman, 1905), 125.

25 Max Weber, 'Der Nationalstaat und die Volkswirtschaftspolitik. Akademische Antrittsrede (1895)', *Gesammelte Politische Schriften*, ed. Johannes Winckelmann, 5th edn (Tübingen: Mohr, 1988), 1–25, here 23. See also Hasse, *Deutsche Weltpolitik*, 16. Weber was a member of the Alldeutsche Verband from 1893 until 1899. See Wolfgang J. Mommsen, *Max Weber und die deutsche Politik, 1890–1920*, 2nd edn (Tübingen: Mohr, 1974), 58–9.

26 The known cases are Max Koch in Breslau and Alfred Israel in Hamburg. On Koch, see Chickering, *We Men Who Feel Most German*, 160, 233; on Israel, see Rainer Hering, 'Juden im Alldeutschen Verband?' in *Aus den Quellen: Beiträge zur deutsch-jüdischen Geschichte. Festschrift für Ina Lorenz zum 65. Geburtstag*, ed. Andreas Brämer (München: Dölling und Galitz, 2005), 291. See also Ernst Hasse to Prof. Viereck, 24 September, 1901, BAB, R 8048/661, 6–7; Alfred Roth to his bride, 20 November 1904, Forschungsstelle für Zeitgeschichte Hamburg, Alfred Roth Collection, 11/R 14, quoted in Hering, 'Juden im Alldeutschen Verband', 294; Julius Friedrich Lehmann to Konstantin von Gebsattel, 15 July 1916, BAB, N 2089/3, 289.

27 On these cases, see Hering, *Konstruierte Nation*, 190; Johannes Leicht, '"Alldeutsch – vielleicht alljüdisch?" Rassistische und antisemitische Semantiken in der Agitation des Alldeutschen Verbandes in den Jahren 1891 bis 1919', *Jahrbuch für Antisemitismusforschung* 13 (2004): 111–37, here 120. See also letter from Ernst Hasse to Ortsgruppe Frankfurt am Main, 23 August 1901, BAB, R 8046/661, 2–4.

28 As Hering did in *Konstruierte Nation*, 219; 'Juden im Alldeutschen Verband', 291. Also, though less emphatically, Chickering, *We Men Who Feel Most German*, 232; Leicht, 'Alldeutsch – vielleicht alljüdisch', 120.

29 A biographical study of Ernst Hasse is an important desideratum. For some condensed information, see Björn Hofmeister, 'Ernst Hasse', in *Handbuch des Antisemitismus: Judenfeindschaft in Geschichte und Gegenwart*, ed. Wolfgang Benz, vol. 2/1 (Berlin: K. G. Saur, 2010), 336–7. On Claß, see Leicht, *Heinrich Claß*.

30 *Stenographische Berichte über die Verhandlungen des Reichstags*, vol. 139, 6 March 1895, 1277 (henceforth StBR). Hasse's declaration that he opposed the antisemitic movement 'in certain respects' and that he would not hold the Jews accountable 'for all the harm inflicted on our public life' should be understood as a coded avowal of antisemitism. See also, for instance, Ernst Hasse, *Das Deutsche Reich als Nationalstaat* (München: Lehmann, 1905), 139–46.

31 See, for example, Hasse to Viereck, 24 September 1901.

32 Eduard von Liebert, 'Besprechung von Friedrich Lange, Reines Deutschtum, 4. Auflage', *Alldeutsche Blätter*, 3 December 1904, 416–7; P. S. [Paul Samassa], 'Was "national" ist. Eine Antwort an Herrn Professor Alfred Kirchhoff in Halle', *Alldeutsche Blätter*, 3 May 1902, 153–5.

33 Hasse to Ortsgruppe Frankfurt am Main, 23 August 1901, BAB, R 8048/661, 3.

34 See, for example, 'Der Allgemeine Deutsche Verband und der der Antisemitismus (1891)', BAB, R 8048/2; Hasse to Ortsgruppe Frankfurt am Main, 23 August 1901; 'Protokoll über die Sitzung des Geschäftsführenden Auschusses in Berlin vom 26. und 27. Oktober 1901', BAB, R 8048/30. The strategic muting of antisemitism remained the policy under Heinrich Claß's leadership until 1918; see, for instance, 'Verhandlungsbericht über die Sitzung des Geschäftsführenden Auschusses des Alldeutschen Verbandes in Breslau am Freitag, den 6. September 1912 im Erfurter Hof in Erfurt', BAB, R 8048/86.

35 Another role which the pan-German antisemites assigned to the Jews was, of course, that of the internationally minded socialist.

36 StBR, vol. 139, 27 February 1895, 1144–53, 6 March 1895, 1277–1306. All the motions were eventually dismissed. However, Hasse also voted in favour of the openly antisemitic bill put forward by the members of the Deutschkonservative Partei. See ibid., 1304.

37 StBR, vol. 141, Erster Anlagenband, 89, 101, 233.

38 All quotations taken from StBR, vol. 139, 6 March 1895, 1277–9.

39 See, for example, 'Die Sprach- und Rassenfremden im Deutschen Reich', *Alldeutsche Blätter*, 18 March 1894, 50–1; E. H., 'Sind Polen, Dänen und Franzosen Teile des "deutschen Volkes"?' *Alldeutsche Blätter*, 6 June 1897, 109–11; Ernst Hasse, 'Zweierlei Maß', *Alldeutsche Blätter*, 9 January 1898, 5–7; E. H., 'Die Gefahren des russischen Handelsvertrages', *Alldeutsche Blätter*, 2 January 1904, 4; Heinrich Claß, 'Deutsche Grenzpolitik', *Alldeutsche Blätter*, 27 January 1906, 30–3; Paul Dehn, 'Ein Vorschlag gegen den Zuzug vom Osten', *Alldeutsche Blätter*, 16 June 1906, 190–1; Heinrich Claß, 'Die Zukunft des deutschen Volkstums', *Alldeutsche Blätter*, 22 December 1906, 410–2; 'Alldeutscher Verbandstag in Berlin', *Alldeutsche Blätter*, 18 September 1908, 323–5; Alfred Piech, 'Die slawische Bewegung unter den Juden Österreichs', *Alldeutsche Blätter*, 2 November 1912, 389–91; 'Schluß der Reichsgrenzen gegen unerwünschte Einwanderung', *Alldeutsche Blätter*, 11 March 1916, 97–100.

From Colonialism to Antisemitism and Back 153

40 'Zur Frage einer Universität in Posen (Kleine Mitteilungen)', *Alldeutsche Blätter*,
5 April 1902, 124.

41 See the editors' comment on the statement earlier. See also Hasse, 'Zweierlei Maß'.
This changed considerably after 1912 and especially once the First World War
began.

42 H. Wendland, 'Ein Hauptstück nationaler Politik', *Alldeutsche Blätter*, 29 September
1906, 313–4, here 314. See also 'Alldeutsche Verbandstag in Breslau (Fortsetzung
und Schluss)', *Alldeutsche Blätter*, 20 September 1913, 317–29.

43 See E. H. 'Ein neuer Kolonialdirektor', *Alldeutsche Blätter*, 15 September 1906,
300–1; P. S., 'Der Sieg vom 25. Januar', *Alldeutsche Blätter*, 2 February 1907, 33–5.
On Dernburg and how he was perceived among colonialists and antisemites, see
Christian S. Davis, *Colonialism, Antisemitism, and Germans of Jewish Descent in
Imperial Germany* (Ann Arbor: University of Michigan Press, 2012), 196–245. See
also the chapter by Axel Stähler in this volume.

44 P. S., 'Die nächsten Aufgaben unserer Kolonialpolitik', *Alldeutsche Blätter*, 11 May
1907, 153–5; Wilhelm Lattmann, 'Von Bismarck bis Dernburg', *Alldeutsche Blätter*,
12 March 1909, 92–3, and 2 April 1909, 118–9, 'Der Alldeutsche Verbandstag
in Schandau (Fortsetzung und Schluß)', *Alldeutsche Blätter*, 18 September 1909,
317–31.

45 Paul Samassa, 'Dernburgs südwestafrikanische Politik', *Alldeutsche Blätter*, 21 May
1910. See also StPR, vol. 231, 18 March 1908, 4066–73 (Eduard von Liebert); Paul
Samassa, 'Dernburg und die Südwestafrikaner. Diamantenfrage. Selbstverwaltung.
Landeshilfe', *Alldeutsche Blätter*, 18 February 1911, 53–4.

46 Ernst Hasse, 'Der Großkapitalismus in den deutschen Schutzgebieten', *Alldeutsche
Blätter*, 10 June 1900, 229–31; Paul Samassa, 'Ziele und Wege deutscher
Weltpolitik', *Alldeutsche Blätter*, 20 April 1901, 189–92; 'Der Verbandstag in
Eisenach', *Alldeutsche Blätter*, 31 May 1902, 185–92; Emil Theodor Förster, 'Das
Konzessionsunwesen in den deutschen Schutzgebieten', *Alldeutsche Blätter*,
3 October 1903, 361–8; 'Der Alldeutsche Verbandstag in Dresden', *Alldeutsche
Blätter*, 8 September 1906, 285–95; Samassa, 'Dernburgs südwestafrikanische
Politik'.

47 Lattmann, 'Von Bismarck bis Dernburg', 119. See also StPR, vol. 231, 18 March
1908, 4066–73.

48 See, for example, Ernst Vohsen, 'Denkschrift über die Vorgänge in Ostafrika
während meiner Leitung der Geschäfte der Deutsch-Ostafrikanischen Gesellschaft
vom 14. Mai 1888 bis 16. Januar 1889', 12 April 1889, BAB R 8124/3; 'Protokoll
der Sitzung des Kolonialrats vom 21.11.1901', BAB R 8023/142; Ernst Vohsen,
'Der Kongostaat und die Revision der Kongoakte', *Deutsche Kolonialzeitung*,
17 September 1903, 379–81; 'Negerarbeit in Afrika: I. Der afrikanische Neger als
Lohnarbeiter' (Editorial), *Koloniale Rundschau* 1 (1909): 65–75; 'Zur Jahreswende'

(Eitorial), *Koloniale Rundschau* 3 (1911): 1–4; 'Zum neuen Jahr!' (Editorial), *Koloniale Rundschau* 4 (1912): 1–4; 'Bericht über die Sitzung des Ausschusses der Deutschen Kolonialgesellschaft vom 3. April 1914, BAB R 8023/920. For more details on Vohsen, see Stefan Vogt, 'Juden in der Deutschen Kolonialgesellschaft: Eine Fallstudie zu Ernst Vohsen', *Zeitschrift für Geschichtswissenschaft* 68 (2020): 1012–27.

49 See, for example, Ernst Vohsen and Dietrich Westermann, 'Unser Programm', *Koloniale Rundschau* 1 (1909): 3; 'Bericht über die Hauptversammlung der Deutschen Kolonialgesellschaft in den Räumen des Künstlervereins in Bremen am 12. Juni 1908', BAB, R 8023/524a, 26.

50 Ernst Vohsen, 'Vorwort', in *Vom Sklaven empor. Eine Selbstbiographie*, ed. Booker T. Washington (Berlin: Reimer, 1902), VI. Other books by Booker T. Washington published by Vohsen included: *Charakterbildung. Sonntags-Ansprachen an die Zöglinge der Normal- und Gewerbeschule von Tuskegee* (Berlin: Reimer, 1910); *Handarbeit* (Berlin: Reimer 1913).

51 'Die Südwestafrikanische Siedlungsgesellschaft des Herrn Vohsen', *Deutsche Kolonialzeitung*, 24 June 1905, 242; Max Robert Gerstenhauer and Ernst Vohsen, 'Erklärung', *Deutsche Kolonialzeitung*, 1 July 1905, 261; 'Die Siedlungsgesellschaft für Deutsch-Südwestafrika in der Hauptversammlung in Essen', *Deutsche Kolonialzeitung*, 1 July 1905, 261–5; Max Robert Gerstenhauer, 'Die Angriffe gegen die Siedlungsgesellschaft II', *Deutsche Kolonialzeitung*, 22 July 1905, 312–6; Rundschreiben der Abteilung Meiningen der Deutschen Kolonial-Gesellschaft an die verehrl. Abteilungen der Gesellschaft, 15 September 1905 (Meiningen 1905). Gerstenhauer's attacks were seconded by Emil Theodor Förster, the editor of the journal *Die Deutschen Kolonien*, who, for instance, attested that Vohsen spoke 'for a man of Jewish descent, remarkably refined German'. E. Th. Förster, 'Die Siedlungsgesellschaft für Deutsch-Südwestafrika und Herr Konsul Vohsen', *Die Deutschen Kolonien* 4 (1905): 355.

52 Ernst Hasse, *Die Zukunft des deutschen Volkstums* (München: Lehman, 1907), 61–2, 65, 68.

53 Hasse, *Das Deutsche Reich als Nationalstaat*, 142–3, 143, 145; Raphaël Marchand, 'Max Nordau. Juifs contre Juifs', *La libre parole*, 21 December 1903, 1–2. While it seems that the interview did indeed take place, there is no way to verify whether Nordau actually said these things. Nevertheless, this quotation has been regularly reproduced in antisemitic and anti-Zionist publications up to the present day. See Desmond Stewart, *Theodor Herzl. Artist and Politician* (London: Hamilton, 1974), 322; Lenni Brenner, *Zionism in the Age of Dictators: A Reappraisal* (London: Croom Helm, 1983), 26; Tony Greenstein, 'Unholy Alliance', *Weekly Worker*, 22 June 2006. The interview appeared only two days after the failed attempt on Nordau's life by Chaim Selig Louban, who blamed Nordau for supporting the Uganda proposal,

which suggested considering part of British East Africa as a temporary homeland for the Jews, as long as Palestine remained unavailable. Herzl supported this proposal, but it was eventually rejected by the majority of the Zionist movement.

54 Hasse, *Das Deutsche Reich als Nationalstaat*, 145. Hasse noted that these passages had been omitted in a new edition of Moltke's works and applauded the antisemites Theodor Fritsch and Friedrich Lange for disclosing this omission.

55 Hasse, *Die Zukunft des deutschen Volkstums*, 62.

56 Ibid., 67.

57 StBR, vol. 139, 6 March 1895, 1280.

58 Heinrich von Treitschke, 'Unsere Aussichten', *Preußische Jahrbücher* 44 (1879): 560–76. Quotations on pages 572–3, 575. The best analyses of Treitschke's antisemitism are Klaus Holz, *Nationaler Antisemitismus: Wissenssoziologie einer Weltanschauung* (Hamburg: Hamburger Edition, 2001), 165–247; and Uffa Jensen, *Gebildete Doppelgänger: Bürgerliche Juden und Protestanten im 19. Jahrhundert* (Göttingen: Vandenhoeck & Ruprecht, 2005), 197–268.

59 Frymann [Claß], *Wenn ich der Kaiser wär*, especially 30–9, 74–8. See also Einhart [Heinrich Claß], *Deutsche Geschichte* (Leipzig: Dieterich, 1909). On Claß's antisemitism, see Leicht, *Heinrich Claß*; Hering, *Konstruierte Nation*, 197–201.

60 Frymann [Claß], *Wenn ich der Kaiser wär*, 32.

61 See ibid., 75.

62 Ibid., 38.

63 Ibid., 31.

64 See ibid., 75–6.

65 On this process, see especially Geoff Eley, *Reshaping the German Right: Radical Nationalism and Political Change after Bismarck* (New Haven: Yale University Press, 1980).

66 Heinrich Claß was by no means the only pan-German to promote radical antisemitism. See, for example, the report by Theodor Reismann-Grone, 'Verhandlungsbericht über die Sitzung des geschäftsführenden Ausschusses des Alldeutschen Verbandes in Breslau am Freitag, den 5. September 1913', BAB, R 8048/90, 28–9; Konstantin von Gebsattel, 'Gedanken über den notwendigen Fortschritt in der inneren Entwicklung Deutschlands, Oktober 1913', BAB, N 2089/6, 5–10.

67 Hasse, *Deutsche Weltpolitik*, 15. Max Weber also used the term *Ellenbogenraum* to denote the goal of pan-German politics. See Weber, *Der Nationalstaat und die Volkswirtschaftspolitik*, 12, 14.

8

'Our Dernburg' – 'The New Moses'

The German Empire's 'Jewish' colonial director and the satirical press

Axel Stähler

After much turmoil, mismanagement and vicious colonial conflict in the early years of the twentieth century, a new colonial director was appointed in imperial Germany in September 1906. An unlikely choice, the banker Bernhard Dernburg nevertheless assumed his new position with immediate resolve and aplomb. Not identifying as Jewish, Dernburg was all the same widely perceived as such, though, as the critic and political writer Maximilian Harden ironically maintained: 'What seems so *shocking* about the new man' – his alleged Jewishness – 'is actually barred by limitation. Family baptized about 40 years ago; dyed-in-the-wool Christian mother and wife; uncle since [18]66 in the House of Lords; of almost rough-hewn Chattic type.'[1] Soon after, in the campaign for the elections of January 1907, the new 'Jewish' colonial director became a very visible public figure. Invoking the colonial endeavour as a unifying project that had the potential of transcending political, religious and social differences, Dernburg lectured on the colonies to large audiences in the major German cities. The financier-turned-politician thus appeared to be a willing and indeed an inspired and inspiring collaborator in the German colonial project.[2]

The new colonial director's appointment was initially met with muted interest, but Dernburg's assertive stance in the Reichstag in December 1906 made an immediate splash, not only in the House and the daily press but also in the satirical magazines of the empire. Bernhard von Bülow, the chancellor of the Reich, explained Dernburg's appointment to the House with his pedigree in the world of finance.[3] He felt that someone with expertise in economics was required – someone, moreover, who was able to address the blunders and scandals rampant in the Colonial Office.[4] To this end, he asked that the members of the House extend their trust to the new colonial director.

It was not long, however, until Dernburg was attacked in the Reichstag by Hermann Roeren.[5] Enumerating a litany of arbitrary and brutal transgressions of the law in the African protectorates, the deputy of the Catholic Zentrum (Centre Party) suspected Dernburg of cover-ups and, on a personal level, not only deprecated the 'stockjobber and office tone' allegedly introduced by the colonial director to the Reichstag but – without corroboration – also hinted at dark secrets in his past and accused him of having a 'robust conscience'.[6] Dernburg's rejoinder was prompt and, it was widely perceived, completely destroyed his detractor.[7]

The confrontation with Roeren was frequently taken up in the satirical press. It in fact raised a number of issues which continued to dominate the debate about Germany's overseas possessions throughout Dernburg's incumbency, such as the treatment of the natives, the remit of missionaries and the economic viability of the colonies. Roeren's altercation with the new colonial director did not, however, deteriorate at any point into an explicitly antisemitic harangue. Indeed, Dernburg's alleged 'Jewishness' was not an impediment to his meteoric rise which saw him elevated to State Secretary for the Colonies in May 1907. As Christian S. Davis puts it quite succinctly:

> Dernburg was widely perceived to be a Jew. Even so, he gained a reputation as a patriot and a man above politics, a crusader against colonial critics and the special interests of Catholicism and Social Democracy. For a time, he enjoyed unprecedented public popularity for a colonial director. Moreover, he helped alleviate many problems plaguing German colonialism, instituting reforms that fulfilled some of the long-standing wishes of colonial enthusiasts, antisemites among them.[8]

Indeed, Davis emphasizes that Dernburg's tenure exemplified that the colonial enterprise facilitated the cooperation of those otherwise divided by antisemitism and that colonialism 'provided a common enemy in the opponents of empire and furnished common identities as colonizers'.[9]

Conversely, this meant that to adversaries of the colonial enterprise, Dernburg – as a powerful cog in the system that supported it – became a common foe as well. Consequently, once the colonial director's upbringing as a commoner, his mercantile experience and his alleged flights of fancy with regard to the profitability of the colonies had been exhausted, his perceived Jewishness was exploited, in blatant violation of the 'limitations' ironically declared by Harden.

158 *Colonialism and the Jews in German History*

Highly sensitive to the power struggles in the Reichstag, on which the large majority of its engagements with Dernburg rely, the satirical press reflected this development to varying degrees and with different political objectives.

This chapter traces the representation of Dernburg in satirical magazines of the Kaiserreich across the political spectrum in relation to the perception of both the German colonial project and the construction of his alleged Jewishness, from his inauguration to his resignation in June 1910.[10] Its focus is mainly on the liberal-conservative *Kladderadatsch*, the moderately progressive *Lustige Blätter*, the Social Democratic *Der wahre Jakob*, the culture critical *Die Jugend* and the liberal *Simplicissimus* as well as the Zionist *Schlemiel*. I suggest that it was in particular the perceived Jewishness of the colonial director and his representation as an Oriental outsider which was used to critique German colonialism whereas pro-colonial voices frequently elided Dernburg's Jewish descent. More specifically, I interrogate the tense interrelation between Jewishness, Germanness and colonialism as it is negotiated in the engagement of the imperial satirical press with the figure of Bernhard Dernburg.

'Jewish', but not a 'Jew'

Among the more intriguing representations of Dernburg is Max Slevogt's seated portrait (Figure 8.1). Not really a cartoon, the image – dating back to 1904 – was prominently displayed on the cover of *Die Jugend* (1907) within a week of the sitter's elevation to ministerial status.[11] It shows Dernburg in informal attire with dark trousers and waistcoat and a light-coloured jacket, leaning back into a high-backed armchair in the antique Spanish style. His posture is relaxed, all the tension in his body concentrated in the rigid neck and face. There are no overt indications of the sitter's Jewish descent; and yet the image exudes an aura of Jewishness. The effect is subtle but nevertheless deliberate.

The artist, who was a regular contributor to *Die Jugend*, cautiously exaggerates facial features and expressions associated with Jewishness. Yet the ensuing image is neither a caricature nor overtly antisemitic, because Slevogt eschewed the use of any stereotypes associated with eastern European Jews. Rather, the three-quarter portrait, supported by the Iberian provenance of the throne-like chair, evokes notions of Sephardic nobility – no less a stereotype, perhaps, but with very different connotations. As John Efron has observed, '[t]here simply was no antisemitic iconography that formulated a negative stereotype of Sephardic Jews'.[12] To the contrary, '[j]ust as the Ashkenazic Jews

Figure 8.1 Max Slevogt, *Bernhard Dernburg* (1904), *Die Jugend*, 22 May 1907, cover image. © Public Domain.

served as a countertype to Christian manhood, so too did the Sephardim serve as a beautiful, noble, and healthy countertype to the Ashkenazim',[13] characterized by a 'long skull', black or brown hair and eyes, a 'graceful nose' and a sense of pride and dignity.[14]

The most expressive features used by the artist to this purpose are the elongation of Dernburg's face and its resulting gauntness, highlighted in particular by the shadows playing on his cheek and temple; the full-lipped and well-shaped mouth, with lips firmly compressed and the lower lip faintly protruding; the hooded eyes, which, deceptively, suggest a downward glance, as if the sitter were literally looking down his nose at the beholder; and the high-drawn arched eyebrows. The overall impression – further enhanced with the slight backward tilt of the sitter's head and the exaggerated, quickly receding perspective from a

160   *Colonialism and the Jews in German History*

point just below it – is one of calm aloofness, even understated disdain or pride. Dernburg, as he is portrayed here, may be 'Jewish', but he is not a 'Jew'.

A few months after the prominent display of the painting in *Die Jugend*, Hans Rosenhagen emphasized its informality and vitality. The art historian's evocative description in *Die Gartenlaube* offers a contemporary appreciation of its style and elaborates on the character of the sitter as it was projected by the critic in extrapolation of the esteem Dernburg ostensibly enjoyed among the popular magazine's predominantly bourgeois readership. Rosenhagen enthused that Slevogt

> represents a man of action, of bold decisions, and of shrewd calculation without any environs, as it were, in and of himself. . . . He muses while he is smoking; but because a merchant – for when the portrait was painted, Dernburg still was one – needs to keep his counsel to himself, so that no others take advantage of his ideas and plans, he also has his facial expression under control. Only self-confidence and energy speak from these half-closed, proud eyes, from these firm features.[15]

The art critic makes no mention of Dernburg's perceived Jewishness. It is obviously of no consequence to him – nor, apparently, to the readers of *Die Gartenlaube* and *Die Jugend*. It was eclipsed by the positively imagined characteristics of Dernburg which emerged during his tenure as colonial director and which were projected retrospectively onto his earlier mercantile persona. The widely perceived Jewishness of Dernburg, subtly painted by the artist into the portrait, was elided by Rosenhagen in his praise not only of the painting but also of the man and politician into which the sitter had evolved.

In his treatment of Dernburg, Slevogt may have taken inspiration from the well-known Wolfenbüttel portrait of Baruch Spinoza by an unknown artist.[16] If in mirror image, the painting of the Jewish philosopher of Sephardi origin displays a similar gauntness as well as similarly raised eyebrows, hooded eyes and prominent lower lip; though in this instance the sitter seems more accessible, even though his face is partially obscured by his long hair.

The comparison with another portrait of Dernburg by Slevogt is instructive in this context. Completed in 1923, the artist's later rendering shows Dernburg's face in much more realistic proportions, if also in a more sketchily impressionist, and impressionistic, style.[17] Perhaps more significantly, all the allusions to Jewishness have been excised from this painting, as has the palpable sense of superiority. Dernburg, after his brief tenure as Secretary of the Treasury in 1919, during which he contributed substantially to the negotiations of the Treaty of Versailles,[18] is still portrayed as inscrutable but shows a restrained smile as he faces the beholder directly and on the same level. This is the portrait of an approachable and amicable man, rather than a calculating mastermind.

The use of Slevogt's earlier portrait for the cover of *Die Jugend* in the month of Dernburg's promotion to ministerial status entails its contextual reconfiguration, which is supported with the inclusion, in the same issue, of four additional pieces referring to the colonial secretary. None of them alludes to Dernburg's perceived Jewishness. Instead, the majority feature his tour of inspection to German East Africa planned for later in the year.[19]

Indeed, Dernburg's determination to form his own opinion on the colonial enterprise through inspection tours, a significant factor to the formulation of his alternative policies, was a frequent topic in the satirical press. 'Der Khaki-Kaftan oder: Dernburgs Reise' (1907; The Khaki-Caftan; or, Dernburg's Voyage) in *Lustige Blätter* is particularly pertinent in this context because it unfolds a coherent narrative, in both text and image, which addresses a range of topical issues in implicit relation to Dernburg's perceived Jewishness.[20]

Wilhelm Lattmann of the antisemitic Deutschsoziale Partei (German Social Party), for instance, had decried in the Reichstag the influx into the South-West African protectorate of allegedly suspicious and criminal Jews from the Capeland and Russia.[21] Taking his prompt from Lattmann, Friedrich Bindewald of the similarly antisemitic Deutsche Reformpartei (German Reform Party) maintained with reference to the government's memorandum on the German protectorates that, attracted by the war in the colony, foreigners were moving in like 'hyenas of the battlefield', among them many Jews.[22] Indeed, Bindewald claimed that obviously a fortune was to be made in the colony, because otherwise the Jews would not descend upon it.[23]

His speech, intermittently punctuated with the mirth of the House, culminated in his appeal to the colonial secretary to see to it that the 'racially alien' Jews be kept away.[24] Given the perceived Jewishness of Dernburg, the inherent irony of this proposition, which seems to have escaped the speaker, produced outright laughter on the left of the House (among the Social Democrats) and some mirth also on the right (among the Conservatives).[25] Yet it also shows the extent to which Dernburg's perceived Jewishness could conveniently and, it seems, quite sincerely be forgotten.

The illustrated narrative in *Lustige Blätter*, clearly stimulated by this occurrence, was a product of the collaboration of the writer Max Brinkmann and the cartoonist Franz Jüttner. Offering a satirically refracted explanation of the alleged Jewish influx in South-West Africa, it not only portrays this as greatly exaggerated but also imputes it to the capitalistic machinations of the Otavi Minen- und Eisenbahn-Gesellschaft (Otavi Mining and Railway Company, OMEG). Presumably inspired by Bindewald's speech, the company is shown to infiltrate the protectorate with twelve 'dyed-in-the-wool' Russian Jews with tropical issue khaki caftans from Tippelskirch. The manufacturers of khaki cloth and other military equipment had an exclusive contract for supplying the Schutztruppe (colonial troops). They were accused not only of bribery and profiteering but also of supplying substandard material. One of Dernburg's first decisive actions in his new office was therefore the cancellation of contracts with monopolists such as Tippelskirch, the shipping line of Carl Woermann and the pharmacy Dr Kade. It was a move which ensured him much acclaim both in the House and in the public but which is subversively countered in the satirical narrative by OMEG.

When the cartoon Dernburg arrives in the protectorate, he is met by a ubiquitous Jewish presence. However, reminiscent of the fable of the hare and the hedgehog, it is in fact always the same Jewish dozen in the service of OMEG whom he meets time and again. As the first indicator of Jewish immigration and supposed economic hegemony, the colonial secretary encounters advertisements for the 'Department Store of the South-West' – an allusion to the recent opening, in March 1907, of the *Kaufhaus des Westens* (also known as KaDeWe) in Berlin and to the Jewish predominance in this economic sector. The luxury department store was the latest and brightest jewel in the crown of the mercantile empire of the Jewish entrepreneur Adolf Jandorf. In fact, the great majority of department stores across Germany was established by Jews and it is estimated that before the First World War Jewish enterprise accounted for more than 80 per cent of the country's total department store sales volume.[26] Clearly, the Department Store of the South-West is an illustration of Bindewald's allegation that wherever anything was to be had, the Jews would go and have it – be it in the metropolitan centre or in the colonial periphery.

The cartoon Dernburg then inadvertently eavesdrops on a bogus board meeting at which unrealistic profits of almost 40 per cent are announced and subsequently comes across a haulage company engaged in the transport of crates of dried dates, once again schemes devised by the Jewish dozen. In the latter instance, the allusion is to Dernburg's encomium on the fertility and productivity of the South-West African protectorate. In one of his speeches, the colonial director had embarked on the anecdote of a crate of dried dates, lost somewhere along the road, from which, after a few years, date palm trees had grown that were already beginning to bear fruit.[27]

Dernburg was frequently mocked about his allegedly fanciful effusion. It is no surprise that the Social Democratic *Der wahre Jakob* in particular would not let the matter rest.[28] After all, it was August Bebel, with Paul Singer joint leader of the party, who brought the matter up in the Reichstag, where it gave rise to acerbic debates about Dernburg and the profitability of the protectorates,[29] and to whom Dernburg responded with characteristic bluntness.[30] In Brinkmann's narrative, the colonial secretary is taken in by the associations evoked by the crates; it suggests Dernburg's gullibility not only in the story but also in reality.

Hardly any less fanciful is the next scheme encountered by the colonial director in the narrative. One of the more bizarre efforts to advance economic development in German South-West Africa was the systematic attempt to find water in the arid protectorate through dowsing.[31] Brinkmann's text participates imaginatively in the satirical engagement with this practice. In his narrative, hot springs are discovered and Dernburg chances upon Jewish surveyors planning the spa of New-Karlsbad and a casino.

Beyond the stereotypical association of Jews with profitable monetary schemes, the very name of New-Karlsbad carried connotations of a mostly antisemitic nature which, moreover, establish a link also to the final scheme presented to Dernburg in the protectorate. Offering a well-developed 'Jewish infrastructure',[32] the Bohemian spa of Karlsbad (Karlovy Vary), like nearby Marienbad (Mariánské Lázně), attracted a large Jewish clientele of diverse cultural and social background; simultaneously German and Austrian spa culture was rife with antisemitism.[33] The laxative effect of the curative waters at both spas elicited a plethora of supposedly humorous postcards. Jews of all descriptions, but mostly conforming to rampant stereotypes of eastern European Jewish peddlers, featured prominently in many of them.[34]

Exploiting the scatological dimension, caricatures delighted in picturing visitors from across the social spectrum as they wait in varying degrees of urgency in front of occupied lavatories.[35] The stereotypically drawn Jewish figures among them are usually shown to be unable to contain themselves. Bodies bent and strained and their hands reaching behind, their faces register shocked surprise as those next to them hold their noses in disgust.[36] To the contemporary reader of *Lustige Blätter*, the abundance of postcards of this kind would have been an easy point of reference.

Brinkmann's narrative additionally insinuates that the Jews know to turn into profit even the basest form of human waste. One of the Jewish dozen in the South-West African protectorate holds the franchise for public lavatories, and

164   *Colonialism and the Jews in German History*

a very profitable franchise it appears to be – he is bedecked with diamonds and golden rings.

The political precedent referred to in this instance was an item in the budget for the colonies which specified under the heading of 'cultural progress' an expenditure of 8,000 Marks for the erection of public lavatories in Cameroon.[37] Brinkmann and Jüttner's narrative, suggesting the scheme's exploitation by Jewish entrepreneurs, is only one of a number of engagements with the innocuous topic turned scatological especially in *Lustige Blätter*.[38] Ernst Stern, for instance, linked the lavatory debate to the new native regulations introduced in German South-West Africa in August 1907.[39]

With the objective of gaining complete control over their mobility, natives were required to carry a passport at all times, while simultaneously being barred from possession of any heavy livestock and riding animals.[40] The cartoonist enumerates in his 'Eingeborenen-Recht in Südwest' (1907; Native Legislature in South-West) increasingly silly examples of the repressive nature of the new regulations.[41] In the final panel, a native woman, drawn very much in analogy to the Jewish defecators queuing in front of the occupied Karlsbad and Marienbad privies, is confronted by soldiers of the Schutztruppe at bayonet point and barred from reaching the safe haven of the wooden structure – not because it is occupied but because she cannot produce the necessary documents for entering the 'extraterritorial area'.

The iconographic parallel may not have been intended; it nevertheless suggests the Jews to occupy a liminal space between the colonizer and the subaltern. Whereas they have access to the blessings of civilization, they lack the necessary refinement to engage successfully in the relevant cultural practices and are consequently othered. The native woman, in turn, is excluded by the gatekeepers of colonial rule from enjoying the benefit of the facility, which is suggested to be entirely alien to her. The Jews emerge by implication as a collaborators' group which, as in Brinkmann and Jüttner's illustrated narrative, profits from its liminal position but nevertheless remains at the margins, excluded from full assimilation.

This last point is relevant in particular in relation to the figure of Dernburg himself. He too is a collaborator in the colonial enterprise, if on a different level. Again, the colonial secretary is represented as Jewish but not as a 'Jew'. In Jüttner's fourth panel, he appears to be an evolved, if significantly more corpulent, double of one of the Jewish dozen, shown in the second panel aboard ship on their way to the protectorate. Though the stereotypical visor cap and long gabardine of the Jew on the far right of the image are translated into a fashionable overcoat and

'Our Dernburg' – 'The New Moses'   165

top hat, the latter is set back at a somewhat too careless angle; Dernburg's posture and gestures, if more refined, moreover closely mimic those of his Jewish avatar, and his profile associates the other's physiognomy.

However, Dernburg, though variously associated with his fraudulent alleged compatriots, is not himself accused of any misconduct or complicity. The illustrated narrative in this way offers a perceptive commentary on the acceptance of Dernburg in conservative, and even in overtly antisemitic, political circles. This is perfectly illustrated by Bindewald's blindness to the perceived Jewishness of the colonial secretary, whom he fully supported in his executive role. The antisemitic deputy's racial 'schizophrenia', though exposed by the hilarity of his colleagues during the parliamentary debate, appears nevertheless to have affected also other 'colonial enthusiasts' – an epithet applied to himself by the strident antisemite Wilhelm Lattmann.[42]

Brinkmann and Jüttner's illustrated narrative is intriguing in this context because it already registers the precarious balance of Dernburg's tenure on sufferance. The Jewish dozen may be ambivalent in their portrayal in that they challenge Bindewald and Lattmann's allegations of Jewish invasion and exploitation. And yet, they emerge as instruments of capitalist intrigues which, implicitly, were linked back to the antisemitic idea of 'Jewish' capital. The Exploration Company of the London Rothschilds had a significant stake in OMEG;[43] Jewish financiers, though not exclusively, were also involved in its other co-owners, the South-West Africa Company (London) and the Disconto-Society (Berlin).[44]

Dernburg, albeit not in the same way as the Jewish dozen, unwittingly becomes another collaborator. He emerges as their dupe, acting involuntarily in the interest of the devious capitalists. He eventually reports to the Reichstag in apparent confirmation of Bindewald's antisemitic claim: 'All over the place, I found Jews in the most propitious financial situation, a sign – that fortunes are to be made there! – Let us make them, gentlemen!' Yet Brinkmann's denouement reveals everything to have been a cynical ploy of OMEG to multiply tenfold the value of their shares.

Given their model's successful banking career, the naivety of Brinkmann and Jüttner's Dernburg is surprising. Indeed, Ludwig Stutz offered in *Kladderadatsch* a very different view of the persistence of the colonial secretary's past in the financial sector. Published even before Lattmann and Bindewald made their point in the Reichstag, the cartoonist implicitly suggested the Jewish presence in – and the 'Jewification' of – the African protectorates as well as Dernburg's collusion in, or even instigation of, the process.

'Dernburgs Vortragserfolge' (1907; The Success of Dernburg's Lectures; Figure 8.2) depicts a stock exchange in the wastelands of Africa.[45] All the traders are represented as animals. Without exception their anthropomorphized physiognomies as well as posture and gestures suggest rampant Jewish stereotypes.[46] Though Dernburg does not appear in the cartoon, he is nevertheless

Figure 8.2 Ludwig Stutz, 'Dernburgs Vortragserfolge', *Kladderadatsch*, 3 February 1907, n.p. © Public Domain.

'Our Dernburg' – 'The New Moses'   167

presented in title and caption as the instigator of the new financial procedures. The stereotypical representation of the Jewishness of the traders and its suggestion of capitalist exploitation is unmistakably associated with the former banker. The cartoon evidently relies on what is left unsaid. Even so, it presents the colonial project essentially as a Jewish venture of economic exploitation orchestrated by the 'Jewish' colonial secretary.[47]

Orientalizing Dernburg

As criticism of the colonial enterprise became more pronounced, references to the colonial secretary's supposed Jewishness multiplied in the satirical press. Dernburg was frequently Orientalized and, occasionally, overtly Jewified. In *Der wahre Jakob*, for instance, Hans Gabriel Jentzsch sketched the colonial secretary as he was travelling in German East Africa in Oriental costume and with an Orientalized physiognomy in 'Exzellenz Pascha Ben Dernburg in Neudeutschland' (1907; His Excellency Pasha Ben Dernburg in New-Germany; Figure 8.3).[48] Against a jungle background, the cartoonist added, moreover, a motley crowd of armed natives with an imperial flag whose physiognomies combine all the stereotypically exaggerated features and who have been supplied with various attributes of German provenance which appear, however, in incongruous ensembles: a copy of the conservative and very influential *Kreuzzeitung* as a loincloth; a beer barrel and steins tucked under the arms of an African belle with a petticoat, collar and voluminous fashionable hat of European provenance, but otherwise nude. Dernburg, taking the salute of the assembled crowd in a liquid, swaying walk and brandishing a whip, is accompanied by stiff officers in uniform as various wild animals scurry for shelter.

The image as a whole offers a sort of simulacrum of Germany on different levels, a notion which is suggested by the fictitious name of New-Germany in the cartoon's title and by the caption in which the natives are addressed as 'new Teutons'. The cartoon (re)presents a degraded copy of life in the colonial periphery as a copy of life in the metropolitan centre and emerges as a simulacrum that challenges conceptions of the original.[49]

The natives are bedecked in a senseless and meaningless way with cultural artefacts not of their own making. Dernburg, implicitly associating his perceived Jewishness, reverts to an Oriental persona. The German officers, in contrast, remain true to their militaristic essence; they are a projection of rigid authoritarianism.

Figure 8.3 Hans Gabriel Jentzsch, 'Exzellenz Pascha Ben Dernburg in Neudeutschland', *Der wahre Jakob*, 28 August 1907, 5525. © Public Domain.

Crucially, 'Pasha Ben Dernburg' once again occupies a liminal position; he is a Protean collaborator with the German authoritarian establishment but is at the same time clearly distinct from its immutable representatives, even as he exerts the authority it bestows on him over the natives, who pose in a fractured and imaginary, but entirely impossible Germanness. At the same time, the notion of collaboration is also extended to the metropolitan context, the simulacrum employed as a distorting mirror. The 'new Teutons' are admonished to refrain from any subversive and revolutionary activities; they are infantilized with the threat of being caned on the posterior in case of transgression.

Beyond the evocation of the notorious debate about corporal punishment in the colonies, the simulacrum character of the cartoon suggests, more specifically, that the 'original' Teutons are similarly degraded to the quasi-infantile level of the natives in relation to the representatives of imperial authority. Given its Social Democratic provenance, the cartoon arguably seeks to denounce the authoritarian imperial 'system' by associating it with the Oriental despotism embodied by the cartoon Dernburg and projected back onto the 'original'. By seeking to create such an awareness, the artist invested the 'original' with new meaning. Its Teutons are not admonished to submit to authority, as in the cartoon, but to reassert their difference from the 'new' Teutons and thus to challenge imperial authority. Confronted with its uncanny simulacrum, the degraded 'original' is called upon to re-form itself. The Oriental Dernburg has no place in this scenario.

The New Moses and the biblical spies

When Bebel launched his attack on Dernburg's crate of dates anecdote in the Reichstag, this was part of a wider campaign to discredit the colonial director for his allegedly fanciful colonial imagination.[50] Lattmann, an unlikely but spirited champion for the colonial director, took up the challenge and in the process quoted from an election leaflet authorized by Bebel and Singer in which Dernburg's anecdote was linked to the biblical narrative of Moses: 'When the Jewish people, as legend tells us, left Egypt and wandered in the desert and were in danger of dying of thirst, Moses struck a rock, from which gushed forth a spring that saved people and cattle. This was a wonder.'[51] A few days later, Hermann Kreth of the Deutschkonservative Partei (German Conservative Party) quoted from another Social Democratic election leaflet, according to which Dernburg 'appears to have inherited the rod of Moses.'[52]

No more likely a supporter of the colonial director than Lattmann and yet, as another 'colonial enthusiast', staunchly taking his side, Kreth was quick to point out with some glee that the bold print of 'inherited' in the leaflet savoured of antisemitism. In fact, the mere suggestion of the biblical point of reference, which appears to be predicated on the perceived Jewishness of Dernburg, is in itself already prejudiced. It not only initiated the cynical identification of Dernburg with Moses on the grounds of their supposedly shared 'racial' identity and prophetic vision. It moreover opened colonial discourse in imperial Germany to (ironic) constructions of the colonies as promised lands and thus, mapping the German colonial endeavour onto the Jewish wanderings and eventual fulfilment of the divinely sanctioned conquest of Canaan, projected the debate about the colonial enterprise onto the Jewish-identified figure of Dernburg-Moses.

With the mentioned leaflets and the ensuing parliamentary debate, the satirical press were presented with a ready-made angle on Dernburg; the prompt was indeed picked up and creatively developed. Perhaps inevitably, it was also linked with the dowsing practice in the South-West African protectorate. In *Der wahre Jakob*, the Social Democratic campaign was continued with 'Dernburg in Afrika' (1907; Dernburg in Africa) by the monogrammist 'Kga'.[53] The cartoon's caption, simultaneously suggesting fraudulent Jewish mercantile practices, elaborated: 'After having purchased from the antique dealers Veilchenstock and Rosenbaum the genuine rod of Moses, Moses-Dernburg went forth into the desert to search for water.'[54]

The visual representation of Dernburg is striking for its physiognomic Orientalization and its historicizing element, which shows him in the imagined costume of an ancient Hebrew with which he inappropriately wears white cuffs. Paradoxically, these align him with the African natives, who were frequently portrayed in ethnographic representations and satirical engagements with such cuffs, their nude Black skin ironically substituting for the otherwise required formal black jacket. In such representations, the cuffs emphasize the failure of the Black natives to assimilate civilization by means of the incongruous appropriation of its markers. The cuffs of Dernburg-Moses hence suggest another distorted simulacrum; the 'Jewish' colonial secretary is denied full whiteness and is, once again, firmly consigned to a liminal position between white and black.[55]

Whereas opinions about dowsing remained divided, Dernburg's colonial optimism was to some extent vindicated with the discovery of diamonds in the South-West African protectorate in June 1908. The half-American cartoonist Arthur Johnson conjoined the figure of Dernburg with this occurrence in 'Südwestafrikanischer Zauber (Der Wüsten- oder Felsen-Automat)' (1909; South-West African Magic (The Desert- or Rock-Automaton)).[56] Dernburg, in the black frock coat of a magician, nonchalantly taps his desert rock-automaton with his wand in order to produce at will coffee, petroleum, gold, copper, coconut spirits, cigars, palm fronds and diamonds. The apparition of the biblical Moses marvels: 'Blast it, *Dernburg*, you did *ten times* better than I did! *Blessed*

'Our Dernburg' – 'The New Moses'   171

the nation led into the desert by *you!*'[57] The identification with Moses is created
here by implication, and with a tongue-in-cheek understanding of the colonial
secretary even surpassing the biblical precedent.

Dernburg's representation as a magician – also a well-established trope in
the satirical engagement with the colonial secretary[58] – may be indebted to the
widespread notion that the Jews 'were particularly suited to being magicians
on account of their knowledge of Kabbalah', which 'increased their popular
attraction and proved to be an advantage over non-Jewish colleagues'.[59] In this
manner, the cartoon once again implicitly reasserts the notion of Dernburg's
Jewishness, while simultaneously suggesting not only a certain glamorous
mystery but also a whiff of demystification and even fraudulence in that it carries
associations of the shady hocus-pocus of a variety performance without real
substance. The concluding sentence of Moses then gains further significance; it
evokes a sarcastic sense of the people being seduced by his latter-day simulacrum
into a desert obscured by the fata morgana of its rich produce.

Dernburg's identification with Moses appeared frequently in conjunction
with the motif of the biblical spies sent out to search the land of Canaan (see
Num. 13). In *Simplicissimus*, for instance, the Norwegian-born Olaf Gulbransson
styled the colonial secretary in his eponymous drawing as 'Der neue Moses'
(1907; The New Moses).[60] Wrapped in voluminous faux biblical robes, Dernburg
welcomes the two spies as they carry on their pole an old opened tin can, the
meagre exploits of their expedition. The caption reads:

> And Dernburg went forth to explore the Promised Land which is called Africa.
> And he sent forth spies and they returned, after they had explored the land, after
> forty days. And they had found a tin can, and it was empty. Then Dernburg said:
> 'The land is good, which the Lord our God has given to us.'[61]

In this persiflage of the biblical promise of the Land, Africa is another land
allegedly promised by divine grace; and the promise, it is implied, has been made
to Germany through the mediation of the Jew. The cartoon mocks celebratory
discourse on the colonies by equating it with the conquest of Canaan which,
in the early twentieth century, was of course still largely a mythical projection,
its biblical fertility contrasted with its latter-day desolation.[62] Simultaneously,
it ridicules the notion of chosenness and of the legitimation derived from the
supposedly divine promise. The land is barren, its only fruits the refuse of
civilization in the shape of the empty tin. Less obviously, the cartoon moreover
mocks the Jewish propensity to believe in chosenness and the promise of the
land. As a perceived Jew, Dernburg appears to be predestined to adopt the

role of the visionary Moses, but if so, he is a 'false prophet', his affirmation of the goodness of the land is a blatant untruth. Again, the suggestion seems to be that it is the Dernburg-Moses who seduces the Germans into the desolate protectorate. Yet in Gulbransson's cartoon no miracle is forthcoming.

The motif of the biblical spies was picked up somewhat later by Ludwig Stutz in *Kladderadatsch* in 'Die Heimkehr aus Ostafrika' (1907; Return from East Africa; Figure 8.4).[63] Dernburg having concluded his inspection tour to German East

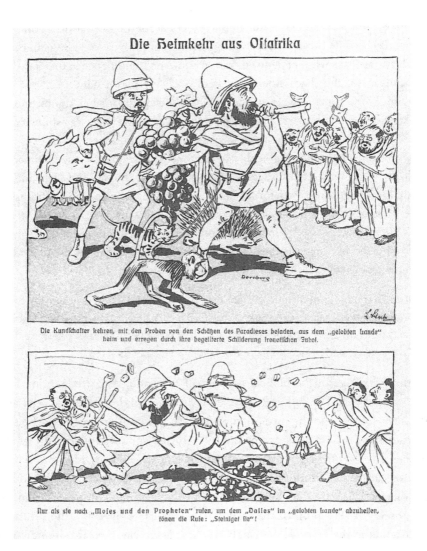

Figure 8.4 Ludwig Stutz, 'Die Heimkehr aus Ostafrika', *Kladderadatsch*, 17 November 1907, n.p. © Public Domain.

'Our Dernburg' - 'The New Moses'   173

Africa on which he had invited the industrialist and banker Walther Rathenau, the cartoon links its outcome to the biblical precedent: 'The spies return from the "Promised Land" with samples of the treasures of paradise and with their enthusiastic account stir up frenetic euphoria.'[64] In contrast to Gulbransson's earlier use of the biblical motif, the giant vine borne by Rathenau and Dernburg (who is no longer associated with Moses in this cartoon) in the first of Stutz's two panels would indeed appear to satisfy the most fanciful expectations.

Both are attired in short tunics with tropical helmets, modern shoes and binocular cases, leading a menagerie of animals. They are received jubilantly by the crowd, dressed in flowing Oriental garments; but when Dernburg and Rathenau 'call on "*Moses* and the *prophets*," in order to remedy the "*dalles*" in the "Promised Land", the suddenly angry mob cries: 'Stone them with stones!'[65] The second panel depicts the two 'spies' being pelted with stones and running for their lives, the vine trampled underfoot and the animals they brought along scattering rapidly.

'Dalles' is a Yiddish word for 'poverty'.[66] The occasional use of Yiddish in satirical engagements with the colonial secretary served at the very least as a reminder of his perceived Jewishness.[67] Both Dernburg and Rathenau were of Jewish descent and active in the banking sector before entering the political stage.[68] In contrast to Dernburg, Rathenau openly identified as Jewish, yet the pseudo-biblical setting of the cartoon once more appears to be motivated with the perceived 'racial' identification of both, which seems to suggest the racialization also of the colonial project itself. The cartoon remains ambivalent about whether the wrath of the crowd is provoked by the financial implications or by the supposed 'Jewification' of the colonial endeavour which was also indicated in some of the cartoons already discussed.

The identification of individuals in the crowd is tenuous, yet Otto Wiemer, Julius Kopsch and Richard Eickhoff - all of the Freisinnige Volkspartei (Free-minded People's Party) - appear to be among the throng. The cartoon's publication preceded the return of the Reichstag after the summer recess. Though the budget for the colonies was a perennially divisive issue, the scene presented by the artist therefore seems not to be based on any immediate precedent in the House. It nevertheless is prescient. Wiemer, if less churlishly than his cartoon double, expressed his concerns about the expenditure the colonies occasioned as soon as the Reichstag reconvened in November 1907.[69]

The motif of the spies was revisited once more in an apparent vindication of the colonial enterprise that seemed to be diametrically opposed to the earlier disenchantment. In February 1909, Thomas Theodor Heine's 'Karneval 1908'

(1909; Carnival 1908) offered in a cartoon sequence in *Simplicissimus* a review of momentous events of the past year among which it includes also a pair of panels commemorating the discovery of diamonds in South-West Africa.[70]

The first panel depicts Dernburg, encumbered with an enormous sabre and with cavalry boots and spurs. Like one of the biblical spies, he carries a pole on his shoulder, sharing the burden with a stereotypically drawn Black native in a loincloth. This time, instead of the empty tin or an actual vine, a colossal diamond is suspended from the pole. Its companion drawing shows a blind hog with spectacles and wearing a fool's cap following the trail of a sheep's droppings. The caption for both reads:

> We can also report a happy occurrence. Our Dernburg has found diamonds in our colonies.
>
> Now we only need to send a blind hog there, then we'll also get pearls.[71]

Heine, who was an acculturated Jew himself, secularized the motif of the spies. Dernburg is not sketched overtly as Jewish in his cartoon. Rather, he is appropriated to the German mainstream as 'Our Dernburg'. Yet the reference to the blind hog carries uncomfortable associations of the motif of the *Judensau*, the Jewish Sow, which, as it devours the unclean droppings of the sheep, evokes rampant stereotypes of insatiable Jewish greed and, once again, the Jewification of the colonial project which challenges the inclusive pronoun.[72]

Finally, a 'Jew'

Dernburg is portrayed at his most 'Jewish' in 'Talmudistischer Marine-Verwaltungs-Unterricht' (1909; Talmudic Navy-Administration-Instruction; Figure 8.5) in *Kladderadatsch*.[73] Indeed, in Gustav Brandt's cartoon he is no longer merely Jewish but finally has metamorphosed into a 'Jew'. Alfred von Tirpitz, State Secretary of the Imperial Naval Office, asks Dernburg what 'rabbi I and II', 'balbos' and 'meshores' means. To which the colonial secretary responds: 'Enough already, you know it not? And so you want to make a "rebes" in your ministry?'[74] Like his speech, Dernburg's facial features and gestures are blatantly 'Jewified' in a manner very different from Slevogt's. The words about which Tirpitz inquires are *rotwelsch* (thieves' cant) but originate in Yiddish.[75] They mean 'master' (rabbi), 'instructor of thieves and cutpurses' (balbos) and 'servant' (meshores);[76] 'rebes' denotes profit.[77]

A fortnight later, a related cartoon by Johnson in the same magazine showed the navy secretary at the bows of a ship with the imperial eagle for its figurehead.

Figure 8.5 Gustav Brandt, 'Talmudistischer Marine-Verwaltungs-Unterricht', *Kladderadatsch*, 5 December 1909, n.p. © Public Domain.

The vessel is tossed about by high waves in the guise of fists and heads of the Social Democratic opposition: Paul Singer and August Bebel can easily be identified. Further back, not individually recognizable, the waves take the shape presumably of deputies of the left-liberal Free-minded People's Party. Tirpitz is bound with ropes to the railing, yet loses his dispatch case and uniform hat in what the cartoon's title identifies as 'Der Interpellations-Sturm' (1909; The Interpellation-Storm); in an emergency telegram, he invokes the (imaginary) saints 'Balbos' and 'Meshores'.[78]

Tirpitz was interpellated by the Reichstag in early December 1909 on allegations of financial irregularities and corruption at his office and at the imperial shipyard at Kiel.[79] Both cartoons refer to the proceedings. The target in either case was Tirpitz. Yet it is hardly a coincidence that in Brandt's caricature Tirpitz addresses Dernburg. The colonial secretary had demonstrated in his own office how to deal efficiently with scandals; more importantly, to the artist he clearly was Jewish or, perhaps, after all, a 'Jew' – an impression re-enforced by the reference of the cartoon's title to the Talmud.[80]

The connection to the Yiddish words used in either cartoon was suggested to the artists by the investigation, subsequent court case and resulting interpellation in the Reichstag. Some of the defendants had used the soubriquets 'Rabbi I', 'Balbos' and 'Meshores'.[81] The further application of thieves' cant to the case, also in the extended parliamentary debate, is intriguing. Kreth noted the non-German origin of the relevant words with amused condescension: 'It is quite edifying to anyone who feels German: when sharp practices occur, the German language lacks the apposite term; in such a case, it is necessary to borrow from other languages.'[82] The implicit belittling and othering of Yiddish, the 'other' language which offers the relevant vocabulary, in effect its criminalization, and, by association, that of its speakers, extends, as in Brandt's cartoon, potentially also to Dernburg.

The antisemitic application of the sentiment was further pursued by Lattmann and Max Liebermann von Sonnenberg of the German Social Party. Remonstrating against the encroaching 'meshores spirit' and denouncing the firm of Frankenthal, which was accused of having defrauded the imperial shipyard at Kiel,[83] Lattmann insisted that the 'mercantile spirit' as it had been introduced to the colonial administration should take the shape of 'the solid German merchant spirit of yore'.[84]

Even without explicitly mentioning Frankenthal's widely recognized Jewish ownership, Lattmann's antisemitic trajectory is apparent. His simultaneous reference to the colonial administration and its commercial reorientation under Dernburg is ambivalent. Dernburg, as Bülow had styled him in his introduction to the Reichstag three years earlier, was of a new mercantile breed of American provenance, one of the *'capitains [sic] of industry'*;[85] he was also, a detail the former chancellor chose to leave unsaid at the time, widely perceived to be a Jew. Lattmann's ambiguous reference to Dernburg is indicative of the fissures that were beginning to show after the fall of Bülow's coalition government of the so-called Hottentot block (1909) in the postament onto which the colonial director had been raised in the wake of his striking debut.

Liebermann von Sonnenberg went even further and alleged that 'wherever the odd sign of corruption may occur in the German civil service, . . . almost invariably those people were implicated who represent the spirit of meshores in a hereditary manner'.[86] In other words, the Jews – which in the Kiel shipyard affair was a gross simplification.

Dernburg, lacking the wholehearted support of the new chancellor, Theobald von Bethmann-Hollweg, may well have recognized that the increasing criticism aimed at him from the parliamentary right and centre, be it direct or indirect, eroded the foundations of his position. His overtly antisemitic representation in the cartoon by Stutz was symptomatic of the trajectory of this process. It eventually led to the resignation of the colonial secretary in June of the following year.

Frequently represented in the satirical press as the result of his relentless harassment,[87] Dernburg's resignation elicited not only regret and sympathy. Especially in the Social Democratic press, he emerged not as a victim of the system but as its collaborator.[88] It was precisely this notion of 'Jewish' complicity in the colonial enterprise which prompted a distancing from Dernburg and the reversal of the process of his Jewification in the Jewish satirical press already at the beginning of his short tenure.

The Jewish countermove: Reversing Dernburg's 'Jewification'

Though of limited impact in the wider context of the Kaiserreich, the short-lived *Schlemiel* (1903–7) was a significant voice in early Zionist discourse in the German-speaking countries.[89] Yet by the time Dernburg became colonial director, the satirical magazine was already ailing; only its final issue appeared during the period of his tenure, at Purim 1907, barely five weeks after the elections.

The issue included an anonymously published satirical travesty of the parliamentary debates, presumably written by the magazine's editor, Max Jungmann. The 'Parlamentsbericht' (1907; Parliamentary Report) alludes to Dernburg and Bülow, as well as – only thinly disguised – the antisemitic deputy Liebermann von Sonnenberg, called von Mondberg in the parody;[90] it also appears to be a response to allegations of the noxious Jewish invasion of the German protectorates, even as it expands on the assumption that, in pursuance of the abortive Uganda Plan (1903–5), a Jewish republic was in fact established adjacent to German East Africa.[91] Written by Jungmann, *Schlemiel* included from its first issue onwards, if intermittently, letters from the fictitious orthodox Jewish colony 'New-Newland', which were attributed to its similarly fictitious former native chief Mbwapwa Jumbo after his conversion to orthodox Judaism.[92]

In the parliamentary report, Mondberg challenges the production in, and the import to, the empire and its protectorates of Jewish kreplach. The dumplings are traditionally eaten on Purim, which commemorates the deliverance of the Jewish people from persecution in the ancient Persian Empire. Mondberg alleges that they are subversive revolutionary tools, which, disguised as a national dish, glorify a bygone revolution and threaten to kill a multitude of people. The antisemitic deputy's claim is confirmed when the colonial director blames the previous colonial administration for allowing German East Africa to have been inundated with the pernicious dumplings. Indeed, he attributes the latest colonial insurrection to the

178   *Colonialism and the Jews in German History*

death by kreplach of ten natives loyal to the Reich and asserts that the rebellion was successfully suppressed only once all the dumplings had been destroyed.

In 'Briefe aus Neu-Neuland' (1903–5; Letters from New-Newland), Jungmann warned Zionism of the dangers of emulating German colonial practice. In the mock parliamentary report, the critical stance of *Schlemiel* towards Zionist involvement in colonialism shifts towards collusion in the German colonial project. It is confronted primarily in the guise of the colonial director.

On the very day before its publication, Liebermann von Sonnenberg – the model for Mondberg – asserted that he gave Dernburg 'without any reservation full recognition for the energetic manner in which he has begun to redress the insalubrities in his office.'[93] In *Schlemiel*, Dernburg is portrayed as an enthusiastic collaborator in the colonial project, but he is divested of any residual Jewishness. The colonial director is baptized and promises perpetual Christian dominance in the colonies: 'In future nothing of the sort needs to be feared; because our colonies are daughterlands of a Christian state, Christian they shall remain.'[94] He effectively precludes further 'Jewish' participation in the colonial endeavour and confirms the Christian nature of colonialism. Ultimately, in order to explain and reject his complicity, *Schlemiel* appears to reverse the Jewification of Dernburg in public discourse and to invalidate his stylization as a 'New Moses' in relation to the promised lands of German colonial expansion.

Conclusion

The relationship between German Jews and colonialism in the Kaiserreich was complex. Responses to colonialism of Germans of Jewish descent ranged from enthusiastic collaboration and commercial pragmatism to political and ethical criticism to outright rejection. They reflected the political, social and cultural certainties and anxieties of wider society and sometimes coexisted uneasily even on an individual level. More specifically, as political antisemitism gained momentum, the colonial project offered an opportunity of patriotic identification and cohesion. And yet, as notions of Germanness were painfully renegotiated in relation to the challenges of the colonial enterprise, such identifications became increasingly ambivalent. At the same time, Jewishness itself emerged as a flexible category in relation to both the controversial colonial venture and the proliferating antisemitism in political discourse.

The perceived Jewishness of the colonial secretary was considered an ambivalent marker of the colonial project in imperial Germany. Mirrored in the satirical press, its critics increasingly emphasized Bernhard Dernburg's alleged Oriental and, more specifically, Jewish descent – either to denounce German colonial practice or to challenge – via the colonial simulacrum – the authoritarian system in the metropole. By insisting on its capitalist underpinning, the colonial enterprise was in some instances 'Jewified', that is, ideologically identified as 'Jewish', in parallel to the former banker Dernburg. The colonial secretary's identification with Moses and the adaptation of the narrative of the biblical spies in particular was employed to devaluate its idealistic foundation and, paradoxically, once it had been vindicated with the 'fruits' borne by the spies, to denigrate its materialistic motivation. In support of its anti-colonial stance, the Zionist *Schlemiel* sought to reverse the Jewification of Dernburg so as to reject any notion of Jewish complicity in what it perceived to be a deeply flawed practice.

The German colonial project was short-lived, but against the background of the fierce colonial debate in imperial Germany it provided a significant platform also for negotiations of Jewishness and Germanness. The tenure of the German Empire's supposedly Jewish colonial director, though influential and transformative, was even more short-lived. Yet Bernhard Dernburg's liminality between the appropriation as 'Our Dernburg' and his othering as 'The New Moses' initiated the momentous intervention in these negotiations in the satirical press.

Notes

1 [Maximilian Harden], 'Moritz und Rina', *Die Zukunft*, 6 October 1906, 7. If not otherwise indicated, all translations are mine. The Chatti referenced in Harden's text were a Germanic tribe. For Dernburg's biographical background, see Werner Schiefel, *Bernhard Dernburg, 1865–1937: Kolonialpolitiker und Bankier im wilhelminischen Deutschland* (Zurich: Atlantis, 1974), 12.

2 For Dernburg, see chapter 4 in Christian S. Davis, *Colonialism, Antisemitism, and Germans of Jewish Descent in Imperial Germany* (Ann Arbor: University of Michigan Press, 2012) and Schiefel, *Bernhard Dernburg*.

3 See *Stenographische Berichte über die Verhandlungen des Reichstags*, vol. 218, 28 November 1906, 3957–60 (henceforth StBR). All references to *Stenographische Berichte* are to the online facsimile edition available at http://www.reichstagsp rotokolle.de/index.html (accessed 21 November 2019).

4 See ibid., 3959.

5 See StBR, vol. 218, 3 December 1906, 4085–95; 4113–16; 4120.

180   *Colonialism and the Jews in German History*

6   See ibid., 4114–15.

7   See ibid., 4096–4103; 4116–18. The Social Democratic *Vorwärts* described the confrontation as a 'caning execution'. *Vorwärts*, 5 December 1906, 1.

8   Davis, *Colonialism*, 199.

9   Ibid., 200.

10   In the course of this chapter, a number of visual representations will be discussed, not all of which it is possible to include in print. However, with the exception of *Schlemiel*, digitized versions of all of these magazines have become available in recent years. For *Kladderadatsch*, see https://digi.uni-heidelberg.de/diglit/kla; for *Lustige Blätter*, so far digitized from 1899 to 1919 (with some lacunae), see https://digi.uni-heidelberg.de/diglit/lb; for *Der wahre Jakob*, *Die Jugend*, and *Simplicissimus*, see http://www.simplicissimus.info/index.php?id=5.

11   See *Die Jugend*, 22 May 1907, title page.

12   John M. Efron, *German Jewry and the Allure of the Sephardic* (Princeton: Princeton University Press, 2016), 84.

13   Ibid.

14   See ibid., 96–7, where Efron quotes from the anthropologist Ignacy Maurice Judt's *Die Juden als Rasse* (1903), and 100.

15   Hans Rosenhagen, 'Vom Betrachten moderner Bilder', *Die Gartenlaube*, 1 August 1907, 639. The art historian Karl Voll, discussing the painting after Dernburg's resignation, was reminded of a *condottiere*, a comparison steeped in associations of conquest but also implying a mercenary dimension; see *Max Slevogt: 96 Reproduktionen nach seinen Gemälden* (Munich and Leipzig: Müller, 1912), 26.

16   See Anonymous, *Portrait of Baruch de Spinoza* (Dutch or German, final quarter of the seventeenth century to first half of the eighteenth century); oil on canvas; 74.0 × 59.8 cm; Gemäldesammlung der Herzog-August-Bibliothek, Wolfenbüttel, Germany. For the image, see http://diglib.hab.de/wdb.php?dir=gemaelde/b-117 (accessed 21 July 2021).

17   See Max Slevogt, *Staatssekretär Bernhard Dernburg* (1923); oil on canvas; 75.0 × 61.5 cm; Nationalgalerie, Staatliche Museen zu Berlin, Germany. For the image, available online: http://www.galerie20.smb.museum/werke/960473.html (accessed 21 July 2021).

18   See Schiefel, *Bernhard Dernburg*, 165–7.

19   See Adolf Münzer, 'Der Kolonialbeamte', *Die Jugend*, 22 May 1907, 435; 'Dernburg in der Wüste Kalahari', *Die Jugend*, 22 May 1907, 455; Monogrammist 'Frosch', 'Glückliche Reise!', *Die Jugend*, 22 May 1907, 455; A[lbert] Weisgerber, 'Dernburg in der ersten Klasse der Usambara-Bahn', *Die Jugend*, 22 May 1907, 458.

20   Max Brinkmann and Franz Jüttner, 'Der Khaki-Kaftan oder: Dernburgs Reise', *Lustige Blätter*, 22 May 1907, 4–5.

21   See StBR, vol. 227, 6 March 1907, 279.

'Our Dernburg' – 'The New Moses'

22 Ibid., 295. See 'Denkschrift über die Entwickelung der deutschen Schutzgebiete in Afrika und in der Südsee. Berichtsjahr 1. April 1905 bis 31. März 1906', in *Verhandlungen des Reichstags. XII. Legislaturperiode. I. Session*, vol. 238: *Anlagen zu den Stenographischen Berichten. Nr. 1 bis 106* (Berlin: Sittenfeld, 1907), 23–433.

23 See StBR, vol. 227, 6 March 1907, 295.

24 Ibid.

25 See ibid.

26 Paul Frederick Lerner, *The Consuming Temple: Jews, Department Stores, and the Consumer Revolution in Germany, 1880–1940* (Ithaca and London: Cornell University Press, 2015), 25; see also Gudrun M. König, *Konsumkultur: Inszenierte Warenwelt um 1900* (Vienna: Böhlau, 2009), 92–124.

27 See Bernhard Dernburg, *Zielpunkte des deutschen Kolonialwesens: Zwei Vorträge* (Berlin: Mittler, 1907), 17.

28 See, for example, in *Der wahre Jakob*: 'Koloniale Wunder', *Der wahre Jakob*, 30 January 1907, 5318; A. M., 'Dernburg als Zauberer', *Der wahre Jakob*, 30 January 1907, 5324; 'Aus der Zeit der Wunder', *Der wahre Jakob*, 27 February 1907, 5343; J. S., 'Der Wüstenkönig', *Der wahre Jakob*, 8 October 1908, 5970; J. S., 'Der Lockvogel', *Der wahre Jakob*, 30 January 1909, 6107; Eugen Lehmann, 'Dernburg', *Der wahre Jakob*, 3 July 1910, 6690. See also, in *Die Jugend*: Monogrammist 'Frosch', [no title], *Die Jugend*, 8 April 1907, 307; Karlchen [pseud.], 'Zu Dernburgs Abschiedsgesuch', *Die Jugend*, 11 June 1910, 577; in *Kladderadatsch*: 'An Dernburg', *Kladderadatsch*, 17 March 1907, 42; 'Die Kiste. Aufsatz des Quartaners Karlchen Mießnick', *Kladderadatsch*, 24 March 1907, no pagination; 'Aus Südafrika. Jubelgesang der Schwarzen', *Kladderadatsch*, 22 September 1907, 151; L[udwig] St[utz], 'Dernburg, der südwestafrikanische Prestidigitateur oder "Die Gewinnung von Diamanten"', *Kladderadatsch*, 27 September 1908, no pagination; and in *Lustige Blätter*: Brinkmann and Jüttner, 'Khaki-Kaftan', 4–5; F[ranz] J[üttner], 'Preisausschreiben für neue Briefmarken', *Lustige Blätter*, 12 February 1908, no pagination.

29 See StBR, vol. 227, 26 February 1907, 47; 28 February 1907, 136; 1 March 1907, 129, 157; 6 March 1907, 277–8, 296; 12 March 1907, 400.

30 See ibid., 6 March 1907, 296.

31 See, for example, Erich Wilke, 'Dernburg in der Wüste Kalahari', *Die Jugend*, 20 May 1907, 455; 'Ein Trost', *Kladderadatsch*, 13 September 1908, no pagination; and J. S., 'Lockvogel', 6107.

32 Rachel Dipper, '"Einmal muß der Mensch ins Bad!" Grüße aus Karlsbad und Marienbad', in *Abgestempelt: Judenfeindliche Postkarten*, ed. Helmut Gold and Georg Heuberger (Heidelberg: Umschau/Braus, 1999), 194–204.

33 See Frank Bajohr, *'Unser Hotel ist judenfrei': Bäder-Antisemitismus im 19. und 20. Jahrhundert* (Frankfurt am Main: Fischer, 2003), 149.

34 For a contextualization of antisemitic postcards and the spas of Karlsbad and Marienbad, see Mirjam Zadoff, *Next Year in Marienbad: The Lost Worlds of Jewish*

182   *Colonialism and the Jews in German History*

Spa Culture, trans. William Templer (2007; Philadelphia: University of Pennsylvania Press, 2012), 99–105. See also Dipper, 'Einmal muß der Mensch ins Bad!'; and Axel Stähler, *Zionism, the German Empire, and Africa: Jewish Metamorphoses and the Colors of Difference* (Berlin: de Gruyter, 2019), 152–62.

35 See Salo Aizenberg, *Hatemail: Anti-Semitism on Picture Postcards* (Philadelphia: Jewish Publication Society, 2013), 202 and Figures 9-2 and 9-3.

36 See ibid.

37 See StBR, vol. 227, 27 February 1907, 81.

38 See, for example, M[ax] Br[inkmann], 'Zwischen den Kaktus', *Lustige Blätter*, 13 March 1907, 6; m., 'Das Abkommen mit den Bondelzwarts', *Lustige Blätter*, 20 March 1907, 3; [Ernst] Stern, 'Eingeborenen-Recht in Südwest', *Lustige Blätter*, 12 November 1907, 5; see also 'Briefe von der Reise Dernburgs', *Der wahre Jakob*, 9 October 1907, 5574; A[rthur] J[ohnson], 'Die vier Aborte für Kamerun', *Kladderadatsch*, 20 December 1908, 202.

39 See G[ustav] H[ochstetter], 'Neues Recht in Afrika', *Lustige Blätter*, 29 October 1907, no pagination.

40 See Jürgen Zimmerer, 'Deutscher Rassenstaat in Afrika: Ordnung, Entwicklung und Segregation in "Deutsch Süd-West" (1884–1915)', in *Gesetzliches Unrecht: Rassistisches Recht im 20. Jahrhundert*, ed. Micha Brumlik, Susanne Meinl, and Werner Renz (Frankfurt am Main: Campus, 2005), 135–53, 138–40.

41 Stern, 'Eingeborenen-Recht', 5.

42 StBR, vol. 227, 6 March 1907, 278.

43 See Niall Ferguson, *The House of Rothschild* (London: Weidenfeld and Nicolson, 1998), 879; for the Exploration Society, see 876–81.

44 See *Deutsches Kolonial-Lexikon*, ed. Heinrich Schnee (Leipzig: Quelle & Meyer, 1920), II, 692.

45 L[udwig] Stutz, 'Dernburgs Vortragserfolge', *Kladderadatsch*, 3 February 1907, no pagination.

46 For representations of Jews as animals and vice versa, see Jay Geller, *Bestiarium Judaicum: Unnatural Histories of the Jews* (New York: Fordham University Press, 2018).

47 For '[t]he narrative of a distinctly Jewish form of colonialism that treated colonies as things to be "plundered" through rapacious capitalism' in relation to Dernburg and Paul Kayser, the first director of the imperial Colonial Office and also of Jewish descent, see the contribution of Christian S. Davis in this volume.

48 H[ans Gabriel] J[entzsch], 'Exzellenz Pascha Ben Dernburg in Neudeutschland', *Der wahre Jakob*, 28 August 1907, 5525.

49 See Jean Baudrillard, *Simulacra and Simulation*, trans. Sheila Faria Glaser (1981; Ann Arbor: University of Michigan Press, 1994), 3.

50 See StBR, vol. 227, 26 February 1907, 47.

51 Ibid., 6 March 1907, 277.

'Our Dernburg' – 'The New Moses'

52 Ibid., 15 March 1907, 523.

53 Kga., 'Dernburg auf der Afrikafahrt', *Der wahre Jakob*, 10 April 1907, 5384.

54 Ibid. For the practice of dowsing in German South-West Africa, see Georg Franzius, *Schriftwechsel des Verbandes mit dem Reichs-Kolonialamt über Erfolge mit der Wünschelrute in Deutsch-Südwestafrika* (Stuttgart: Wittwer, 1912).

55 For the semantic potential of cuffs, see Stähler, *Zionism*, 114–16, 158–9, 296.

56 A[rthur] Johnson, 'Südwestafrikanischer Zauber (Der Wüsten- oder Felsen-Automat)', *Kladderadatsch*, 31 January 1909, no pagination.

57 Ibid.

58 See, for example, A. M., 'Dernburg als Zauberer', 5324 and Stutz, 'Dernburg, der südwestafrikanische Prestidigitateur', no pagination.

59 Klaus Hödl, *Entangled Entertainers: Jews and Popular Culture in Fin-de-Siècle Vienna*, trans. Corey Twitchell (New York: Berghahn, 2019), 7. Moses himself constitutes a biblical precedent for a Jewish magician; see, for example, Exo. 7:10–12 and Num. 20:10–13. Samuel Bellachini (born Berlach) and Samuel Thiersfeld, known as Professor St. Roman, were celebrated nineteenth-century magicians of Jewish descent, both of whom performed before Kaiser Wilhelm I. While neither seems to have been openly referenced in Johnson's cartoon, their popularity may nevertheless indicate the diffusion of the notion of a Jewish affinity with magic which the image implicitly confers onto Dernburg and which, in turn, adds to the cartoon's semantic potential.

60 Olaf Gulbransson, 'Der neue Moses', *Simplicissimus*, 11 March 1907, 806.

61 Ibid. This text was published separately also in *Vorwärts* (*Unterhaltungsblatt*), 12 March 1907, 200.

62 See Stähler, *Zionism*, 261, 21–7.

63 L[udwig] Stutz, 'Die Heimkehr aus Ostafrika', *Kladderadatsch*, 17 November 1907, no pagination.

64 Ibid.

65 Ibid. See also Num. 13:23–4 and 14:10.

66 See *Duden: Deutsches Universalwörterbuch*, 3rd edn (1983; Mannheim: Dudenverlag, 1996), 314.

67 See, for example, J. S., 'Freisinns Glück und Ende', *Der wahre Jakob*, 27 February 1907, 5342 and 'Woher? Wohin?', *Der wahre Jakob*, 13 March 1907, 5356.

68 See Walther Rathenau, *Reflexionen* (Berlin: Hirzel, 1908).

69 See StBR, vol. 229, 30 November 1907, 1931.

70 Thomas Theodor Heine, 'Karneval 1908', *Simplicissimus*, 22 February 1909, 796–7.

71 Ibid., 797.

72 See Stähler, *Zionism*, 262–4.

73 G[ustav] B[randt], 'Talmudistischer Marine-Verwaltungs-Unterricht', *Kladderadatsch*, 5 December 1909, no pagination.

74 Ibid.

184   *Colonialism and the Jews in German History*

75   For the influence of Yiddish on *rotwelsch*, see, for example, Salcia Landmann, *Jiddisch: Das Abenteuer einer Sprache* (Frankfurt am Main: Ullstein, 1988) and Roland Girtler, *Rotwelsch: Die Sprache der Gauner, Dirnen und Vagabunden* (Göttingen: Vandenhoeck & Ruprecht, 2019).

76   See Friedrich Avé-Lallemant, *Das Deutsche Gaunerthum in seiner social-politischen, literarischen und linguistischen Ausbildung zu seinem heutigen Bestande* (Leipzig: Brockhaus, 1862), 452; 138; 143; 134.

77   See Wilhelm Polzer, *Gauner-Wörterbuch für den Kriminalpraktiker* (Munich: Schweitzer, 1922), 72.

78   Arthur Johnson, 'Der Interpellations-Sturm', *Kladderadatsch*, 19 December 1909, no pagination.

79   See StBR, vol. 258, 4 December 1909, 46. See also Gary E. Weir, *Building the Kaiser's Navy: The Imperial Naval Office and German Industry in the von Tirpitz Era, 1890–1919* (Annapolis: Naval Institute Press, 1992), 104.

80   Following the publication of August Rohling's rabidly antisemitic pamphlet *Der Talmudjude* (The Talmudic Jew) in 1871, the association of Dernburg with the Talmud would have evoked the image of the 'Talmudic Jew' as of a 'race born from Satan' that 'mocks the sacred' and indulges in 'corrupted morality'; August Rohling, *Der Talmudjude: Zur Beherzigung von Juden und Christen aller Stände* (1871; Münster: Russell, 1876), 10, 4.

81   See 'Die großen Kieler Werftunterschlagungen vor dem Schwurgericht', *Vorwärts*, 30 October 1909, 9. See also StBR, vol. 258, 7 December 1909, 118.

82   Ibid., 6 December 1909, 94.

83   See Weir, *Building the Kaiser's Navy*, 104.

84   StBR, vol. 258, 7 December 1909, 112.

85   StBR, vol. 218, 28 November 1906, 3959.

86   StBR, vol. 258, 11 December 1909, 235.

87   See, for example, Arthur Krüger, 'Halali', *Kladderadatsch*, 12 June 1910, 94.

88   See, for example, Lehmann, 'Dernburg', 6690.

89   See, for example, Michael Berkowitz, *Zionist Culture and West European Jewry before the First World War* (Chapel Hill: University of North Carolina Press, 1993), 180.

90   See [Max Jungmann], 'Parlamentsbericht', *Schlemiel*, 28 February 1907, 5–6; see also Stähler, *Zionism*, 215–25.

91   For the Uganda Plan and its relevance to *Schlemiel*, see ibid., 3.

92   See Max Jungmann, 'Briefe aus Neu-Neuland', *Schlemiel*, 1 November 1903, 2 and Stähler, *Zionism*, 42.

93   StBR, vol. 227, 27 February 1907, 96.

94   Ibid., 5–6; see also Dernburg's insistence that 'our body politic is built on a Christian foundation and … we live in a Christian culture', StBR, vol. 218, 3 December 1906, 4103.

9

A paradigm for repatriation projects

The African-American and the Zionist examples and their interrelationship

Mark H. Gelber

In the nineteenth and early twentieth centuries, the term '*Negerfrage*' was commonly utilized in German-language discourses to refer to the particular situation and future possibilities of the African-American, African-British and African-European populations.[1] This term can no longer be used. Some commentators utilize the expression 'N-word' instead, in order to demonstrate sensitivity to the racialist or racist dimensions of the issue at hand. However, in my view, it is neither advisable nor even possible to enunciate an 'N-word', even as a quotation, for fear of hurting the feelings and insulting or alienating certain individuals or audiences by employing racist terminology. In this chapter, I use the terms 'African', 'African-American', 'African-British' and so forth. They do not reflect faithfully nineteenth-century discourses regarding categories of race, nation and difference pertaining to African peoples resident outside of the African continent, who were depicted and categorized in a vast literature on the basis of ostensibly different and dark or darker skin colour, in contrast to others of lighter skin colour, who were designated sometimes as white. But, these terms evidence awareness and a certain sensitivity to a very painful and tragic history. This issue, especially as it pertains to scholarship, is extremely complicated and problematical in western anthropological science and racial-cultural studies – namely the attempt to categorize humanity into specific racial groups by means of degrees of difference in skin colour or by employing colour variations, as opposed to, or in addition to, other physical or genetic markers, as primary tools for attempting to draw racial boundaries and to discriminate against those whose origins may be African, or in general 'other'.

The issue of race is an important one in historical studies which concern the Jews, Zionism, Germany and especially German colonialism. Virtually all recent attempts to comprehend the Zionist movement in Germany, as well as in central and eastern Europe, especially its ideological varieties and historical subtleties, but also its practical settlement policies and pre-state-building activities, take colonial and post-colonial theory and perspectives into account. This is true, even if an argument against viewing Zionism primarily as a form of colonialism is advanced.[2] Very often, critical postcolonial perspectives are the foundation and point of departure for many such studies. However, the emergence of 'settler-colonial' theory, which as a methodological tool and a particular variety of postcolonial theory, may be understood as supplementary to criticism of imperialism and colonialism worldwide, ushered in a new phase in the debate about Zionism and colonialism.[3] 'Settler-colonialism' pinpoints and analyses particularly nefarious and exploitative forms of colonialism, characterized by the displacement or murder of indigenous peoples, in addition to the submission or enslavement of those peoples, and the denigration, marginalization or erasure of native cultures by 'settler-colonialist' projects. Numerous examples throughout the world have been cited in these studies, including Australia, Central America, the United States, South Africa, Palestine/Israel and others.[4] In all fairness, it must be said that a lively, if sometimes acrimonious debate – which frequently appears to include politically charged polemics – has been and continues to be conducted in scholarly and non-scholarly forums, arguing for and against the different positions. Racialist or racist terminologies are regularly employed in this discussion. Taking the previous discussion into account here, I attempt to contextualize the discussion of the emergence and development of modern Zionism in Germany and Central Europe by recasting it or by viewing it principally as a repatriation movement. Admittedly, in order to comprehend Zionism in all of its complexity, it must be considered and analysed from numerous vantages and with critical tools derived from various disciplines. Indeed, it is fair to say – and it has been said – that there are numerous Zionisms and different Zionist ideologies. But, while colonialism and repatriation are not necessarily mutually exclusive, they may be considered as independent or singular projects to a degree. By focusing on repatriation, a different or unique point of view regarding Zionism in its entirety may be achieved.

Furthermore, by linking an aspect of the racialist perspective, specifically the African one, to the Jewish national dimension and by utilizing this linkage to offer a comparative study, a compelling case may be made for viewing Zionism as more of – or just as much of – a repatriation movement than a colonialist or 'settler-colonist' enterprise. The African repatriation movement, which like Zionism was an internationalist movement, has not generated the kind or quality or range of scholarly attention that it deserves, despite recent attempts to redress this situation. Moreover, the particular relationship between Zionism as a repatriation movement and the African repatriation movement has been hardly studied or analysed closely. Nevertheless, it is not my intention here to offer an historical study of this fascinating and complicated relationship, or even to sketch the outlines and chapters of its history. Given the limited space at my disposal and the specific focus on Zionism within German imperialism and colonialism, it is rather my intention to offer a general paradigm of repatriation, based on the African and Zionist examples. My aim is to argue that Zionism as repatriation may be measured against African repatriation and resettlement in order to derive a sense of the extent to which it pertains to and resonates with repatriation as a concept and ideology, over against colonialism. Subsequently, the utility of this model may be realized in future applications to specific historical interrogations of colonial enterprise characteristic of Imperial Germany and Central Europe.

My argument begins with a reference to a passage in Theodor Herzl's utopian Zionist novel *Altneuland*, published in 1902 towards the end of his Zionist career, before his early death. Herzl (1860–1904), who was a luminary among the Viennese cultural elite of the fin-de-siècle, a dramatist, journalist, editor and critic of stature, is considered in Zionist historiography to be the visionary whose dream of a Jewish state began to take concrete form as he initiated some decisive steps towards its realization. Perhaps his two most important accomplishments were the founding of the World Zionist Organization under his leadership and the organization of the annual or biannual World Zionist Congresses, over which he presided from their inception until his death (1897–1903). The particular passage in *Altneuland* under discussion may be found in the Third Book of the novel, set in Tiberius on the Sea of Galilee in the future Jewish homeland, during which the protagonists visit the Research Institute of Professor Steineck. German science and technology inform the background of Herzl's novel, similar to their function in German colonialism in general; they will ostensibly play a central role in the new Jewish (i.e. Zionist) society which will be established in the Jewish homeland, that is, in the land of Israel/Palestine. In the novel Steineck works as a bacteriologist, who seeks cures for harmful and devastating illnesses, including diphtheria, tuberculosis, cholera and malaria, which plagued late nineteenth and early-twentieth-century humanity. At the point during the tour when the guests arrive at Steineck's own laboratory, he

188   *Colonialism and the Jews in German History*

is asked about the nature of his current research project. His reply surprises the guests. He states simply: 'die Erschliessung Afrikas' (the development or opening up of Africa).[5] When pressed about what he might possibly mean by this response – since the connection to Africa is by no means patently obvious – he goes into some detail. First, he digresses about how malaria was brought under control in Palestine, but he adds that the conditions in Africa are very different from those in Palestine. In any case, Africa, like Palestine, can only be developed and opened up to civilization after malaria is eliminated. Steineck's idea is that Europeans would stream to Africa after malaria and other infectious and deadly diseases have been erased or brought under control. Kingscourt, one of the more memorable characters in the novel, expresses astonishment that Steineck's idea is to ship white Europeans ('weisse Menschen') to the Black continent. Steineck replies:

> Not only the whites, but the blacks too. There is an unsolved national problem, a great tragedy of human suffering that only we Jews can fully understand. I mean the African Question. I am not at all ashamed to say. . . . Now that I have lived to see the return of the Jews, I wish to help prepare the way for the return of the Africans.[6]

Kingscourt, one of whose roles in the second part of the novel is to function as a mouthpiece for the happy astonishment and enthusiastic non-Jewish approval of virtually everything that transpires in the New Jewish Society projected twenty years into the future, expresses his approbation and admiration for these 'Zionist' efforts regarding the 'African question'. In a final remark, Steineck explains his reasoning in universalist and decidedly sentimental terms: 'All people should have a homeland. Then they will be kinder to each other. Then people will love and understand each other better.'[7] This passage is but one of many in the novel which underscores Herzl's broadly humanistic and international vision, which projects a sense of the universal beneficiality of Zionist endeavour. However, it must be said that the fictional character Kingscourt was originally a German aristocrat named Königshoff. Before he enters the narration, he had spent years in the United States, working very hard to become an extremely rich man, and as a result he became Americanized to a degree. His retinue at the beginning of Herzl's novel includes two servants 'of colour', one an African-American and one a native of Tahiti. Thus, both the German background of privileged aristocracy and race and the American background of racialist relations and the superior position of the white man – here a figure both German and American in one – play important roles in this Zionist novel.

The linkage in Herzl's novel between the Jewish and African repatriation projects was emphasized and problematized in a very well-known, scandal-provoking review of the novel, written shortly after its publication by one of his major antagonists within the Jewish national spectrum, namely Ahad Ha-am (1856–1927).[8] A Hebraist, and in Zionist historiography considered to be one of the major proponents of spiritual or cultural Zionism, Ahad Ha-am rejected Herzl's novel peremptorily and criticized it scathingly, owing especially to the dearth of unique Jewish national characteristics in the utopian Zionist society depicted in it. In his review, he rejected forcefully Herzl's vision, lamenting that there was little to no difference between Herzl's Zionist repatriation project and the African one.[9] For Ahad Ha-am this prospect was absolutely untenable. He claimed there was nothing particularist in a Jewish sense to be found in the novel: 'Nowhere a specific Jewish trace'.[10] According to Ahad Ha-am, the realization of a unique and specifically or essentially Jewish – in the sense of Jewish-national – society is what makes the Zionist project in theory desirable and even necessary. It allows for the fostering of an authentic Jewish culture and the development of authentic Jewish human beings. This is, for him, in fact its *raison d'être*. Concomitantly, the same would be true for African repatriation to the degree that theoretically only in Africa can those Africans who reside in their diasporas worldwide achieve authentic African culture and realize authentic African existence. The neo-Romantic character of Ahad Ha-am's cultural view contrasts with Herzl's more political and diplomatic approach, even if many of the pragmatic or practical ideas incorporated into Herzl's Zionist vision, as presented in the novel, were no doubt flawed.

Herzl's interest in Africa extended well beyond his incorporation of one passage that referred to it in *Altneuland*,[11] and there was certain overlap between this interest and his concerted efforts to win Wilhelm II and Imperial Germany over to the Zionist cause. Herzl and leading German Zionists were strong supporters of German colonialism, in Africa and elsewhere, and some of them belonged to the German Colonial Society and were active members in it. One of the most prominent examples in this regard is Otto Warburg (1859–1938), who participated in German colonialist projects.[12] He was born in Hamburg, and he became an expert in industrial agriculture. Also, he was a professor of botany in Berlin and a Zionist activist, who later became the president of the World Zionist Organization (1911–21). Herzl and other Zionists were enthusiastic about the so-called civilizing and modernizing impulses associated with European colonialism in general, and they were especially excited by projects and activities associated with German colonialism. For a time Herzl favoured the idea of a

German protectorate over Palestine, which would be mediated by the Kaiser. He would limit Ottoman sovereignty and allow for the mass immigration of Jews. Herzl's model in this regard was Egypt, which functioned as an autonomous province within the Ottoman Empire, but in effect Egypt was controlled by Britain.[13] Accordingly, Herzl strove to arrange a meeting with Wilhelm II to enlist his support for Zionism. He eventually succeeded to meet him in 1898 with the help of the German ambassador in Vienna, Philipp zu Eulenburg, who was a close friend of Kaiser Wilhelm.[14] Herzl also met with the German foreign minister Bernhard von Bülow to persuade him to intercede with the Ottoman sultan on behalf of Zionism. In fact, the Kaiser developed a positive attitude towards Herzl and Zionism, while Herzl expressed his delight at the prospect of the Jews living in Palestine under the protection of 'this strong, great, moral, splendidly governed, rightly organized Germany'; this situation, if realized, would likely have the most beneficial impact on Jewish national character.[15]

After Herzl's death in 1904, the Zionist leadership relocated to the German Kaiserreich, hoping to continue more effectively the effort first coordinated by Herzl to garner sympathy for the movement with this key world power at the same time that Germany was at an important stage regarding its own colonialist ambitions. While the Zionist leadership endeavoured to maintain allegiance to Herzl's vision and to his priorities for the movement, especially the securing of a charter and receiving approval for repatriation from a world power through diplomatic and political means, the new leadership was forced to accommodate itself to a degree to other tendencies and factions within German Zionism and the larger Jewish-national and Zionist movements, especially those which favoured practical settlement initiatives. David Wolffsohn (1856–1914), who succeeded Herzl as president of the World Zionist Organization, was born in Lithuania, but he grew up and was educated in the Kaiserreich, in east Prussia. He later settled in Cologne and became a successful businessman. As a disciple of Herzl, he continued to seek opportunities to negotiate a charter which would enable Jewish repatriation to Palestine in the Ottoman Empire. He orchestrated the transfer of the headquarters of the movement to Cologne, although he had at first considered Berlin also to be a good option in this regard. Next, he secured Hamburg as the site of the Eighth Zionist Congress in 1909. But, despite the prospect of compatibility, shared discourses and mutual approval of certain colonialist tendencies and projects in both German imperialism and Zionist endeavour, nothing concrete came to fruition in Germany to help realize Zionist goals during Wolffsohn's tenure as president of the World Zionist Organization from 1905 to 1913.[16]

At this point it is useful to provide an outline of the general components of a grand repatriation project, in order to establish a paradigm and arrive at a thesis concerning the early Zionist response and relationship to the 'African Question' and to repatriation in general. In the following I quote or paraphrase from James T. Campbell's *Middle Passages: African American Journeys to Africa, 1787–2005* (2006), which deals largely with African repatriation movements.[17] Overall, I attempt to generalize what in his account is presented as historically specific. According to Campbell, the dream of return or repatriation must have been, and must be, kept alive over long stretches of time among a displaced, oppressed or disenfranchised and dispersed population, in other words a diasporic people. There are numerous strategies – educational, artistic, cultural – that may be employed to this end. The original land or territories, from which the once mostly indigenous population was removed, that is also the apparent and designated future destination of the returning groups, must remain a palpable presence in the life of the dislocated and disenfranchised nation. An emotional allegiance and desire regarding return to the land must be cultivated, forged and maintained. At the same time other possible locations or regions in the world may be considered as alternative destinations or secondary options. This is especially true if it appears that they might be more practical immediate choices or otherwise viable for repatriation and resettlement, either as a temporary asylum or on a permanent basis. Means of galvanizing sectors of the population for the cause must be broadly nourished, while as much of the population as possible needs to be convinced of the necessity or at least of the concrete advantages and beneficialities of the project both for individuals and for the masses of people. This dimension of the process is important, even though a complete repatriation of an entire displaced people would be an unrealistic goal. Various compelling narratives regarding common descent or national and racial commonalities need to be fashioned and disseminated, including a direct identification with proponents of earlier or prehistoric and mythical liberation and well-known repatriation movements, for example, the classic case of the exodus of the ancient, biblical Israelites from Egyptian bondage. A compelling rhetoric of heroic nation building in a future homeland needs to be articulated, sometimes with reference to ancient mottos taken from or reminiscent of the biblical models, for example one which resonates deeply with passages in the biblical Book of Numbers or the Book of Joshua: 'The land is ours; there it lies with inexhaustible resources; let us go and possess it.'[18]

National or racial pride and ideas regarding the supreme suitability and quality of the human material itself are to be instilled and repeatedly emphasized, usually by attempts to establish a link to mythic or glorious achievements far back in time. Socially or politically oriented action groups, clubs and societies need to be founded in order to help organize and propel the endeavour, to rally the adherents, as well as to secure an organizational structure in place which might coordinate eventually the repatriation on the ground. One particularly useful tool, related to these, is the national convention, which may be convened in order to project a sense of the solidarity or unified purpose of the nation and its ultimate goal of repatriation. Education and training programmes need to be devised in order to prepare for the technical work and to develop skilled labour which will be essential in the future, while providing a framework for national endeavour in the present in the diaspora. Influential political or cultural figures outside the movement need to be courted and won over for the cause, even if there is no unanimous agreement about which candidates would be the most useful for this purpose. Also, generous benefactors or sources of financial support need to be secured. Sources which keep on giving, so to speak, are normally hard to win for any such movement. Efforts in this vein which resemble begging or pandering should be avoided to the extent that they impinge on the image of a proud and viable nation and national cause. Vicious attacks and discrimination experienced in the countries of residence should be resisted bravely and resolutely by actions of self-defence or by any other means, while the greater goal of repatriation is simultaneously trumpeted as the ultimate solution to the condition of the permanently or eternally disdained outsider nation. Journalistic instruments – newspapers and magazines especially – need to be utilized in order to create a loyal following and to aid in building a community with equal access to information and to transmit widely the ideology and progress being registered by the movement. New adherents may also be won this way, while a spectrum of opinion expressed by faithful followers or even bitter opponents may be communicated to an extensive readership. Different, critical and contrary opinions may be discussed in order to arrive at a positive outcome. Also, a range of supportive written texts, from reports concerning current events to polemical tracts and including poetry or fictional works, perhaps even novels, which tend to promote the repatriation project, are part and parcel of this overall effort.

Exploration missions or commissions, inspired by the travels and efforts of missionaries and nineteenth-century explorers throughout the underdeveloped world, need to be organized and dispatched under the aegis of the repatriation movement. These missions would invite and include well-educated, articulate and competent technical experts and scientists who are able to report back authoritatively regarding the conditions on the ground and to recommend specific policy or particular tracts of land for settlement, given the agronomic or industrial potential and the geophysical, climatic and human realities in place. If premature settlement attempts are risked, then these need to be contextualized and viewed positively as pioneering, even if flawed, but in any case they should be regularly covered in the press or other media established by the movement. A charismatic leader needs to take control of the movement. This leader, while politically savvy and broadly acceptable to a majority or to an influential segment of the nation as an authority figure, may at the same time evidence various problematical personal instabilities or idiosyncrasies. But, the leaders serve as symbols and motivational rallying points for the movement. They present themselves or fashion an image as born leaders with royal lineage and an aristocratic habitus. They are valiant and proud liberators in the mould of the biblical Moses, who, although a former Egyptian prince, directed the liberation movement of Israelite slaves from Egyptian bondage. These leaders are explicitly acclaimed as reincarnations of 'Moses, leading his wayward people to the promised land'.[19] Concomitantly, the charismatic leaders will attempt to meet and establish a dialogue or working relationship with other political leaders and admired royalty, projecting a sense of equality with their aristocratic or privileged peers. Treaties or agreements with recognized leaders may be signed in the name of the movement or nation. Importantly, this movement needs to be depicted as possessing the capacity to import modern civilization and the most advanced technologies and industrial techniques to a relatively backward region, which will elevate and ameliorate the condition of the local population already in residence. These activities elevate and solidify the status of the leader of the repatriation movement within the fold as well as outside of it. Nonetheless, at the same time, infighting, challenges or bitter criticism directed at the leader and leadership, as well as attempts to undermine it, and disputes over the priorities, competing agenda and methods appear to be constant and ineluctable features of the endeavour. While all of the above is going on, it should be made clear that the repatriation project is nonetheless 'the grandest prospect for the regeneration of a people that was ever presented in the history of the world'.[20]

This outline in effect constitutes a paradigm of a grand repatriation project. It is taken virtually verbatim, that is, as quotation or as paraphrase with some minor deviations and additions, from James T. Campbell's study of African-American repatriation to and colonization in Africa cited earlier. More specifically, this summary gives an overview of the career, efforts and projects spearheaded

M. R. DELANEY.

Figure 9.1 Martin R. Delany (1812–85). Courtesy of the Louis Round Wilson Special Collections Library, the University of North Carolina at Chapel Hill. © Public Domain.

by Martin Robinson Delany (1812–1885), perhaps the most important and fascinating leader of the African-American repatriation and resettlement project in the nineteenth century (Figure 9.1). Although not nearly as well known as he deserves to be outside of the specific movement he inspired and led, he has been considered, arguably, to be the first proponent of Black Nationalism.[21] By removing the specific references to Delany in the above paragraphs, including the exact titles of his writings, the names of the organizations or newspapers he established and the specific details of his numerous repatriation and liberation activities, I have attempted to suggest that the African-American repatriation project associated with him may be understood – to a great extent – as a model. I submit that this model runs parallel to the early Zionist project, especially to the specific endeavour associated with the name of Theodor Herzl, but also taking into account pre-Herzlian and post-Herzlian or anti-Herzlian Jewish-national voices and activities, many of which were expressed already during his lifetime. One who knows the Zionist project well and in detail, especially in its earliest phases, might get the impression from this paradigm that early Zionism modelled itself consciously as a repatriation movement according to the patterns established by Delany. He died just as the modern Zionist movement was coming into existence. To be absolutely clear: I make no such a claim. However, familiarity with Delany's career naturally allows for unbiased observers to establish numerous parallels between it and the career of Herzl and the history of the early Zionist movement. The many striking parallels are illustrative of a certain structural compatibility. And, the African-American repatriation project overall, which extends well beyond Delany and his activities, shared much in common with the Zionist endeavour to repatriate diaspora Jews to the land of Israel. Furthermore, as early as 1852 Delany had expressed positively and in proto-Jewish nationalist, territorialist or Zionist language his view of the desired repatriation of the Jewish people. For him, the historical predicament of the Jews was akin to that of African-Americans:

> such also are the Jews, scattered throughout not only the length and breadth of Europe, but almost the habitable globe, maintain their national characteristics, and looking forward in high hopes of seeing the day when they may return to their former national position of self-government and independence, let that be in what ever part of the habitable world it may.[22]

At this point it is useful to identify some of the specific parallel activities and goals pursued by Delany and Herzl in their careers, which is tantamount to tracing the shared trajectory between African repatriation and early Zionism, in order to make clear how similar they truly are. When Delany entered the national political arena, only Haiti (1804) and Liberia (1848) were independent Black nations, that is, self-governing republics. There was no independent Jewish state, when Herzl took up the Jewish national/Zionist cause in the last years of the nineteenth century. The State of Israel, the first and until today the only Jewish nation state on the globe, was established in 1948, some fifty years after Herzl began his Zionist work. While slavery was legal and institutionalized in the southern states of the United States until the Civil War (1860–5), the Jews were mostly liberated and enfranchised citizens throughout the world by the time modern Zionism came into existence. The process of Jewish emancipation took place gradually and with occasional setbacks beginning in the late eighteenth century and lasting through the nineteenth century. Nevertheless, vicious and rampant antisemitism in its various nefarious forms continued apace, limiting Jewish opportunities, imposing restrictions and often presenting life-threatening dangers, even after Jewish enfranchisement had been legally secured. Thus, the historical backgrounds in which these two figures emerged were relatively or even considerably different as they took up their individual causes, despite some remarkable parallels.

Delany claimed that he penned his first sensation-arousing publication, *The Condition, Elevation, Emigration and Destiny of the Colored People of the United States* in 1852 within one month.[23] Similarly, Herzl claimed to have written his first Zionist brochure, *Der Judenstaat* (The Jewish State) within a few weeks in 1895. It was received enthusiastically in some quarters, although it was criticized in others, to be sure, even among readerships sympathetic to Jewish nationalism. The idea of voluntary mass relocation is usually difficult for settled populations to embrace, as the historical record shows time and again. It may be that the notion of a feverish pace of authorship in these two cases lends the causes they propagate added urgency. Between 1848 and 1854, more than forty ships embarked for Liberia from the United States, loaded with some four thousand African-American would-be settlers. Although Herzl claimed famously in retrospect not to have known anything about Zionism or proto-Zionist activities or publications when he wrote *The Jewish State*, the first Zionist clubs, organizations and newspapers had come into existence, and the earliest settlement activities of the first waves of Jewish immigration to Palestine – according to Zionist historiography the First and Second 'Aliyot' – had already transpired. Furthermore, Herzl employed the term 'Zionismus' (Zionism) in *The Jewish State*, his first Zionist publication. One must question how he came upon this specific term, since it was a neologism coined in Vienna which had come into use a little more than a decade before Herzl emerged on the Jewish nationalist scene. Thus, Herzl's claims must be taken *cum grano salis*. In both Delany's *The Condition* and in Herzl's brochure, the target readerships are confronted with the notion that each of these diasporic populations constitutes a nation in its own right. For Delany, African-Americans are 'a nation within a nation'.[24] For Herzl, the Jewish nation is precisely that, a nation, 'ein Volk': 'Wir sind ein Volk, ein Volk'.[25] The Jews need to be understood above all as a people *sui generis*, rather than merely a certain population identifiable by religious difference or a unique set of beliefs and traditional laws and teachings. Delany believed that African-Americans would never command respect until they created a nation or political entity of their own, where they constituted the ruling element. The same notion was advanced by Herzl and other early Zionists who argued in favour of establishing a homeland with a Jewish majority population as a way of countering or negating rampant antisemitic prejudice, as well as institutionalized antisemitism and discrimination. In his book *The Condition*, Delany discussed the various options for resettlement, and in this first work he argued against Liberia, favouring rather Central or South American destinations over African ones. As a matter of fact, throughout his career he changed his mind more than once about this issue and he was quite mercurial regarding which location might be the best one for African-American resettlement.[26] In this regard, Herzl was very similar. In *The Jewish State*, Herzl included a section entitled 'Palestine or Argentina' (Palästina oder Argentinien), in which he rhetorically raised the question about which location might match best Jewish national resettlement goals.[27] He claimed to be a pragmatist in this regard, stating (on behalf of his people) that the Jews would accept whatever land they were given. Nevertheless, the bountiful resources and extensive open spaces of Argentina, 'one of the naturally richest lands on the earth' with a negligible indigenous population, were very appealing to him, and it seemed like it would be a very good choice.[28] At other times, Herzl considered relocation to North America and to South Africa. Later, in 1903, Herzl was favourably predisposed to accept the offer of the British colonial secretary Joseph Chamberlain, to resettle the Jewish people in territory in East Africa, at the time a British colony. But, it may have been a tactic on Herzl's part in order to curry favour or court the British government, while viewing the East-African option – or as it was called within Zionism, the Uganda plan – as merely a temporary solution. At the time, the Jewish condition seemed particularly dire, given the recent vicious outbreak of murderous antisemitism in the form of a deadly pogrom in Kishinev (1903), which received worldwide attention and underscored the pitiful vulnerability and virtually defenceless condition of Jews throughout the diaspora.[29] It must be emphasized that Herzl personally opposed rash settlement plans which were promoted by certain factions in the Zionist movement; he consistently urged caution and pleaded for patience in this regard until such time that a treaty or charter or great power support for such a plan were to be approved. Unlike Delany, who managed to sign a treaty granting resettlement rights to African-American repatriates, Herzl failed in his attempts to achieve the same. However, during the First World War, Chaim Weizmann, who was one of the rising stars in the Zionist ranks, as well as an important figure who opposed Herzl in numerous ways, managed to receive the equivalent of a charter. During the war, he resided in Britain and he managed to lobby successfully for official British support to establish a Jewish home in Palestine, which came under British mandateship following the British military defeat of the Ottoman Empire in the First World War. The Balfour Declaration (2 November 1917), as the document was subsequently called, expressed clearly in the words of the Foreign Secretary Lord Arthur Balfour

198   *Colonialism and the Jews in German History*

that the British government 'view with favour the establishment in Palestine of a national home for the Jewish people, and will use their best endeavor to facilitate the achievement of this object'.[30] This statement represented at the time a major diplomatic breakthrough and triumph for the Zionist movement. Weizman, who later became president of the World Zionist Organization, was chosen to be the first president of the State of Israel.

Both Delany and Herzl called for and organized major convocations of supporters to project the sense of mass movements under their leadership and to coordinate ideology and policy. Delany initiated a National Emigration Convention, which took place in Cleveland in 1854. A second and third convention followed in two-year intervals and one was held in Canada. One of Herzl's most important achievements according to Zionist historiography was his success in convening the First Zionist Congress in Basel in 1897 and to establish the annual or biannual Zionist Congresses, which took place in different countries in Europe, as permanent features of this international movement. The Congress became an important Zionist institution and a useful instrument for the practical realization of Zionist goals. In fact, the term 'Congress Zionism' is regularly used to give singular credit to this political vehicle and to acknowledge Herzl's leadership in its establishment. Furthermore, the speeches by Delany and Herzl given at the respective mass gatherings were important or sometimes even electrifying events in their own right, and their impact could be registered long after the convocations came to an end in the form of publication.

Both Delany and Herzl utilized their talents as writers in service of their repatriation movements. Also, both authored novels in order to reach a wide and diverse audience. Delany's novel, *Blake, or the Huts of America*, was published serially in the *Anglo-African Magazine* between 1859 and 1862. In some ways it may be read as an answer to Harriet Beecher Stowe's *Uncle Tom's Cabin, or Life among the Lowly* (1852), the great bestselling novel of the nineteenth century in the United States and Britain; it exerted a major impact on the abolitionist movement in the United States. At the end of the novel, the escaped slaves and Tom's survivors eventually reach Liberia, while in Delany's novel, the Americas displace Africa as the choice location for African-American resettlement. In *Uncle Tom's Cabin*, one of the protagonists who decides to resettle in Liberia, states: 'The desire and yearning of my soul is for an African nationality. I want a people that shall have a tangible separate existence of its own.'[31] Regarding Delany, it was only later, after he visited Africa and following his signing a treaty concerning African-American settlement in the Niger Valley, did he change his mind and give primacy to Africa for a while.

Both Delany and Herzl cultivated images of themselves as Mosaic figures, that is, they understood or presented themselves and were viewed by many of their supporters as following in the footsteps of the biblical Moses, that is as liberators from bondage, leading their enslaved or disenfranchised people to the promised land (Figure 9.2). In their work for their peoples, they appeared as self-styled ambassadors, equal to princes or royalty, representing their nations in foreign courts or houses of government and engaging in diplomatic negotiations in order to secure a treaty or a charter which would permit repatriation and settlement projects. Delany traced his lineage to African royalty,[32] and Herzl was saluted by numerous admirers as a Jewish prince or the uncrowned king of the Jews, and

Figure 9.2 In his depiction of the biblical Moses (1908), the Zionist artist Ephraim Moses Lilien (1874–1925) gave Moses the facial features of Herzl. © Public Domain.

occasionally hailed as a messianic saviour who would achieve redemption for his nation. When Delany signed a treaty in 1859 to secure a grant of land at Abeokuta in West Africa, he understood himself to be negotiating 'on behalf of the African race in America'.[33] Herzl likewise strove to meet with influential aristocrats and government leaders in order to score a major diplomatic achievement for the Zionist movement by securing a charter or a treaty or a protectorate which would permit Jewish resettlement. His one and only visit to Jerusalem and the land of Israel in 1898 was timed exactly in order to orchestrate a meeting with the German Kaiser, who would be visiting in the Holy Land precisely at the same time. Herzl had high hopes that the German Kaiser and his government would be able to convince the Ottoman sultan to agree to Jewish immigration to Palestine and Herzl favoured a German protectorate in Palestine in order to advance the Zionist cause.

The particular paradigm of repatriation, as I have distilled it from the career of Martin Delany (and as presented by Campbell), constitutes an anatomy of repatriation that goes beyond the two individual cases. Methodologically, I follow here the classic study of revolutions authored by the American historian Crane Brinton, entitled *The Anatomy of Revolution*.[34] Written in 1938 and revised twice (1952 and 1965), it was for decades a standard work for the understanding of revolutionary movements in the United States and elsewhere. What interested Brinton were the patterns and historical processes and especially the uniformities or affinities and the similar cyclical movements which could be found in the English, French, American and Russian revolutions – that is, in all of them. Even though he admitted that each revolution was unique in its own way, it was possible nevertheless to identify structural parallels and common patterns. Understanding the individual deviations from the paradigm in each case made possible more complete and subtle understandings of each one, as well as of the historical processes which defined revolution. An anatomy of repatriation movements may potentially accomplish the same results. In this chapter I have presented two specific examples. Regarding repatriation and colonialism, Martin Delany was exceedingly concerned and actively committed to preclude the possibility of the African-American repatriation movement becoming a colonial movement in Africa.[35] Repatriation does not preclude colonialism. While it understands and presents itself as a national self-liberation project and human rights movement, it has the potential to curtail or impinge on the human rights of others by means of colonial exploitation. There are even cases on record where African-American settlers in Africa were guilty of enslaving indigenous Africans.[36] But, these seem to be exceptional or isolated cases. Were one to

A Paradigm for Repatriation Projects   201

measure the extent to which early Zionism might be seen to have followed or deviated from this same course as set by Delany, it might be possible to shed light on an important and contentious aspect of the Zionist project, namely its fraught relationship to colonialism and the indigenous population of Palestine.

In conclusion, I would like to observe that the historical relationship between the two repatriation movements was, as seen from the Zionist side, extremely limited or restrained. One finds occasional approbation of African-American repatriation and resettlement in Africa in the early Zionist press or early Zionist literature, as the example from Herzl's *Altneuland* clearly illustrates. However, it is fair to state that the African-American repatriation movement was of only marginal or very limited interest within early Zionism. Historically, the Jewish and Zionist examples probably prove to be of more interest to the later incarnations of Black nationalist struggle and African-American repatriation in the twentieth century than the Black repatriation movement was to early Zionism in the nineteenth century. In this context one may mention the better-known names of W. E. B. Du Bois (1868–1963) and Marcus Garvey (1887–1940). Both were proponents of Black Nationalism and prominent voices in favour of the resettlement of African-Americans and other Africans in Africa. Both of these important figures tended to appropriate the biblical Exodus narrative for the African repatriation movement, while expressing consistent support for the Zionist cause.[37]

Perhaps it is possible to speculate on the failure or reluctance of early Zionism to develop a more tangible or concrete relationship with the African-American repatriation movement. It may be that the early Zionist reticence – relative reticence, that is – regarding African-American repatriation can be explained partially in relation to the racially charged and racist-antisemitic discourses characteristic of late nineteenth- and early-twentieth-century European societies. Late nineteenth-century European society largely viewed the Jews as a race, and racist antisemitism was extremely pernicious from the time it came into existence in the last decades of the nineteenth century until the Holocaust and even afterwards. In this regard, Jews suffered from racist prejudice in a manner similar to the suffering of Blacks in white European and white American society. But, Jewish nationalist claims, as well as Jewish racialist claims, which nourished certain factions within early Zionism – if it may be put that way – tended to posit the national and racial viability of the Jewish nation and/or Jewish race vis-à-vis other races in Europe, in face of antisemitic polemics which argued for the inferiority, diseased nature and nefariousness of the Jewish nation or Jewish race.[38] Still, a broad spectrum of those who utilized

202   *Colonialism and the Jews in German History*

the racist rhetoric and formulated the racist polemics of the late nineteenth century deprecated in similar and different ways the Black African nation or Black African race, often considering Black Africans to be of an inferior status, primitive and sometimes a passive race or an effeminate race, but certainly one not capable of accomplishing major achievements or of creating true culture. According to this racist rhetoric, Africans were not racially equipped to create outstanding or lasting cultural products or of contributing to and developing civilization in the western sense or according to western models. In the racist-antisemitic discourse, Jews were regularly depicted as an inferior, defective and dangerous racial group. Towards the end of the century they came to be considered by many to be the most degenerate and contaminated, mongrel racial strain possible, for example, in Houston Stewart Chamberlain's authoritative, influential and very popular racist work *Die Grundlagen des 19. Jahrhunderts* (The Foundations of the Nineteenth Century, 1899).[39] Chamberlain claimed that Jewish racial admixture with African blood during their sojourn in Egypt was a primary cause for Jewish racial degeneration and depravity. Furthermore, Chamberlain argued that the downfall of the superior and meritorious ancient civilizations – Greek and Roman – had been caused directly by racial mixing with the poisonous, contaminated blood of Africans and Jews.[40] The fusion of stereotypically negative Jewish and African facial and physical features was common in the racist and antisemitic visual culture dating back to the eighteenth century, especially in the tradition of western caricature. Moreover, there was a widely disseminated myth about the Jews themselves being in truth racial Africans, that is, an African race (and Black).[41] Thus, it may have appeared politic to some early Zionists to maintain a certain distance from the African racial groupings, in order to help make the case and to emphasize that the Jews and the Africans were racially separate and distinct groups and also to strengthen the counterclaim in favour of Jewish national strength and racial health or racial-cultural viability. In this framework some Jewish racialist thinkers argued for the salubriousness of Zionism since it would bring Jewish racial Semites in close territorial proximity with other racial Semites, namely the Arab Semites, and thus help effect a Jewish racial regeneration. These varieties of dubious racial discourse may have been persuasive within the framework of various popular racial discourses which were by and large accepted at the time. Alternately, by the very end of the nineteenth century and at the beginning of the twentieth, the chances for the broad success of African repatriation may have seemed bleak. Thus, to align the Jewish repatriation movement with another enterprise, whose prospects for success appeared to be remote at best, would have made little sense

A *Paradigm for Repatriation Projects*   203

to early Zionists solely from a pragmatic point of view. At the same time, the self-fashioning of Zionism as a repatriation movement was but one of many possible self-fashionings within Zionism, and among certain sectors or groupings within early Zionism other options for self-understanding, self-presentation, myth-making and propaganda may have appeared to be more promising.

Notes

1 I would like to thank my colleague, Yael-Ben Zvi, an expert in African-American studies and critical racial theory, for her assistance while I conducted my research for this chapter.

2 See Arnon Golan, 'European Imperialism and the Development of Modern Palestine: Was Zionism a Form of Colonialism?', *Space and Polity* 5 (2001): 127–43; Derek Penslar, 'Zionism, Colonialism and Postcolonialism', *Journal of Israeli History* 20 (2001): 84–98; Gideon Shimoni, 'Post-Colonial Theory and the History of Zionism', *Israel Affairs* 13 (2007): 859–71; Avi Bareli, 'Forgetting Europe: Perspectives on the Debate about Zionism and Colonialism', *Journal of Israeli History* 20 (2001): 99–120; Tuvia Friling, 'What Do Those Who Claim Zionism Is Colonialism Overlook?', in *Handbook of Israel II*, ed. Eliezer Ben-Rafael, Julius Schoeps, Yitzhak Sternberg, and Olaf Glöckner (Oldenbourg: De Gruyter, 2016), 847–72; Yitzhak Sternberg, 'The Colonialism/Colonization Perspective on Zionism/Israel', ibid., 823–47; cf. Ilan Pappé, 'Zionism as Colonialism: A Comparative View of Diluted Colonialism in Asia and Africa', *South Atlantic Quarterly* 107 (2008): 611–33. Pappé categorizes Zionism as 'unconventional colonialism' (ibid., 612).

3 See Lorenzo Veracini, *Settler Colonialism: A Theoretical Overview* (Basingstoke: Palgrave Macmillan, 2010); Lorenzo Veracini, 'Introducing: Settler Colonial Studies', *Settler Colonial Studies* 1 (2011): 1–12; Lorenzo Veracinie, 'Introduction: Settler Colonialism as a Distinct Mode of Domination', in *The Routledge Handbook of the History of Settler Colonialism*, ed. Edward Cavanaugh and Lorenzo Veracini (London and New York: Routledge, 2017), 1–8; David Lloyd, 'Settler Colonialism and the State of Exception: The Example of Palestine/Israel', *Settler Colonial Studies* 2 (2012): 59–80; Patricia Wolfe, 'Settler Colonialism and the Elimination of the Native', *Journal of Genocide Research* 8 (2006): 387–409; Omar Jabary Salamana et al., 'Past Is Present: Settler Colonialism in Palestine', *Settler Colonial Studies* 2 (2012): 387–409. See also Joseph Massad, 'The Ends of Zionism. Racism and the Palestinian Struggle', *Interventions. International Journal of Postcolonial Studies* 5 (2003): 440–8.

4 See *Making Settler Colonial Space: Perspectives on Race, Place and Identity*, ed. Tracy Banivanua Mar and Penelope Edmonds (Basingstoke: Palgrave Macmillan, 2010);

204   *Colonialism and the Jews in German History*

also, *The Routledge Handbook of the History of Settler Colonialism* presents a wide range of case studies, including South Africa, French Algeria, Liberia, southern Rhodesia, Ethiopia, Angola, Australia, New Zealand and others. The case of Palestine is represented in the *Routledge Handbook* by Gershon Shafir, 'Theorizing Zionist Settler Colonialism in Palestine', ibid., 339–52.

5 Theodor Herzl, *Altneuland* (Haifa: Haifa Publishing Company, 1962), 129. Unless noted otherwise, all translations are mine.

6 Ibid. The German original reads: 'Nicht nur die Weissen! Die Schwarzen auch. Es gibt eine ungelöste Frage des Völkerunglücks, die nur ein Jude in ihrer ganzen schmerzlichen Tiefe ermessen kann. Das ist die Negerfrage … Ich schäme mich nicht, es zu sagen … nachdem ich die Rückkehr der Juden erlebt habe, möchte ich auch noch die Rückkehr der Neger vorbereiten helfen.'

7 Ibid., 130. 'Alle Menschen sollen eine Heimat haben. Dann werden sie gegeneinander gütiger sein. Dann werden sich die Menschen besser lieben und verstehen.'

8 Ahad Ha-am's review, 'Altneuland', originally appeared in Hebrew in *Ha-Shiloah*. A German translation followed shortly thereafter in *Ost und West* 3 (1903): 227–44. Citations which follow are from the German translation. For more on Ahad Ha-am and the controversy in wake of his review of Herzl's *Altneuland*, see Steven J. Zipperstein, *Elusive Prophet. Ahad Ha'am and the Origins of Zionism* (Berkeley: University of California Press, 1993), 194–201.

9 Achad Ha-am, 'Altneuland', 243. 'We could certainly imagine a movement of the Africans, with the Zionist leader at its helm, who writes an "Altneuland," in which he envisions the realization of the African ideals twenty years from now – we just wonder how this African Altneuland would be different from the Zionist one.' The German version reads: 'Wir könnten uns also sehr wohl eine Negerbewegung ausmalen, mit dem Zionistenführer an der Spitze, der ein 'Altneuland' schreibt, um uns die Verkörperung des Negerideals nach 20 Jahren zu versinnlichen – wir fragen nun, wodurch würde sich das Neger-Altneuland vom zionistischen unterscheiden?' Interestingly, in the Hebrew original Ahad Ha-am utilizes the word ניגרים (nigarim) for Africans (for Blacks), instead of the biblical term for Africans and Blacks: כושים (kushim). See Ahad Ha-am, *Kol kitvei Ahad Ha-am* (Tel Aviv and Jerusalem: Dvir and Ivrit Publishing, 1956), 319–20.

10 Achad Ha-am, 'Altneuland', 241. 'Nirgends eine besondere jüdische Spur.'

11 Derek Penslar, *Theodor Herzl. The Charismatic Leader* (New Haven: Yale University Press, 2020), 139–40.

12 See Stefan Vogt, *Subalterne Positionierungen. Der deutsche Zionismus im Feld des Nationalismus in Deutschland 1890–1933* (Göttingen: Wallstein, 2016), 174–7. Vogt argues persuasively for and documents the compatibilities between German colonialism and German Zionism. Warburg was one of the editors of the Zionist magazine *Altneuland*, which appeared under the auspices of the Zionist

Commission for the Study of Palestine. He also propagated and embodied the scientific-technological impulse, which characterized both German colonial discourse and German Zionist activity. See Vogt, 177. Cf. Axel Stähler, 'Zionism, Colonialism, and the German Empire: Herzl's Gloves and Mbwapwa's Umbrella', in *Orientalism, Gender, and the Jews,* ed. Ulrike Brunotte, Anna-Dorothea Ludewig, and Axel Stähler (Berlin: De Gruyter, 2015), 98–123.

13 Penslar, *Theodor Herzl*, 138.

14 See Alex Bein, 'Memoirs and Documents about Herzl's Meeting with the Kaiser', *Herzl Year Book* 6 (1964/65): 39–60; David Vital, *Zionism: The Formative Years* (Oxford: Clarendon Press, 1982), 74–105.

15 Penslar, *Theodor Herzl*, 144.

16 For more on Wolffsohn and the Zionist leadership following the death of Herzl, see Adolf Böhm, *Die Zionistische Bewegung. II Teil* (Berlin: Welt-Verlag, 1921), 165–80; Walter Laqueur, *A History of Zionism* (New York: Schocken, 1976), 136–55; David Vital, *Zionism: The Formative Years*, 412–75.

17 James T. Campbell, *Middle Passages: African American Journeys to Africa, 1787–2005* (New York: Penguin Press, 2006), 20–95.

18 Ibid., 80.

19 Ibid., 76, 87.

20 Ibid., 71.

21 See *Martin R. Delany: A Documentary Reader*, ed. Robert S. Levine (Chapel Hill: University of North Carolina Press, 2003). See also Ifeoma Kiddoe Nwankwo, *Black Cosmopolitanism. Racial Consciousness and Transnational Identity in the Nineteenth Century Americas* (Philadelphia: University of Pennsylvania Press, 2005). In contrast to the caption of the illustration above, Delany spelled his name without an -ey.

22 Campbell, *Middle Passages*, 71.

23 Ibid., 72.

24 Ibid., 73. See Martin R. Delany, *The Condition, Elevation, Emigration, and Destiny of the Colored People of the United States and Official Report of the Niger Valley Exploring Party* (Amherst: Humanity Books, 2004).

25 Campbell, *Middle Passages*, 73.

26 Delany also contemplated temporary solutions for resettlement as a first stage towards the ultimate repatriation. A good option in this regard to his mind was Canada. See his discussion of 'The Canadas' in Delany, *The Condition*, 189–92.

27 Theodor Herzl, *Der Judenstaat*, 9th edn (Wien: R. Löwit, 1933), 13.

28 Ibid.

29 Ibid.

30 'Balfour Declaration', en.wikipedia.org/wiki/Balfour_Declaration (last accessed 26 August 2020).

31 Harriet Beecher Stowe, *Uncle Tom's Cabin or Life Among the Lowly* (Garden City: Doubleday, 1960), 498.

32 Campbell, *Middle Passages*, 95.

33 Delany, *The Condition*, 298.

34 Crane Brinton, *The Anatomy of Revolution* (New York: Vintage, 1965).

35 Campbell, *Middle Passages*, 71.

36 Ibid.

37 See the following: Edmund David Cronon, *Black Moses. The Story of Marcus Garvey and the Universal Negro Improvement Association* (Madison: University of Wisconsin Press, 1955); Wilson S. Moses, 'Marcus Garvey. A Reappraisal', *The Black Scholar* 4, no. 3 (1972): 38–49; David Levering Lewis, *W.E.B. Du Bois. Biography of a Race* (New York: Henry Holt, 1993); David Levering Lewis, *W.E.B. Du Bois. A Biography* (New York: Henry Holt, 2009).

38 See Vogt, *Subalterne Positionerungen*, 113–96; Mark H. Gelber, 'The Rhetoric of Race and Jewish-National Cultural Politics: From Birnbaum and Buber to Brieger's Rene Richter', in *Melancholy Pride. Nation, Race, and Gender in the German Literature of Cultural Zionism* (Tübingen: Niemeyer, 2000), 125–60.

39 Houston Stewart Chamberlain, *Die Grundlagen des Neunzehnten Jahrhunderts. Volksausgabe*, 9th edn (München: Verlagsanstalt F. Bruckmann, 1909).

40 Ibid.

41 See Sander Gilman, *The Jew's Body* (New York: Routledge, 1991), 174–6; Neil MacMaster, '"Black Jew – White Negro" Antisemitism and the Construction of Cross-Racial Stereotypes', *Nationalism and Ethnic Politics* 6, no. 4 (2000): 65–82; Abraham Melamed, *The Image of the Black in Jewish Culture. A History of the Other* (London: Routledge, 2003); Ran Ha-Cohen, 'The "Jewish Blackness" Thesis Revisited', *Religions* 9, no. 7 (2018), https://doi.org/10.3390/rel9070222 (accessed 3 September 2020). Even Herzl, who declined to understand the Jews primarily as a race, evidently subscribed partially to this view. For example, after he met the Anglo-Jewish author Israel Zangwill, he wrote in his diary on 22 November 1895 that Zangwill appeared to him to be the African ('Negroid') racial type: 'Israel Zangwill hat einen langnasigen Negertypus, sehr wollige tiefschwarze in der Mitte gescheitelte Haare.' ('Israel Zangwill is of a long-nosed Negroid type, he has very wooly and deep black hair which is parted in the middle.') See Theodor Herzl, *Zionistisches Tagebuch 1895–1899* (Berlin: Propyläen Verlag, 1983), 281.

Part III

The postcolonial era

10

The predicaments of non-nationalist nationalism

The case of Hans Kohn, Robert Weltsch and Hannah Arendt

Christian Wiese

In an article written on the occasion of the seventieth birthday of the Zionist politician, publicist and historian Robert Weltsch on 20 June 1961,[1] the well-known doyen of academic historiography on nationalism, Hans Kohn,[2] reminisced about their lifelong friendship since their youth as members of the student association Bar Kochba in Prague, recalling the intellectual influences that had once formed the basis of their shared views on the ideological and political implications of Jewish nationalism in Europe and Palestine before the Second World War and the Shoah. He pointed out that, despite a certain difference of temperament, their relationship had always been characterized by an agreement on the most fundamental questions. 'If my memory does not deceive me', he continued, 'we have never been separated by fundamentally opposed opinions.'[3] He then praised Weltsch's 'realistic assessment of the Palestinian situation', his consistent rejection of any form of Jewish chauvinism and his awareness that the Zionist project could only be carried out within the context of an increasingly self-conscious Arab world.[4] In a concluding passage, Kohn quoted a passage from an article Weltsch had published in 1935 in the Zionist journal *Jüdische Rundschau*, characterizing it as a true expression of his friend's moral and humane political attitude:

> If we didn't voluntarily – and not because we are forced to do so – include the rights of the Arabs in our concept of Palestine . . . we would have forfeited the right to raise our voice on behalf of the Jews in the Diaspora at a time of affliction. Nothing else seems more reprehensible to us than a politics characterized by

210   *Colonialism and the Jews in German History*

double standards. . . . This is the one and only hope that we have and from which all of us draw our strength, . . . that we will not subsequently prove those right who consider Jewish ethics just as an expedient, born out of the situation of a weak minority, whilst – under different external circumstances, the pagan will to power is prevailing also among us. In this case, according to our view, Zionism would lose its soul.[5]

Interestingly enough, Kohn's tribute to Weltsch does not even allude to any disagreement between them, conveying instead the image of unrestricted proximity and harmony. Whether, due to the occasion, Kohn deliberately decided to emphasize the common ground rather than pointing to differing biographical experiences and ideological decisions in the past, or whether he did, in fact, attach more weight to their fundamental consensus than to occasional differences, is not entirely clear. In this regard, it is illuminating to look at a text Weltsch wrote on the occasion of Kohn's seventieth birthday that same year. In his reflections on his friend's 'winding path' from Prague to New York, Weltsch seems to echo Kohn's perception when accentuating their shared experiences, values and ideological turns since their early student years in Prague.[6] Full of admiration, Weltsch characterized Kohn's sober approach to the political realities in Palestine, his unusually clear awareness of the circumstances in the changing Arabic world in the 1920s and 1930s which prompted him to take a stance that was considered 'an outright heresy' by the Zionist majority. He then gave a very empathetic interpretation of his friend's subsequent dissociation from Zionism and Palestine:

With inner agitation he saw the advent of the disaster of an imminent clash. When the development he feared eventually came true, Hans Kohn came to the conclusion that he was unable to continue going along this path. To him, political striving for power that led to violence appeared as the opposite of what we had once, during the era of liberalism, understood as Jewish nationalism. Hans Kohn was defeated in his fight for the only kind of Zionism that seemed acceptable to him, and he drew the consequences.[7]

Weltsch emphasized that decades later many in the Zionist camp who had used to think differently had come to appreciate Kohn's vision that Israel had 'to become a loyal part of the Middle Eastern world'.[8] Nevertheless, in a eulogy he published ten years later, after Kohn's death in 1971, he expressed at least a slight hint of implicit criticism: 'Hans Kohn may sometimes have been mistaken, but he was always seeking for truth. . . . He was a non-conformist and an independent thinker who drew from his – at times bitter – insights the conclusions he considered to be correct without allowing personal or materialistic considerations to influence him.'[9]

What is interesting here is that Weltsch, despite his great respect for his friend's intellectual and moral integrity, seemed to remember a time in which they were, indeed, separated by differing views as well as by diverging political assessments and personal choices. Even though Weltsch did not specify which errors he was actually referring to, it would seem plausible to interpret this passage as an allusion to an important episode in their friendship around 1929/30: their dissent during and in the wake of Kohn's decision to leave Zionism – and Palestine – behind, thus profoundly questioning what had been the very basis of their joint conviction, shared over decades, that a Jewish nationalism guided by ethical standards rather than considerations of power was, indeed, possible, that is, a Zionist project whose main aspiration was the spiritual and humanist revival of Judaism both in the Diaspora and in Palestine, a project based on respect for the rights of the Arab population and the vision of a peaceful coexistence in the Middle East.

In the many-voiced reflections of contemporary research into the origins, nature and moral character of nationalism, the insight into its essentially contradictory nature is almost ubiquitous. Historically, Tom Nairn argues, nationalism – 'the modern Janus' – assumed the shape of a 'morally and politically positive force in modern history', particularly where it was the expression of weaker nations liberating themselves from foreign oppression;[10] but it is 'contradictory in its very nature', since it is morally and politically susceptible to aggressive tendencies.[11] One of the central aspects of the theoretical discourse on nationalism is an ethical reflection on how to overcome or limit its darker side and how to strengthen its liberal and liberating elements.[12] Hans Kohn, Robert Weltsch and Hannah Arendt were representatives of what has been termed a 'non-nationalist nationalism',[13] that is, a form of Jewish nationalism that was particularly aware of the destructive implications of European nationalism in the age of imperialism and that envisioned Zionism as a potentially liberating counter-force against any chauvinistic motifs. The problem of the potential links between this variant of Jewish nationalism and (anti-)colonialism, however, is a complicated one; the same applies to the historically contested questions regarding the colonial character of the Zionist settlement in Palestine and the establishment of the State of Israel that have been raised by critics of Zionism in the Arab and Muslim world as well as by historians who contributed to the post-Zionist debates in recent decades.[14] It is not the latter question that this chapter is devoted to. Rather, it asks whether Kohn's, Weltsch's and Arendt's

212   *Colonialism and the Jews in German History*

critique of political Zionism's nationalist policies in the 1930s and 1940s and their characteristic rejection of the concept of Jewish national sovereignty was in any way informed by insights into the impact of colonialism on the colonized nations in the Middle East and to what extent anti-colonial attitudes played a role in their assessment of the political situation in Palestine.

I.

As is well known, the origins of Weltsch's and Kohn's friendship lay in the Prague Zionist student association *Bar Kochba* that included a number of other prominent intellectuals such as Hugo Bergmann, Max Brod, Felix Weltsch and Franz Kafka.[15] Before the First World War, this circle immersed itself in the study of Hebrew, the Bible and Jewish literature, at the same time absorbing a wealth of other influences – irrationalism, Herder and Fichte, neo-romanticism, Henri Bergson's philosophy of life, Nietzsche, Gustav Landauer's socialist social theory and Ahad Ha'am's plea for *tehiyat ha-levavot*, that is, the revival of the heart, the inner detachment from *galut* even before any external political liberation of the Jewish people. However, it was the young Martin Buber who made the strongest impression on the circle with his *Drei Reden über das Judentum*, delivered in Prague between 1909 and 1911. In these lectures, Buber addressed the emaciation of Jewish identity in exile and advocated a fundamental cultural revival of the spiritual and ethical values of the Jewish people, which alone could, he believed, provide the basis for a living Jewish nationality.

The First World War and the experience as soldiers of the Austrian army in eastern Europe marked a crucial caesura with far-reaching consequences for both Weltsch's and Kohn's political thought in the 1920s and 1930s.[16] In his correspondence with friends since 1917/18, Weltsch expressed optimism that, after the violent culmination of European imperialistic politics, democracy and the self-determination of the nations would become an irresistible force in international politics, and that, after the Balfour Declaration in 1917, Theodor Herzl's vision of *Altneuland* had become an imminent opportunity. What occupied him most, however, and what became a recurring theme in his writings and political activism after the war was the question how the Zionist movement could avoid developing into the kind of chauvinistic nationalism that had been responsible for the brutality of an unprecedented war in Europe. When he took over the responsibility as editor-in-chief of the *Jüdische Rundschau* in Berlin in 1919, Weltsch entered the very centre of the Zionist movement in

Germany. From that point onwards, for a period of almost twenty years, he was confronted with the challenge of implementing the convictions formulated in pre-war Prague within the complex reality of Zionist politics in Europe and in Palestine. During that period, he became a close ally of those within German cultural Zionism, including his friend Hans Kohn, who struggled to strike a balance between what they saw as legitimate Jewish interests in Palestine and the endeavour to make Zionism a creative, non-nationalist movement and to do justice to the fundamental principles of peace and mutual respect between different nations.[17]

Kohn's intellectual and political path that underwent different – and sometimes dramatic and contradictory – metamorphoses, from an enthusiastic follower of Buber's ideas to a dissenting Zionist in Jerusalem and later a scholar of nationalism and ideologue of the Cold War in the United States after the Second World War,[18] was even more strongly shaped by the experience of the Great War. After a brief episode as an officer in the Austrian army, he had spent several years in Russian captivity from which he returned only in 1920. His political development during those crucial years in Samarkand, Turkmenistan and later in Novosibirsk and Krasnojarsk is documented particularly in his correspondence with Robert Weltsch and Martin Buber between 1915 and 1920. What can be noted in those letters are the strongly universalistic and ethical overtones that eventually became central to his Zionist convictions. He criticized the narrow national perspective dominating political Zionism and suggested the Zionist movement should become aware that Jewish nationalism was not only aiming at a liberation of the Jewish people but also had general implications for the intellectual and social problems of a humankind stricken by chauvinism and brutality.

There were mainly four elements that became central to his thought during the years of his captivity. First of all, in Samarkand, as he recalls in his autobiography, he encountered the dehumanizing effects of colonialism – 'the clash of two different civilizations, a relationship not of rival peers but of master and subject'.[19] Second, at a time when British politics in the Middle East made the creation of a Jewish homeland by the Zionist movement suddenly appear as a realistic goal, Kohn underwent an 'anarchistic phase', reading Bakunin and Kropotkin and developing, as he wrote to Weltsch in 1919, a fierce aversion to the idea of national sovereignty. He had become 'an anarchist, particularly an absolute opponent of the state' – a self-understanding he developed further after the war and that made him a fierce critic of the very concept of a Jewish national state.[20] Third, this attitude was complemented by a turn to socialist ideas, which he tried to combine with his notion of Prophetic Judaism, and which caused his temporary sympathy for the Soviet Union. The fourth and most important element, however, was his pacifist turn. 'Since World War I', Kohn remembered in his autobiography, 'I was wary of power, bureaucracy, and saber-rattling. I hated the excesses of national pride and self-righteousness, and I dreaded the hardening, inhuman nature of the war.'[21] After his return from Russia, therefore, he became involved with the organization *War Resisters International* in London and served as the latter's representative in Palestine.

During the early 1920s, Kohn was, like Weltsch and Hugo Bergmann, profoundly inspired by Martin Buber's warnings against the dangers of national ideology to which, in his eyes, Zionism had also fallen prey, and by his call to embrace a 'true nationalism', a 'Hebrew humanism' that would turn away with disgust from the methods of European power politics and satisfy the expectations of a 'supra-national ethical requirement'.[22] In an essay entitled 'Zur Araberfrage', Kohn severely criticized Zionism's lack of awareness of the actual situation in Palestine, underscored the historical rights of the Arab population and demanded that the Jews of the *yishuv* must familiarize themselves with Arabic language and culture, and refrain from setting themselves up, in relation to the Arabs, 'as the ruling nation, as the people of the state':

> Let us not be beguiled by nationalist chauvinism; let us not become, after having been the slaves of yesteryear, the imperialists of tomorrow. Jewish nationalism was always a moral nationalism; duties and not rights: responsibility to humanity. Let us remain serious and clear, and true to ourselves! Let us guard against any fetishism, let us guard ourselves above all against the fetishism of the national master race![23]

In 1925, Kohn became the secretary of the newly founded association *Brith Shalom*. Dominated by German cultural Zionists, this group of intellectuals advocated a binational Arab-Jewish society shaped by the distinctiveness of two culturally autonomous nationalities, with political rule being shared equally under the supervision of the international community.[24] The fundamental orientation was a pacifist one: The Jews should enter Palestine not as invaders, nor should they aim to rapidly form the majority of the population, but should settle the land cautiously, in a peaceable manner, and win the Arab population over through cultivating work and the joint development of a socialist society. According to the members of *Brith Shalom*, it was Zionism's task to build a morally legitimized community in Palestine, not a state like any other that served only the interests of power. It was Kohn who formulated the political

The Predicaments of Non-Nationalist Nationalism   215

goals of the association, based on elements of Swiss federalism and the minority policies of the Habsburg monarchy, and who drafted a bold vision of the future development of Palestine:

> Historically and geographically, Palestine is a land of peace. . . . This should also find expression in its outward position; it should become a neutral country under the protection of the League of Nations, a site of national and international peace, which through history and location should, in the near future, also become the seat of the League of Nations. . . . A Palestine that is peaceful and prosperous in its internal life, and autonomous in its cultural diversity, that also outwardly always guards and spreads peace, neutrally, inviolably and unarmed, can be the first great deed of the League of Nations on its arduous path to its true form and task.[25]

Kohn's pacifist, cosmopolitan ideals and his ethical interpretation of Zionism also shaped much of his historical analysis of the phenomenon of nationalism itself, including nationalistic movements emerging in eastern Europe, Asia and among Islamic nations in the postcolonial world he envisioned in the wake of the Great War. However, Kohn's vision was a minority position within the Zionist movement whose persuasive power was inevitably small in the face of the conflicts of interest in Palestine. The profound crisis that the year 1929 meant for the members of *Brith Shalom* in general and for Kohn in particular becomes apparent in the latter's radicalization during this period and in his decision to leave Zionism and Palestine behind. Already at the beginning of this fateful year, the first differences between Weltsch and Kohn began to crystallize. Kohn voiced fears that *Brith Shalom* might inadvertently contribute to concealing the truth about the situation in Palestine, since the organization pretended that it actually represented Zionism, whereas in reality, he indicated, Zionism was ever more clearly emerging as a form of colonialism – as the long arm of European imperialism. What was needed in order to do justice to the political realities in Palestine and the Middle East, he suggested, was a determined return to the ideals of their youth, even though he was now deeply sceptical about their practical prospects:

> But that is Buber-Zion.[ism]. If anyone thinks this is Zionism, that is just a lie, and I am implicated there too. . . . No-one wants to take this one path, I mean no-one apart from you, Hugo [Bergmann], me, [Ernst] Simon; a small handful! And [Kurt] Blumenfeld probably does not think much of Buber and A.[had] Ha.[am]. My God, into what company did we unwittingly fall in 1910 and 1919? Is that the company we keep?![26]

Since, at this point, Kohn regarded 'Buber-Zionism' ultimately as a lofty literary ideal that was practically doomed to failure, he turned against Weltsch's hope that *Brith Shalom* and the peace-oriented forces in Palestine might be strengthened should they succeed in convincing Buber to accept an offer by the Hebrew University and to move to Jerusalem. He pointed out that he would actually regret Buber's settling in Palestine, not only because it was his 'fate', as it were, 'to realize himself as a German' but because he, Kohn, was firmly convinced that one could be 'a much better Jew – and it is only thus that the word Zionist has any meaning: a person who desires the renewal of Judaism – in Frankfurt than in Eretz Israel'. In Palestine, the philosopher, whose influence in the Zionist movement had, he felt, become very small, could only lose: 'Here, he would be silenced, or soon be regarded as a fool.'[27]

Kohn's remarks resulted from a process of self-reflection which in 1929/30 prompted him to detach himself from Zionism, including *Brith Shalom*. His feeling that Buber should not settle in Palestine can be understood as symbolically expressing a growing conviction that the struggle to shape Zionist policy in the sense of the philosopher's teachings had failed. The letters of 1929 often express a despairing sense that most Zionists were now striving for a 'Jewish state': even the moderate Zionists such as Weltsch wanted 'to take from the Arabs as much as possible, without any limits other than those set by bitter Arab resistance'. In this way, he maintained, they were heading for violence; in the long term they were making any peace impossible, indeed they were provoking a war in which 'the Arabs would be in the right'.[28] In Kohn's view, the only route to peace lay in a programmatic renunciation of efforts towards achieving a Jewish majority and, connected to this, an agreement with the Arabs regarding a protected minority status for the Jews in Palestine.

Kohn's uncompromising ethical interpretation of Jewish nationalism and his disillusionment with the moral potential of the Zionist movement during his eight-year stay in Palestine cannot be isolated from his historical work on imperialism, colonialism and the awakening nationalism of the colonized nations in the Middle East and the Far East. As Zohar Maor has pointed out, Kohn's sharp critique of colonialism and his ideological struggles with Zionism are indissolubly linked. His increasingly critical perspectives on Zionism made him sensitive to the fateful impact of the post-First World War colonial order on the unique route of the east towards national identity. He anticipates several perspectives of later postcolonial theory – particularly in his complex dialectical interpretation of the process in which the colonized nations of the east internalized and appropriated western nationalism as a means of decolonization.[29] Kohn's

The Predicaments of Non-Nationalist Nationalism 217

critique of what he perceived as the colonial nature of Zionist politics under the British Mandate and his partial justification of Arab violence as an expression of legitimate anti-colonial resistance since 1929 seem to be a result of the profound anti-colonialism that distinguished him from the majority of his co-Zionists, including most of his friends in *Brith Shalom*.[30]

Since Kohn felt he could not deceive himself any longer, he decided in 1930 to withdraw from both *Brith Shalom* and all Zionist activity. He explained to Berthold Feiwel, one of the leaders of the *Keren Hayesod*, that in his opinion Zionism had failed as a 'moral spiritual movement' based on pacifism, liberalism and humanism, the ideals of *Bar Kochba*, succumbing instead to colonial tendencies. Zionism, he argued, had not used the crisis triggered by the violence of 1929 as an opportunity for reorientation but had retreated into lies and violence. Certainly, the Arabs had committed all manner of barbaric acts 'that are typical of a colonial uprising', but the Jews had, he insisted, not recognized the deeper causes: 'We have been in Palestine for twelve years without having once made a serious effort to obtain the agreement of the people, to negotiate with the people that live in the country.'[31] It was indeed possible that with the aid of the British 'and later with the aid of our own bayonets' the Jews would remain in and spread throughout Palestine, even in the absence of peace with the Arabs. But then, he observed,

> We shall never be able to do without the bayonet. The means will have determined the ends. Jewish Palestine will have nothing of that Zion which I supported. . . . If we do not achieve peace with the Arabs in the near future, if we do not make every effort towards this goal with wholehearted truthfulness and sincerity, then it is better for us to admit that through our culpability, Zionism cannot be realized in the only sense in which it deserves to be realized. Otherwise, we shall have to continue, over many years, to develop our Zionist settlement work on the basis of our ability to defend ourselves, internal militarisation, and outwardly directed inflammatory rhetoric.[32]

Kohn's stance represented a challenge to Buber and to his friends of *Brith Shalom*. Hugo Bergmann, for instance, reacted touchily. He took special exception to Kohn's questioning not only of Zionist reality on Palestine but also of the original intentions of Bar Kochba. It was, he protested, not the Zionist idea itself but its falsification by radical forces that was responsible for the current crisis. Kohn responded that before the war, they had all 'made up [their] own Zion.[ism] to suit themselves', that they had all been blind to the 'true face of Zion.[ism]'. There had not, Kohn indicated, been any intentional falsification

218   *Colonialism and the Jews in German History*

here, a bloody conflict with the Arabs rather emerging from the movement's 'historical dialectic'. The failure to recognize this, he argued, was the 'fault' of Bar Kochba. Although Weltsch, Kohn asserted, was aware of this, he was avoiding this dilemma 'like the plague', whereas Bergmann was too embroiled in equating Judaism and the Jewish people with Zionism – a consequence of the 'blinkered view of 1910'.[33]

II.

Weltsch too fell into conflict with Kohn. In numerous letters, he expressed his own deep-seated doubts regarding developments in Palestine, stressing how closely his feelings matched those of his friend; but he also offered reasons why, despite everything, he wished to hold fast to Zionism and did not want to abandon his hopes. On the one hand, he was convinced that Jewish nationalism would be, as he put it, 'the most dreadful in the world', 'as everything is most dreadful with this people; the Jewish state, if there were one, would be completely unbearable'. On the other hand, there were also counter-forces, and one had to fight 'against all the stifling atmosphere that holds sway there'.[34] 'I often feel,' he wrote in October 1929, 'that our struggle has been lost once and for all, and that we must disappear. The struggle that we have been engaged in since 1910, and particularly in the last 10 years – it seems that it has been in vain.' But Weltsch then proceeded to cast doubt on such feelings: what was at play was not simply a matter of basic conviction but also of 'what actually happens'; in history there were forces 'that often act invisibly and underground, and perhaps do more than much superficial activity, so perhaps they are not entirely lost'.

Even if everything seemed appalling, Weltsch wrote – quite in the spirit of Buber – one could not simply regard oneself as 'superior', thus refusing to use one's personal influence in the struggle with political Zionism.[35] In January 1930, he even admitted to Kohn 'that we actually stand outside Zionism', which, it seemed, had to be based on power and violence, as was the rest of the world. However, Weltsch did not want to abandon a cautious confidence that with time, the peace-oriented strand of Zionism would prevail.[36] In his view, Kohn's letters were sometimes 'quite hysterical', evidently on account of a lack of distance.[37] Kohn countered Weltsch's charges of 'doctrinarism' and unpolitical rigorism[38] with his own accusation of self-deception. As Kohn saw things, Weltsch underestimated the dimensions of Arab displacement;[39] beyond that he did not understand that the Zionists simply did not want peace. Just as the Arabs wanted to destroy the Zionists because they feared them, the Zionists wanted to destroy the Arabs because they stood in the way of the 'Jewish state'.[40] No one could keep Zionism from striving for power and a Jewish majority, as such a process was necessarily embedded in the nature of national movements. 'When we were young and immature, we allowed ourselves to be ensnared by something whose true nature we had not seen through. Now we are still mired in it.'[41] Although Kohn always made it clear that he respected Weltsch's position, he also tried to convince him 'to leave Zionism' and seek another sphere of political activity.[42]

Kohn had become ever more convinced that there was no longer any place for him in Palestine. Whoever stayed there as a Zionist, he indicated, even if he struggled against injustice, would share responsibility for what was going to happen: the 'creation of eternal discord . . . of a Levantine Balkan [state]', always 'armed to the teeth' and a 'seed-bed of nationalism that was exaggerated because . . . it felt weak'.[43] In some letters he expressed at least understanding for the motives of those who, having escaped their pariah status, antisemitism, pogroms and subjugation in eastern Europe, joined the revisionist camp of the Zionist movement: their wish 'to be rulers themselves' resulted from a search for liberty and dignity; but unfortunately, Kohn pointed out, they had come to a land in which 'the Arabs were already there'. On moral grounds, establishing an autonomous Jewish entity somewhere in Europe or elsewhere in the world, as suggested, for instance, by Simon Dubnow, or by the so-called ideology of 'territorialism', was the only sensible alternative.[44]

This was, in fact, the abandonment of the dream of a Jewish state, meaning withdrawal into the Diaspora, continued exile. Despite his shared criticism of the situation in Palestine, Weltsch saw things differently. He attempted to explain his perspective in a letter dated 14 August 1930. Over the course of decades, he argued, Arab-Jewish relations would not be as troubled and violent as Kohn assumed; the Arabs would soon catch up with the Jews culturally and economically. Beyond that, burning all bridges with the Zionists as a result of criticism of nationalism was to be avoided: doing so would be the same as condemning oneself to ineffectuality. Weltsch thus saw no betrayal of his ideals at work in his moderating position:

> But if I were to stand up today and speak to the people in the style of your letters, then I would be finished from the first minute, and opponents would find it very easy to conclude that their path is the one that must be followed. Just how all this will develop, I do not know; for what is to become of this *furor judaicus* now raging, and how it will be quelled, we cannot imagine at all. But I am after

220   *Colonialism and the Jews in German History*

all caught up in it, and I must take the consequences and battle it out; fate has seen to it that I am already too entangled in the whole business [of Zionism] to simply abandon it.[45]

After the September 1930 elections, Weltsch also referred to his responsibility for the German Jews: in a Germany that would soon be Nazi, he indicated, they could 'no longer be certain of their lives'[46] – a perspective he felt Kohn, from the distance of his life in Palestine, took too little into account:

> What is to happen to the Jews? It is entirely possible that the *German Jews* will shortly be forced to emigrate, of course only partially; every single one of them is in for it; what is going to happen here? In response to this question, we cannot comfort ourselves with the answer that *nothing at all* can happen (the answer that you are always ready to give). Naturally it is the easiest thing to assume this; but if one's own people, in closest proximity, have to starve or are expelled (it has not yet come to that, but it could, and it is in this 'could' that the terrible spectre lies!), one cannot be satisfied with this.[47]

III.

The dilemma Robert Weltsch faced as a dissenting Zionist who continued to advocate a very cautious process of immigration to Palestine and, at the same time, was painfully aware of the Nazi threat to Jewish life in Europe is reflected in his correspondence with Hans Kohn from the years 1933 to 1938. As can only be indicated here, the letters convey an impression of Weltsch's sense of despair given the situation in Europe and the worsening conflict in Palestine.[48] In September 1938, a few weeks before the pogrom, Weltsch was eventually permitted, as a Czech citizen, to leave Germany. Shortly before his departure, on 30 August 1938, he wrote to Kohn: 'Yes, Palestine! In fact, I have only one thought in my mind, how to get away from it again!'[49] He nevertheless remained in Palestine until the end of the war. His letters from that period reveal his disappointment about the deepening rifts between Arabs and Jews, the ever-present violence, about the political events that made the concept of a binational state obsolete and about the Biltmore program in 1942 – the first official proclamation of the Zionist movement's goal to establish a Jewish state in Palestine. For Weltsch, the partition decision by the UN in November 1947 by no means meant jubilation. He feared that the proclamation of a Jewish state would lead to a war which the Jews would either lose or – in the event of victory – would use 'to really drive the

The Predicaments of Non-Nationalist Nationalism 221

Arabs out, just as the Czechs [did] with the Sudeten Germans'.[50] 'It can only end badly', he wrote on 20 May 1948 and predicted an endless war in which the very nature of Zionism as a humanist version of nationalism was in peril.[51]

Weltsch's perception of the events in the Middle East made him a close ally of Hannah Arendt's post-war writings on Zionism in the 1940s. This is shown in his unpublished correspondence with her after the war. Arendt had originally adopted a Zionist perspective under the impression of Nazi policy, and the influence of the Zionist activist and theorist Kurt Blumenfeld had prompted her to promote youth immigration to Palestine while she was living in France as a refugee in the 1930s. What had first attracted her to Zionism was the readiness of the Zionists to take political responsibility for their own fate and actions rather than succumbing to powerless passivity in view of discriminatory practices and the emergence of a powerful antisemitic ideology in the Diaspora since the late nineteenth century. During the early years of the Second World War, Arendt had enthusiastically embraced and promoted the idea of a Jewish army – not only to defend Palestine but also to fight Hitler everywhere in Europe and thereby to guarantee Jewish survival and restore Jewish dignity and honour.[52] However, she embraced Jewish nationalism only rather reluctantly and, interestingly enough, never articulated the view that the creation of such an army implied the goal of Jewish political sovereignty in Palestine.

Only a few years after her urgent call for a Jewish army, Arendt became an outspoken critic of Zionism and fiercely rejected the idea that Jewish freedom from persecution depended on the creation of a Jewish state, most prominently in her article 'Zionism Reconsidered', a polemical essay she published in 1944 in the American journal *Menorah*. Even though she praised the Zionist movement for overcoming 'the mentality of enslaved peoples, the belief that it does not pay to fight back, that one must dodge and escape in order to survive',[53] she accused it of having embraced a politics of the wrong kind. It was disturbing, she argued, that the Zionists would entrust the future of the Zionist project to a model of chauvinistic nationalism and imperial power – the 'rude force of the nation'[54] – at the very moment when imperialism had revealed its horrifyingly brutal potential during the Second World War. As Jews had been the victims of the nation state system in Europe, it was their particular responsibility to reject political aims they knew to be unjust and find a morally more adequate alternative to a Jewish state.[55]

Arendt's article expressed a sharp critique of the main assumptions of Herzl's political Zionism, particularly his conception of the *Judenstaat* as *the* answer to antisemitism and, most importantly, his fixation on an alliance with imperialism instead of with oppressed and discriminated groups and peoples. A recurring *leitmotif* of her argument was that the Zionists – as members of a national movement – 'could think only in national terms, seemingly unaware of the fact that imperialism was a nation-destroying force, and therefore, for a small people, it was near-suicide to attempt to become its ally or its agent'.[56] Instead of seriously attempting to 'integrate the Jewish people into the pattern of Asiatic politics', that is, seeking 'an alliance with the national revolutionary peoples of Asia and participation in their struggle against imperialism',[57] political Zionism, she warned, had engaged in the dangerous game of achieving its goals under the protection of the imperial powers:

> The erection of a Jewish state within an imperial sphere of interest may look like a very nice solution to some Zionists, though to others as something desperate but unavoidable. In the long run, there is hardly any course imaginable that would be more dangerous, more in the style of an adventure. It is, indeed, very bad luck for a small people to be placed without any fault of its own in the territory of a 'sphere of interest', though one can hardly see where else it could be placed in the economically and politically shrunken world of today. But only folly could dictate a policy which trusts a distant imperial power for protection, while alienating the goodwill of neighbors. What then, one is prompted to ask, will be the future policy of Zionism with respect to big powers, and what program have Zionists to offer for a solution of the Arab-Jewish conflict?[58]

Anticipating views later expressed in *The Origins of Totalitarianism*, she thus warned against the blindness of the Jewish leadership, who had surrendered to European colonial discourse and interests, rather than challenging them. Reliance on imperialist power, to her, seemed as an adoption of the same principles that enabled the political influence and victory of modern antisemitism. Her critique of nationalism, including Zionism, was rooted in the historical experience of the 1930s and 1940s – an experience that inspired in her a sense of obligation to oppose discrimination, persecution, human rights violations, deportations and genocide on a universal level rather than focusing on the Jewish people alone.

One of the most challenging elements of Arendt's essays on Zionism from the 1940s lies in the conviction that the relationship with the Arab population in Palestine and the Arab nations in the Near East constituted the main political and moral issue of contemporary Zionist politics. Similar to Kohn and Weltsch, she struggled with the fundamental predicament they had faced since the 1930s at the latest: how to preserve the moral character of Jewish nationalism in a situation in which the survival of millions of Jews in Europe was at stake while a tragic conflict between Jewish immigrants and the Arab population was unfolding in Palestine. Arendt's post-war essays on Zionism are dominated by powerful statements of the dangers which would threaten a potential Jewish state if it came into being without the consent of Palestine's Arab population. The inalterable reality was that the Arabs were the Jews' neighbours and that the Jews had to come to an agreement with them, at least if they did not want to choose living under the protection of one of the great imperial powers and thus ironically become little more than a bastion of imperial interests in a region that was supposed to liberate itself from colonialism. On the other hand, Arendt criticized that Arab policies equally ignored the needs of the Jewish settlements in Palestine. She believed that cooperation between Jews and Arabs in the Near East could form the basis for true sovereignty and independence, but the only way for this to occur was if both sides gave up their nationalistic ambitions and explored alternative models of coexistence, for instance in a political federation in the Middle East or the Mediterranean region.

When the War of Independence broke out in 1948, Arendt feared that the hopes of the Jewish survivors from the Shoah would be extinguished in another historical tragedy. But even if the Jews were to win the war, she predicted, a long period of military insecurity would make military self-defence the eternal priority of the Jewish state and cause nationalistic aggressiveness. The Jewish state, she asserted, would not solve the 'Jewish problem', its tragic result being that antisemitism would in the long run be transformed into anti-Zionism and that the Jewish people, the pariah people, would have created nothing else than a 'pariah-state' that would be constantly threatened by and involved in bloody conflicts. Arendt's views were clearly the product of a time and context quite different from our own, and neither a simplistic condemnation nor an undifferentiated anti-Zionist appropriation of her ideas would do justice to her intentions. Whatever the perspective on her views might be, the least one can argue is that Arendt's insistence on the political centrality and relevance of the moral aspect of the relationship to the Palestinian people belongs to a legacy that cannot be easily ignored.

Weltsch fully agreed with Arendt's 1948 essay 'To Save the Jewish Homeland'. In this article, she deplored the destructive violence that had recently erupted between Jews and Arabs and particularly the change of political perceptions within the Jewish public – in America as well as in Palestine – with regard to militaristic attitudes and the affirmation of a Jewish state instead of earlier visions of a Jewish homeland based on peaceful coexistence with the Arab majority. She strongly criticized the 'growing unanimity of opinion' among Jews that the moment had now come 'to get everything or nothing', that Arab and Jewish claims were irreconcilable and only a military victory could settle the issue.[59] This unanimity, according to Arendt, signified a tragic response to the catastrophe of European Jewry, based on the 'cynical and deep-rooted conviction that all gentiles are antisemitic, and everybody and everything is against the Jews' – an unalterable, eternal fact of Jewish history that required ruthless decisions in the fight for a Jewish state. 'Obviously', she continued, 'this attitude is plain racist chauvinism and it is equally obvious that this division between Jews and all other peoples – who are to be classed as enemies – does not differ from other master-race theories.'[60] One of the tragic elements Arendt diagnosed in her essay was the loss of relevance of those non-nationalist dissenting voices that had opposed the establishment of a Jewish state at the expense of the Arab population since the 1920s and that had insisted that 'the only permanent reality in the whole constellation was the presence of Arabs in Palestine, a reality no decision could alter – except perhaps the decision of a totalitarian state, implemented by its particular brand of ruthless force.'[61] The price for this, Arendt argued, would be a final tragedy, the loss of the hope of the Jewish people for a Jewish homeland, either through a military defeat, a catastrophe 'almost beyond imagining' that could even become the 'beginning of the self-dissolution of the Jewish people',[62] or through a military victory that would destroy the unique opportunities and achievements of Zionism in Palestine. 'The land that would come into being would be something quite other than the dream of world Jewry, Zionist and non-Zionist. The "victorious" Jews would live surrounded by an entirely hostile Arab population, secluded inside ever-threatened borders, absorbed with physical self-defense to a degree that would submerge all other interests and activities.'[63] The alternative to these two dark scenarios, Arendt suggested in early 1948, was the deliberate renunciation of the dream of sovereignty, even in the guise of a small Jewish state resulting from the partition of Palestine, and a compromise based on mutual concessions. While the ideal solution of a Middle Eastern federation no longer appeared realistic to her, she advocated – at least temporarily – a United Nation trusteeship backed by the United States and Great Britain and a model of Jewish-Arab coexistence based on a very limited Jewish immigration to Palestine, and she concluded: 'It is not too late.'[64]

From Weltsch's point of view, however, it was already too late. On 1 June 1948, two weeks after the establishment of the State of Israel, he wrote a letter to Arendt, thanking her for her 'brave and prudent article' and emphasizing that this was the first really accurate analysis of the current political situation he had encountered. He underlined that he himself had, since 1940, warned against the spreading suicidal 'ideology of Massada' and diagnosed the existence of a 'horrible mystical notion burdening the Jewish people with the responsibility for its heroic downfall – an inversion of the Christian notion that burdened the Jewish people with the metaphysical responsibility for the death of Jesus'. While he shared Arendt's gloomy portrayal of the developments in Palestine, he was much less optimistic that her model was realistic. After the acknowledgement of the Jewish state by the main world powers, he argued, her vision was obsolete: the entire future of the Jewish homeland had tumbled 'into the wild sea of irrationalism', and prudent, realistic arguments would simply no longer be heard. 'This is the hard and terrible truth' that, Weltsch argued, was partly the fault of the Jews and partly that of 'thoughtless "friends" who have driven the unfortunate Jewish people into this rage instead of forcing it to adopt a more sober attitude'.[65] Arendt responded to his 'warm and sad letter' by acknowledging his diagnosis but urging him not to yield to despair: 'I have made it a rule never to give anything up for lost in politics as long as it is not really lost and not to believe in my own prophecies. Whatever I can do (nebbich) I will do as long as it can be done; but then I am also strongly determined not to hang myself if things go terribly wrong'.[66]

IV.

The inner conflict reflected in the political thinking of the intellectuals presented in this chapter can be understood as the expression of the tragedy of a movement that belonged to the dreamed, utopian elements of Zionism that were eventually destroyed by the political developments in Europe and in the Middle East before and after the Shoah. The idealistic construction of a humanist anti-imperialist nationalism faced the dilemma of a historical crisis of unprecedented proportions that was more powerful than the lofty visions of peace developed after the First World War. Whether the attempt to make Palestine into a model for the coexistence of two distinct nations on one territory might have been successful under different historical circumstances remains speculation. The same applies to the question of whether the ideal of 'Buber-Zionism', as Hans Kohn called it, might have proven to be politically realistic had the Zionist settlement of Palestine taken place under democratic and peaceful conditions rather than in the midst of excessive, violent nationalisms that made *galut* into a place of destruction. The events in Palestine leading to the establishment of the State of Israel and the ensuing conflicts in the Middle East took place in the shadow of a devastating war and an unprecedented genocide, whose political consequences made the ideas of *Bar Kochba* and of *Brith Shalom* seem, from the point of view of the majority of Zionists, to be an unworldly ideal. The experience that during the years of persecution and destruction of European Jewry, the entire world had closed its doors to the Jewish refugees, and that the survivors were often able to enter Palestine only illegally, discredited the voice of ambivalent, dissenting or former Zionists such as Kohn, Weltsch and Arendt, corroborating the conviction that only an independent Jewish state possessing military supremacy in the midst of a hostile Arab environment could ensure the survival of the Jewish people. Throughout his life Robert Weltsch continued to mourn the failure of the political hopes he had harboured before they were brutally shattered by the catastrophic events during the Second World War. In 1972, in an article on the history of German Zionism, he concluded with the following passage:

> In retrospect, it must be admitted that the ideas that have characterized German Zionism . . . have fallen at the hurdle of reality. . . . The notion that a developing nationalism need not necessarily mutate into an aggressive form, and that the idea of a spiritual renaissance, moral renewal, personal human dignity, and national creativity can also – and in fact only – be realized in the context of peaceful coexistence with other free peoples, was an illusion. World history has taken a different turn. Armaggedon has triumphed. The Jewish people has been drawn into an unimaginable catastrophe. A nationalism of infernal origin tore the whole world to pieces and unleashed evil. Brute force appeared to rule. This cynical insight has shaped the thoughts and actions of the generation.[67]

Nevertheless, recent historical research on those disillusioned protagonists of a 'non-national nationalism' such as Hans Kohn, Robert Weltsch or Hannah Arendt,[68] even though confirming that their visions failed in view of historical reality, still tends to take a more nuanced approach and to ascribe to their ideas at least a certain degree of political relevance for current ethical and political debates. Historian George L. Mosse, for instance, asked in his 1995 essay 'Can Nationalism be Saved?': 'Is then there hope? Have these attempts been totally in vain?' His sceptical and yet positive answer is:

> Scholarship has a task here, to discover and evaluate such efforts so that we may learn what has to be overcome. The obstacles to a humanized nationalism are not solely *realpolitik* or even social injustice . . . Movements which try to defeat all nationalism have had as little success as pacifism could boast even in our bloody century. Here we have no real choice. We are dealing, after all, with the

existence of a powerful civic religion which, unlike many traditional religions, does not seem to have lost its political force. And if we study the thought of the men just mentioned, and are impressed by their lack of realism, then this itself might in the end prove to be their real strength: for men must dream before they can act.[69]

In a similar vein, historian Steven E. Aschheim argues in his article on 'Bildung in Palestine: Zionism, Binationalism and the Strains of German-Jewish Humanism' that the study of figures such as the Prague Zionists or Arendt 'provides us with an alternative foundational perspective when not only was statehood not a certainty but other options did not seem to contradict historical reality and it was possible to envisage alternative future social orders'.[70] His final conclusion is no less thought-provoking:

Their legacy may help us not to rationalize and justify past actions but to retain a critical and humanizing impulse in the midst of increasing desperation, violence, and inhumanity. These thinkers sought not to abolish nationalism but rather provide it with a more tolerant, gentle face – a goal that, in the present circumstances, may be exceedingly difficult but is no less admirable for that.[71]

Notes

1 For Robert Weltsch, see Ernst Simon, 'Robert Weltsch als Politiker, Historiker und Erzieher im Vergleich mit Buber und Scholem', *Bulletin des Leo Baeck Instituts* 64 (1983): 15–28; Herbert A. Strauss, 'Robert Weltsch und die Jüdische Rundschau', in *Berlin und der Prager Kreis*, ed. Margarita Pazi and Hans Dieter Zimmermann (Würzburg: Königshausen & Neumann), 31–43; Herbert A. Strauss, 'Zum zeitgeschichtlichen Hintergrund zionistischer Kulturkritik: Scholem, Weltsch und die jüdische Rundschau', in *Juden in Deutschland: Emanzipation, Integration, Verfolgung und Vernichtung*, ed. Peter Freimark, Alice Jankowski, and Ina Lorenz (Hamburg: Christians, 1991), 375–87; Stefan Vogt, 'Robert Weltsch and the Paradoxes of Anti-Nationalist Nationalism', *Jewish Social Studies* 16 (2010): 85–115. This essay draws on a number of articles on Weltsch I published in recent years.
2 For recent works on Hans Kohn, see Noam Pianko, *Zionism and the Roads Not Taken: Rawidowicz, Kaplan, Kohn* (Bloomington: Indiana University Press, 2010); Romy Langeheine, *Von Prag nach New York: Hans Kohn. Eine intellektuelle Biographie* (Göttingen: Wallstein, 2014); Adi Gordon, *Toward Nationalism's End: An Intellectual Biography of Hans Kohn* (Waltham: Brandeis University Press, 2017).

228   *Colonialism and the Jews in German History*

3 Hans Kohn, 'Rückblick auf eine gemeinsame Jugend', in *Robert Weltsch zum 70. Geburtstag von seinen Freunden*, ed. Hans Tramer and Kurt Loewenstein (Tel Aviv: Bitaon, 1961), 113–29, here 113.

4 Ibid., 118.

5 Ibid., 120. See Robert Weltsch, 'Rechenschaft', *Jüdische Rundschau* 40 (1935), No. 31/32, 18 (separate pagination).

6 Robert Weltsch, 'Hans Kohn (1961)', in *An der Wende des modernen Judentums: Betrachtungen aus fünf Jahrzehnten* (Tübingen: Mohr Siebeck, 1972), 280–6, here 280. Weltsch conceded that during their initial encounter with Zionism both of them had passionately embraced elements, such as an 'unconcealed Romantic attitude', which 'two or three decades later appeared questionable or even detrimental to us' (282).

7 Ibid., 285.

8 Ibid.

9 Ibid., 288. As an assessment of Kohn's biography and work, see also Robert Weltsch, 'Hans Kohn on Nationalism', *Orbis, a Quarterly Journal of World Affairs* 10 (1967): 1310–26; for a comparative interpretation of Weltsch's and Kohn's interpretation of Zionism before the Shoah, see Christian Wiese, 'The Janus Face of Nationalism: The Ambivalence of Zionist Identity in Robert Weltsch and Hans Kohn', *Leo Baeck Institute Yearbook* 51 (2006): 103–30.

10 Tom Nairn, *The Break-Up of Britain: Crisis and Neo-Nationalism* (London: NLB, 1977), 331.

11 Ibid., 148. See Tom Nairn, *Faces of Nationalism: Janus Revisited* (London: Verso, 1997), particularly 71–2.

12 See, for example, *The Morality of Nationalism*, ed. Robert McKimm and Jeff McMahan (New York: Oxford University Press, 1997).

13 See Raluca Munteanu Eddon, 'Gershom Scholem, Hannah Arendt and the Paradox of "Non-Nationalist" Nationalism', *Journal of Jewish Thought and Philosophy* 12 (2003): 55–68.

14 See, for example, Laurence J. Silberstein, *Postzionism Debates: Knowledge and Power in Israel Culture* (New York: Routledge, 1999), 102–11.

15 For the context, see Dimitry Shumsky, *Zweisprachigkeit und binationale Idee: Der Prager Zionismus 1900–1930* (Göttingen: Vandenhoeck & Ruprecht, 2012).

16 For the details of their war experience, see Christian Wiese, 'Martin Buber und die Wirkung des Ersten Weltkriegs auf die Prager Zionisten Hugo Bergmann, Robert Weltsch und Hans Kohn', in *Texturen des Krieges: Körper, Schrift und der Erste Weltkrieg* (Tel Aviver Jahrbuch für deutsche Geschichte, vol. 43), ed. Galili Shahar (Göttingen: Wallstein, 2015), 181–222.

17 See, for example, Robert Weltsch, 'Unser Nationalismus. Eine Chanukka-Betrachtung', *Jüdische Rundschau* 30 (1925): 805–6.

The Predicaments of Non-Nationalist Nationalism   229

18 See Adi Gordon, 'The Ideological Convert and the "Mythology of Coherence": The Contradictory Hans Kohn and His Multiple Metamorphoses', *Leo Baeck Institute Year Book* 55 (2010): 273–93.

19 Hans Kohn, *Living in a World Revolution: My Encounters with History* (New York: Simon and Schuster, 1964), 95.

20 Hans Kohn to Robert Weltsch, 16 July 1919, Archives of the Leo Baeck Institute, New York (henceforth LBIA), Hans Kohn – Robert Weltsch Correspondence, AR 6908. All the letters between Kohn and Weltsch quoted in this chapter are, if not indicated otherwise, part of this collection.

21 Kohn, *Living in a World Revolution*.

22 Martin Buber, 'Nationalismus: Rede in Karlsbad anlässlich des XII. Zionistischen Kongresses', in *Ein Land und zwei Völker: Zur jüdisch-arabischen Frage*, ed. and with an introduction by Paul R. Mendes-Flohr (Frankfurt am Main: Jüdischer Verlag, 1993), 73–86, here 85.

23 Hans Kohn, 'Zur Araberfrage', *Der Jude* 4 (1919/1920): 567–9, here 569.

24 For this circle, see, for example, Hagit Lavsky, 'German Zionists and the Emergence of Brit Shalom', in *Essential Papers on Zionism*, ed. Jehuda Reinharz and Anita Shapira (New York: New York University Press, 1996), 648–70; Shalom Ratzabi, *Between Zionism and Judaism: The Radical Circle in Brith Shalom, 1925–1933* (Leiden: Brill, 2002).

25 Hans Kohn, 'Zur künftigen Gestaltung Palästinas', in *Zionistische Politik: Eine Aufsatzreihe von Hans Kohn und Robert Weltsch* (Mährisch-Ostrau: Verlag Dr. R. Färber, 1927), 268–91, here 290–1.

26 Hans Kohn to Robert Weltsch, 25 January 1929.

27 Hans Kohn to Robert Weltsch, 29 January 1929 [emphasis in the original].

28 Hans Kohn to Robert Weltsch, 27 February 1929.

29 For Kohn's views on the ambivalent impact of European colonialism on the Middle East, see Hans Kohn, *Orient und Okzident* (Berlin: Zentral-Verlag, 1931); *A History of Nationalism in the East* (New York: Harcourt, Brace and Company, 1929); *Nationalismus und Imperialismus im Vorderen Orient* (Frankfurt: Societas-Verlag, 1931); *Die Europäisierung des Orients* (Berlin: Schocken, 1934).

30 See Zohar Maoz, 'Hans Kohn and the Dialectics of Colonialism: Insights on Nationalism and Colonialism from Within', *Leo Baeck Institute Year Book* 55 (2010): 255–71. While before 1933 Kohn's interpretation of Zionism at the same time shaped and was shaped by his anti-colonialism, Maor argues, his later break with the Zionist cause and emigration to the United States was accompanied by an increasing identification with the West and an abandonment of his previous rejection of the latter's continuing colonial policies.

31 Hans Kohn to Berthold Feiwel, 21 November 1929, reprinted in Buber, *Ein Land und zwei Völker*, 137–41, here 138–9.

230   *Colonialism and the Jews in German History*

32 Ibid., 140.

33 Hans Kohn to Shmuel H. Bergman, 21 January 1930, LBIA, Robert Weltsch Papers, AR 7185. With this phrase Kohn alluded to Buber's second speech in Prague in 1910 ('Judaism and Humankind'), which put particular emphasis on the theme of Zionism's reflection on ethnic-cultural distinctiveness and uniqueness. Bergmann later accused Kohn (in a letter of 21 October 1933) of exaggerated cosmopolitanism and 'hatred for Jewish Palestine'; see Schmuel Hugo Bergman, *Tagebücher & Briefe*, *vol. 1: 1901–1948* (Königstein/Ts: Athenäum, 1985), 345.

34 Robert Weltsch to Hans Kohn, 26 September 1929.

35 Robert Weltsch to Hans Kohn, 10 October 1929.

36 Robert Weltsch to Hans Kohn, 9 January 1929.

37 Robert Weltsch to Hans Kohn, 28 May 1930.

38 Robert Weltsch to Hans Kohn, 17 February 1931.

39 Hans Kohn to Robert Weltsch, 21 January 1930.

40 Hans Kohn to Robert Weltsch, 7 March 1930.

41 Hans Kohn to Robert Weltsch, 21 January 1930.

42 Hans Kohn to Robert Weltsch, 12 June 1931.

43 Hans Kohn to Robert Weltsch, 21 April 1930.

44 Hans Kohn to Robert Weltsch, 21 May 1930.

45 Robert Weltsch to Hans Kohn, 14 August 1930.

46 Robert Weltsch to Hans Kohn, 30 September 1930.

47 Robert Weltsch to Hans Kohn, 4 February 1931.

48 For Weltsch's activities in Nazi Germany and his emigration to Palestine, see Christian Wiese, 'Das "dämonische Antlitz des Nationalismus": Robert Weltschs zwiespältige Deutung des Zionismus angesichts von Nationalsozialismus und Shoah', *Zeitschrift für Geschichtswissenschaft* 60 (2012): 618–45.

49 Robert Weltsch to Hans Kohn, 30 August 1938.

50 Robert Weltsch to Hans Kohn, 7 March 1948.

51 Robert Weltsch to Hans Kohn, 20 May 1948.

52 See, among other essays, Hannah Arendt, 'The Jewish Army: The Beginning of Jewish Politics?' (1941), in *The Jewish Writings*, ed. Jerome Kohn and Ron H. Feldman (New York: Schocken Books, 2007), 136–8.

53 Hannah Arendt, 'Zionism Reconsidered', *Menorah-Journal* 33 (1945): 162–96 (reprinted in *The Jewish Writings*, 343–74, here 361).

54 Ibid., 344.

55 For Arendt's attitude towards Zionism and nationalism, see, for example, Richard J. Bernstein, *Hannah Arendt and the Jewish Question* (Cambridge, MA: The MIT Press, 1996), 102–22; Ronald Beiner, 'Arendt and Nationalism', in *The Cambridge Companion to Hannah Arendt*, ed. Dana Villa (Cambridge: Cambridge University Press, 2000), 44–61; Moshe Zimmermann, 'Hannah Arendt: The Early Post-

The Predicaments of Non-Nationalist Nationalism 231

Zionism', in *Hannah Arendt in Jerusalem*, ed. Steven E. Aschheim (Berkeley: University of California Press, 2001), 181–93; Seyla Benhabib, *The Reluctant Modernism of Hannah Arendt* (Lanham: Rowman & Littlefield, 2003), 35–46, 75–85.

56 Arendt, 'Zionism Reconsidered', 364.

57 Ibid., 366.

58 Ibid., 372.

59 Hannah Arendt, 'To Save the Jewish Homeland' (1948), in *The Jewish Writings*, 388–404, here 389.

60 Ibid., 393.

61 Ibid., 394.

62 Ibid., 394–35. 'There is no Jew in the world whose whole outlook on life and the world would not be radically changed by such a tragedy' (ibid., 395).

63 Ibid., 396.

64 Ibid., 401.

65 Robert Weltsch to Hannah Arendt, 1 June 1948, LBIA, AR 7185.

66 Hannah Arendt to Robert Weltsch, 23 June 1948, LBIA, AR 7185.

67 Robert Weltsch, 'Deutscher Zionismus in der Rückschau' (1972), in *Die deutsche Judenfrage: Ein kritischer Rückblick* (Königstein: Jüdischer Verlag, 1981), 95–107, here 105.

68 See Eddon, 'Gershom Scholem'.

69 George L. Mosse, 'Can Nationalism Be Saved? About Zionism, Rightful and Unjust Nationalism', *Israel Studies* 2 (1997): 156–73, here 171.

70 Steven E. Aschheim, '*Bildung* in Palestine: Zionism, Binationalism, and the Strains of German-Jewish Humanism', in *Beyond the Border: The German-Jewish Legacy Abroad* (Princeton: Princeton University Press, 2006), 9.

71 Ibid., 43.

11

Colonial revisionism and the Emin Pasha legend in Weimar and Nazi Germany

Christian S. Davis

In 1942, a second edition of the book *Höre Israel!* ('Hear O Israel!') by the Nazi historian Walter Frank appeared in print in Germany. Frank, who is well known to historians as a leading producer, editor and organizer of anti-Jewish scholarship during the Third Reich, augmented the original chapters on Maximilian Harden and Walther Rathenau from the first edition with a new essay on Eduard Schnitzer, better known to contemporaries as Emin Pasha: the colourful Jewish-born German adventurer and explorer who captured Europe's imagination in the 1880s when he became trapped in Equatoria by the Islamic fundamentalist Mahdist uprising against Egypt while serving as the region's Egyptian-appointed governor.[1] In his 127-page essay on Emin's life and career, Frank moulded him into the archetypical Jew of the National Socialist imagination. The Emin Pasha that emerged from Frank's account was not just vain, materialistic, idle, indecisive, cowardly and self-serving. He was also a snake in the grass who masked his cruelty, vindictiveness and murderous rage towards racial betters with a sickening veneer of obsequiousness and self-deprecation. Above all, Frank's Emin Pasha was the wandering Jew extraordinaire: 'he was Ahasverus, the cursed, who ran through the lands of Europe, Asia, and Africa without faith, without commitment, without God, and without Fatherland.'[2] In his preface, Frank wrote that the purpose of *Höre Israel!* was to disseminate to the wider public scholarly research on the Jewish question that would otherwise be accessible to only a 'circle of specialists'.[3]

Frank's essay is the most thorough attempt by any Nazi propagandist or spokesmen to remove Emin Pasha from the pantheon of German colonial heroes of the Kaiserreich.[4] In it, Frank painted a picture of the former governor of Equatoria that was the diametrical opposite of the popular image of Emin that had emerged in Germany in the 1880s after news of his plight filtered back to Europe: an image that, despite the awkward facts of his conversion to Islam, his voluntary service to a foreign power and his adoption of a Turkish name and title, presented Emin as a German patriot. This idealized picture stressed Emin's Germanness and German sentiment, his penchant for natural study, his paternalistic concern for the Africans he governed and his ability to survive in the 'uncivilized' heart of Africa. In short, it identified Emin as the embodiment of Germany's civilizing mission.[5] It became standard fare in the publications of German pro-colonial pressure groups that advocated for a German rescue expedition to him in the hopes that it would lead to Germany's acquisition of Emin's Equatorial province. And it continued after newspaper reports on his Jewish roots appeared in 1888.

Emin's stature only grew with the passage of time. Although the ensuing German expedition to him led by the explorer Carl Peters failed, German nationalists became ecstatic when, after reaching German East Africa in 1891 through the intervention of the British adventurer Henry Morton Stanley, Emin turned his back on his British rescuers. Awarded the Crown Order of the second class by Wilhelm II, Emin quickly entered German service and returned to the wilderness, this time to help solidify German control over the hinterland of the colony. With this turn of events, Emin became not just a symbol of German colonizing prowess but also of German defiance against an overbearing England. After Emin was murdered in 1892 at the hands of slave traders – likely as a reprisal for his earlier actions against slavers – reports emerged that he died while trying to traverse the African interior in order to create a German-controlled land bridge connecting German Cameron with German East Africa, an idea that thrilled colonialism's advocates back home.[6] Even before this turn of events, the popular adventure novelist Karl May had immortalized Emin in the serialized novel *Die Sklavenkarawane* (*The Slave Caravan*). May used him as a template for his protagonist, Emil Schwarz, who, like the real Emin, was a scholar-warrior who collected specimens of the local flora and fauna for German museums and fought Arabic slavers. May's novel also praised Emin directly, characterizing him as a model of white paternalistic colonialism.[7]

That a Nazi fanatic like Frank would attempt to dismantle the reputation of a well-known Jewish figure from Germany's recent past is, of course, unsurprising. What is of interest is the fact that the celebratory legend of Emin Pasha persisted not only into the Weimar Republic but even into the Nazi period. Although Emin's fame faded in the decades after his death and critical accounts of his life emerged that chipped away at his legend, his name continued to command respect in many pro-colonial publications both up to and after 1933 – in the latter period, in books and articles written especially by older members of the colonial revanchist movement that emerged during the early Weimar Republic.[8] Astoundingly, even some National Socialist publications lauded Emin Pasha as late as 1940 (see later), identifying him as one of the great colonial actors of the imperial era alongside men like the German East Africa governor Hermann von Wissmann and the explorer Carl Peters. It was undoubtedly the stubborn endurance of the positive image of Emin that drove Frank to try to lay it to rest in 1942 with his additional essay in *Höre Israel!*. For a Nazi like Frank, Emin Pasha represented a problem analogous to that posed by the German-Jewish soldiers of the First World War.[9] Both contravened the idea that Jews could never be German patriots who purposefully advanced German national causes.

This chapter uses the contested memory after 1933 of the participation of Germans of Jewish descent in the colonial efforts of the Imperial era to trace the emergence of National Socialist narratives reconciling the fact of Jewish involvement in Wilhelminian colonialism with the Nazi world view: a world view that identified Jews as a colonizing people of a sort but argued that Jews could never positively contribute to the German nation. From the Nazi perspective, Emin Pasha was the German-Jewish colonial actor whose remembrance needed the most refashioning. But there were other individuals widely seen as Jewish from Germany's colonial past who also drew the attention of authors during the Third Reich. One was Paul Kayser, a Jewish-born jurist in the Foreign Office who was highly active overseeing colonial affairs from the mid-1880s until 1896, becoming the head of the Foreign Office's Colonial Division in 1890. Kayser's later successor, Bernhard Dernburg, was a third. The Christian son of a Jewish-born father, Dernburg took the reins of the colonial administration in 1906, heading a newly formed Colonial Office from 1907 to 1910.[10] The participation of these men in the patriotic project of colonial empire building not only had to be squared with Nazi antisemitic beliefs but also with the idea – pushed by the Nazi state – that Germany's colonial empire had been a resounding success, an example of European colonialism worthy of admiration.

As will be shown further, the National Socialist narratives developed by Frank and others acknowledged the involvement of men of Jewish descent in German colonialism. But they identified them as inauthentic German colonizers: as having worked against Germany's true colonial interests while pursuing a form of overseas colonialism informed by Jewish, rather than Aryan, racial instincts and practices. In so doing, Frank and others advanced a revisionist version of the colonial past, one that attempted to wipe out any positive remembrance of Jewish participation

Colonial Revisionism

in Germany's colonial projects. These efforts ran up against persistent good feelings for Emin Pasha, however, and the insistence among an older generation of antisemites that Emin had been the exceptional 'good' Jew who was a true German patriot. The fact that Emin has been the object of the failed rescue expedition by the violent Carl Peters – a man widely celebrated during the Third Reich as a precursor to the National Socialist masculine type – presented men like Frank with an additional challenge: that of vilifying Emin without darkening Peters's star and calling into question Peters's judgement. It was a much simpler task to fashion a memory of Paul Kayser that served Nazi aims. Kayser's reputation during the colonial period as an advocate of a strictly capitalist form of colonialism, and his involvement in developments that led to Peters's downfall, made it easy for propagandists to present him in a way that validated Nazi ideology.

Persistent admiration for Emin Pasha

One of the most romanticized articles on Emin Pasha in the colonial revanchist press of the Weimar Republic appeared in the *Deutsche Kolonial-Zeitung* in December of 1930. In 'A Hour of Tea with Dr. Emin Pasha's Sister', the anthropologist Max Grühl detailed a visit to the explorer's 89-year-old sibling in observation of Emin's ninetieth birthday. In describing his encounter with Melanie Schnitzer, Grühl repeated major components of the celebratory legend of Emin that began with the public campaign of the late 1880s undertaken by Carl Peters and his associates. On a wall of Melanie's apartment, Grühl wrote, hung a painting showing Emin's 'modest little house in Lado on the upper Nil, where he lived only for the fulfillment of his duty, cut off from the rest of the world, to protect the territory of the Sudan entrusted to him from the fanatical harm of the Mahdi'. Grühl recounted Melanie's description of Emin as a precocious child 'who collected useful natural history specimens and felt in himself from his youth an urge toward distant zones'. Towards the end of his piece, Grühl narrated the story of Emin's assassination, painting him as defiant and fearless to the end. 'Three people entered' his tent, Grühl wrote, 'and helped to hold Emin, who struggled violently to free himself and grasp his revolver which lay on the table; his efforts were in vain'. Subdued by his assassins, 'Emin gave no sign of fear' as he faced imminent death. Grühl's piece presents Emin as duty-bound, scholarly minded, adventurous and courageous, harking back to parts of the pre-war Emin Pasha legend that had electrified pro-colonial advocates decades earlier.[11]

236   *Colonialism and the Jews in German History*

Grühl's essay evinces the continuation of this legend throughout the Weimar years, a development that was surprising for several reasons. First, the memory of Emin Pasha had faded both in the lead-up to and aftermath of the First World War. By the dawn of the Weimar Republic, the Emin Pasha craze of the last century seemed like something from a distant past, and the earth-shattering events of 1914–19 had turned the public's attention away from the old colonies.[12] Second, accounts of Emin's life and career appeared after the war that threatened to dull his reputation. Occasional articles appeared about his personal life before he volunteered his services to Egypt that highlighted unsavoury parts of his biography, like his abandonment of dependents in Germany for a life of adventure abroad.[13] More significantly, in 1925, the Austrian novelist Ernst W. Freißler published a book attempting to overturn the conventional take on him. In *Emin Pascha* (Emin Pasha), Freißler argued that Emin's reputation as a capable administrator and brave commander was almost entirely unfounded. Emin had virtually no skill for leadership, Freißler claimed, and his survival in the Equatorial province during the Mahdist rebellion was the result of his remarkable good fortune and capable underlings.[14] Yet as Grühl's 1930 essay shows, these efforts to disrupt the Emin Pasha legend failed. The colonial revanchist movement that emerged after the war continued to identify Emin as an important hero of the lost colonies.[15] Radio programme lectures in the late 1920s paired discussions of Emin with Napoleon and other historical luminaries.[16]

The fortieth anniversary of Emin's death occasioned new celebratory remembrances of him. In 1932, Munich's city government christened an 'Emin-Pascha-Platz' (Emin-Pasha-Square), and Emin was the subject that year of three radio programme lectures in Germany: one in Berlin, one in Munich and one in Königs Wursterhausen.[17] An incredibly effusive and partially fictionalized biography of Emin, titled *Die Schwarze Sonne: Leben, Schaffen und Sterben deutscher Kolonialhelden* (The Black Sun: The Life, Work, and Death of a German Colonial Hero), then appeared in print in 1933. Written by Ehm Welk, the book details Emin's career from his days as a medical doctor in Khartoum, through his governorship of Equatoria during the Mahdist rebellion, to his death at the hands of slave traders in the hinterland of German East Africa. Welk emphasized Emin's bravery, his skill in colonizing peacefully and paternalistically, his scholarly interest in the surrounding environment and his German patriotism. Welk used imaginary conversations and invented scenes to evince his hero's outstanding qualities. In a passage representative of the book's tenor, one of Emin's companions implores him to colonize with 'a sword' like the English, to which Emin replies that he had 'hitherto managed to do without brutality' and would 'continue to do so in the future'.[18] Welk elaborated on how Emin, a trained physician, provided medical care for the Africans around him, even sacrificing his own health and comfort for their well-being towards the end.

Laudatory accounts of Emin during the Weimar Republic often omitted the fact of his Jewish heritage. Welk made no mention of it, and references to Emin in colonial revanchist periodicals elided this part of his biography. Even Freißler virtually ignored Emin's Jewish background, referring ambiguously and only once to Emin's 'tribe' in his highly critical account of him. Yet Emin's Jewish roots were not forgotten.[19] Indeed, some nationalists with pro-colonial sentiments identified Emin as an exceptional Jew, one whose German patriotism put other Jews to shame. This was the sentiment of the retired naval commander Max W. L. Foß, whose antisemitic-tinged books *Enthüllungen über den Zusammenbruch* (Revelations about the Collapse) and *England als Erzieher* (England as Educator) appeared in print in 1920 and 1921, respectively. In both, Foß repeated a litany of antisemitic tropes, accusing Jews of shirking direct action during the war and lacking German national sentiment. Yet Foß boldly declared, 'I am not an antisemite', and he cited Emin Pasha as one Jew he admired, calling him 'the most loyal German that I can imagine' and 'a loyal German-minded Jew'.[20] Several years later, the racial theorist and antisemite Albrecht Wirth issued a new version of his pre-war book *Weltgeschichte der Gegenwart* (World History of the Present). In it, Wirth retained from the 1913 edition highly complementary sections on Emin Pasha's activities in the Sudan that also identified him as 'a Silesian of the Mosaic race'.[21]

Positive accounts of Emin continued well into the Nazi era. The colonial revanchist movement that began in the early years of the Weimar Republic continued after Hitler's rise to power, persisting in its mission of keeping the memory of the old colonies alive with the expectation of their eventual return to Germany. Although the president of the movement's leading organization, former governor of German East Africa Heinrich Schnee, joined the Nazi Party in 1933, and under his leadership, the Deutsche Kolonialgesellschaft (German Colonial Society) expelled its 'non-Aryan' members, movement publications identified Emin Pasha as a colonial hero worth remembering until the end of the decade. In November of 1933, an advertisement for *Emin Paschas Leben und Sterben* (Emin Pasha's Life and Death) by Georg Schweitzer appeared in the *Deutsche Kolonial-Zeitung*. The advertisement celebrates 'the German student Eduard Schnitzer' who 'with spirit and sword . . . withstood the storm of the Madhi attack' to eventually 'carry the black-white-red flag through the unexplored territory of East Africa'.[22] In 1934 and 1935, the youth-oriented magazine *Jambo* listed Emin's birthday in its regular feature 'What shall we Remember this Month?', as it had done in the 1920s.[23] In 1936, the *Kolonial-Post* identified Emin's arrival with Stanley in German East Africa as a date to remember.[24] In 1937, the anthology *Das Buch der deutschen Kolonien* (The Book of the German Colonies), composed by former colonial governors, briefly described Emin's activities in German East Africa, labelling him an 'Africa researcher'.[25] The following year, *Kohler's illustrierter deutscher Kolonial-Kalender* (Kohler's Illustrated German Colonial Calendar) listed Emin as one of the great heroes of the old colonial empire, describing him as 'the scholar, who pressed forward, researching into the last riddles of the Dark Continent'.[26]

Emin's name was most commonly evoked during the Third Reich in connection with Carl Peters. Although Peters lost out to Stanley in the race to Emin in 1888, and he failed to secure Emin's Equatorial province for Germany, the Emin Pasha Relief Expedition became a central part of the Peters legend both before and after 1933 – in part, because the failed rescue mission encompassed a treaty-signing trek across the East-African interior and also because it symbolized Peters's fanatical devotion to expanding Germany's African territories at Great Britain's expense. Carl Peters became a celebrated figure during the Third Reich both within the colonial revanchist movement and by the National Socialist state, and remembrances of his life and work frequently mentioned his expedition to Emin Pasha.[27] In the summer of 1934, an article in the *Afrika-Nachrichten* titled 'Dr. Carl Peters: Der deutschen Jugend ins Gedächtnis!' (Dr. Carl Peters: The German Youth to Remember) lauded the trek to Emin as 'the most important magnificent chapter in the conquest voyage of Carl Peters . . . the crowning of his devoted achievements for the fatherland'.[28] In 1939, the Hitler Youth yearbook briefly mentioned the Emin Pasha Relief Expedition when discussing Peters in the article 'Bismarck und die jungen Männer von 1880' (Bismarck and the Young Men of 1880).[29]

Biographies of Peters published during the early years of the Third Reich not only detailed his expedition to Emin Pasha but also maintained a positive image of Emin, sometimes with explicit praise. Undoubtedly, the continued respect for Emin shown by the colonial revanchist press influenced this approach, but Peters's own laudatory accounts of him were probably more decisive. In addition to the pro-Emin propaganda that the German Emin Pasha Committee propagated in the lead-up to the expedition, Peters had written positively about Emin in his post-expedition memoirs. Peters briefly met him in 1890 after the latter had entered German service, and he described Emin as 'a good and honorable German' who 'had all of the characteristics our people display'.[30]

Peters's biographer Paul Baecker advanced this narrative in his 1934 book *Carl Peters: Der Wiking der deutschen Kolonialpolitik* (Carl Peters: The Viking of German Colonial Politics) while acknowledging Emin's Jewish heritage. 'Of Jewish descent,' Baecker wrote, 'this one possessed not only an un-Jewish nature; but also the perilous career that he chose instead of creating for himself, using his unusual intellectual gifts, a life of comfortable prosperity as a doctor in Germany speaks to the fact that other currents in his blood must have prevailed than that in the mass of the racially-disunited Jewish nationality.'[31] Baecker omitted the fact of Emin's Jewish heritage in a second Peters biography the next year but continued to praise him. According to *Der letzte Wiking: Carl Peters erobert Ostafrika* (The Last Viking: Carl Peters Conquers East Africa), Emin 'worked his way up through his own initiative to the governorship of the Equatorial province, where he created an almost entirely independent position with Waderlei as its middle point'. After news of Emin's plight during the Mahdist rebellion reached Europe, Peters became 'occupied with the thought of bringing help to the German countryman Emin Pasha', Baecker wrote, 'and using this assistance to further German colonial interests'.[32]

Other biographies of Peters from the post-Weimar 1930s either lauded Emin outright or refrained from attacking him. In *Dr. Carl Peters: Der Weg eines Patrioten* (Dr. Carl Peters: The Path of a Patriot), published in 1934, Richard Wichterich labelled the 'German Emin-Pasha Expedition' a 'page of glory for German history'.[33] Wichterich reproduced the original announcement from the German Emin Pasha Committee from 1888 identifying Emin as 'our German countryman' who had been able to 'maintain the Equatorial province . . . against the Mahdist onrush' and who was 'the last bulwark of European culture' in the region. Wichterich added that this call to action 'appealed to human compassion to not permit the heroic countryman to be delivered to destruction'.[34] In *Carl Peters: Der Begründer von Deutsch-Ostafrika* (Carl Peters: The Founder of German East Africa), published in 1939, the military historian Hermann Böhme called Emin a 'born Jew' but said nothing negative about him.[35] To the contrary, Böhme mentioned Emin's support for Peters's efforts to bring Uganda under German influence. He noted that Emin had interceded with a Ugandan king to this end on Peters's behalf, underscoring Emin's devotion to the German colonial cause.[36] Böhme's positive depiction of Emin at such a late date was not unique. In 1940, the *Innsbrucker Nachrichten*, subtitled *Parteiamtliches Organ der NSDAP* (Official Party Organ of the NSDAP), listed Emin along with 'Barth, Nachtigall, Schweinfuhrt . . . v. Wissmann and Carl Peters' as 'German names' that 'jut out' from the history of distinguished European explorers of Africa.[37]

240 *Colonialism and the Jews in German History*

The Hitler Youth yearbook also maintained a positive image of Emin until the late 1930s. In an article on Carl Peters in 1938, the publication romanticized Emin as sitting 'in a lonesome tent on the upper Nile with the German flag' in the lead-up to the German relief expedition. The clear implication is that Emin was a German patriot.[38]

It was precisely these perceptions of Emin Pasha that Walter Frank felt compelled to dispel. The legend of the deeply patriotic and eminently capable German-Jewish colonizer of central Africa had to be shattered, given the incongruity from the Nazi perspective of Jewishness with Germanness and its associated positive qualities, like bravery and patriotism. Even before Frank's updated edition of *Höre Israel!* appeared in 1942, however, other authors had already taken shots at Emin, poking holes in the popular legend of him. In his 1938 book *Carl Peters: Ein deutsches Schicksal* (Carl Peters: A German Destiny), *Hochschulgruppenführer* (University Group Leader) Erich zu Klampen labelled Emin a 'Jewish adventurer' and claimed that Carl Peters had 'artificially made . . . Emin Pasha into a German national hero' to drum up public support for an expedition to him.[39] The following year, the Vienna-based *Illustrierte Kronen Zeitung* published a short salacious piece of fiction presenting Emin as a kidnapper of women.[40] In the story, two male protagonists travelled to Constantinople to rescue a woman whom Emin had spirited away after she rebuffed his advances. In 1940, the Nazi military theorist and geographer Ewald Banse briefly attacked Emin in his book *Unsere großen Afrikaner: Das Leben deutscher Entdecker und Kolonialpioniere* (Our Important Africans: The Life of German Explorers and Colonial Pioneers). Emin 'didn't do much for the young colony' of German East Africa after entering German service, Banse claimed, and Emin died at the hands of Arabs because he 'didn't understand how to treat' them.[41] According to Banse, Carl Peters's primary motive for creating the Emin Pasha Relief Expedition was not, in fact, to rescue Emin Pasha but to seize the Equatorial province for Germany. Banse stressed Emin's Jewishness, remarking upon his 'Semitic face'.[42]

The year 1942 witnessed more thorough attempts to dismantle Emin's reputation. In addition to Frank's essay in *Höre Israel!*, an article by the Nazi prosecutor Theodor Klinkhardt attacking Emin appeared that year in the *Afrika-Nachrichten*. Klinkhardt began his piece by identifying one of the central problems Emin Pasha posed for National Socialists: that 'the German Emin-Pasha-Expedition . . . is forever tied with the name of its spiritual author and ingenious leader, Carl Peters who always and always again commands our admiration'. Asking the question, 'Emin Pasha, who was this man?' Klinkhardt

Colonial Revisionism 241

then detailed the basic facts of Emin's life, undercutting several components of the legendary image of him. Klinkhardt attacked the idea that Emin was unusually courageous, arguing that he fled south from the approaching Mahdists even though his position in the north was 'well-fortified'. Klinkhardt rejected the notion that Emin was a capable administrator. He insisted that the governor-general of the Sudan put Emin in charge of the Equatorial province because he 'had nobody else available for the post'. Emin was of 'a pronounced passive nature, fickly-courageous, easily influenceable, and without any active initiative', and this was all because 'Emin was a Jew', Klinkhardt wrote. 'Herein lies the key to his essence and his entire personality.' Klinkhardt granted Emin some positive qualities, though. He prefaced his insistence that Emin 'completely lacked organizational or military talent' by admitting that 'it is true that one cannot deny him a certain capability as a researcher'. Klinkhardt labelled Emin as 'perhaps not timid' even though 'he can just as little be called brave'.[43]

The takedown by the historian Frank is far more substantial. His vitriolic essay details Emin's life from birth to death, using Emin's own letters and accounts by his contemporaries as primary sources, and it leaves readers with nothing to admire. Most of the piece focuses on Emin's activity in the Equatorial province, and it closely mirrors Freißler's earlier interpretation: Emin had been a weak, indecisive and ineffective leader, Frank claimed, who survived the Mahdist uprising through luck and the brave actions of his subordinates. He 'lacked the courage of the soldier in battle' and he 'also lacked the courage of a political leader . . . He was . . . not born to heroism', Frank wrote. Emin 'was only a clever merchant and the parasite of a foreign power'.[44]

Unlike Freißler, Frank explicitly grounded Emin's supposed character flaws in his Jewishness, and he attributed Emin with all the negative characteristics ascribed to Jews in Nazi ideology: among them, vanity, arrogance, deceitfulness, jealousy, greed and a carefully hidden murderous rage. Frank also explained away Carl Peters's well-known praise for Emin by noting that Peters encountered him only once and that the meeting had lasted 'barely three days'. Other contemporaries who dealt with Emin longer reached a better understanding of what he was, Frank insisted, finding him 'strange and repulsive'.[45] The portrait of Emin as 'a soldierly fighter of great stature and wild audacity' who 'maintained the flag of Christian culture and European civilization in the southernmost region of the Sudan' was the invention of an 'international press', Frank wrote, that had said little about Emin's Jewishness.[46]

Frank eviscerated the idea that Emin had been an exceptional Jew who expressed true German patriotism. He claimed that Emin had initially asked

242   *Colonialism and the Jews in German History*

England to protect his Equatorial province even though he knew that Germany was a colonial power, too.[47] Although Emin entered German service after reaching German East Africa, he gave offers from Britain equal consideration, Frank insisted, proving that 'this Pasha was not bound to a fatherland'.[48] Frank also argued that the idea that Emin died while attempting to create a German-controlled land bridge across the African interior was likely false: more probably, his final trek westward out of German East Africa was meant to retrieve vast stores of ivory left behind in the southern Sudan.[49] Material greed, therefore, not patriotic fervour had led to Emin's death. In this telling, Emin exhibited no love for Germany.

Nazi-era visions of Jewish colonialism

The Emin Pasha legend inherited from Wilhelminian times was incompatible with Nazi antisemitism generally. More specifically, it conflicted with Nazi ideas about what Jewish overseas colonialism entailed. During the Third Reich, authors like the propagandist Hermann Seifert articulated a fantasy of a distinctly Jewish form of colonialism inflicted on non-European peoples, one that reduced them through exploitative capitalism to a situation 'barely different from slavery'.[50] Emin Pasha's reputed paternalism towards Africans contravened this narrative, yet it was the part of the Emin Pasha legend to which his character assassins paid the least attention. Frank did not dispute the well-publicized accounts of Emin using his medical expertise to treat Africans around him, something Welk played up in his celebratory biography. Instead, Frank countered the legend of Emin's benevolence more indirectly. He accused Emin of planning to offer his own Black troops to the king of Uganda in return for safe passage to German East Africa. He also told how Emin plotted the murder of an African ruler, attributing him with the 'laughing cruelty of the Orient'.[51] In this way, Frank attempted to undercut the idea that Emin was a paternalistic colonizer, bringing his activities more in line with what Seifert and others imagined Jewish-style colonialism to be. The idea that Emin was a capitalist exploiter of indigenous peoples whose profit-fuelled colonial methods harmed those he governed was not pushed by his detractors, however, possibly because very little in the public record about Emin's activities could be used to bear this out. As shown earlier, this was not the case when it came to contesting other parts of Emin's reputation. Given the reality of his service to foreign powers, it was easier to challenge his German patriotism.

The narrative of a distinctly Jewish form of colonialism that treated colonies as things to be 'plundered' through rapacious capitalism was applied more readily to Paul Kayser and Bernhard Dernburg, two other Germans of Jewish descent who figured large in the history of the pre-war colonial empire.[52] Contemporaries of both men had criticized them for pursuing policies during their leadership of the colonial bureaucracy that favoured big business. Paul Kayser's preferred path to colonial development had been concessionary policy: the granting of terrific land rights and privileges to private companies with the expectation that the companies would undertake development projects. Although Dernburg initially took steps to limit the power of concession companies, towards the end of his tenure he, too, pursued a similar policy, giving monopolistic control over German South-West Africa's diamond fields to a consortium of banks and a German corporation. In addition, Dernburg came from the world of high finance, having helped run the Darmstädter Bank before becoming colonial director. Assuredly with these facts in mind, Nazi-era authors accused both men of promoting a strictly capitalist and commercial form of colonialism. In 1937, Peters biographer Alfred Funke contrasted Kayser's approach with Peters's vision of 'a colonial policy that was not a matter of "business" but rather . . . of the worldwide greatness, standing, self-confidence of the German people'.[53] In 1938, the *Deutsche Kolonial-Zeitung* wrote that German colonial policy became 'stamped' with the face of 'speculative capital' once 'Jewry' installed Dernburg as colonial director.[54]

Of the two men, Nazi-era authors paid far less attention to Dernburg. His name surfaced only occasionally and briefly in books and articles published after 1933 about the lost colonies. The reason for this is unclear, but it may have had to do with how Dernburg was remembered both within the colonial revanchist movement and by the general public. Like Emin Pasha, Dernburg had been widely admired by colonial advocates for much of his time in office, even though his Jewish heritage had been public knowledge. His tenure witnessed a series of developments that colonial advocates deemed quite positive, like an expansion of the railroad network in German Africa and an upswing in colonial enthusiasm among the public. The contemporary colonial movement credited Dernburg for these improvements, and memory books about the old colonies made passing references to his accomplishments well into the Nazi period, suggesting a lingering admiration for him.[55] Unlike Emin Pasha, though, Dernburg never became a long-term fixture in the German imaginary landscape: nothing like Emin's celebratory immortalization in a Karl May novel happened to him.[56] Nazi authors who wrote about the colonial past may therefore have seen little reason to focus much ire on him.[57]

244   *Colonialism and the Jews in German History*

Nazi and Nazi-era authors who wrote on colonial matters paid considerably more attention to Paul Kayser. They frequently cast him as a Jewish villain in their books and articles, and he was also presented this way in the 1940 feature film *Carl Peters*. As with Emin Pasha, it was Kayser's connection to Peters that drew the most attention during the Third Reich. As a jurist in the Foreign Office charged with overseeing certain colonial affairs, and then as colonial director, Kayser had worked closely with Peters in the 1880s and early 1890s. But unlike with Emin, the public memory of the connection between the two men was largely negative because Peters's contemporary allies and admirers had blamed Kayser for the former's removal from colonial service. With some justification, they alleged that Kayser had betrayed Peters during the *Reichstag* inquiry of 1896 into executions that Peters ordered while serving as an imperial commissioner in German East Africa: during the Reichstag proceedings, Kayser had revealed embarrassing information about Peters's sexual relationships with Africans, information that helped discredit him.[58] Warm feelings for Kayser generally did not exist, therefore, in either the colonial movement of the Kaiserreich or in the colonial revanchist movement after the war. This undoubtedly encouraged the targeting of Kayser with antisemitic invective both before and after 1933. It probably made a difference as well that Kayser was ostensibly much more 'Jewish' than either Emin or Dernburg: Kayser converted to Christianity at the age of thirty-seven, whereas Emin converted as a child and Dernburg was born a Christian.[59]

Colonial-themed Nazi-era works attacking Kayser reduced him to a Jewish stereotype and highlighted his supposed opposition to Peters. In his 1934 Peters biography where he called Emin a 'heroic countryman', Richard Wichterich described Kayser as 'a Jew' who cared nothing for the German colonial cause. Instead, he was a 'careerist' for whom 'the young colonial politics only appeared as a path toward fulfilling his ambition within officialdom'. Kayser 'misused his position to hound the conqueror of German East Africa with the skill of the cabal', Wichterich wrote, because Peters's desire to see the colonies self-govern threatened Kayser's power.[60] For zu Klampen, Kayser's animosity towards Peters was more a matter of racial programming. 'Who fought and intrigued against Peters?' zu Klampen asked in his Peters biography of 1938. 'Minister director Kayser' who 'obeys the same inner voice' as Jews like Karl Marx and August Bebel 'that orders him to hate and destroy everything German'.[61] Zu Klampen also painted Kayser as a traitor to German colonialism, insisting that Kayser had been behind the Heligoland-Zanzibar Agreement of 1890 that ceded vast territories north of German East

Africa to Britain in exchange for a tiny archipelago in the North Sea.[62] The historian Walter Frank reiterated most of these accusations in a long article in the *Historische Zeitschrift* in 1943. Like zu Klampen, Frank presented Kayser as an ambitious Jewish striver concerned only with his own career who was driven by 'racial hatred' to destroy Peters.[63]

The *Carl Peters* film propagated this image of Paul Kayser to a national audience. Released in 1940 and staring Hans Albers in the Peters role, the film was the culmination of Peters's rehabilitation by the Nazis, and it was shown to large crowds across Germany.[64] The movie tells the story of Carl Peters up to his departure from colonial service following the Reichstag investigations of 1896, and the conflict between 'Jew' and 'German' has a central role. Throughout the film, a government official named Leo Kayser – an unmistakable stand-in for the real Kayser – undermines Peters at every turn, from withdrawing official protection for him during his first treaty-signing expedition to denying Peters the governorship of the colony created from his efforts. Leo's Jewishness is established early on. In the initial meeting between the two, Peters mimics one of Leo's gestures and remarks sarcastically about his baptism.[65]

The movie posits two opposing colonialisms: one Jewish, allied with Britain, that sees colonial work as a capitalist venture and that harms colonized Black Africans, the other German, which is idealistic, nationalist and paternalistic towards colonial subjects. Several scenes in the movie establish this contrast. In one, the Peters character forcibly disrupts Arab slave-raiding activities endorsed by the British, freeing the captives. Leo's hostility towards Peters and his strong interest in maintaining Germany's good relations with Britain therefore places the Jewish bureaucrat in stark opposition to the best interests of Black Africans. In a second scene, Leo expresses astonishment that Peters accomplished so much during his initial treaty-signing expedition with so little capital. 'One doesn't conquer a colony with 2,000 marks!' Leo exclaims. To this, Peters's representative replies, 'One cannot conquer with money alone. Peters took much more than this with him. Namely, personal courage and the power of an idea.'[66]

Any challenge that the Emin Pasha legend might have posed to the division established within the film between 'Jewish' and 'German' colonialism is sidestepped, as the film makes no reference to either Emin Pasha or Peters's expedition to him. The historical Peters's second trip to East Africa – the Emin Pasha Relief Expedition in real life – is presented in the film as only another treaty-signing endeavour. Within the world of the movie, the problematic association of Peters with Emin is obliterated.

The contested remembrance of Emin Pasha

The 1922 novel *Ruland* by the German author Otto Flake provides additional evidence of the transference of the Emin Pasha legend from Wilhelminian times to Weimar. While contemplating the greats of human history who had rebelled against God and, in so doing, separated themselves from the unheroic masses who were mere 'gelatin', Flake's protagonist spontaneously writes down a list of names. In the list, which includes Cleopatra, Pandora, Wotan, Siegfried, Cortes and Don Juan, among others, Ruland places Emin Pasha between Napoleon and Crusoe, following Crusoe with Winnetou, the fictional Native American hero of Karl May's novels. Upon completion, Ruland remarks that these figures had transcended the status of legend to become myth and, in so doing, represented not just great deeds but also great ideas.[67]

Emin Pasha became a legend during his own lifetime, due in part to the efforts of Carl Peters and his supporters to gin up public support for their proposed expedition to him. The legend of the patriotic, paternalistic, brave German colonizer of central Africa whose Jewish ancestry was public knowledge persisted into both the Weimar and Nazi periods. As the novel *Ruland* suggests, it did indeed take on mythical qualities at times, embodying certain truths for some people. For Emin's Wilhelminian admirers, the Emin Pasha story illustrated Germany's civilizing mission in Africa and Germany's defiance towards an overbearing Britain. For individuals like Max Foss and Paul Baecker, it confirmed the idea of the 'exceptional Jew' who showed true German patriotism.

The Emin Pasha legend also came to resemble a myth when it assumed fictionalized elements in some retellings. Emin became a fictionalized character in Karl May's *Die Sklavenkarawane* (The Slave Caravan). Ehm Welk's exuberant biography created an Emin Pasha decades later that was somewhere between fact and fiction. But it was National Socialists like Frank who did the most to treat the Emin Pasha legend as a myth, albeit as a pernicious one. For them, the Emin Pasha story handed down from before the war contained ideas inimical to National Socialist ideology. In the world without Jews that the Third Reich was actively creating, the story of the patriotic German-Jewish colonizer of central Africa was a myth that needed revision. It had to be brought in line with a world view grounded on the lie of an unbridgeable divide between Jew and German and the ascription onto an unchanging Jewish nature of everything that the Nazis hated.

For Nazis like Frank, the Emin Pasha legend inherited from the Kaiserreich era presented a problem similar to that of the German-Jewish veterans of the

First World War: both challenged the National Socialist racialist understanding of history. As historian Tim Grady has shown, the Nazi state dealt with the inconvenient fact of Jewish participation in the patriotic struggle of 1914–18 by prohibiting the placement of Jewish names on newly erected war memorials and disbanding the Reichsbund jüdischer Frontsoldaten (Reich Association of Jewish Combat Veterans), among other measures. As seen here, some efforts were made during the Third Reich to erase Emin Pasha from public memory as well. Colonial revanchist periodicals like *Jambo* eventually stopped listing moments from Emin's life as dates to remember. More importantly, the popular *Carl Peters* film never mentioned him.

But Emin's place in the imaginary landscape was far deeper than that of the German-Jewish First World War veterans, dating to the childhoods of the men who came to power in 1933. It was also bound up with the legend of Carl Peters, a man whom the Nazis venerated. It was likely for these reasons that Frank saw Emin Pasha as a problem that had to be actively addressed, not just ignored. He attempted to replace the Emin Pasha legend with a new counter myth: that of Emin as a modern 'Ahasverus the cursed', a wandering Jew in colonial spaces who served only himself and had no fatherland. Frank and others manipulated the memory of Paul Kayser for a similar purpose. Although there was no positive popular remembrance of Kayser with which they had to contend, they distorted the facts of his career as well so to fit the Nazi caricature of the self-serving disloyal Jew for whom colonialism was only another form of capitalism.

These retellings of the recent past reconciled the reality of Jewish participation in German colonialism with National Socialist knowledge about the supposed differences between Germans and Jews, creating a narrative that made sense from the Nazi perspective. Whether or not Frank and others like him succeeded in destroying the Emin Pasha legend and replacing it with their own myth is unclear, however. One example suggests that they may not have: while all other streets and places in Munich named after Jews were renamed for so-called Aryans during the Third Reich, Emin-Pascha-Platz remained unchanged.[68] Whether this was an oversight or a sign that the Emin Pasha legend lingered at some level even in this most brown of German cities remains an open question.

In closing, some Jewish and Jewish-allied groups used the Emin Pasha legend to challenge Nazi antisemitism. The Viennese periodical *Gerechtigkeit*, published by the outspoken anti-Nazi crusader Irene Harand, printed laudatory articles on Emin before the *Anschluss* as a response to 'the slanders that German Jewry is subject to' in the contemporary age.[69] The First World War Jewish veterans group, the Reichsbund jüdischer Frontsoldaten, devoted a chapter to Emin in the 1936 book, *Heroische Gestalten jüdischen Stammes* (Heroic Figures of the Jewish Tribe). He was a German patriot, the book declared: 'The life goal of Emin Pasha was to create a colonial Reich for his fatherland that offered stability in economic and geographical respects and to help procure for the motherland a world ranking.'[70] Harand and the compilers of *Heroische Gestalten* interpreted the Emin legend differently from men like Walter Frank. But they all understood that it was an affront to the antisemitic beliefs of the Hitler state.

Notes

1 Max Weinreich, *Hitler's Professors: The Part of Scholarship in Germany's Crimes Against the Jewish People* (New Haven: Yale University Press, 1999).

2 Walter Frank, *'Höre Israel!' Studien zur modernen Judenfrage*, 2nd edn (Hamburg: Hanseatische Verlagsanstalt, 1942), 126.

3 Ibid., 11.

4 For the most thorough scholarly treatment of Emin Pasha, see Christian Kirchen, *Emin Pascha: Arzt – Abenteurer – Afrikaforscher* (Paderborn: Ferdinand Schöningh, 2014). See also Patricia Clough, *Emin Pascha, Herr von Äquatoria: Ein exzentrischer deutscher Arzt und der Wettlauf um Afrika*, trans. Peter Torberg (Munich: Deutsche Verlags-Anstalt, 2010); Harald Lordick, 'Isaak Eduard Schnitzer – Emin Pascha. Erinnerungssplitter aus einem Jahrhundert Literature', in *Memoria – Wege jüdischen Erinnerns: Festschrift für Michael Brocke zum 65. Geburtstag*, ed. Birgit E. Klein and Christiane E. Müller (Berlin: Metropol, 2005).

5 See, for example, 'Vortrag des Herrn Direktors im Reichs-Postamt Sachse über die Emin Pascha-Expedition gehalten in der Vorstandssitzung der Deutschen Kolonialgesellschaft am 11. September 1888', Bundesarchiv Berlin R 1001, 249/3.

6 Christian S. Davis, *Colonialism, Antisemitism, and Germans of Jewish Descent in Imperial Germany* (Ann Arbor: The University of Michigan Press, 2012), 147–63.

7 Wolfram Pyta, 'Kulturwissenschaftliche Zugriffe auf Karl May', in *Karl May: Brückenbauer zwischen den Kulturen*, ed. Wolfram Pyta (Berlin: LIT Verlag, 2010), 16.

8 The continued relevance of the one-time colonies to post-imperial German politics, culture and society has drawn increasing attention in recent years. See Willeke Sandler, *Empire in the Heimat: Colonialism and Public Culture in the Third Reich* (New York: Oxford University Press, 2018); Britta Schilling, *Postcolonial Germany: Memories of Empire in a Decolonized Nation* (Oxford: Oxford University Press, 2014); *Weimar Colonialism: Discourses and Legacies of Post-Imperialism in Germany after 1918*, ed. Florian Krobb and Elaine Martin (Bielefeld: Aisthesis Verlag, 2014); and Jared Poley, *Decolonization in Germany: Weimar Narratives of Colonial Loss and Foreign Occupation* (Bern: Peter Lang, 2005). The Nazis had an ambiguous

relationship with the colonial revanchist movement. Leading party members hindered its publicity efforts, 'seeing them as representative of a discarded past and as irrelevant when compared with Eastern European *Lebensraum*'. Sandler, *Empire in the Heimat*, 10. Yet the government allowed the colonial revanchist movement to continue until 1943, and it also harnessed the memory of the colonies for its own purposes.

9   Tim Grady, *The German-Jewish Soldiers of the First World War in History and Memory* (Liverpool: Liverpool University Press, 2011).

10 For extensive coverage of the colonial activities of Emin Pasha, Paul Kayser and Bernhard Dernburg, see Davis, *Colonialism*.

11 Max Grühl, 'Eine Teestunde bei Dr. Emin Paschas Schwester', *Deutsche Kolonial-Zeitung*, 1 December 1930, 467–8.

12 In 'Eine Teestunde', Grühl presented Melanie Schnitzer's apartment as a portal to a lost nineteenth century: 'As I climbed the stairs to her apartment in the rear building, it seemed too as if the glittering present was left behind and a sunken, more peaceful, more pleasant Berlin arose.'

13 Bernhard Szana, 'Emin-Paschas Frau. Der Eheroman des Afrikaforschers', *Neues Wiener Tagblatt*, 29 April 1923, 21–4.

14 Ernst W. Freißler, *Emin Pascha*, 2nd edn (Munich: C. H. Beck'sche Verlagsbuchhandlung, 1925).

15 See, for example, v. Ny., 'Dem Gedenken Emin Paschas und Dr. Karl Peters', *Der Kolonialdeutsche*, 16 March 1927, 87.

16 'Dienstag, den 5. April 1927', *Die europaischen Sende-Programme. Beilage der Zeitschrift Radio-Wien* 2, no. 14, 3 April 1927, 8; 'Radio-Programme. Dienstag, 7. Feber.', *Prager Tagblatt*, 7 February 1928, 11.

17 Gerhard M. Nawratil, 'Berühmte Mediziner im Spiegel der Münchner Straßennamen', Ph.D. diss., Ludwig-Maximilians Universität München, 2003, 106; 'Ausland', *Radio Wien* 9, no. 3, 14 October 1932, 65; 'Ausland', *Radio Wien* 9, no. 4, 21 October 1932, 37; 'Ausland', *Radio Wien* 9, no. 5, 28 October 1932, 37.

18 Ehm Welk, *Die schwarze Sonne: Leben, Schaffen und Sterben deutscher Kolonialhelden* (Berlin: Ullstein, 1933), 101.

19 Freißler, *Emin Pascha*, 40.

20 Max W. L. Foß, *Enthüllungen über den Zusammenbruch: Eine Betrachtung über die Ursachen, daß es so gekommen ist* (Halle: Richard Mühlmann Verlagsbuchhandlung, 1920), 18; Max W. L. Foß, *England als Erzieher* (Berlin: Verlag der Täglichen Rundschau, 1921), 268.

21 Albrecht Wirth, *Weltgeschichte der Gegenwart (1879–1924)* (Braunschweig and Hamburg: Georg Westermann, 1924), 34.

22 Advertisement for *Emin Pashas Leben und Sterben*, *Deutsche Kolonial-Zeitung*, 1 November 1933, 237.

23 'Woran sollen wir uns in diesem Monat erinnern?', *Jambo* 11, no. 3 (1934): 90; 'Woran sollen wir uns in diesem Monat erinnern?', *Jambo* 12, no. 3 (1935): 88.

24 'Gedenktage im Dezember', *Kolonial-Post*, no. 11 (November 1936): 211. That year, the *Kolonial-Post* also listed Emin's murder in 1892 in the same section. See 'Gedenktage im Oktober', *Kolonial-Post*, no. 9 (September 1936): 162.

25 Dr. Heinrich Schnee et al., *Das Buch der deutschen Kolonien* (Leipzig: Wilhelm Goldmann Verlag, 1937), 48.

26 Harald von Beringe, 'Koloniales Deutschland', *Köhlers illustrierter deutscher Kolonial-Kalender* 17 (1938): 82.

27 The colonial revanchist movement maintained a degree of autonomy from the Nazi state until 1936, when the various pro-colonial organizations were absorbed into a unified Reich Colonial League. Discernible differences between the revanchist movement and the Nazi state remained, however. In particular, the former continued to emphasize Africa as the location for German expansion as opposed to eastern Europe. See Sandler, *Empire in the Heimat*.

28 Ch. Blume, 'Dr. Carl Peters: Der deutschen Jugend ins Gedächtnis!', *Afrika-Nachrichten* 15, no. 7 (July 1934): 172.

29 Ludwig Alwens, 'Bismarck und die jungen Männer von 1880', *Jungen – eure Welt! Das Jahrbuch der Hitler-Jugend* 2 (1939): 88.

30 Carl Peters, *Afrikanische Köpfe: Charakterskizzen aus der neueren Geschichte Afrikas* (Berlin: Ullstein & Co., 1915), 158.

31 Paul Baecker, *Carl Peters: Der Wiking der deutschen Kolonialpolitik* (Berlin: De Vo Verlag Volksbuch, 1934), 89.

32 Paul Baecker, *Der letzte Wiking: Carl Peters erobert Ostafrika* (Berlin: Junge Generation, 1935), 49–50.

33 Richard Wichterich, *Dr. Carl Peters: Der Weg eines Patrioten* (Berlin: Keil Verlag, 1934), 109.

34 Ibid., 112.

35 Hermann Böhme, *Carl Peters: Der Begründer von Deutsch-Ostafrika* (Leipzig: Philipp Reclam, 1939), 47.

36 Ibid., 54.

37 'Afrika als Ergänzungsraum Europas', *Innsbrucker Nachrichten: Parteiamtliches Organ der NSDAP. Gau Tirol-Vorarlberg*, 14 December 1940, 3.

38 Karlheinz Dahlfeld, 'Kolonien für Deutschland', *Jungen – eure Welt! Das Jahrbuch der Hitler-Jugend* 1 (1938): 92.

39 Erich zu Klampen, *Carl Peters: Ein deutsches Schicksal* (Berlin: Hans Siep, 1938), 140, 142.

40 Oswald Heydenhausz, 'Katja ist Frei', *Illustrierte Kronen Zeitung*, 12 November 1939, 10–11.

41 Erwald Banse, *Unsere großen Afrikaner: Das Leben deutscher Entdecker und Kolonialpioniere* (Berlin: Haude & Spenersche Buchhandlung Max Paschke, 1940), 197.

Colonial Revisionism

42 Ibid., 203.

43 Staatsanwalt Klinkhardt, 'Peters greift nach dem oberen Nil', *Afrika-Nachrichten* 23, no. 7 (July 1932): 109–11.

44 Frank, *'Höre Israel!'*, 59.

45 Ibid., 83.

46 Ibid., 65.

47 Ibid., 61–2.

48 Ibid., 108.

49 Ibid., 45.

50 Hermann Erich Seifert, *Der Jude zwischen den Fronten der Rassen, der Völker, der Kulturen* (Berlin: Zentral Verlag der NSDAP, 1942), 164.

51 Frank, *'Höre Israel!'*, 111.

52 Seifert, *Der Jude*, 165.

53 Alfred Funke, *Carl Peters: Der Mann, der Deutschland ein Imperium schaffen wollte* (Berlin: Metten, 1937), 46–8, quoted in Constant Kpao Sarè, 'Abuses of German Colonial History: The Character of Carl Peters as a Weapon for *völkisch* and National Socialist Discourses. Anglophobia, Anti-Semitism, Aryanism', in *German Colonialism and National Identity*, ed. Michael Perraudin and Jürgen Zimmerer (New York: Routledge, 2011), 167.

54 Alfred Funke, 'Cecil Rhodes und Carl Peters', *Deutsche Kolonial-Zeitung*, 1 October 1938, 334–5.

55 *Das Buch der deutschen Kolonien* acknowledged the expansion of railroads under Dernburg in the colonies. See Schnee et al., *Das Buch der deutschen Kolonien*, 132.

56 Dernburg did, however, undergo a short-lived period of public idolization while in office. See Davis, *Colonialism*, 197–8.

57 Dernburg remained largely unmolested during his retirement until his death in 1937. Werner Schiefel, *Bernhard Dernburg, 1865–1937: Kolonialpolitiker und Bankier im wilhelminischen Deutschland* (Zurich: Atlantis, 1974), 179.

58 Arne Perras, *Carl Peters and German Imperialism 1856–1918: A Political Biography* (Oxford: Clarendon Press, 2004), 214–30.

59 Of course, National Socialists and the likeminded needed little pretence to attack anyone, even non-Jews, with antisemitic diatribes.

60 Wichterich, *Dr. Carl Peters*, 98.

61 zu Klampen, *Carl Peters*, 194.

62 Ibid., 156, 194.

63 Walter Frank, 'Der Geheime Rat Paul Kayser', *Historische Zeitschrift* 168 (1943): 560. Compared to his earlier essay on Emin Pasha, this piece is less polemical, likely because there was no competing narrative celebrating the subject as a patriotic and empire-loving German Jew. In addition, the colonial revanchist press had already adopted a negative picture of Kayser. See Hans Gerd Esser, 'Der Weg eines

Revolutionärs: Jud Kayser brachte Dr. Carl Peters zu Fall', *Afrika-Nachrichten* 18, no. 10 (October 1937): 246–7.

64 Sandler, *Empire in the Heimat*, 259.

65 In discussing the film, I refer to the Kayser character by his first name, Leo, to distinguish him from the real Paul Kayser.

66 Herbert Selpin (director), *Carl Peters* (1941).

67 Otto Flake, *Ruland Roman* (Berlin: S. Fischer, 1922), 413–14.

68 The detailed records from the Nazi period concerning the name changes preserved at Munich's city archive contain no discussion of the *Platz*.

69 A. W., 'Deutsch-jüdisches Forscherschicksal: Emin Pascha', *Gerechtigkeit* 5, no. 188 (April 1937): 4; 'Der vergessene Emin Pascha', *Gerechtigkeit* 2, no. 46 (July 1934): 3.

70 Reichsbund Jüdischer Frontsoldaten, *Heroische Gestalten jüdischen Stammes* (Berlin: Erwin Löwe, 1937), 45.

12

Trauma, privilege and adventure in transit

Jewish refugees in Iran and India

Atina Grossmann

This chapter explores the unexpected and quite unintended places and intersections that research, initially focused on Jewish survivors in post-war Germany, can reveal. The larger history I address links two stories central to the history of the Shoah and the wartime Jewish experience but generally told and understood separately: on the one hand, the fate of East European, mostly Polish, Jews who escaped the Final Solution in involuntary exile in the Soviet Union, first in Stalinist special camps in the Soviet interior and then in Central Asia – also an 'Orient' – and who, numbering somewhere around 200,000, eventually came to form the (unmarked) majority of the *She'erith Hapleta*, the surviving remnant in the Displaced Persons Camps of post-war occupied Europe,[1] and, on the other hand, the flight from comfortable bourgeois Central European homes to 'exotic' non-European sites of refuge all over the globe, in this case Iran and India, of German-speaking Jews. It is also an integral part of the history of Zionism, Palestine and the State of Israel because of the *Teheran Children*, and their journey from Uzbekistan through Iran and India to Palestine,[2] and constitutes a crucial if quite under-recognized piece of the history of the JDC (JOINT, the American Jewish Joint Distribution Committee) relief efforts for Jews stranded in Central Asia via its Tehran headquarters.[3]Moreover, the passage of the exile Polish Anders Army, some 115,000 strong, from Uzbekistan into Iran and eventually via Palestine to the front in Italy, as well as the establishment of Polish orphanages in Iran (notably Isfahan) and in India, especially on the princely estate of the Maharajah of Nawanagar, situate these experiences within Polish and Polish-Jewish as well as Iranian and Indian history.

In a further step, therefore, that only clarified as I followed the trail of the refugees, this project is also a history of the anxieties of empire. Refugee fates were shaped by a defiant, vulnerable Great Britain and British Empire fighting on multiple fronts: confronting the German onslaught, competition from their Soviet and, to some degree, US allies, in the context of growing nationalist and anti-colonialist movements in India as well as occupied Iran during wartime. In that sense, my work fits into what one might term a colonial (or imperial) turn in Holocaust studies, as especially younger scholars start to focus on the entangled problems of race, class, gender and racism in the encounter between desperate Jewish refugees and colonial subjects as well as authorities, or more generally non-European, 'people of colour' in mostly (and not accidentally) temporary flight destinations.[4] This research highlights the critical role of empires (most obviously British but also French as well as the more informal Soviet and American spheres) in both facilitating and impeding rescue for European Jews – whether in Mandate Palestine and the Indian subcontinent or in Africa, the Caribbean and the Middle East more broadly, including Iran. These 'transits' of variable duration must be integrated more firmly into *both* the history of the Holocaust and of colonialism (and its fracturing).[5]

Finally, this is also a personal story, a kind of family memoir of my parents, two German Jews who, as they often insisted, never would have intersected 'at home' in Berlin. They met as refugees in Teheran in the mid-1930s where their relationship developed against the dual backdrop of the emerging European catastrophe and their paradoxical experience – excruciatingly ambivalent – as uprooted refugee Jews. They were homeless, displaced, having lost livelihoods and professions and with little to no sense of their families' fate or what the future held for them. But they were also Europeans, oddly privileged, adventurers in exotic non-western, colonial and quasi-colonial societies.

Here I present some pieces from a family history that, framed by archival research, is based on the experiences of those parents who remained always a rather unlikely pair, joined by the intersection of Orientalist desire, romantic passion, the desperation of refugees trying to escape the Nazis and the complexities of interwar and wartime geopolitics. In many ways, my Berlin-born and raised parents were perhaps paradigmatic in their differing motivation for turning to the 'Orient'. My father was a 'salon Communist', a brash young lawyer for the party legal aid association *Rote Hilfe* who needed to exit Germany quickly, as a leftist even more urgently than as a 'non-Aryan' expelled from the Berlin courts. When the Nazis came to power, he just happened to have an Armenian girlfriend whose family lived in Tehran and was willing to host a refugee disguised as a tourist. The two had apparently cut a striking figure in late 1920s Berlin; they accompanied KPD street demonstrations in style, he driving a big late model American Buick, she sporting a striking streak of white in her dark hair.[6]

My mother, by contrast, was a decade younger and a reluctant toiler in the family pharmacy located in the 'Red Wedding', a working-class district of Berlin. Not unlike other Jewish Weimar cultural radicals, she was fascinated by the 'Orient'. Banned by Nazi restrictions from the further education to which she aspired, she became a hanger-on at the Humboldt University (and perhaps at the radical chic mosque in Charlottenburg)[7] where she met Persian students and began the study of Farsi that served her well during eleven years in Iran and accompanied her entire life. A wannabee Orientalist, fluent in Farsi but never academically trained, she eventually became the (eccentric but cherished) department secretary of the Columbia University Middle East Department. Never fully separated from her Persian sojourn, where she encountered my father, her future husband, she displayed a Koran under the glass of our Danish Modern coffee table, slept on Persian rugs and never failed to celebrate *Nowruz*, the multi-ethnic Persian New Year's festival. My father, on the other hand, was an accidental refugee who, chastened by a 1932 foray to the Soviet Union which revealed the dark side of the 'workers' paradise', would surely have preferred to go west, presumably a more appropriate destination *'für einen Berliner Rechtsanwalt'*. In that peculiar context, they – and fellow refugees who remained lifelong friends – produced and collected a quite vast 'archive' of letters, documents and objects that now serve me as sources along with other ostensibly more 'conventional' research materials. By taking this 'micro' social and family history approach, I hope to contribute to putting 'flesh', as it were, on a discussion of the Holocaust, colonialism and postcolonialism that has for the most part – although that is now changing – been addressed in terms of cultural theory, to investigate how Michael Rothberg's formulation of multidirectionality functions in concrete historical contexts.[8]

Iran

'We are all uprooted and put down in this utterly alien culture . . . replete with "adventurers, spies, foreign agents" and the "wildest rumors"', where 'we were very visible; we were suddenly something special', recalled the German refugee paediatrician Marianne Leppmann in her unpublished memoirs, written decades later in Berkeley, California.[9] German and other Central European Jews, who generally arrived in the 1930s, were able to find first refuge and then work in the forcibly modernizing Iran of the upstart Reza Shah Pahlavi (and then occupied Iran) as engineers, architects, construction managers, teachers, legal advisers, multilingual secretaries and physicians. The rationalizing Pahlavi project offered opportunities for professors and scientists at Tehran University, only established in 1934, as well as technical and professional experts for the Trans Iranian Railroad, and other reform programmes in a new national Ministry of Justice and Education. Even the new National Dress Law which banned the traditional *Chador* created business for merchants, designers and skilled seamstresses or tailors.[10]

Persia offered shelter and adventure – 'things were so much more colorful then than they would have been under "normal" circumstances at home', Leppmann reflected – but also danger; friends contracted tropical diseases, committed suicide, children drowned in the pools of Iranian courtyards. The 'hunt' for 'rare' and coveted 'young European girls', like my mother, became, one male refugee observed, like a 'cult'.[11] Indeed, acquiring visas for Persia (Iran as of 1935) was particularly difficult for young single women precisely because of fears that they would constitute a sexual threat as prostitutes or at least women of loose morals, a gender-specific aspect of immigration possibilities, particularly perhaps to 'non-western' destinations, that requires further investigation.

These German-Jewish refugees, themselves often quite varied in their levels of identification with the religious/racial designation that had driven them from home, lived in a multicultural enclave, socializing with other foreigners, non-Jewish Germans, Americans (notably Protestant missionaries), British, Russians, Armenians and, after the Anglo-Soviet occupation in 1941, with British and American military personnel. Close contacts with Persians, even Persian Jews, were limited. Everyday life involved multiple daily encounters with domestic servants, chauffeurs, shopkeepers and professional or business colleagues, Persian language tutors and landlords (often Persian Jews). The reading room of the Alliance Israélite Universelle which traditionally served local Jews attracted both Persian and European Jews and provided an important conduit for JDC and Jewish Agency contact to the Tehran Jewish community. However, the few genuinely intimate relationships were mostly tied to the particular liminal world of mixed couples and families who tended to socialize with Europeans. Moreover, while refugees learned basic Farsi, French was the common language of diplomacy and elite society.

For the most part then, stranded in precarious safety on the margins of their collapsing and devastated Jewish European world, refugees lived as hybrids, themselves on the margins, simultaneously émigré, expat and refugee, caught uneasily, more or less comfortably, between colonizer and colonized. In flight from homelands that had condemned them as racially inferior they nevertheless carried with them a fraught sense of racialized superiority. Driven out of Europe by one form of racism they now encountered, and benefitted from, a different colonial form of racialized hierarchy in which they occupied a peculiar in-between position, definitely European but, as refugees and Jews, not part of a colonial or occupier elite. Expelled from the 'West' they never really left it behind, remaining for variable and sometimes considerable lengths of time in 'global transit', never relinquishing the dream of returning to the world they had lost or at least a new version of past homes in which they would be welcome.

With exceptions such as my border-crossing mother, a mix of semi-colonialist and Central European refugee customs prevailed. The archive of refugee ephemera features programmes for classical chamber music programmes, amateur cabarets and light opera. Letters report reading English paperbacks (my mother was particularly taken with the *Well of Loneliness*, the then scandalous interwar lesbian novel) and, a sign of the rapid urbanization under Reza Shah, going to the cinema, which offered a wide repertoire from Chaplin, the comedian Harold Lloyd and the tap-dancing Maurice Chevalier to German UFA costume dramas. In Tehran, both before and after the 1941 Anglo-Soviet occupation, this mixed expat/refugee milieu enabled for the most part a good life, punctuated by the news of Nazi measures and then war, ominous if carefully coded letters from home, and eventually, even more ominously, the absence of letters arriving at the *Poste Restante* of the Main Post Office. The relative safety and comfort enjoyed by pre-war refugees were only highlighted by the unexpected influx of emaciated Polish refugees from the Soviet Union in 1942.

'Thin indeed was the ice which we were skating on in wartime Iran', wrote Dr Leppmann, referring to an unstable and sometimes inscrutable if exciting life-navigating internal upheaval and the differing national and cultural interests and agendas of foreign powers. The Iranian capital might have been the only place in the world where refugee Jews asked German diplomats to stamp 'Js' in their passports in order to evade the rumoured British round-up (repatriation for women and children and internment, mostly in Palestine, of males) of German nationals as enemy aliens which accompanied occupation in summer 1941. Those German passports renewed with a 'J' (apparently with some surprise from mission officials) were, as she remembered, 'worth their weight in gold' as signs of anti-Nazi bona fides for the British occupiers but not, as my father would discover, for British colonial officials in India.[12] The German mission in Tehran was not fully Nazified and had maintained contact with the refugee community,

250   *Colonialism and the Jews in German History*

including Jews. Tehran hosted a relatively small German-speaking world, marked by both interaction and suspicion between 'Aryans' and 'non-Aryans'. In the late 1930s, the German mission was still recommending my Jewish father as a legal consultant (*Rechtsberater*) to all Germans in Tehran at the same time as he was consulting for the Iranian *Palais de Justice* on constitutional issues and conducting, together with an Iranian Muslim partner, an extensive 'import/export' trade from the Bazaar, selling a variety of goods from rugs to discarded military paraphernalia.[13] Both the suspicious travel – back to Europe at least twice and throughout the Middle East (including Palestine and a journey to Medina accompanying his business partner on a *Haj*) – until October 1938 with a regular German passport and purported 'trading with the enemy' later got him into trouble with the British when in May 1941 he crossed into India hoping to make his way to the United States. He had concluded, in contrast to my mother who remained in Tehran for what turned out to be another five and half years, that 'Asia' was indeed 'no place for a [disbarred] Berlin lawyer'.

Shortly after the outbreak of war in Europe, in October 1939, he wrote to his mother trapped in Berlin, 'I hope that you are doing relatively well', but also expressed his anxiety about finances, the disruption of trade and the future of the postal service – the remarkably efficient if agonizingly slow lifeline among the refugees in Iran, their friends and relatives now scattered across the globe, and above all, with those still in Germany. These letters have been preserved because like many who had escaped Nazi Germany, fearing that the letters might not arrive or with grave delays, he saved carbon copies of typed letters.[14] In a December 1940 letter he commented hopefully (with, I wonder, what degree of scepticism) on how cheerful her letters were, including a sprightly rendition of her birthday party. This regular correspondence was made possible until 1941 by Iran's adherence, quickly declared on 4 September 1939, to what the British envoy, with typical scorn, described as a 'manic neutrality'.[15] This official neutrality, a source of increasing concern for the Allies, did not, however, prevent the activities of 'Brown Houses' by local NSDAP affiliates. According to the anxious reports of the British 'political residents' which set the stage for the occupation, covert pro-German military training took place under cover of hiking trips in the Tehran environs, propaganda occasionally blared from loudspeakers in central squares or in cinema newsreels, and the Persian language programmes broadcast from Berlin included some anti-Jewish content. My hyper-observant father who recorded every film he saw or book he read, every excursion to the mountains or sea, did not, however, mention this German infiltration or any of the 'anti-Jewish articles . . . appearing in the local papers and causing considerable perturbation among the Jewish community' noticed by British diplomatic officials, neither, unsurprisingly, in his letters to Berlin but also not in those dispatched to his older brother Walter, already safely settled as a physician in Hartford, Connecticut.[16]

Reports focused rather on the pleasures of urban life – cabaret, cafés and films – and the indignities of adaptation to the Orient – endless stomach troubles, recalcitrant drivers, maddingly slow time rhythms and minor shortages.[17] He was thrilled with his motorcycle, itself a product of the long-standing trade relations with Germany which took my parents into the desert, with my mother Erika, the new Berlin girlfriend he had acquired in Tehran, perched glamorously in the sidecar (Figure 12.1). Europeans frequented cafes, restaurants and cabarets in the more 'western' areas, along Avenue Khibiane, consuming vodka and caviar and dancing until 3.00 am at the Café Pars. They went sightseeing, skied in the mountain resort of Derband which also attracted affluent Persians, swam in the Caspian, explored Isfahan and Persepolis and lounged around the pools in courtyards of established refugee families (Figure 12.2). They also sought the familiar, in the bed and breakfast pensions offering Central European-style food and a sense of home to single men (albeit not without danger since some of the

Figure 12.1 Erika and Hasigro on motorcycle in desert, 1939. © Atina Grossmann.

Figure 12.2 Erika birthday excursion to Ghan, Fars Province, fall 1940. © Atina Grossmann.

best were apparently equally popular with Nazified Germans) as well as income especially for refugee women; such lodgings were also important in Bombay – and surely in other refugee sites.

Fears of war loomed; would the escape routes via the Trans-Siberian Railroad or to Bombay and on to the port to San Francisco remain open? But Erika had found her place in the 'desert' and despite the romance with my father refused to accompany his attempted further emigration to the United States via India. Erika, Dr Leppmann complained, 'exasperated us by her foolhardy noncha-la[e]nce with which she spent summer moonlit nights in the fields outside Teheran – all alone!!'[18] (Figure 12.3). At the same time, this no-nonsense German-Jewish paediatrician did disrupt her flow of salacious tales and clinical judgements about fellow refugees, to tellingly acknowledge, even if only in passing, the shadow of the menacing events in a now remote 'there', unclear developments that letters mostly avoided mentioning (sometimes explicitly noting the evasion): 'of course we realize that she is worrying frightfully about her left behind parents, as we all do who have people there.'[19] Already in 1935,

Figure 12.3 Erika on donkey in desert, fall 1939. © Atina Grossmann.

another refugee, from southern Germany, realizing that he would not succeed in persuading his Catholic 'Aryan' mother and partially 'non-Aryan' – like himself – sister to join him in Tehran, had pointedly noted, 'The newspaper reports have at least one good effect, I no longer suffer from any homesickness', an assertion that was both only partly accurate and more and more potent over time.[20]

India

In May 1941, just as unbeknownst to him, the Soviets and British were plotting an invasion to short-circuit any further flirtation with the Germans by Reza Shah, my father, British transit visa issued in Tehran, precious American affidavit and visa and fully paid ticket on the SS General Gordon sailing from Bombay for San Francisco, in hand, hopefully made his way towards the border to India from Tehran. He had just noted for the first time an influx of desperate Polish Jews fleeing Soviet Central Asia. On 23 May 1941, a vigilant British political resident recorded laconically that 'Dr. Hans Grossmann, German Jewish Barrister, arrived in Meshed from Tehran on 22nd May en route India and the U.S.A', with no hint of the troubles just ahead.[21] Hasigro – the Dadaist name he invented for himself

262 *Colonialism and the Jews in German History*

in Weimar Berlin to replace the Germanic 'Hans Sigismund Grossmann' – did not know that he would have the 'bad luck' – a particularly unlucky convergence of the personal and the geopolitical – to pass the border at Quetta just a short time before the planned 'occupation of Persia'. He had stumbled into 'one of the hottest and most guarded spots in India . . . when everybody arriving from there was suspected as a Fifth Columnist and thus immediately becoming suspect as one of possibly thousands of German agents seeking to flee to India'.[22] His correspondence, a stream of almost daily letters from 1941 through 1946, typed and in English – for the censor – to Erika in Tehran and Walter in Hartford as well as to other scattered friends and relatives in Palestine, South Africa, Latin America as well as, thanks to a kind of prisoner of war status, Germany, record an intensely ambivalent and paradoxical set of experiences, sensibilities and emotions. His lengthy and entirely unwanted Indian interregnum began with his arrest at the border in June 1941, 'when I was for 20 days the only European prisoner in the Quetta District Jail' with the 'whole Jail Hospital' at his 'disposal together with 2 servants and cook specially engaged for preparing my meals'. He is bemused, horrified, frustrated and hardly grateful for this racialized colonial privilege. The poor cook prepared the 'most awful stuff' so that he subsisted on 'liquid milk and soda water and one Penguin book a day lent by the sympathetic Muslim Deputy Superintendent'. [23]

Only shortly thereafter, in August 1941, when the invasion finally arrived in Iran, my mother's friend Gisela, another young single Jewish refugee from Berlin, gaily embarked on an adventurous new life as a driver for the American Red Cross. For her, the occupation, deeply unpopular with Iranians, was an opportunity to do something meaningful – and exciting – for the Allied war effort, and not coincidentally to start a hot if ultimately ill-starred romance with an American colonel. Leppmann echoed her excitement, describing the arrival of the Persian Gulf Command: 'Streets all thronged with British, Russian, Indian, American, Polish soldiers, British nurses in resplendent white, archbishops in uniform, Rabbis in uniform . . . sitting in restaurants watching the many coloured crowds.'[24]

Indeed, Iran was one of the most important – albeit non-combat – theatres of the Second World War. Alarmed by German influence in officially neutral Iran, the invasion of the Soviet Union and Axis victories in North Africa and determined to protect vital oil supplies, British and Soviet forces had, in August 1941, divided the monarchy into southern and northern occupation zones. Reza Shah Pahlavi, deemed a potential German collaborator, was deposed and his son Mohammad Reza Pahlavi installed as titular leader. At the end of September

1941, President Roosevelt ordered the formation of a US Military Mission in Iran, launching what would become the Persian Gulf Command (under none other than General Norman Schwarzkopf Sr.). This crucial Allied supply operation brought some 30,000 (mostly African-American) US uniformed personnel and thousands of civilian workers into Iran from 1942 to 1944 (supplementing a British force with mostly Indian troops and the Soviets in the north) and shipped millions of tons of material, including some 5,000 planes and 200,000 trucks, to the beleaguered Soviets.

Iran emerged also as the epicentre of an early Allied confrontation with the ravages of war. Polish military and refugees – now estimated at somewhere between 114,000 and 300,000, including soldiers, women and children – poured in from Soviet Central Asia. The influx confronted the occupiers with a geopolitical dilemma as they sought to navigate competing Allied claims pitting the virulent anti-communism of the Poles against the US commitment to Lend-Lease and support of the Soviet war effort, in the context of British semi-colonial efforts at control – but also with a perceived humanitarian disaster. The Americans, placed, rather to their annoyance, in charge of relief efforts by the 'official' British occupiers, scrambled to contain hunger and epidemic disease among these 'haunting shadows' or 'walking skeletons', 'literally skin and bones', in a situation that the US Red Cross head for the Middle East, hastily summoned from Cairo, referred to in spring 1942 (right after the first Polish Exile Anders Army wave arrived) as 'this awful holocaust'.[25] Tehran, a centre of wartime intrigue, before and especially after the overthrow of Reza Shah, quickly became the centre for transit camps of especially child refugees headed for Palestine and a relief operation that shipped packages with vital goods for consumption and trading to the much larger number of Jews trying to survive the war in the unoccupied Soviet Union. Iran thus served as a key site for the rescue of some 200,000 Polish Jews stranded in Central Asia and several thousand Polish Jews attached to the Anders Exile Army who actually made it into Iran. A much smaller number of resident Axis nationality Jews, some of whom were actively engaged in that relief project, worked with the JDC, the Jewish Agency and Allied forces.[26]

My father in the meantime had become one of 223 refugees (out of hundreds more who were released) detained in British India after the recommendations of the Aliens Advisory Committee on 1 August 1941 and eventually one of only 119 aliens transferred to parole centres as 'undesirables of one brand or another'. New stringent instructions for the arrest or re-internment of enemy aliens, first issued in May 1940 after the shock of Nazi success in France and the low countries, had technically provided for the 'continued liberty of doctors, dentists, skilled workers, potential emigrants, and, whether Jews or not, persons who could show that they had taken an active part against Nazism and Fascism'. In an indication of the gendered nature of detention policies, the orders also foresaw 'the removal from ports and other places of strategic importance of women of enemy origin not specially permitted to remain in those places'.[27] In fact, the suspect undesirables were a rather motley crew, including Leopold/ Muhammad Asad-Weiss, age forty-three, with wife and son, 'Master Tal', listed as a 'German convert to Islam, Suspected German agent', as well as someone interned on account of his association with Communists and the marriage of one of his daughters to a well-known Communist. Or in my father's case, Nr. 32 of the transferred (transitist) internees, 'Grossmann, Dr. H.S. 41. German. Merchant. From Persia. Reported to have been trading with Germany while in Persia. Also suspected to be an enemy agent.'[28] Five years later, while trying to reactivate his long-forfeited US visa, he managed to examine his case file and concluded that he was indeed the victim of bad timing and some incautiously chatty remarks about his activities in Iran made to the Hungarian wife of a local British officer who served as his rather mysterious interrogator in Quetta.

Traces of that story have survived, not only in the India Office records in the British Library and the German Foreign Office Archives but also in multiple artefacts, somehow preserved and eventually deemed worthy of transport to the Upper West Side of New York. Fraying papers, stamped as the property of the Library, Wing 2, Central Internment Camp, Dehradun, include a tattered 'Home Section' of *The Illustrated Weekly of India*, from 7 December 1941 (of all days), with a page on 'Unusual Saris', of interest, I suspect, to the former Tehran bazaar salesman who had sensed business opportunities for ladies' hats and shawl sales when Reza Shah banned the *Chador* in 1936. The personal archive also includes a 4 October 1941 *Picture Post* article by Edward Thompson, illustrated with a half-page photo of Gandhi, titled 'What We Should Offer India' and warning that as 'Hitler drives toward India, Japan awaits her opportunity on the other side. Yet we leave the vital problem of India unsolved, keep some of her people's leaders in prison, disturb world opinion by failing to give her the benefits of the Atlantic Charter . . . India is the test of whether we fight for democracy.'[29] Were these texts that he discussed with his fellow inmate Leopold Weiss, aka Muhammad Asad, already deeply involved with Muslim politics in India with whom he shared the dubious and relatively rare, certainly for 'non-Aryans', distinction of being marked not only as an 'enemy alien' but also as a 'suspect enemy agent?' Other crumbling fragments include a view of the new film 'Forty-

Ninth Parallel', photos from a British magazine of a still undestroyed Berlin and a small map of Palestine.

As in other British internment camps from the Isle of Man to New Zealand, the inmates tried to entertain each other, chafing against their restrictions: 'DEH-RA-DU-UN Wonderful camp for fools / We will leave you/With all your bloody rules / We ask from Maxwell the keys / As we want to enjoy release. O DEHRA DUN, O DEHRA DUN! We want to leave you soon' (the ditty is preserved on a scrap of paper dated 5 October 1942). Letters, with sections scissored out by the censor, chronicled the curious existence of the uprooted anti-fascist enemy alien. A letter to his brother dated 2 April 1942 described a small Seder, bereft of wine and bitter herbs but brimming with tentative hopes for freedom. 'Waiting,' he observed, 'is the main occupation of an internee, waiting for mail, for the different meals and eventually for the great miracle of getting back freedom, of being put back in normal circumstances of living and working and of not furthermore being deemed as a convict and an enemy of the cause' and expressed 'envy at you having found refuge and the start of a new life in USA'. Reading regularly the *Aufbau* and *Readers Digest* he 'didn't know what to do without books'. Non-interned Polish and Hungarian Jewish refugees and freed German or Austrian Jews, together with the highly diverse local Indian Jewish community, were able to work with the JDC and the Jewish Agency in the Bombay Jewish Relief Committee to support relief efforts for the Polish Jews who had evacuated to Iran with the Anders Army or remained – in much larger numbers – trapped in Central Asia. Enemy aliens, however, struggled to prove their anti-Nazi credentials even as they remained suspect as a potential 'fifth column' of German agents attempting to exploit anti-colonial sentiment for the benefit of the Reich.

A year later, however, on 2 April 1943, Hasigro announced a sudden and decided improvement in his living conditions; after jail in Quetta and two internment camps, he had arrived in Purandhar

> six days ago from Dehra Dun with all my stuff, 8 big boxes and trunks . . . Together with 2 old Dehra Duniaans I am living in a small flat of 3 rooms, 1 verandah, 1 small bathroom and 1 small kitchen . . . looks rather nice . . . Although we have here neither electric light nor running water, I am very glad to be transferred to this place. You can't imagine the big difference between living in a barbed wire camp, male in every respect, and this camp where I met for the first time since almost two years women . . . to have always the most beautiful view upwards to surrounding valleys and to be able again to think at least of a future in freedom without being a phantast.

He wrote regularly to his brother in Hartford and almost daily to his 'fiancée' in Tehran, in imperfect English for the British military censor. The letters were carefully numbered, in a kind of reproach, I imagine, to my mother, who sent hasty scrawled missives from the Main Tehran Post Office, often apologizing for not conveying any concrete details of her own everyday life in occupied wartime Iran. Her more infrequent letters were couched in obscure, or as he liked to recall, 'dreamy' language, using initials and nicknames, full of allusions, covering up perhaps her ecstasy at living in the place of her Orientalist fantasies while her ostensible betrothed was locked up in India, reduced to writing letters while she was free to pursue her own adventures.

On 30 April 1943, as the war in Europe and the Pacific raged and the ghettos of eastern Europe were being liquidated, Hasigro once again recorded his relief about the move to new quarters with no barracks and no barbed wire. Purandhar was a 'family camp' set up for women and families (including Asad and his wife and young son). As a camp designated for Europeans it provided servants, tablecloths in the dining room and the privilege of an 11.00 am roll call. Notwithstanding the disturbing presence of 'c. 70 Nazis with families' who were apparently also housed in Purandhar, despite the official policy of maintaining order by separating 'fascist' and 'anti-fascist' internees, he, otherwise, rather enjoyed this 'well-known hill station and health resort' which featured '2 churches, 1 school, 1 dancing room (where we had thrice Passover services) . . . and a coffee-house . . . nice walking roads, even with opportunity for climbing steep rocks'. He remained sharply attuned to the absurdities of racialized colonial hierarchy in an internment camp, noting rather haughtily that 'not a few of the inmates here did never ago know such a life of "luxury", served by waiters, man-servants, sweepers, even without being bound to clean their shoes themselves'. As for himself, 'I, notwithstanding all these advantages would prefer to be released as soon as possible.' At the same time, the war and the news of genocide generated an insistent rollercoaster of emotions. 'No news from Mother and [his younger brother] Franz.' 'I am definitely convinced of the worst. Shall even we ever see us again?'

On 30 September 1943, the former lawyer from Berlin who had clearly been listening to BBC reports on the unfolding of the 'final solution' offered his Rosh Hashanah sermon to Jewish refugees saved from the Nazis now stranded behind British barbed wire:

> In this solemn hour we remember our fathers and mothers who instead of enjoying a well-earned evening of life full of quiet and happiness among their children

either put their life to an end themselves, or fell victim to murder, we remember our brothers and sisters who, unlike ourselves, had not the opportunity to escape the disaster and whom we shall never see again, we remember all the hundred thousands and millions of our Jewish brethren who died as suffering heroes, and we remember all the Jewish and non-Jewish soldiers who died in all the five parts of the world and all the seven seas fighting for humanity and freedom.

He expressed explicit regret that, trapped by the British who should have recognized them as allies, 'we are here only a small number of Jews who up to now, contrary to our hopes and wishes, could do little so that their death will be avenged, that the foundation-stone for a new and better world will be laid'. Adapting the High Holiday prayers for God and Country that he had learned at the liberal Fasanenstrasse Synagogue in Berlin, he was careful to add, 'Give Thy blessing to His Majesty King George VI and the Royal Family. Bless his Excellency Lord Wavell, Viceroy of India, bless all the Leaders of the United Nations and their Ministers, and give them power and wisdom . . . let the tyrants perish so that we may live in righteousness and peace.'

The Jewish internees continued their peculiar daily life marked by simultaneous 'white skin' privilege and imprisonment, always accompanied by thoughts of lost homes and family, oscillating between hope and despair. On 6 December 1943, Hasigro recorded his daily routine: one hour of tennis, bridge games, walking, reading, gossiping and always waiting. 'Life could be much worse!' he conceded to his physician brother, noting that 'people here received news that deported relatives wrote reassuring letters from Bohemia [Theresienstadt], even acknowledging parcels. Is there is still some hope of our beloved ones?' News and rumours circulated, through letters and crucially, the transnational German-Jewish refugee weekly *Aufbau*.[30] On 17 January 1944, 'Jews and other anti-Nazis have, for the first time since my internment, been asked for filing new applications, stating their pro-British attitude and usefulness for employment. I offered again unreservedly my willingness to join armed forces or Pioneer Corps or to accept every job in the war effort.' He confirmed once again the benefits of being an interned trapped European in the Raj: 'playing tennis and even football . . . I enjoy my rather nice flat with its most beautiful views . . . our good Purandhar, which under, quite different circumstances, might rightly be called a small paradise.' But he was ever more frustrated by his 'paradise cage', his forced exclusion from both the anti-Nazi war effort and the possibility of building a new and more permanent new life.

On 3 April 1944, he dared hope that the war's end might be coming closer: 'Some people here have indirect news from Theresienstadt and similar places.

Contrary to our expectations, these news are not 100% bad, thus allowing at least a small chance of meeting some of our beloved ones again . . . What a life of continuous strain and expectancy, hope and dejection.' As the war was finally about to be won and further news of the Jewish catastrophe trickled in, desperate searches for loved ones began; Hasigro's first queries via the British Red Cross were sent from Purandhar Parole Center in spring 1945. At its annual General Meeting in March 1945, the Jewish Relief Association of Bombay reported that 1,300 Jewish refugees in British India were searching for some 3,000 displaced and missing persons (Figure 12.4).

On 8 May 1945, with the unconditional surrender of the European theatre, a holiday was declared in Purandhar Parole Center and the flags hoisted in nearby Poona. On 13 May 1945, my father turned a VE Day speech to fellow internees into a painfully ambivalent *Kaddish*, noting that 'we who, against our expressed will, were not permitted to participate actively in this battle for the freedom of all peoples can feel no true joy' and recalled, 'Our parents and siblings, our relatives and friends, who unlike us were not able to escape destruction.'

Finally, on 11 December 1945, a full half year after VE Day, having been granted a conditional release, he was able to write from Bombay: 'This is my very first letter written in freedom since more than 54 (!!!) months.' He was living in a boarding house managed by Berlin refugees with 'very good food, a nice single room and bath . . . marvelous view on the Indian Ocean 100 m away . . . Rupees 10/ -p day ($3.30)'.

He had been freed from the camps but, visa-and-asset-less, was still not free to leave India. His *Wunschtraum* (wish dream) *after ten years Inner Asia, five years India and six months Bombay* list, typed on blue aerogram paper, reflected the desires of a quintessential Berlin Jew, nostalgic for the accoutrements of a bourgeois European life long since left behind. At the same time, it piercingly articulated the classic yearnings of a stateless refugee (and former prisoner), without a passport or papers, living out of suitcases, speaking the patois of the uprooted, without money or property, condemned to idleness (except the busyness of trying to free oneself and find a place in the world), reduced to writing applications pleading for a return to individual agency and political identity and citizenship. He yearned to 'sleep at night under a woolen blanket . . . Sit at the wheel of a car . . . Be able to unpack all my suitcases . . . Live without mosquitoes, cockroaches, and moths . . . Be liberated from the attribute *"refugee"* . . . Know where I will find myself in 6 months . . . Eat gooseberry tart with whipped cream'.[31]

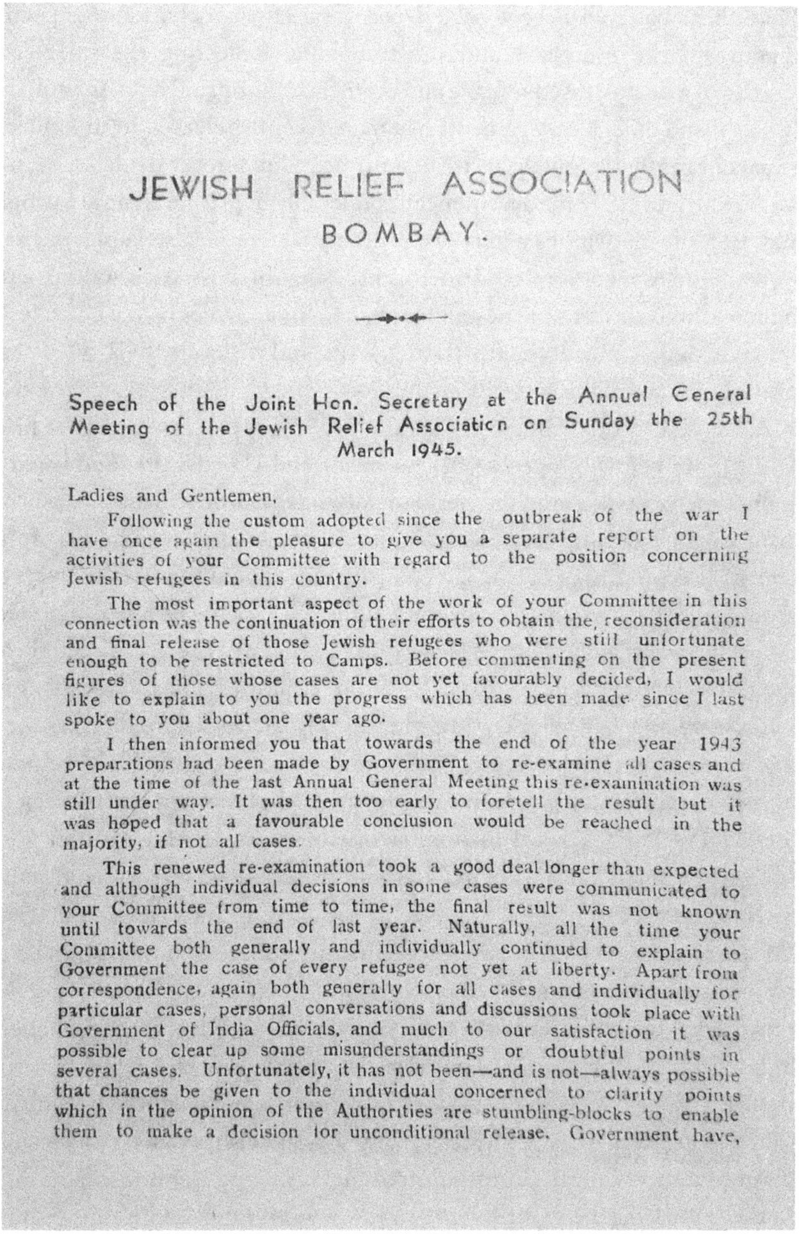

JEWISH RELIEF ASSOCIATION
BOMBAY.

—◆•◆—

Speech of the Joint Hon. Secretary at the Annual General Meeting of the Jewish Relief Association on Sunday the 25th March 1945.

Ladies and Gentlemen,

Following the custom adopted since the outbreak of the war I have once again the pleasure to give you a separate report on the activities of your Committee with regard to the position concerning Jewish refugees in this country.

The most important aspect of the work of your Committee in this connection was the continuation of their efforts to obtain the reconsideration and final release of those Jewish refugees who were still unfortunate enough to be restricted to Camps. Before commenting on the present figures of those whose cases are not yet favourably decided, I would like to explain to you the progress which has been made since I last spoke to you about one year ago.

I then informed you that towards the end of the year 1943 preparations had been made by Government to re-examine all cases and at the time of the last Annual General Meeting this re-examination was still under way. It was then too early to foretell the result but it was hoped that a favourable conclusion would be reached in the majority, if not all cases.

This renewed re-examination took a good deal longer than expected and although individual decisions in some cases were communicated to your Committee from time to time, the final result was not known until towards the end of last year. Naturally, all the time your Committee both generally and individually continued to explain to Government the case of every refugee not yet at liberty. Apart from correspondence, again both generally for all cases and individually for particular cases, personal conversations and discussions took place with Government of India Officials, and much to our satisfaction it was possible to clear up some misunderstandings or doubtful points in several cases. Unfortunately, it has not been—and is not—always possible that chances be given to the individual concerned to clarity points which in the opinion of the Authorities are stumbling-blocks to enable them to make a decision for unconditional release. Government have,

Figure 12.4 Pamphlet documenting meeting of Jewish Relief Association, Bombay, 25 March 1945. © Public Domain.

270   *Colonialism and the Jews in German History*

My father's battered *Regent Table Diary* for 1946 also charted this peculiar zigzagging of the mundane and the traumatic. Reflecting the intersecting itineraries of a dispossessed refugee and privileged European, it documented the daily social and official engagements of a man, recently released from four and a half years of captivity, acutely aware of a prime of life forever denied, not in the best of health and eager for decent meals, preferably in private Central European homes. But, the meticulous habits of a jurist still active, he also kept track of his daily reading (Armed Services Paperbacks, Penguin classics as well as letters with increasingly devastating news). He tracked his activities by the hour: Jewish Relief Association meetings, frustrating waits and visits to the United States Consulate, Friday night services at the Fort Synagogue, performances at the YMCA, dinners at the Chinese restaurant 'Sea View', endless rounds of bridge and Skat (with fellow refugees, a British major and US advisers) and listed the acquaintances who were finally permanently released or leaving. In February he read *Kim* by Kipling. He filled his days with American films (Tracy and Hepburn) at the Metro or Strand Cinema, doctor's appointments (the fevers that came and went), occasionally a meeting at the Taj Lounge or lunch/high tea at the Majestic, walks along Marine Drive or to Gateway of India. One could chart a topography of these refugee passages in India, in the camps, in Bombay and Calcutta but also in the countryside and princely estates where refugees served as physicians, factory owners, architects and engineers, as they did in Tehran.

Jewish organizations provided employment; he was appointed secretary of the Central Jewish Board of Bombay established in 1944, with Sir Victor Sassoon as president, as an umbrella group for some 30,000 local and refugee Jews. He organized the 1945 Passover celebration for 'our boys', 200 Jewish-Allied servicemen, so as to assure 'a certain atmosphere of home, cosiness and gaiety, pleasant for them as well as for me who spent his last Ceder [*sic*] Night just five years ago together with Erika in a Russian Jewish home in Teheran. With knedelach, gefillte Fisch, First class US Army Matzoh (best ever), wine, cigarettes, kosher sweets, hagadahs, prayer books', and a dance for which he recruited 'daughters of Israel' (presumably local Jewish women) as hostesses, followed by a merry third Zionist inspired night, singing Hebrew songs.

At the same time, he was revelling in his new-found freedom to explore the Indian city. Despite warnings not to 'live dangerously', he ventured to Frant Road, with its 'street hawkers, fortune-tellers, hair-dressers and beggars', and opium dens as well as the byways of 'cages' with Indian prostitutes who were 'practically slaves'. Armed with a British Guide for servicemen in India, *Hello Chaps! This Is BOMBAY*, which offered warnings about 'germs' and admonitions never to 'stare at girls' along with maps, sightseeing tips, postal and telephone locations and rates, plus 'Have You Written Home?' reminders, he was an aghast and fascinated tourist, a European voyeur, a refugee, a traumatized survivor, a man with no knowable future – all at the same time. He mused, 'When I saw this first . . . I was deeply shocked. But after having seen so many strange and awkward things here in this fairy-land India I would rather be surprised not to find all and everything quite different to all I have seen and experienced in the first 34 years of my life' (Figure 12.5).

Always, despite his striving for what he considered objective observation, he articulated a bath of emotions – hopeful and crushed, never reconciled to being stuck forever in India but, like most, although not all, Jewish refugees, even more determined to resist repatriation to Germany. 'For many many years, I am "an unemployed," "a transitist" or "a displace[d] person" by profession. I would like very much to get rid for good of all these "honourable" titles and to start anew something more reasonable, permanent, promising, and decent.' Still, statelessness was preferable to repatriation to that 'ghastly' European home from which, after all, a barbarism had emanated that he now feared was once again rearing its head in different form on the decolonizing subcontinent. The JRA finally managed to convince the Government of India that the status of Jewish refugees from Germany and Austria should be changed from 'enemy' to 'refugee

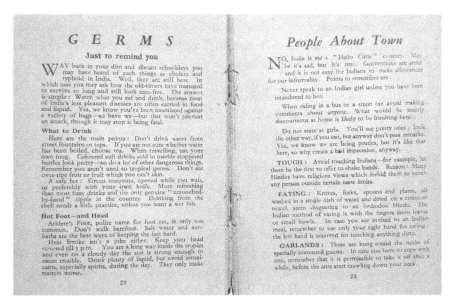

Figure 12.5 From the pamphlet *Hello Chaps! This Is BOMBAY, The Times of India* Press (n.d.). Tourist guide for allied forces. © Public Domain.

272 *Colonialism and the Jews in German History*

alien', a move that granted a kind of 'Displaced Person' protection against forced repatriation. However, other – more local – politics intruded as, with the defeat of fascism, the anti-colonial independence struggle with its spectre of ethnic/ religious violence gained steam. In one letter from Bombay on 23 February 1946, my father ruefully noted that having finally achieved his parole, he might actually have been safer as a British internee than in the streets of Bombay. 'For six years I missed the war, didn't hardly catch a glimpse at all of soldiers and tanks, planes, and warships. During the last five days I was more than recompensated for all that' with curfews (no cinemas, no cabarets) and 'R.A.F. bomber squadrons flying over the city' coupled with labour unrest, demonstrations, riots, looting and 'assaults on many Europeans and European-dressed Indians'.

The mood among the refugees darkened; more of them wanted to leave, fearing that the anti-colonial rage, now freed from any obligation to support the British anti-fascist war effort, would not only be directed at the Raj (a sentiment with which many sympathized) 'but against all white-skinned people'. 'Muslims and Hindus,' he mused, 'can agree at least on their hatred against all non-Indians.' He was convinced that as Edward Thompson had predicted, the British would not be able to 'suppress by force this nationalism of 400 Millions, 90% of them illiterate'. Racism became an ever more entangled category – not only the antisemitic variant that had devastated his home and family or the contempt of the colonizer for the colonized he had observed for over a decade but also, he reflected, the hatred between 'subaltern' groups as well as between the colonizers and the colonized, 'a racial consciousness' that in late December 1945 he rather remarkably deems 'formerly quite unknown to me':

> There is no possibility of friendship or of understanding between different races. It is not only the racial feeling alone but the feeling of each race and nation to be 'the master race or nation'. Thus, it proves that Nazism was only one of the symptoms of a world-wide phenomenon which hardly can be overcome during the next decades. This subcontinent called India reflects only as a microcosm the happenings all over the earth . . . the venomous hatred of one community against the other.

He wanted out from the chaos and encroaching violence in Bombay. After the memorial service for A. W. Rosenfeld, the revered leader of the JRA who had died at age forty-four during a visit to London, held in the Baghdadi Fort Synagogue, 'in that part of the city where most of the Continental Jewry is dwelling', Hasigro confessed (in cringeworthy language – a hazard of family history) to his now American brother:

Trauma, Privilege and Adventure in Transit 273

For the first time since 8 years (Yom Kippur service in Fasanenstrasse) I saw an assembly of almost 400 white people and for the first time since then I saw exclusively well and very well dressed people. For somebody unaccustomed to the life in the East it may sound snobbish and priggish when they learn that I enjoyed very much such a picture.

Ready to leave, although still not at the price of repatriation, most of his Bombay excursions were now emigration errands, with repeated appearances at the US consulate, Palestine Office and Central Jewish Board, as he hedged his bets about which permit would come through first, balancing a new fascination with the possibility of a Jewish state with the pull to the United States. But he also displayed an acute interest in the tense political situation throughout the failing British Empire in the Middle East as well as South Asia. His calendar listed a Muslim League Meeting on the evening of March 19 while the next morning he was off to WIZO, the Women's Zionist Organization bazaar. By March he was exhausted and frustrated by the refugees' bureaucratic catch-22; time was running out for a full release conditional on leaving India, which in turn depended on a visa from a sceptical US consulate waiting for political clearance from the British. On 11 March 1946, he hastened to a breakfast meeting in the Sea Lounge of the Taj Mahal Hotel with Sydney Silverman, a left-wing Labour MP from the East End, and Camille Honig, director of the British section of the World Jewish Congress. They had come to India on a dual mission, to aid the remaining Jewish internees and to raise money from the local Jewish community, especially wealthy Baghdadi Jews, to support relief measures for Jewish survivors in Europe.[32] The chance to explicate his own case and the plight of the seventy Jewish refugees still interned was, despite his 'deficient' English, 'a real pleasure' for the disbarred Berlin lawyer (who had been reading Indian and British law). Silverman, who had already in 1940 negotiated the release of Axis refugees interned in the UK with Churchill, spoken passionately in Parliament about the extermination of European Jews and been quickly on the ground at the liberation of Belsen, reacted immediately with a widely publicized press conference calling for the release of remaining internees. Much to the consternation of his more decorous colleague from the World Jewish Congress, he then took off for the hill stations, spending three hours in Purandhar, after which he visited Gandhi in Poona, who provided an eloquent statement of support for the survivors in Europe. Thus fortified, Silverman and Honig worked to collect funds for Jewish survivors in Europe from wealthy Baghdadi Jews and Parsees in Bombay and Calcutta, with support also from Nehru and leaders of princely states including the 'Moslem'

274 *Colonialism and the Jews in German History*

Nawab of Bhopal and the Maharajah of Nawanagar on whose estates Polish orphans escaped from the Soviet Union had found shelter.[33]

As the larger dramas of decolonization and Hindu/Muslim conflict played out in India and a 'refugee nation' of displaced persons emerged in Allied-occupied Europe, the refugees remaining in India continued to plot their departures while processing the ever more horrific news from Europe, sometimes communicated directly by British servicemen who had themselves been in Germany. Hasigro spent an 'Oneg Shabbat' after services in the Bombay Palestine Office, joining protests against the British blockade on Jewish immigration; the diary recorded another high fever, dysentery and sulfa drugs. Friends from the camps were leaving. He was still waiting for visas. In June he read *Lady Chatterley's Lover*. In July there was a telegraph strike. On 30 July, the latest visit to the US consulate yielded 'no news'; in August a quota number finally arrived, with the promise of a visa. At the same time, Hasigro was insistently trying to convince my mother to leave the 'Orient' she had embraced and join him in the new world where he hoped, even in middle age, to start anew. By refusing to join her fiancé on his ill-fated initial 1941 journey to the 'West' she had remained free to pursue her adventures as a young unattached European woman in multinational wartime Iran. Moreover, she had escaped the humiliation and frustration of British internment and been able to use her linguistic and secretarial skills to support the Anglo-American war effort in Iran as well as the JDC relief mission for Polish-Jewish refugees in Soviet Central Asia or in transit to Palestine via Iran.[34] Erika's reluctance to relinquish the Orientalist Weimar dreams she had by a cruel irony been able to fulfil after 1933 were surely not assuaged by my father's excited promise in August 1946 that 'Hartford is a very nice place surrounded by a landscape exactly to your taste. Mountains and green valleys, flowers and a river. Soon I hope to have a car and we will make our excursions as we were accustomed to.' She would have much preferred the motorcycle sidecar in the Persian desert. Erika did depart Tehran, very reluctantly, on a snowy 2 December 1946, taking a months-long circuitous route via Palestine and London that, at least temporarily, reunited her with scattered pieces of her surviving family. When she finally rejoined, in mid-1947, the partner who had, as he reminded her, kissed her goodbye on 20 May 1941, they settled, not in small-town Hartford but in the metropolis New York, another object of Weimar fantasies. As Hasigro had confessed in an earlier letter in December 1945, even as he struggled to secure passage to the United States he too knew how much the ruptures of National Socialism, war and the years in transit outside of Europe had shaped them, 'certainty in every respect has left me more than 12 years ago'. Indeed, 'the thought of being condemned to a quiet, uneventful, secure bourgeois life in an American middle town with its "Mainstreet" and all its "Babbits"[35] terrifies me from time to time'. His determination to leave was tinged with regret and fascination, for the 'cosmopolitan' Bombay he was only just discovering, with its 'variety of races, colours, dresses . . .' and 'huge contrasts between "indescribable poverty and dirt" and the "hypermodern"'.

Nonetheless, after a celebratory dinner at the Taj, multiple vaccinations and farewell visits, by noon on 20 August 1946, he was on board the General W. H. Gordon, a still unconverted troopship, almost exactly five years later than intended; now the journey cost only $350, much less, he noted with trademark irony, than in 1941. The ship's manifest identified his occupation as 'lawyer, merchant', his nationality as 'stateless', his 'race or people' as 'Hebrew' and his 'last permanent [*sic*] residence' as Bombay. And in a final indication of ambivalent and ongoing ties to the Orient, he wrote, to his brother, 'This letter ends, *inshallah*, our 8 years correspondence and separation'. Simultaneously, he was marking time via the Jewish calendar, planning to reach Hartford on 25 September, which he knew was Rosh Hashanah.

By 5:00 p.m. on Thursday August 22, 1946, he was 'sailing to AMERIKA'. August 31, playing poker, he reached the bay of Manilla with its sunken ships and encountered 'American style' jeeps, bars, bands, beer, and cokes, beginning the transformation of refugees and survivors into citizens of new homes. On September 10 came a landmark sign that the Orient has been left behind, 'first use of woolen trousers, pillows and woolen blankets'. And then the long-awaited day: 'Up at 5:30 to a beautiful sunrise under the Golden Gate Bridge, the ship docked Pier 46 at 10:10'. Two valises took several hours to locate, $3.65 customs duty had to be paid, and eventually, on dry land, he phoned his brother in Hartford, 'the first since 8 years'. Fulfilling a long-deferred plan from 1941, he purchased American Express travelers' checks, and went sightseeing, to Chinatown, to the Cliff Restaurant, and the Golden Gate Bridge, and then on the next evening, boarded the cross-country Pullman. His last entry listed all the books he read on that last refugee journey, from *Animal Farm* to *Pocket History of the US* by Allan Nevins and Henry Steele Commager. *Inshallah* he would make it to Hartford for Rosh Hashanah.

Notes

1   *Shelter from the Holocaust: Rethinking Jewish Survival in the Soviet Union*, ed. Mark Edele, Sheila Fitzpatrick, Atina Grossmann (Detroit: Wayne State University Press, 2017).

276   *Colonialism and the Jews in German History*

2 See Mikhal Dekel, *Tehran Children: A Holocaust Refugee Odyssey* (New York: Norton, 2019), which traces both her father's journey and her own as she uncovers his wartime and post-war story.

3 See Atina Grossmann, "'Joint Fund Teheran'': JDC and the Jewish Lifeline to Central Asia', in *The JDC at 100: A Century of Humanitarianism*, ed. Avinoam Patt, Atina Grossmann, Linda G. Levi, Maud S. Mandel (Detroit: Wayne State University Press, 2019), 205–44.

4 See, for example, the exciting doctoral research of Kimberly Cheng (New York University) on the encounter between Jewish refugees and local residents as well as Japanese occupiers in Shanghai and Pragya Kaul (University of Michigan) on similar processes in Calcutta (Kolkata) among Jewish refugees, Indian Jews, other local residents and British colonials.

5 See among a growing list, work on southern Africa, for example, Shirli Gilbert, *From Things Lost: Forgotten Letters and the Legacy of the Holocaust* (Detroit: Wayne State University, 2017), the Caribbean, the Philippines, Singapore, Shanghai and in a different register, throughout Central and South America.

6 These impressions of my father's political activities and his relationship with his Armenian-Iranian partner in Berlin are based on oral history interviews with Rosa Meyer Leviné, London, 1978. See also Meyer Leviné's memoirs, *Inside German Communism: Memoirs of Party Life in the Weimar Republic* (London: Pluto Press, 1977).

7 On the quite glittering mix of Islam, Weimar *Lebensreform* and Berlin radical culture in the 1920s and its development in the 1930s, see Marc David Baer, 'Muslim Encounters with Nazism and the Holocaust: The Ahmadi of Berlin and Jewish Convert to Islam Hugo Marcus', *American Historical Review* 120 (2015): 140–71, and Gerdien Jonker, *Zwischen Juden und Muslimen: Eine Europäische Familiengeschichte 1836–2016* (Göttingen: Wallstein, 2018) and Gerdien Jonker, *The Ahmadiayya Quest for Religious Progress: Modernizing Europe 1900–1965* (Leiden: Brill, 2015). Germany and Persia had a long-established history of economic and cultural ties, which clearly impacted the ability of refugees to gain admittance to Iran in the 1930s as well as the lives they were able to establish. See Jennifer Jenkins, 'Hjalmar Schacht, Reza Shah, and Germany's Presence in Iran', *Iran Nameh* 30 (2015): XX–XLVI; Jennifer Jenkins, 'Experts, Migrants, Refugees: Making the German Colony in Iran, 1900–1934', in *German Colonialism in a Global Age*, ed. Bradley Naranch and Geoff Eley (Durham: Duke University Press, 2014), 147–69.

8 Michael Rothberg, *Multidirectional Memory: Remembering the Holocaust in the Age of Decolonization* (Stanford: Stanford University Press, 2009).

9 Marianne Leppmann memoirs, unpublished typescript (by kind permission of family), 80. Leppmann's recollections as well as correspondence with Walter Maria Guggenheimer, a refugee who had joined the Free French Forces, offer insight into

the Iran refugee world, the impact of the occupation and the role of gender and sexuality in structuring everyday life and emotions.

10 On the history of Pahlavi rule and Reza Shah's seizure of power, see among many sources, Ervand Abrahamian, *A History of Modern Iran*, rev. edn (New York: Cambridge University Press, 2018). On Jews' place in that history, sees Lior Sternfeld, *Between Iran and Zion: Jewish Histories of Twentieth Century Iran* (Palo Alto: Stanford University Press, 2018), 15–39. The Iranians tried to recruit German refugee scientists and physicians, drawing from a list of about 200 (see Sternfeld, *Between Iran and Zion*, 16, 137), but it is not clear how many (if any) actually arrived.

11 Letter Guggenheimer to his mother in Bad Tölz, 26 August 1935, Walter Maria Guggenheimer papers, Deutsches Exil Archiv Frankfurt, NL 146, EB 99/70.

12 Quotes from Leppmann memoirs, 161–2, 120.

13 Politisches Archiv des Auswärtigen Amts, Berlin, Deutsche Gesandtschaft Teheran, Passport Division, Parcel 21, III.4, vols. 7–9. German officials maintained files on most German nationals in Iran and communicated with their hometown Gestapo as to whether there was any reason (political, not racial) not to renew. Even though the files were clearly marked '*Jude*' if deemed appropriate, the passports were virtually always reauthorized – only, starting in 1939, with the proviso that they not be used for travel back to Germany.

14 The originals were indeed lost when his mother slipped into hiding in 1942 and then was denounced and deported to Auschwitz a year later. Unless otherwise indicated, all letters, texts (sometimes on ripped scraps of paper) and artefacts are from my private family collection. For reflections on the letters exchanged between my parents in Tehran and their respective mothers in Berlin, see Atina Grossmann, 'I Thought She Was Old But She Was Really My Age: Tracing Desperation and Resilience in my Grandmothers' Letters From Berlin – Fragments', in *On Being Adjacent to Historical Violence*, ed. Irene Kacandes (de Gruyter, 2021), 467–91.

15 See *Iran Political Diaries 1881–1965*, ed. R. Michael Burrell and Robert L. Jarman (Slough: Archive Editions, 1997). Volume 12: 1943–1945. This is an edited version of the diaries of Sir Reader Bullard, the British envoy. Covert German activity and attempted propaganda and the concomitant fear of a 'fifth column' did not cease with the occupation; see Adrian O'Sullivan, *Nazi Secret Warfare in Occupied Persia (Iran): The Failure of the German Intelligence Services, 1939–45* (Houndmills, Basingstoke: Palgrave Macmillan, 2014); also Jennifer Jenkins, 'Iran in the Nazi New Order, 1933–1941', *Iranian Studies* 49 (2016): 727–51.

16 See BL IOR/L/PS/12/3407. *Political Diary 23*, 26 November 1941 and *Political Diary 21*, 26 October 1941. The British were clearly anxious about the occupation's possible exacerbation of the very pro-German tendency it was intended to curb. Later reports, oozing with colonialist contempt, note that as the tide of the war

278   *Colonialism and the Jews in German History*

turned, pro-German sentiments, fed mostly by long-standing resentment of British interference and fear of Soviet control, subsided once it was clear that the Germans would not be able to provide that protection, a shift interpreted by the British as indicating the childlike unreliability of the Persians.

17   This preoccupation with 'tropical' maladies and occasional requests for advice from physicians still in Germany or emigrated to western locales pervade many refugee reports on life in the Orient.

18   Leppmann memoirs, 132.

19   Leppmann to Guggenheimer, 3 March 1943, 10 October 1943 and 17 February 1944, Walter Maria Guggenheimer papers, Deutsches Exil Archiv Frankfurt, EB 99/70.

20   Guggenheimer to his mother, 8 August 1935, Walter Maria Guggenheimer papers, Deutsches Exil Archiv Frankfurt, EB 99/70.

21   BL IOR/L/PS/12/3407, 23 May 1941, *Political Diary* Nr. 10, p. 3.

22   Hasigro to his brother, Walter Grossmann, in Hartford, Conn., Bombay 11 December 1945.

23   Hasigro to Walter Grossmann, 11 March 1946, Bombay. He noted sarcastically that given the no more than 500–1,700 Germans resident in Iran these fears of an invasion of Axis fifth columnists were totally inflated.

24   Leppmann to Guggenheimer, 20 September 1942, Walter Maria Guggenheimer papers, Deutsches Exil Archiv Frankfurt, EB 99/70.

25   Letters from Maurice Barber, American Red Cross representative in Tehran to ARC, Washington, DC, 2 and 12 April 1942. NARA, State Department Refugee Files 840.48, microfilm box 1284, roll 31.

26   See Grossmann, 'Remapping Survival: Jewish Refugees and Lost Memories of Displacement, Trauma, and Rescue in Soviet Central Asia, Iran, and India', *Simon Dubnow Institute Yearbook* 15 (2016): 71–97, revised version in *Shelter from the Holocaust*, 185–218, and Grossmann, 'Joint Fund Teheran'. See also Lior Sternfeld, '"Poland is Not Lost While We Still Live": The Making of Polish Iran, 1941–1945', *Jewish Social Studies* 23 (2018): 101–27. On British reactions to the Polish evacuees, see also BL IOR/L/PS/12/3047. Interestingly, the standard English-language historiography on Iran during the Second World War period does not, to the best of my knowledge, discuss this visible presence of Jewish and non-Jewish Poles. See, for example, Abrahamian, *A History of Modern Iran*, which covers the period of the 1930s and 1940s in two chapters, on the reign of Reza Shah and the 'Nationalist Interregnum' from 1941 to the overthrow of Mossadegh, 65–125. Sternfeld, *Between Iran and Zion*, does briefly discuss the Polish presence during the war and its post-war legacy, 19–32. Mikhal Dekel's richly detailed family memoir and history tells the story of the Tehran Children. See Dekel, *Tehran Children*.

27   British Library (henceforth BL), IOR: L/PJ/8/67 (India Office), 104. In general, the presence of women of enemy nationality was deemed 'embarrassing' and

Government of India would have much preferred to repatriate (or deport) as many women as possible back to Germany or Italy. See Government India Home Department to His Majesty's Under Secretary of State for India, India Office, London. New Delhi, 13 September 1943.

28 BL, IOR: L/PJ/8/67 (India Office), 125. The list of refugees 'restricted to parole centers who are to continue in detention for the present' also included (together with his wife) Dr M. H[erman] Selzer, a physician in charge of the camp hospital at Purandhar Parole Center, whose (rather problematic to evaluate) memoirs are in the Leo Baeck Institute Archives, New York. Listed as a man of 'pro Axis sympathies', Selzer was nonetheless permitted to serve as medical officer and publish his research on 'Diet in Health and Disease in India', BL, IOR l/PJ/8/35, 248; IOR: L/PJ/8/67, Enemy Aliens, 109.

29 Edward Thompson (father of the historian E. P. Thompson) was a British colonial official who had grown sceptical about the long-term prospects of the Raj.

30 See Peter Schrag, *The World of Aufbau: Hitler's Refugees in America* (Madison: University of Wisconsin Press, 2019).

31 For further reflections on this text, see 'Transnational Jewish Stories: Displacement, Loss and (Non)Restitution', in *Three Way Street: Jews, Germans, and the Transnational*, ed. Jay Geller and Leslie Morris (Ann Arbor: University of Michigan Press, 2016), 362–84.

32 Reports on these meetings and the World Jewish Congress efforts in India veer uneasily between a haughtiness towards 'Asian' (and not only the 'black' *Bene Israel* indigenous) Jews – a total of about 30,000 Indian Jews – and an unabashed desire for their financial support, all complicated by frustration at Baghdadi (or 'Anglo-Indian') Jews' insistence on clearing their actions with Gandhi and Nehru and their desire to support relief in Europe rather than in Palestine, thereby avoiding any direct support for Zionism. See The Jacob Rader Marcus Center of the American Jewish Archives, WJC Papers. Box H189, File 11.

33 Honig, Camille; Silverman, Sydney, trip to India, 1946, The Jacob Rader Marcus Center of the American Jewish Archives, WJC Papers, Box H189 File 11. The Jacob Rader Marcus Center of the American Jewish Archives.

34 See Grossmann, 'Joint Fund Teheran'.

35 A reference to the novels critiquing small-town American life, published by Sinclair Lewis in 1920 and 1922 which would have been familiar to European leftists.

Bibliography

Abrahamian, Ervand. *A History of Modern Iran*, rev. edn. New York: Cambridge University Press, 2018.

Abulafia, Anna Sapir. *Christians and Jews in the Twelfth-Century Renaissance*. London: Routledge, 1995.

Achinger, Christine, and Robert Fine, eds. *Antisemitism and Racism: Current Connections and Disconnections*. New York: Routledge, 2017.

Adorno, Theodor W. 'Prejudice in the Interview Material', in *The Authoritarian Personality*, edited by Theodor W. Adorno, Betty Ruth Aron, Else Frenkel-Brunswik, Daniel J. Levinson, et al. New York: Harper & Brothers, 1950, 605–53.

Ahmed, Shahab. *What Is Islam: The Importance of Being Islamic*. Princeton: Princeton University Press, 2015.

Aizenberg, Salo. *Hatemail: Anti-Semitism on Picture Postcards*. Philadelphia: Jewish Publication Society, 2013.

Ames, Eric, Marcia Klotz, and Lora Wildenthal, eds. *Germany's Colonial Pasts*. Lincoln: University of Nebraska Press, 2005.

Arendt, Hannah. *The Origins of Totalitarianism*. New York: Harcourt Brace Jovanovich, 1973.

Aschheim, Steven E. 'German History and German Jewry: Boundaries, Junctions and Interdependence', *Leo Baeck Institute Yearbook* 43 (1998): 315–22.

Aschheim, Steven E. '*Bildung* in Palestine: Zionism, Binationalism, and the Strains of German-Jewish Humanism', in *Beyond the Border: The German-Jewish Legacy Abroad*. Princeton: Princeton University Press, 2006, 6–44.

Austen, Ralph A., and Jonathan Derrick, eds. *Middlemen of the Cameroons Rivers: The Duala and Their Hinterland, c. 1600–c. 1960*. Cambridge: Cambridge University Press, 1999.

Axster, Felix. 'Arbeit an der "Erziehung zur Arbeit", oder: die Figur des deutschen Kolonisators', in '*Deutsche Arbeit*': *Kritische Perspektiven auf ein ideologisches Weltbild*, edited by Felix Axster and Nikolas Lelle. Göttingen: Wallstein Verlag, 2018, 226–51.

Axster, Felix, and Jana König. 'Nachwort: Multidirektionalität in Deutschland', in *Multidirektionale Erinnerung: Holocaustgedenken im Zeitalter der Dekolonisierung*, edited by Michael Rothberg, Berlin: Metropol, 2021, 361–79.

Baer, Marc David. 'Muslim Encounters with Nazism and the Holocaust: The Ahmadi of Berlin and Jewish Convert to Islam Hugo Marcus', *American Historical Review* 120 (2015): 140–71.

Bajohr, Frank. 'Unser *Hotel ist judenfrei*': *Bäder-Antisemitismus im 19. und 20. Jahrhundert*. Frankfurt am Main: Fischer, 2003.

Bar Yosef, Eitan, and Nadia Valman, eds. *'The Jew' in Late-Victorian and Edwardian Culture: Between the East End and East Africa*. Basingstoke: Palgrave Macmillan, 2009.

Bareli, Avi. 'Forgetting Europe: Perspectives on the Debate about Zionism and Colonialism', *Journal of Israeli History* 20 (2001): 99–120.

Bartal, Israel. *The Jews of Eastern Europe, 1872–1881*. Philadelphia: University of Philadelphia Press, 2005.

Barth, Boris, and Jürgen Osterhammel, eds. *Zivilisierungsmissionen: Imperiale Weltverbesserung seit dem 18. Jahrhundert*. Konstanz: Universitätsverlag Konstanz, 2005.

Bartlett, Robert. 'Illustrating Ethnicity in the Middle Ages', in *The Origins of Racism in the West*, edited by Miriam Eliav-Feldon, Benjamin H. Isaac, and Joseph Ziegler. Cambridge: Cambridge University Press, 2009, 132–56.

Bauche, Manuela. *Medizin und Herrschaft: Malariabekämpfung in Kamerun, Ostafrika und Ostfriesland 1890–1919*. Frankfurt am Main: Campus, 2017.

Baudrillard, Jean. *Simulacra and Simulation*. Translated by Sheila Faria Glaser. Ann Arbor: University of Michigan Press, 1994.

Beddingfield, Meghan: 'Gog and Magog', in *Encyclopedia of the Bible and its Reception*, edited by Constance M. Furey et al., vol. 10. Berlin: De Gruyter, 2015, 504–18.

Bein, Alex. 'Memoirs and Documents about Herzl's Meeting with the Kaiser', *Herzl Year Book* 6 (1964/5): 39–60.

Beiner, Ronald. 'Arendt and Nationalism', in *The Cambridge Companion to Hannah Arendt*, edited by Dana Villa. Cambridge: Cambridge University Press, 2000, 44–61.

Benhabib, Seyla. *The Reluctant Modernism of Hannah Arendt*. Lanham: Rowman & Littlefield, 2003.

Ben-Rafael, Eliezer, Julius Schoeps, Yitzhak Sternberg, and Olaf Glöckner, eds. *Handbook of Israel II*. Oldenbourg: De Gruyter, 2016.

Benz, Wolfgang, ed. *Islamfeindschaft und ihr Kontext: Dokumentation der Konferenz 'Feindbild Muslim – Feindbild Jude'*. Berlin: Metropol, 2009.

Berg, Nicolas. *Der Holocaust und die westdeutschen Historiker: Erforschung und Erinnerung*. Göttingen: Wallstein, 2003.

Berg, Nicolas. '"Weg vom Kaufmannsstande! Zurück zur Urproduktion!" Produktivitätsforderungen an Juden im 19. und frühen 20. Jahrhundert', in *Das nennen Sie Arbeit? Der Produktivitätsdiskurs und seine Ausschlüsse*, edited by Nicole Colin and Franziska Schößler. Heidelberg: Synchron Publishers, 2013, 29–51.

Bergmann, Werner, and Mona Körte, eds. *Antisemitismusforschung in den Wissenschaften*. Berlin: Metropol, 2004.

Berkowitz, Michael. *Zionist Culture and West European Jewry before the First World War*. Chapel Hill: University of North Carolina Press, 1993.

Bernstein, Richard J. *Hannah Arendt and the Jewish Question*. Cambridge, MA: The MIT Press, 1996.

Bildungsstätte, Anne Frank, ed. *Themenheft Geschichtsrevisionismus und Antisemitismus: Wie die Rechten die Geschichte umdeuten*. Frankfurt am Main: Bildungsstätte Anne Frank, 2000.

Bitzan, Amos. 'Leopold Zunz and the Meanings of Wissenschaft', *Journal of the History of Ideas* 78 (2017): 233–54.

Blackbourn, David. *The Conquest of Nature: Water, Landscape, and the Making of Modern Germany*. London: Cape, 2006.

Blackburn, Robin. *The Overthrow of Colonial Slavery 1776–1848*. London: Verso, 1988.

Bloom, Etan. *Arthur Ruppin and the Production of Pre-Israeli Culture*. Leiden: Brill, 2011.

Böhm, Adolf. *Die Zionistische Bewegung: II. Teil*. Berlin: Welt-Verlag, 1921.

Bommarius, Christian. *Der gute Deutsche: Die Ermordung Manga Bells in Kamerun 1914*. Berlin: Berenberg Verlag, 2015.

Borowy, Iris 'Akklimatisierung. Die Umformung europäischer Landschaft als Projekt im Dienst von Wirtschaft und Wissenschaft, 1850–1900', *Themenportal Europäische Geschichte 2009*, https://www.europa.clio-online.de/essay/id/fdae-1493 (last accessed 12 February 2020).

Boyarin, Daniel. *The Jewish Gospel: The Story of the Jewish Christ*. New York: New Press, 2012.

Braese, Stephan. 'Kommentar zu Christian Wilhelm Dohm', in *Theorien über Judenhass – eine Denkgeschichte: Kommentierte Quellenedition (1781-1931)*, edited by Birgit Erdle and Werner Konitzer. Frankfurt am Main: Campus, 2015, 35–43.

Braude, Benjamin. 'The Sons of Noah and the Construction of Ethnic and Geographical Identities in the Medieval and Early Modern Periods', *The William and Mary Quarterly* 54 (1997): 103–42.

Brenner, Michael. *Prophets of the Past: Interpreters of Jewish History*. Translated by Steven Rendall. Princeton: Princeton University Press, 2010.

Brenner, Michael. 'Orchideenfach, Modeerscheinung ode rein ganz normales Thema? Zur Vermittlung von jüdischer Geschichte und Kultur an deutschen Universitäten', in *Jüdische Geschichte: Alte Herausforderungen, neue Ansätze*, edited by Eli Bar-Chen and Anthony D. Kauders. München: Utz, 2013, 13–24.

Brenner, Michael, and Maximilian Strnad, eds. *Der Holocaust in der deutschsprachigen Geschichtswissenschaft: Bilanz und Perspektiven*. Göttingen: Wallstein, 2012.

Breuer, Stefan. *Die Völkischen in Deutschland*. Darmstadt: Wissenschaftliche Buchgesellschaft, 2008.

Brinton, Crane. *The Anatomy of Revolution*. New York: Vintage, 1965.

Bruer, Albert A. *Geschichte der Juden in Preußen*. Frankfurt am Main: Campus, 1991.

Brumlik, Micha, Hajo Funke, and Lars Rensmann. *Umkämpftes Vergessen: Walser-Debatte, Holocaust-Mahnmal und neuere deutsche Geschichtspolitik*. Berlin: Das Arabische Buch, 1999.

Brunotte, Ulrike. 'From *Nehemia Americanus* to Indianized Jews: Pro- and Anti-Judaic Rhetoric in Seventeenth-Century New England, *Journal of Modern Jewish Studies* 15 (2016): 188–207.

Brunotte, Ulrike, 'The Beautiful Jewess as Borderline Figure in Europe's Internal Colonialism: Some Remarks on the Intertwining of Orientalism and Antisemitism', *ReOrient* 4 (2019): 166–80.

Brunotte, Ulrike, Anna-Dorothea Ludewig, and Axel Stähler, eds. *Orientalism, Gender, and the Jews: Literary and Artistic Transformations of European National Discourses.* Berlin: De Gruyter, 2014.

Brunotte, Ulrike, Jürgen Mohn, and Christina Späti, eds. *Internal Outsiders – Imagined Orientals? Antisemitism, Colonialism and Modern Constructions of Jewish Identity.* Würzburg: Ergon, 2017.

Bruns, Claudia. 'Wilhelminische Bürger und "germanische Arier" im Spiegel des "Primitiven": Ambivalenzen einer Mimikry an die kolonialen "Anderen"', *Comparativ. Zeitschrift für Globalgeschichte und vergleichende Gesellschaftsforschung* 9, no. 5 (2009): 15–33.

Bruns, Claudia. 'Antisemitism and Colonial Racism: Transnational and Interdiscursive Intersectionality', in *Racisms Made in Germany*, edited by Wulf D. Hund, Christian Koller, and Moshe Zimmermann. Berlin: Lit Verlag, 2011, 99–121.

Bruns, Claudia. 'Towards a Transnational History of Racism: Interrelationships between Colonial Racism and German Anti-Semitism? The Example of Wilhelm Marr', in *Racism in the Modern World: Historical Perspectives on Cultural Transfer and Adaptation*, edited by Manfred Berg and Simon Wendt. New York: Berghahn, 2011, 122–39.

Bruns, Claudia, and M. Michaela Hampf, eds. *Wissen – Transfer – Differenz: Transnationale und interdiskursive Verflechtungen von Rassismen ab 1700.* Göttingen: Wallstein, 2018.

Buck-Morss, Susan. *Hegel, Haiti, and Universal History.* Pittsburgh: University of Pittsburgh Press, 2009.

Bunzl, Matti. *Anti-Semitism and Islamophobia: Hatred Old and New in Europe.* Chicago: Prickly Paradigm Press, 2007.

Campbell, James T. *Middle Passages: African American Journeys to Africa, 1787–2005.* New York: Penguin Press, 2006.

Cârstocea, Raul, and Éva Kovács, eds. *Modern Antisemitism in the Peripheries: Europe and its Colonies 1880–1945.* Vienna: New Academic Press, 2019.

Cavanaugh, Edward, and Lorenzo Veracini, eds. *The Routledge Handbook of the History of Settler Colonialism.* London, New York: Routledge, 2017.

Cheyette, Bryan. *Diasporas of the Mind: Jewish and Postcolonial Writing and the Nightmare of History.* New Haven: Yale University Press, 2013.

Chickering, Roger. *We Men who Feel Most German: A Cultural Study of the Pan-German League, 1886–1914.* Boston: Allen & Unwin, 1984.

Clough, Patricia. *Emin Pascha, Herr von Äquatoria: Ein exzentrischer deutscher Arzt und der Wettlauf um Afrika.* Translated by Peter Torberg. Munich: Deutsche Verlags-Anstalt, 2010.

Cousin, Glynis, and Robert Fine. 'A Common Cause: Reconnecting the Study of Racism and Antisemitism', *European Societies* 14 (2012): 166–85.

Cronon, Edmund David. *Black Moses: The Story of Marcus Garvey and the Universal Negro Improvement Association*. Madison: University of Wisconsin Press, 1955.

Davis, Christian S. *Colonialism, Antisemitism, and Germans of Jewish Descent in Imperial Germany*. Ann Arbor: University of Michigan Press, 2012.

de Blois, Francois. 'Nasrani and Hanif: Studies on the Religious Vocabulary of Christianity and of Islam', *Bulletin of the School of Oriental and African Studies* 65 (2002): 1–30.

Dekel, Mikhal. *Tehran Children: A Holocaust Refugee Odyssey*. New York: Norton, 2019.

Diner, Dan. *Gegenläufige Gedächtnisse: Über Geltung und Wirkung des Holocaust*. Göttingen: Vandenhoeck & Ruprecht, 2007.

Dipper, Rachel. '"Einmal muß der Mensch ins Bad!" Grüße aus Karlsbad und Marienbad', in *Abgestempelt: Judenfeindliche Postkarten*, edited by Helmut Gold and Georg Heuberger. Heidelberg: Umschau/Braus, 1999, 194–204.

Distelhorst, Lars. *Leistung: Das Endstadium der Ideologie*. Bielefeld: transcript, 2014.

Distelhorst, Lars. 'Die Glühbirne und der Möbelpacker: Über den Begriff der "Leistung" als leere Abstraktion', in *Zonen der Selbstoptimierung: Berichte aus der Leistungsgesellschaft*, edited by Felix Klopotek and Peter Scheiffele. Berlin: Matthes & Seitz Berlin, 2016, 38–52.

Eddon, Raluca Munteanu. 'Gershom Scholem, Hannah Arendt and the Paradox of 'Non-Nationalist' Nationalism', *Journal of Jewish Thought and Philosophy* 12 (2003): 55–68.

Edele, Mark, Sheila Fitzpatrick, and Atina Grossmann, eds. *Shelter from the Holocaust: Rethinking Jewish Survival in the Soviet Union*. Detroit: Wayne State University Press, 2107.

Edthofer, Julia. 'Gegenläufige Perspektiven auf Antisemitismus und antimuslimischen Rassismus im post-nationalsozialistischen und postkolonialen Forschungskontext', *Österreichische Zeitschrift für Soziologie* 40 (2015): 189–207.

el-Aris, Tarek. 'Introduction', in *The Arab Renaissance: A Bilingual Anthology of the Nahda*. New York: Modern Language Association, 2018, xv–xxx.

Eley, Geoff. *Reshaping the German Right: Radical Nationalism and Political Change after Bismarck*. New Haven: Yale University Press, 1980.

Erb, Rainer, and Werner Bergmann. *Die Nachtseite der Judenemanzipation: Der Widerstand gegen die Integration der Juden in Deutschland 1780–1860*. Berlin: Metropol, 1989.

Erlewine, Robert. *Judaism and the West: From Hermann Cohen to Joseph Soloveitchik*. Bloomington: Indiana University Press, 2016.

Feldman, David. *Englishmen and Jews: Social Relations and Political Culture, 1840–1914*. New Haven: Yale University Press, 1994.

Feldman, David. 'The British Empire and the Jews, c. 1900', *History Workshop Journal* 63 (2007): 70–89.

Ferguson, Niall. *The House of Rothschild*. London: Weidenfeld and Nicolson, 1998.

Fischer, Barbara. 'Residues of Otherness: On Jewish Emancipation during the Age of German Enlightenment', in *Insiders and Outsiders: Jewish and Gentile Culture in Germany and Austria*, edited by Dagmar C. G. Lorenz and Gabriele Weinberger. Detroit: Wayne State University Press, 1994, 30–8.

Fomin, E. S. D., and Victor Julius Ngoh. *Slave Settlements in the Banyang Country, 1800–1950*. Buea: University of Buea Publications, 1998.

Foucault, Michel. 'Vorlesung vom 17. März 1976 (Von der Geburt der Bio-Macht, Bio-Macht und Rassismus)', in *In Verteidigung der Gesellschaft: Vorlesungen am Collège de France 1975–1976*. Frankfurt am Main: Suhrkamp, 1999, 276–305.

Foucault, Michel. *The Birth of Biopolitics: Lectures at the Collège de France, 1978–1979*. Basingstoke: Palgrave Macmillan, 2008.

Frech, Stefan. *Wegbereiter Hitlers? Theodor Reismann-Grone. Ein völkischer Nationalist (1863–1949)*. Paderborn: Schöningh, 2009.

Friedrichsmeyer, Sara, Sara Lennox, and Susanne Zantop, eds. *The Imperialist Imagination: German Colonialism and Its Legacies*. Ann Arbor: University of Michigan Press, 1998.

Gann, Lewis H. 'Marginal Colonialism: The German Case', in *Germans in the Tropics: Essays in German Colonial History*, edited by Arthur J. Knoll and Lewis H. Gann. New York: Greenwood Press, 1987, 1–38.

Gelber, Mark H. *Melancholy Pride: Nation, Race, and Gender in the German Literature of Cultural Zionism*. Tübingen: Niemeyer, 2000.

Geller, Jay. *Bestiarium Judaicum: Unnatural Histories of the Jews*. New York: Fordham University Press, 2018.

Gerwarth, Robert, and Stephan Malinowski. 'Der Holocaust als "kolonialer Genozid"?' *Geschichte und Gesellschaft* 33 (2007): 439–66.

Gilbert, Shirli. *From Things Lost: Forgotten Letters and the Legacy of the Holocaust*. Detroit: Wayne State University, 2017.

Gilman, Sander L. *On Blackness without Blacks: Essays on the Image of the Black in Germany*. Boston: G. K. Hall, 1982.

Gilman, Sander L. *The Jew's Body*. New York: Routledge, 1991.

Gilman, Sander L. 'Einführung', in *Rasse, Sexualität und Seuche: Stereotype aus der Innenwelt der westlichen Kultur*. Reinbek bei Hamburg: Rowohlt, 1992, 7–36.

Girtler, Roland: *Rotwelsch: Die Sprache der Gauner, Dirnen und Vagabunden*. Göttingen: Vandehoeck & Ruprecht, 2019.

Golan, Arnon. 'European Imperialism and the Development of Modern Palestine: Was Zionism a Form of Colonialism?', *Space and Polity* 5 (2001): 127–43.

Goldberg, Sylvie Anne. 'On the Margins of French Historiography: Once Again, the History of the Jews', *Shofar* 14, no. 3 (1996): 47–62.

Gordon, Adi. 'The Ideological Convert and the "Mythology of Coherence": The Contradictory Hans Kohn and his Multiple Metamorphoses', *Leo Baeck Institute Year Book* 55 (2010): 273–93.

Gordon, Adi. *Toward Nationalism's End: An Intellectual Biography of Hans Kohn*. Waltham: Brandeis University Press, 2017.

Gow, Andrew Colin. *The Red Jews: Antisemitism in an Apocalyptic Age, 1200–1600,*. Leiden: Brill, 1995.

Gow, Andrew Colin. 'Kartenrand, Gesellschaftsrand, Geschichtsrand: Die legendären *judei clausi/inclusi* auf mittelalterlichen und frühneuzeitlichen Weltkarten', in *Fördern und Bewahren: Studien zur europäischen Kulturgeschichte der frühen Neuzeit. Festschrift anlässlich des zehnjährigen Bestehens der Dr. Günther Findel-Stiftung zur Förderung der Wissenschaften*, edited by Hedwig Schmidt-Glintzer. Wiesbaden: Harrassowitz, 1996, 137–56.

Gow, Andrew Colin. 'Gog and Magog on *Mappae mundi* and Early Printed World Maps: Orientalizing Ethnography in the Apocalyptic Tradition', *Journal of Early Modern History* 2 (1998): 61–88.

Grady, Tim. *The German-Jewish Soldiers of the First World War in History and Memory*. Liverpool: Liverpool University Press, 2011.

Grossman, Avraham. 'The Commentary of Rashi on Isaiah and the Jewish-Christian Debate' in *Studies in Medieval Jewish Intellectual and Social History*, edited by Elliot R. Wolfson, Lawrence H. Schiffman and David Engel. Leiden: Brill, 2012, 47–63.

Grossmann, Atina. 'Remapping Survival: Jewish Refugees and Lost Memories of Displacement, Trauma, and Rescue in Soviet Central Asia, Iran, and India', *Simon Dubnow Institute Yearbook* 15 (2016): 71–97.

Grossmann, Atina. 'Transnational Jewish Refugee Stories: Displacement, Loss and (Non)Restitution', in *Three Way Street: Jews, Germans, and the Transnational*, edited by Jay Geller and Leslie Morris. Ann Arbor: University of Michigan Press, 2016, 362–84.

Grossmann, Atina. '"Joint Fund Teheran": JDC and the Jewish Lifeline to Central Asia', in *The JDC at 100: A Century of Humanitarianism*, edited by Avinoam Patt, Atina Grossmann, Linda G. Levi, and Maud S. Mandel. Detroit: Wayne State University Press, 2019, 205–44.

Grossmann, Atina. 'I Thought She Was Old But She Was Really My Age: Tracing Desperation and Resilience in my Grandmothers' Letters From Berlin – Fragments', in *On Being Adjacent to Historical Violence*, edited by Irene Kacandes. Berlin: De Gruyter, 2021, 467–91.

Gründer, Horst. *Geschichte der Deutschen Kolonien*, 7th edn. Paderborn: Schöningh, 2018.

Ha-Cohen, Ran. 'The "Jewish Blackness" Thesis Revisited', *Religions* 9, no. 7 (2018): https://doi.org/10.3390/rel9070222 (last accessed 3 September 2020).

Hall, Stuart. 'The West and the Rest: Discourse and Power', in *Formations of Modernity*, edited by Stuart Hall and Bram Gieben. Cambridge: Polity Press, 1992, 184–227.

Hamann, Ulrike. *Prekäre koloniale Ordnung: Rassistische Konjunkturen im Widerspruch. Deutsches Kolonialregime 1884–1914*. Bielefeld: transcript, 2016.

Hanke, Christine. 'Zwischen Evidenz und Leere: Zur Konstitution von "Rasse" im physisch-anthropologischen Diskurs um 1900', in *Der Gesellschaftskörper: Zur Neuordnung von Kultur und Geschlecht um 1900*, edited by Christine Hanke, Hannelore Bublitz, and Andrea Seier. Frankfurt am Main: Campus, 2000, 179–235.

Harris, Horton. *The Tübingen School*. Oxford: Clarendon Press, 1975.

Hartwig, Dirk, Walter Homolka, Michael J. Marx, and Angelika Neuwirth, eds. *'Im vollen Licht der Geschichte': Die Wissenschaft des Judentums und die Anfänge der kritischen Koranforschung*. Würzburg: Ergon Verlag, 2008, 65–86.

Heinig, Herbert Louis, ed. *The 'Black Jew': Germans, Nazis, and Nature's Other Creatures*. Bloomington: Author House, 2004.

Henderson, W.O. *Studies in the Economic Policy of Frederick the Great*. London: Frank Cass, 1963.

Heng, Geraldine. *The Invention of Race in the European Middle Ages*. Cambridge: Cambridge University Press, 2018.

Hentges, Gudrun. *Schattenseiten der Aufklärung: Die Darstellung von Juden und 'Wilden' in philosophischen Schriften des 18. und 19. Jahrhunderts*. Schwalbach: Wochenschau Verlag, 1999.

Herbert, Ulrich. 'Der Historikerstreit: Politische, wissenschaftliche, biographische Aspekte', in *Zeitgeschichte als Streitgeschichte: Große Kontroversen seit 1945*, edited by Martin Sabrow, Ralph Jessen, and Klaus Große Kracht. München: Beck, 2003, 94–113.

Herf, Jeffrey. 'Comparative Perspectives on Anti-Semitism: Radical Anti-Semitism in the Holocaust and American White Racism', *Journal of Genocide Research* 9 (2007): 575–600.

Hering, Rainer. *Konstruierte Nation: Der Alldeutsche Verband 1890 bis 1939*. Hamburg: Christians, 2003.

Hering, Rainer. 'Juden im Alldeutschen Verband?', in *Aus den Quellen: Beiträge zur deutsch-jüdischen Geschichte. Festschrift für Ina Lorenz zum 65. Geburtstag*, edited by Andreas Brämer. München: Dölling und Galitz, 2005.

Herrmann, Klaus. 'Das Bild des Islam im Reformjudentum des 19. und 20. Jahrhunderts', in *Orient als Grenzbereich? Rabbinisches und ausserrabbinisches Judentum*, edited by Annelies Kuyt and Gerold Necker. Wiesbaden: Harrasowitz, 2007, 217–47.

Heschel, Susannah. *Abraham Geiger and the Jewish Jesus*. Chicago: University of Chicago Press, 1998.

Heschel, Susannah. 'Revolt of the Colonized: Abraham Geiger's Wissenschaft des Judentums as a Challenge to Christian Hegemony in the Academy', *New German Critique* 77 (1999): 61–85.

Heschel, Susannah. *The Aryan Jesus: Christian Theologians and the Bible in Nazi Germany*. Princeton: Princeton University Press, 2008.

Heschel, Susannah. 'German-Jewish Scholarship on Islam as a Tool of De-Orientalization', *New German Critique* 117 (2012): 91–117.

Heschel, Susannah. *Jüdischer Islam: Islam und jüdisch-deutsche Selbstbestimmung.* Berlin: Matthes & Seitz, 2017.

Hess, Jonathan M. 'Sugar Island Jews? Jewish Colonialism and the Rhetoric of "Civic Improvement" in Eighteenth-Century Germany', *Eighteenth-Century Studies* 32 (1998): 92–100.

Hess, Jonathan M. *Reconstituting the Body Politic: Enlightenment, Public Culture and the Invention of Aesthetic Autonomy.* Detroit: Wayne State University Press, 1999.

Hess, Jonathan M. 'Modernity, Violence and the Jewish Question: Christian Wilhelm Dohm and the Eradication of Jewish Alterity' in *Progrès et violence au XVIIIe siècle*, edited by Valérie Cossy and Deidre Dawson. Paris: Champion, 2001, 87–116.

Hess, Jonathan M. *Germans, Jews and the Claims of Modernity.* New Haven: Yale University Press, 2002.

Hochschild, Adam. *Bury the Chains: Prophets and Rebels in the Fight to Free an Empire's Slaves.* Boston: Houghton Mifflin, 2005.

Hodgson, Peter C. *The Formation of Historical Theology: A Study of Ferdinand Christian Baur.* New York: Harper and Row, 1966.

Hodgson, Peter C. 'F.C. Baur's Interpretation of Christianity's Relationship to Judaism', in *Is There a Judeo-Christian Tradition? A European Perspective*, edited by Emmanuel Nathan and Anya Topolski. Berlin: De Gruyter, 2016, 31–52.

Höfert, Almut. *Den Feind beschreiben: 'Türkengefahr' und europäisches Wissen über das Osmanische Reich 1450–1600.* Frankfurt am Main: Campus, 2003.

Höfert, Almut. 'Das Gesetz des Teufels und Europas Spiegel: Das christlich-westeuropäische Islambild im Mittelalter und der Frühen Neuzeit', in *Orient- und Islambilder. Interdisziplinäre Beiträge zu Orientalismus und antimuslimischem Rassismus*, edited by Iman Attia. München: Unrast, 2007, 85–110.

Hofmeister, Björn. 'Ernst Hasse', in *Handbuch des Antisemitismus: Judenfeindschaft in Geschichte und Gegenwart, 2/1*, edited by Wolfgang Benz. Berlin: K. G. Saur, 2010, 336–7.

Holz, Klaus. *Nationaler Antisemitismus: Wissenssoziologie einer Weltanschauung.* Hamburg: Hamburger Edition, 2001.

Hudson, Nicholas. 'From "Nation" to "Race": The Origins of Racial Classification in Eighteenth-Century Thought', *Eighteenth-Century Studies* 29 (1996): 247–64.

Hund, Wulf D. *Rassismus.* Bielefeld: transcript, 2007.

Jackisch, Barry A. *The Pan-German League and Radical Nationalist Politics in Interwar Germany, 1918–1939.* Farnham: Ashgate, 2012.

Jansen, Sarah. *'Schädlinge': Geschichte eines wissenschaftlichen und politischen Konstrukts, 1840–1920.* Frankfurt am Main: Campus, 2003.

Jenkins, Jennifer. 'Hjalmar Schacht, Reza Shah, and Germany's Presence in Iran', *Iran Nameh* 30 (2015): xx–xlvi.

Jenkins, Jennifer. 'Iran in the Nazi New Order, 1933–1941', *Iranian Studies* 49 (2016): 727–51.

Jensen, Uffa. *Gebildete Doppelgänger: Bürgerliche Juden und Protestanten im 19. Jahrhundert.* Göttingen: Vandenhoeck & Ruprecht, 2005.

Johach, Eva. 'Der Bienenstaat: Geschichte eines politisch-moralischen Exempels', in: *Politische Zoologie*, edited by Anne von der Heiden and Joseph Vogl. Zürich: diaphanes, 2007, 219–33.

Jonker, Gerdien. *The Ahmadiayya Quest for Religious Progress: Modernizing Europe 1900–1965*. Leiden: Brill, 2015.

Jonker, Gerdien. *Zwischen Juden und Muslimen: Eine Europäische Familiengeschichte 1836–2016*. Göttingen: Wallstein, 2018.

Joskowiez, Ari. *The Modernity of Others: Jewish Anti-Catholicism in Germany and France*. Stanford: Stanford University Press, 2013.

Jotschky, Andrew. 'Ethnic and Religious Categories in the Treatment of Jews and Muslims in the Crusader States', in *Antisemitism and Islamophobia in Europe*, edited by James Renton and Ben Gidley. London: Palgrave Macmillan, 2017, 25–49.

Jungcurt, Uta. *Alldeutscher Extremismus in der Weimarer Republik: Denken und Handeln einer einflussreichen bürgerlichen Minderheit*. Berlin: De Gruyter Oldenbourg, 2016.

Kalmar, Ivan Davidson, and Derek J. Penslar. *Orientalism and the Jews*. Waltham: Brandeis University Press, 2005.

Karniel, Josef. *Die Toleranzpolitik Kaiser Josephs II*. Translated by Leo Koppel. Gerlingen: Bleicher, 1985.

Kastein, Josef. *Eine Geschichte der Juden*. Wien: Löwith, 1935.

Katz, Ethan B. 'An Imperial Entanglement: Anti-Semitism, Islamophobia, and Colonialism', *American Historical Review* 123 (2018): 1190–209.

Katz, Ethan B., Lisa Moses Leff, and Maud S. Mandel, eds. *Colonialism and the Jews*. Bloomington: Indiana University Press, 2017.

Katz, Jacob. 'The Term "Jewish Emancipation": Its Origin and Historical Impact', in *Emancipation and Assimilation: Studies in Modern Jewish History*. Westmead: Gregg, 1972, 21–45.

Katz, Steven T. *The Holocaust and Comparative History*. New York: Leo Baeck Institute, 1993.

Katz, Steven T.. *The Holocaust and New World Slavery: A Comparative History*, 2 vols. Cambridge: Cambridge University Press, 2019.

Kirchen, Christian. *Emin Pascha: Arzt – Abenteurer – Afrikaforscher*. Paderborn: Ferdinand Schöningh, 2014.

Klauß, Klaus. 'Die Deutsche Kolonialgesellschaft und die deutsche Kolonialpolitik von den Anfängen bis 1895', Ph.D. diss., Humboldt Universität Berlin, Ostberlin, 1966.

König, Gudrun M. *Konsumkultur: Inszenierte Warenwelt um 1900*. Vienna: Böhlau, 2009.

Kopp, Kristin. *Germany's Wild East: Constructing Poland as Colonial Space*. Ann Arbor: University of Michigan Press, 2012.

Krobb, Florian, and Elaine Martin, eds. *Weimar Colonialism: Discourses and Legacies of Post-Imperialism in Germany after 1918*. Bielefeld: Aisthesis Verlag, 2014.

Bibliography

Kruck, Alfred. *Geschichte des Alldeutschen Verbandes 1890–1939*. Wiesbaden: Steiner, 1954.

Kühne, Thomas. 'Colonialism and the Holocaust: Continuities, Causations, and Complexities', *Journal of Genocide Research* 15 (2013): 339–62.

Kundrus, Birthe, ed. *'Phantasiereiche': Der deutsche Kolonialismus aus kulturgeschichtlicher Perspektive*. Frankfurt am Main: Campus, 2003.

Lamm, Hans. 'The So-Called "Letter of a German Jew to the President of the Congress of the United States of America" of 1783', *Publications of the American Jewish Historical Society* 37 (1947): 171–7.

Landmann, Salcia. *Jiddisch: Das Abenteuer einer Sprache*. Frankfurt am Main: Ullstein, 1988.

Langbehn, Volker M., ed. *German Colonialism, Visual Culture, and Modern Memory*. New York: Routledge, 2010.

Langbehn, Volker M., and Mohammad Salama, eds. *German Colonialism: Race, the Holocaust, and Postwar Germany*. New York: Columbia University Press, 2011.

Langeheine, Romy. *Von Prag nach New York: Hans Kohn. Eine intellektuelle Biographie*. Göttingen: Wallstein, 2014.

Langmuir, Gavin I. *Toward a Definition of Antisemitism*. Berkeley: University of California Press, 1996.

Laqueur, Walter. *A History of Zionism*. New York: Schocken, 1976.

Lavsky, Hagit. 'German Zionists and the Emergence of Brit Shalom', in *Essential Papers on Zionism*, edited by Jehuda Reinharz and Anita Shapira. New York: New York University Press, 1996, 648–70.

Lässig, Simone. *Jüdische Wege ins Bürgertum: Kulturelles Kapital und sozialer Aufstieg im 19. Jahrhundert*. Göttingen: Vandenhoeck & Ruprecht, 2004.

Leicht, Johannes. '"Alldeutsch – vielleicht alljüdisch?" Rassistische und antisemitische Semantiken in der Agitation des Alldeutschen Verbandes in den Jahren 1891 bis 1919', *Jahrbuch für Antisemitismusforschung* 13 (2004): 111–37.

Leicht, Johannes. *Heinrich Claß 1868–1953: Die politische Biographie eines Alldeutschen*. Paderborn: Schöningh, 2012.

Lerner, Paul Frederick. *The Consuming Temple: Jews, Department Stores, and the Consumer Revolution in Germany, 1880–1940*. Ithaca, NY and London: Cornell University Press, 2015.

Levy, Daniel, and Natan Sznaider. *Erinnerungen im globalen Zeitalter: Der Holocaust*. Frankfurt am Main: Suhrkamp, 2001.

Levy, Lital. 'The Nahda and the Haskalah: A Comparative Reading of "Revival" and "Reform"', *Middle Eastern Literatures* 16 (2013): 300–16.

Lewin, Maurycy. 'Geschichte der Juden in Galizien unter Kaiser Joseph II. Ein Beitrag zur Geschichte der Juden in Oesterreich', Ph.D. diss., University of Vienna, 1933.

Lewis, David Levering. *W.E.B. Du Boi:. Biography of a Race*. New York: Henry Holt, 1993.

Lewis, David Levering. *W.E.B. Du Bois: A Biography*. New York: Henry Holt, 2009.

Lewis, Martin W., and Kären Wigen. *The Myth of Continents: A Critique of Metageography*. Berkeley: University of California Press, 1997.

Liberles, Robert. 'From Toleration to Verbesserung: German and English Debates on the Jews in the Eighteenth Century', *Central European Quarterly* 22 (1989): 3–32.

Libson, Gideon. *Jewish and Islamic Law: A Comparative Study of Custom during the Geonic Period*. Cambridge: Harvard University Press, 2003.

Lloyd, David. 'Settler Colonialism and the State of Exception: The Example of Palestine/Israel', *Settler Colonial Studies* 2 (2012): 59–80.

Lohalm, Uwe. *Völkischer Radikalismus: Die Geschichte des Deutschvölkischen Schutz-und Trutz-Bundes 1919–1923*. Hamburg: Leibniz, 1970.

Lordick, Harald. 'Isaak Eduard Schnitzer – Emin Pasha. Erinnerungssplitter aus einem Jahrhundert Literature', in *Memoria – Wege jüdischen Erinnerns: Festschrift für Michael Brocke zum 65. Geburtstag*, edited by Birgit E. Klein and Christiane E. Müller. Berlin: Metropol, 2005.

Lotter, Friedrich. 'Christoph Meiners und die Lehre von der unterschiedlichen Wertigkeit der Menschenrassen', in *Geschichtswissenschaft in Göttingen: Eine Vorlesungsreihe*, edited by Hartmut Boockmann and Hermann Wellenreuther,. Göttingen: Vandenhoeck & Ruprecht, 1987, 30–75.

Löwenbrück, Anna-Ruth. *Judenfeinschaft im Zeitalter der Aufklärung: Eine Studie zur Vorgeschichte des modernen Antisemitismus am Beispiel des Göttinger Theologen und Orientalisten Johann David Michaelis (1717–1791)*. Frankfurt am Main: Peter Lang, 1995.

MacMaster, Neil. '"Black Jew–White Negro". Anti-Semitism and the Construction of Cross-Racial Stereotypes', *Nationalism and Ethnic Politics* 6, no. 4 (2000): 65–82.

MacMaster, Neil. *Racism in Europe 1870–2000*. New York: Palgrave, 2001.

Madley, Benjamin. 'From Africa to Auschwitz: How German South West Africa Incubated Ideas and Methods Adopted and Developed by the Nazis in Eastern Europe', *European History Quarterly* 35 (2005): 429–64.

Malcom, Noel. *Useful Enemies: Islam and The Ottoman Empire in Western Political Thought, 1450–1750*. Oxford: Oxford University Press 2019.

Mangold, Sabine. *Eine 'Weltbürgerliche Wissenschaft': Deutsche Orientalistik im 19. Jahrhundert*. Stuttgart: Steiner, 2004.

Maoz, Zohar. 'Hans Kohn and the Dialectics of Colonialism: Insights on Nationalism and Colonialism from Within', *Leo Baeck Institute Year Book* 55 (2010): 255–71.

Mar, Tracy Banivanua, and Penelope Edmonds, eds. *Making Settler Colonial Space: Perspectives on Race, Place and Identity*. Basingstoke: Palgrave Macmillan, 2010.

Marchand, Suzanne. *German Orientalism in the Age of Empire*. Cambridge: Cambridge University Press, 2009.

Markmiller, Anton. *'Die Erziehung des Negers zur Arbeit.' Wie die koloniale Pädagogik afrikanische Gesellschaften in die Abhängigkeit führte*. Berlin: Dietrich Reimer Verlag, 1995.

Martin, Peter. *Schwarze Teufel, edle Mohren*. Hamburg: Hamburger Edition, 2001.

Bibliography

Massad, Joseph. 'The Ends of Zionism: Racism and the Palestinian Struggle', *Interventions. International Journal of Postcolonial Studies* 5 (2003): 440–8.

McKimm, Robert, and Jeff McMahan, eds. *The Morality of Nationalism*. New York: Oxford University Press, 1997.

Melamed, Abraham. *The Image of the Black in Jewish Culture: A History of the Other*. London: Routledge, 2003.

Mellinkoff, Ruth. *Outcasts: Signs of Otherness in Northern European Art of the Late Middle Ages*. Berkeley: University of California Press, 1993.

Menache, Sophia. 'Tartars, Jews, Saracens and the Jewish-Mongol "Plot" of 1241', *History. The Journal of the Historical Association* 81 (1996): 319–42.

Mendes-Flohr, Paul. 'Fin-de-Siècle Orientalism, the Ostjuden and the Aesthetics of Jewish Self-Affirmation', *Studies in Contemporary Jewry* 1 (1984): 96–139.

Meyer, Michael A., ed. *German-Jewish History in Modern Times*, 4 vols. New York: Columbia University Press, 1996–1998.

Meyer, Michael A. 'From Combat to Convergence: The Relationship between Heinrich Graetz and Abraham Geiger', in: *Reappraisals and New Studies of the Modern Jewish Experience: Essays in Honor of Robert M. Seltzer*, edited by Brian M. Smollett and Christian Wiese. Leiden: Brill, 2015, 145–61.

Michels, Stefanie. 'Schutzherrschaft Revisited: Kolonialismus aus afrikanischer Perspektive', in *Die Vielfalt normativer Ordnungen: Konflikte und Dynamik in historischer und ethnologischer Perspektive*, edited by Andreas Fahrmeir and Anette Imhausen. Frankfurt am Main: Campus, 2013, 243–74.

Miles, William F.S. 'Hamites and Hebrews: Problems in "Judaizing" the Rwandan Genocide', *Journal of Genocide Research* 2 (2000): 107–15.

Minnema, Lourens. 'Different Types of Orientalism and Corresponding Views of Jews and Judaism: A Historical Overview of Shifting Perceptions and Stereotypes', *Antisemitism Studies* 4 (2020): 270–325.

Mommsen, Wolfgang J. *Max Weber und die deutsche Politik, 1890–1920*, 2nd edn. Tübingen: Mohr, 1974.

Moses, Dirk. 'Conceptual Blockages and Definitional Dilemmas in the Racial Century: Genocide of Indigenous Peoples and the Holocaust', *Patterns of Prejudice* 36 (2002): 7–36.

Moses, Dirk. 'The Fate of Blacks and Jews: A Response to Jeffrey Herf', *Journal of Genocide Research* 10 (2008): 269–87.

Moses, Wilson S. 'Marcus Garvey: A Reappraisal', *The Black Scholar* 4, no. 3 (1972): 38–49.

Mosse, George L. *Towards the Final Solution*. London: dent, 1978.

Mosse, George L. 'Can Nationalism Be Saved? About Zionism, Rightful and Unjust Nationalism', *Israel Studies* 2 (1995): 157–73.

Moyn, Samuel. 'German Jewry and the Question of Identity: Historiography and Theory', *Leo Baeck Institute Yearbook* 41 (1996): 291–308.

Mufti, Aamir. *Enlightenment in the Colony: The Jewish Question and the Crisis of Postcolonial Culture*. Princeton: Princeton University Press, 2007.

Müller, Klaus E. *Der Krüppel: Ethnologia passionis humanae*. München: Beck, 1996.

Münkler, Marina. *Erfahrung des Fremden: Die Beschreibung Ostasiens in den Augenzeugenberichten des 13. und 14. Jahrhunderts*. Berlin: Akademie Verlag, 2000.

Münkler, Marina. 'Monstra und mappae mundi: Die monströsen Völker des Erdrands auf mittelalterlichen Weltkarten', in *Text – Bild – Karte: Kartographien der Vormoderne*, edited by Jürg Glauser and Christian Kiening. Freiburg: Rombach, 2007, 149–74.

Münkler, Marina, and Werner Röcke. 'Der ordo-Gedanke und die Hermeneutik des Fremden im Mittelalter: Die Auseinandersetzung mit den monströsen Völkern des Erdrandes', in *Die Herausforderung durch das Fremde*, edited by Herfried Münkler. Berlin: Akademie, 1998, 715–6.

Murray, Pauli, ed. *States' Laws on Race and Color*. Athens: University of Georgia Press, 1997.

Mveng, Engelbert, and D. Beling-Nkoumb. *Manuel d'Histoire du Cameroun*. Yaoundé: Centre d'édition et de production de manuels et d'auxiliaires de l'enseignement, 1978.

Nairn, Tom. *The Break-Up of Britain: Crisis and Neo-Nationalism*. London: NLB, 1977.

Nairn, Tom. *Faces of Nationalism: Janus Revisited*. London: Verso, 1997.

Naranch, Bradley, and Geoff Eley, eds. *German Colonialism in a Global Age*. Durham: Duke University Press, 2014.

Nawratil, Gerhard M. 'Berühmte Mediziner im Spiegel der Münchner Straßennamen', Ph.D. diss., Ludwig-Maximilians Universität, München, 2003.

Neuwirth, Angelika. *Der Koran als Text der Spätantike: Ein europäischer Zugang*. Berlin: Verlag der Weltreligionen, 2010.

Neuwirth, Angelika. *The Qur'an in Context*. Leiden: Brill, 2011.

Neuwirth, Angelika. 'Qur'anic Studies and Philology: Qur'anic Textual Politics of Staging, Penetrating, and Finally Eclipsing Biblical Tradition', in *Qur'anic Studies Today*, edited by Angelika Neuwirth and Michael A. Sells. New York: Routledge, 2016, 178–206.

Nipperdey, Thomas. *Deutsche Geschichte 1800–1866: Bürgerwelt und starker Staat*. München: Beck, 1983.

Nipperdey, Thomas. *Deutsche Geschichte 1866–1918, vol. 1: Arbeitswelt und Bürgergeist*. München: Beck, 1990.

Nipperdey, Thomas. *Deutsche Geschichte 1866–1918, vol. 2: Machtstaat vor der Demokratie*. München: Beck, 1992.

Niven, Bill, ed. *Germans as Victims: Remembering the Past in Contemporary Germany*. Houndmills: Palgrave Macmillan, 2006.

Nwankwo, Ifeoma Kiddoe. *Black Cosmopolitanism: Racial Consciousness and Transnational Identity in the Nineteenth Century Americas*. Philadelphia: University of Pennsylvania Press, 2005.

Nwokeji, Ugo, and David Eltis. 'Characteristics of Captives Leaving the Cameroons for the Americas, 1822–1837', *The Journal of African History* 43 (2002): 191–210.

O'Sullivan, Adrian. *Nazi Secret Warfare in Occupied Persia (Iran): The Failure of the German Intelligence Services, 1939–1945*. Houndmills: Palgrave Macmillan, 2014.

Osterhammel, Jürgen, and Sebastian Conrad, eds. *Das Kaiserreich transnational: Deutschland in der Welt, 1871–1914*. Göttingen: Vandenhoeck & Ruprecht, 2004.

Paget, James Carleton. 'The Definition of the Terms Jewish Christian and Jewish Christianity in the History of Research', in *Jewish Believers in Jesus*, edited by Oskar Skarsaune and Reidar Hvalvik. Peabody: Hendrickson, 2007, 22–52.

Pappé, Ilan. 'Zionism as Colonialism: A Comparative View of Diluted Colonialism in Asia and Africa', *South Atlantic Quarterly* 107 (2008): 611–33.

Parfitt, Tudor. *Hybrid Hate: Jews, Blacks, and the Question of Race*. New York: Oxford University Press, 2020.

Pečar, Andreas, and Damien Tricoire. *Falsche Freunde: War die Aufklärung wirklich die Geburtsstunde der Moderne?* Frankfurt am Main: Campus, 2015.

Penslar, Derek J. *Zionism and Technocracy: The Engineering of Jewish Settlement in Palestine, 1870–1918*. Bloomington: Indiana University Press, 1991.

Penslar, Derek J. 'Zionism, Colonialism and Postcolonialism', *Journal of Israeli History* 20 (2001): 84–98.

Penslar, Derek J. *Theodor Herzl: The Charismatic Leader*. New Haven: Yale University Press, 2020.

Perras, Arne. *Carl Peters and German Imperialism, 1856–1918: A Political Biography*. Oxford: Oxford University Press, 2004.

Perraudin, Michael, and Jürgen Zimmerer, eds. *German Colonialism and National Identity*. New York: Routledge, 2011.

Peters, Michael. *Der Alldeutsche Verband am Vorabend des Ersten Weltkrieges (1908–1914): Ein Beitrag zur Geschichte des völkischen Nationalismus im spätwilhelminischen Deutschland*, 2nd edn. Frankfurt am Main: Lang, 1996.

Pianko, Noam. *Zionism and the Roads not Taken: Rawidowicz, Kaplan, Kohn*. Bloomington: Indiana University Press, 2010.

Pierard, Richard V. 'The German Colonial Society, 1882–1914', Ph.D. diss., University of Iowa, Iowa City, 1964.

Pogge von Strandmann, Hartmut. *Imperialismus vom grünen Tisch: Deutsche Kolonialpolitik zwischen wirtschaftlicher Ausbeutung und 'zivilisatorischen' Bemühungen*. Berlin: Links, 2009.

Polaschegg, Andrea. *Der andere Orientalismus: Regeln deutsch-morgenländischer Imagination im 19. Jahrhundert*. Berlin: De Gruyter, 2005.

Poley, Jared. *Decolonization in Germany: Weimar Narratives of Colonial Loss and Foreign Occupation*. Bern: Peter Lang, 2005.

Polonsky, Antony. *The Jews in Poland and Russia, vol. 2*. Oxford: The Littman Library of Jewish Civilization, 2010.

Postone, Moishe. 'Anti-Semitism and National Socialism: Notes on the German Reaction to "Holocaust"', *New German Critique* 19 (1980): 97–115.

Przybilski, Martin. 'Jüdische Körper als Subjekte und Objekte des kulturellen Transfers in der Vormoderne', in *'Rasse' und Raum: Topologien zwischen Kolonial-, Geo- und Biopolitik: Geschichte, Kunst, Erinnerung*, edited by Claudia Bruns. Wiesbaden: Reichert, 2017, 61–78.

Puhle, Hans-Jürgen. *Agrarische Interessenpolitik und preußischer Konservativismus im wilhelminischen Reich, 1893–1914.* Hannover: Verlag für Literatur und Zeitgeschehen, 1966.

Pulzer, Peter G. *Die Entstehung des politischen Antisemitismus in Deutschland und Österreich 1867 bis 1914.* Göttingen: Vandenhoeck & Ruprecht, 2004.

Pyta, Wolfram. 'Kulturwissenschaftliche Zugriffe auf Karl May', in *Karl May: Brükenbauer zwischen den Kulturen*, edited by Wolfram Pyta. Berlin: LIT Verlag, 2010, 9–47.

Railton, Nicholas M. 'Gog and Magog: The History of a Symbol', *Evangelical Quarterly* 75 (2003): 23–43.

Ratzabi, Shalom. *Between Zionism and Judaism: The Radical Circle in Brith Shalom, 1925–1933.* Leiden: Brill, 2002.

Reed-Anderson, Paulette. *Rewriting the Footnotes: Berlin und die afrikanische Diaspora.* Berlin: Die Ausländerbeauftragte des Senats von Berlin, 2000.

Reimann, Sarah. *Die Entstehung des wissenschaftlichen Rassismus im 18. Jahrhundert.* Stuttgart: Franz Steiner Verlag, 2017.

Ritzmann, Iris. 'Judenmord als Folge des "Schwarzen Todes": Ein medizinhistorischer Mythos?', *Medizin, Gesellschaft und Geschichte* 17 (1998): 101–30.

Robert, L. Nelson, ed. *Germans, Poland, and Colonial Expansion to the East: 1850 Through the Present.* Basingstoke: Macmillan, 2009.

Rohde, Achim. 'Der innere Orient: Orientalismus, Antisemitismus und Geschlecht im Deutschland des 18. bis 20. Jahrhunderts', *Die Welt des Islams* 45 (2005): 370–411.

Römer, Nils. *Jewish Scholarship and Culture in Nineteenth-Century Germany: Between History and Faith.* Madison: University of Wisconsin Press, 2005.

Rommelspacher, Birgit. 'Was ist eigentlich Rassismus?' in *Rassismuskritik, vol. 1: Rassismustheorie und -forschung*, edited by Paul Mecherli and Claus Melter. Schwalbach: Wochenschau-Verlag, 2009, 25–38.

Rosman, Moshe. 'Jewish History across Borders', in *Rethinking European Jewish History*, edited by Jeremy Cohen and Moshe Rosman. Portland: Litman Library of Jewish Civilization, 2009, 15–29.

Rothberg, Michael. *Multidirectional Memory: Remembering the Holocaust in the Age of Decolonization.* Stanford: Stanford University Press, 2009.

Rüger, Adolf. 'Die Duala und die Kolonialmacht 1884–1914: Eine Studie über die historischen Wurzeln des afrikanischen Antikolonialismus', in *Kamerun unter deutscher Kolonialherrschaft*, edited by Helmuth Stoecker. Berlin: VEB Deutscher Verlag der Wissenschaften, 1968, 181–257.

Rürup, Mirjam. *Ehrensache: Jüdische Studentenverbindungen an deutschen Universitäten 1886–1937.* Göttingen: Wallstein, 2008.

Rürup, Reinhard. *Emanzipation und Antisemitismus: Studien zur Judenfrage der bürgerlichen Gesellschaft.* Göttingen: Vandenhoeck & Ruprecht, 1975.

Rürup, Reinhard. 'Emanzipation und Krise – Zur Geschichte der "Judenfrage" in Deutschland vor 1890', in *Juden im Wilhelminischen Deutschland 1890–1914*, edited by Werner E. Mosse. Tübingen: J.C.B. Mohr, 1976, 1–56.

Said, Edward. *Orientalism.* New York: Vintage Books, 1979.

Salamana, Omar Jabary, Mezna Quato, Kareem Rabie, and Sobhi Samour, 'Past is Present: Settler Colonialism in Palestine', *Settler Colonial Studies* 2, no. 1 (2012): 1–8.

Salzborn, Samuel. *Antisemitismus als negative Leitidee der Moderne: Sozialwissenschaftliche Theorien im Vergleich.* Frankfurt am Main: Campus, 2010.

Salzborn, Samuel. *Globaler Antisemitismus: Eine Spurensuche in den Abgründen der Moderne*, 2nd edn. Weinheim: Beltz Juventa, 2020.

Sandler, Willeke. *Empire in the Heimat: Colonialism and Public Culture in the Third Reich.* New York: Oxford University Press, 2018.

Schäfer, Julia. *Vermessen – gezeichnet – verlacht: Judenbilder in populären Zeitschriften 1918–1933.* Frankfurt am Main: Campus, 2005.

Schatz, Holger, and Andrea Woeldike. *Freiheit und Wahn deutscher Arbeit: Zur historischen Aktualität einer folgenreichen antisemitischen Projektion.* Münster: Unrast Verlag, 2001.

Schechter, Ronald. *Obstinate Hebrews: Representations of Jews in France, 1715–1815.* Berkeley: University of California Press, 2003.

Schiefel, Werner. *Bernhard Dernburg, 1865–1937: Kolonialpolitiker und Bankier im wilhelminischen Deutschland.* Zurich: Atlantis, 1974.

Schilling, Britta. *Postcolonial Germany: Memories of Empire in a Decolonized Nation.* New York: Oxford University Press, 2014.

Schoeps, Hans-Joachim. *Das Judenchristentum: Untersuchungen über Gruppenbildungen und Parteikämpfe in der frühen Christenheit.* Bern: Francke, 1964.

Schorsch, Ismar. *Leopold Zunz: Creativity in Adversity.* Philadelphia: University of Pennsylvania Press, 2016.

Schrag, Peter. *The World of Aufbau: Hitler's Refugees in America.* Madison: University of Wisconsin Press, 2019.

Schreier, Joshua. *Arabs of the Jewish Faith: The Civilizing Mission in Colonial Algeria.* New Brunswick, 2010.

Schroeter, Daniel J. *The Sultan's Jew: Morocco and the Sephardic World.* Stanford, 2002.

Schüler-Springorum, Stefanie. *Die jüdische Minderheit in Königsberg/Preußen, 1871–1945.* Göttingen: Vandenhoeck & Ruprecht, 1996.

Sevitch, Benjamin. 'W.E.B. Du Bois and Jews: A Lifetime of Opposing Anti-Semitism', *The Journal of African American History* 87 (2002): 323–37.

Shimoni, Gideon. 'Post-Colonial Theory and the History of Zionism', *Israel Affairs* 13 (2007): 859–71.

Shohat, Ella. 'Taboo Memories and Diasporic Visions: Columbus, Palestine and the Arab-Jews', in *Performing Hybridity*, edited by May Joseph and Jennifer Natalya Fink. Minneapolis: University of Minneapolis Press, 1999, 131–56.

Shooman, Yasemin. 'Islamfeindlichkeit und Antisemitismus – Diskursive Analogien und Unterschiede', in *Antisemitismus: Ein gefährliches Erbe mit vielen Gesichtern*, edited by Milena Detzner and Ansgar Drücker. Düsseldorf: IDA, 2012, 25–7.

Shumsky, Dimitry. *Zweisprachigkeit und binationale Idee: Der Prager Zionismus 1900–1930*. Göttingen: Vandenhoeck & Ruprecht, 2012.

Sieg, Ulrich. *Jüdische Intellektuelle im Ersten Weltkrieg: Kriegserfahrungen, weltanschauliche Debatten und kulturelle Neuentwürfe*. Berlin: Akademie-Verlag, 2001.

Silberstein, Laurence J. *Postzionism Debates: Knowledge and Power in Israel Culture*. New York: Routledge, 1999.

Simon, Ernst. 'Robert Weltsch als Politiker, Historiker und Erzieher im Vergleich mit Buber und Scholem', *Bulletin des Leo Baeck Instituts* 64 (1983): 15–28.

Skolnik, Jonathan. *Jewish Pasts, German Fictions: History, Memory, and Minority Culture in Germany, 1824–1955*. Stanford: Stanford University Press, 2014.

Soénius, Ulrich. *Koloniale Begeisterung im Rheinland während des Kaiserreichs*. Köln: Selbstverlag, 1992.

Speitkamp, Winfried. *Deutsche Kolonialgeschichte*, 3rd edn. Stuttgart: Reclam, 2014.

Speyer, Heinrich. *Von den biblischen Erzählungen im Qoran*. Berlin: Akademie für die Wissenschaft des Judentums, 1924.

Spivak, Gayatri. 'Can the Subaltern Speak?', in *Colonial Discourse and Post-Colonial Theory: A Reader*, edited by Patrick Williams and Laura Chrisman. New York: Columbia University Press, 1994, 66–111.

Stähler, Axel. 'Orientalist Strategies of Dissociation in a German "Jewish" Novel: Das neue Jerusalem (1905) and Its Context', *Forum for Modern Language Studies* 45 (2009): 51–89.

Stähler, Axel. *Zionism, the German Empire, and Africa: Jewish Metamorphoses and the Colors of Difference*. Berlin: De Gruyter, 2019.

Stein, Sarah Abrevaya. *Saharan Jews and the Fate of French Algeria*. Chicago: University of Chicago Press, 2014.

Sternfeld, Lior. *Between Iran and Zion: Jewish Histories of Twentieth Century Iran*. Palo Alto: Stanford University Press, 2018.

Sternfeld, Lior. '"Poland Is Not Lost While We Still Live": The Making of Polish Iran, 1941–1945', *Jewish Social Studies* 23 (2018): 101–27.

Strauss, Herbert A. 'Robert Weltsch und die Jüdische Rundschau', in *Berlin und der Prager Kreis*, edited by Margarita Pazi and Hans Dieter Zimmermann. Würzburg: Königshausen & Neumann, 1991, 31–43.

Strauss, Herbert A. 'Zum zeitgeschichtlichen Hintergrund zionistischer Kulturkritik: Scholem, Weltsch und die jüdische Rundschau', in *Juden in Deutschland: Emanzipation, Integration, Verfolgung und Vernichtung*, edited by Peter Freimark, Alice Jankowski, and Ina Lorenz. Hamburg: Christians, 1991, 375–87.

Tal, Uriel. *Christians and Jews in Germany: Religion, Politics, and Ideology in the Second Reich, 1870–1914*. Translated by Noah Jacobs. Ithaca: Cornell University Press, 1975.

Tolzmann, Don Heinrich. 'The German Image of Cincinnati Before 1830', *Queen City Heritage* 42, no. 3 (1984): 31–8.

Toury, Jacob. 'Emanzipation und Judenkolonien in der öffentlichen Meinung Deutschlands (1775–1819)', *Jahrbuch des Instituts für deutsche Geschichte* 11 (1982): 17–53.

Trouillot, Michel-Rolph. *Silencing the Past: Power and the Production of History*. Boston: Beacon Press, 1995.

van Rahden, Till. *Juden und andere Breslauer: Die Beziehungen zwischen Juden, Protestanten und Katholiken in einer deutschen Großstadt von 1860 bis 1925*. Göttingen: Vandenhoeck & Ruprecht, 2000.

Veracini, Lorenzo. *Settler Colonialism: A Theoretical Overview*. Basingstoke: Palgrave Macmillan, 2010.

Veracini, Lorenzo. 'Introducing: Settler Colonial Studies', *Settler Colonial Studies* 1 (2011): 1–12.

Verheyen, Nina. *Die Erfindung der Leistung*. München: Hanser, 2018.

Vital, David. *Zionism: The Formative Years*. Oxford: Clarendon Press, 1982.

Voß, Rebekka. 'Entangled Stories: The *Red Jews* in Premodern Yiddish and German Apocalyptic Lore', *AJS Review* 36 (2012): 1–41.

Voß, Rebekka. *Disputed Messiahs: Jewish and Christian Messianism in the Ashkenazic World during the Reformation*. Detroit: Wayne State University Press, 2021.

Vogt, Stefan. 'Robert Weltsch and the Paradoxes of Anti-Nationalist Nationalism', *Jewish Social Studies* 16 (2010): 85–115.

Vogt, Stefan. 'Zionismus und Weltpolitik: Die Auseinandersetzung der deutschen Zionisten mit dem deutschen Imperialismus und Kolonialismus, 1890–1918', *Zeitschrift für Geschichtswissenschaft* 60 (2012): 596–617.

Vogt, Stefan. *Subalterne Positionerungen: Der deutsche Zionismus im Feld des Nationalismus in Deutschland 1890–1933*. Göttingen: Wallstein, 2016.

Vogt, Stefan. 'Juden in der Deutschen Kolonialgesellschaft: Eine Fallstudie zu Ernst Vohsen', *Zeitschrift für Geschichtswissenschaft* 68 (2020): 1012–27.

Vogt, Stefan. 'Zwischen Togo und Tel Aviv: Otto Warburg als Jude und Zionist in der deutschen Kolonialbewegung', *Geschichte in Wissenschaft und Unterricht* 72 (2021): 416–30.

Volkov, Shulamit. 'Antisemitism as Cultural Code: Reflections on the History and Historiography of Antisemitism in Imperial Germany', *Leo Baeck Institute Yearbook* 23 (1978): 25–46.

Volkov, Shulamit. 'Die Verbürgerlichung der Juden in Deutschland als Paradigma', in *Jüdisches Leben und Antisemitismus im 19. und 20. Jahrhundert: Zehn Essays*. München: Beck, 1990, 111–30.

Volkov, Shulamit. 'Reflections on German-Jewish Historiography: A Dead End or a New Beginning?', *Leo Baeck Institute Yearbook* 41 (1996): 309–20.

Volkov, Shulamit. *Die Juden in Deutschland, 1780–1918*, 2nd edn. München: Oldenbourg, 2000.

von Braun, Christina. 'Und der Feind ist Fleisch geworden: Der rassistische Antisemitismus', in *Der ewige Judenhass: Christlicher Antijudaismus, Deutschnationale Judenfeindlichkeit, Rassistischer Antisemitismus*, edited by Christina von Braun and Ludger Heid. Berlin: Philo, 2000, 149–213.

von Braun, Christina, and Eva-Maria Ziege, eds. *Das 'bewegliche' Vorurteil: Aspekte des internationalen Antisemitismus*. Würzburg: Königshausen & Neumann, 2004.

von den Brincken, Anna-Dorothee. 'Gog und Magog', in *Die Mongolen: Ein Volk sucht seine Geschichte. Begleitband zur Ausstellung 'Die Mongolen', Haus der Kunst München, 2. März bis 28. Mai 1989*, edited by Walther Heissig and Claudius C. Müller. Innsbruck: Pinguin, 1989, 27–9.

Walkenhorst, Peter. *Nation – Rasse – Volk: Radikaler Nationalismus im Deutschen Kaiserreich 1890–1914*. Göttingen: Vandenhoeck & Ruprecht, 2007.

Wallerstein, Immanuel. 'The Ideological Tensions of Capitalism: Universalism versus Racism and Sexism', in *Race, Nation, Class: Ambiguous Identities*, edited by Immanuel Wallerstein and Etienne Balibar. London and New York: Verso, 1991, 29–36.

Wehler, Hans-Ulrich. *Deutsche Gesellschaftsgeschichte*, 5 vols. München: Beck, 1987–2008.

Wehler, Hans-Ulrich. *Das Deutsche Kaiserreich, 1871–1918*. Göttingen: Vandenhoeck & Ruprecht, 1994.

Weinreich, Max. *Hitler's Professors: The Part of Scholarship in Germany's Crimes Against the Jewish People*. New Haven: Yale University Press, 1999.

Weinryb, Sucher B. *Der Kampf um die Berufsumschichtung: Ein Ausschnitt aus der Geschichte der Juden in Deutschland*. Berlin: Schocken, 1936.

Weir, Gary E. *Building the Kaiser's Navy: The Imperial Naval Office and German Industry in the von Tirpitz Era, 1890–1919*. Annapolis, MD: Naval Institute Press, 1992.

Wiegel, Gerd. *Die Zukunft der Vergangenheit: Konservativer Geschichtsdiskurs und kulturelle Hegemonie*. Köln: PappyRossa, 2001.

Wiese, Christian. 'Struggling for Normality. The Apologetics of Wissenschaft des Judentums as an Anti-colonial Intellectual Revolt against the Protestant Construction of Judaism', in *Towards Normality? Acculturation and Modern German Jewry*, edited by Rainer Liedtke and David Rechter. Tübingen: Mohr Siebeck, 2003, 77–101.

Wiese, Christian. *Challenging Colonial Discourse: Jewish Studies and Protestant Theology in Wilhelmine Germany*. Leiden: Brill, 2005.

Wiese, Christian. 'The Janus Face of Nationalism: The Ambivalence of Zionist Identity in Robert Weltsch and Hans Kohn', *Leo Baeck Institute Yearbook* 51 (2006): 103–30.

Wiese, Christian. 'Das 'dämonische Antlitz des Nationalismus': Robert Weltschs zwiespältige Deutung des Zionismus angesichts von Nationalsozialismus und Shoah', *Zeitschrift für Geschichtswissenschaft* 60 (2012): 618–45.

Wiese, Christian. 'Martin Buber und die Wirkung des Ersten Weltkriegs auf die Prager Zionisten Hugo Bergmann, Robert Weltsch und Hans Kohn', in *Texturen des Krieges:*

Bibliography

Körper, Schrift und der Erste Weltkrieg, (Tel Aviver Jahrbuch für deutsche Geschichte, vol. 43), edited by Galili Shahar. Göttingen: Wallstein, (2015): 181–222.

Winkler, Heinrich August. *Der lange Weg nach Westen*, 2 vols. München: Beck, 2000.

Wintle, Michael J. *The Image of Europe: Visualizing Europe in Cartography and Iconography Throughout the Ages*. Cambridge: Cambridge University Press, 2009.

Wirz, Albert. *Vom Sklavenhandel zum kolonialen Handel: Wirtschaftsräume und Wirtschaftsformen in Kamerun vor 1914*. Zurich: Atlantis-Verlag, 1972.

Wisnovsky, Robert. 'Islam', in M.W.F. Stone and Robert Wisnovsky, 'Philosophy and Theology', in *The Cambridge History of Medieval Philosophy*, vol. 2, edited by Robert Parnau. Cambridge: Cambridge University Press, 2010, 687–706.

Wolfe, Patricia. 'Settler Colonialism and the Elimination of the Native', *Journal of Genocide Research* 8 (2006): 387–409.

Young, Robert J.C. *Colonial Desire. Hybridity in Theory, Culture and Race*. London: Routledge, 1995.

Young, Robert E. *Postcolonialism: A Very Short Introduction*. Oxford: Oxford University Press, 2003, 14–16.

Yuval, Israel. *Two Nations in Your Womb: Perceptions of Jews and Christians in Late Antiquity and the Middle Ages*, Translated by Jonathan Chipman. Berkeley: University of California Press, 2006.

Zachhuber, Johannes. *Theology as Science in Nineteenth-Century Germany*. Oxford: Oxford University Press, 2013.

Zadoff, Mirjam. *Next Year in Marienbad: The Lost Worlds of Jewish Spa Culture*. Translated by. William Templer. 2007. Philadelphia: University of Pennsylvania Press, 2012.

Zantop, Susanne. *Colonial Fantasies: Conquest, Family, and Nation in Precolonial Germany, 1770–1870*. Durham: Duke University Press, 1997.

Zimmerer, Jürgen. 'Holocaust und Kolonialismus: Beitrag zur Archäologie des genozidalen Gedankens', *Zeitschrift für Geschichtswissenschaft* 51 (2003): 1098–119.

Zimmerer, Jürgen. 'Deutscher Rassenstaat in Afrika: Ordnung, Entwicklung und Segregation in "Deutsch Süd-West" (1884–1915)', in *Gesetzliches Unrecht: Rassistisches Recht im 20. Jahrhundert*, edited by Micha Brumlik, Susanne Meinl, and Werner Renz. Frankfurt am Main: Campus, 2005, 135–53.

Zimmerer, Jürgen. *Von Windhuk nach Auschwitz?* Berlin: Lit, 2011.

Zimmermann, Moshe. *Wilhelm Marr: The Patriarch of Anti-Semitism*. New York: Oxford University Press, 1986.

Zimmermann, Moshe. 'Hannah Arendt: The Early Post-Zionism', in *Hannah Arendt in Jerusalem*, edited by Steven E. Aschheim. Berkeley: University of California Press, 2001, 181–93.

Zipperstein, Steven J., and Elusive Prophet. *Ahad Ha'am and the Origins of Zionism*. Berkeley: University of California Press, 1993.

Index of Names

Abduh, Muḥammad 89
Abraham 99
Abulafia, Anna Sapir 96
Adorno, Theodor W. 123–5, 128, 133 n.42
Ahad Ha-am 189, 204 n.9, 212
Ahmed, Shahab 105
Akwa, Ludwig Mpundo 127
Albers, Hans 245
Ambrose 31
Améry, Jean 6
Arendt, Hannah 6, 14, 25, 66, 113, 209, 211, 221–7
el-Ariss, Tarek 102
Asad, Muhammad 264, *see also* Weiss, Leopold
Aschheim, Steven E. 2, 227
Augustine 29, 31, 53 n.93

Baeck, Leo 103
Baecker, Paul 239, 246
Balfour, Arthur 197
Banse, Ewald 240
Baur, Ferdinand Christian 92–3, 95
Bebel, August 163, 169, 175, 244
Beecher Stowe, Harriet 198
Bell, Rudolf Duala Manga 118, 124, 126–7
Bellachini, Samuel 183
Bergmann, Hugo 212, 214, 217–18, 230 n.33
Bergson, Henri 212
Bigland, John 35
Bindewald, Friedrich 161–2, 165
Bitzan, Amos 98
Blumenbach, Johann Friedrich 57, 71
Blumenfeld, Kurt 215, 221
Böhme, Hermann 239
Boyarin, Daniel 105
Braese, Stephan 79, 81
Brandt, Gustav 174–6
Braude, Benjamin 56

Brinkmann, Max 161, 163–5
Brinton, Crane 200
Brod, Max 212
Brumlik, Micha 110 n.71
Brunotte, Ulrike 8, 91
Bruns, Claudia 73–4
Buber, Martin 212–18, 225, 230 n.33
Bunzl, Matti 46

Campbell, James T. 191, 193, 200
Césaire, Aimé 6
Chamberlain, Houston Steward 44, 202
Chamberlain, Joseph 197
Chaplin, Charles 257
Cheng, Kimberly 276 n.4
Chevalier, Maurice 257
Cheyette, Bryan 25
Churchill, Winston 273
Church Terrell, Mary 114–17, 121, 127, 129 n.9, 130 n.9
Chwolson, Daniel 94
Claß, Heinrich 136, 139, 143, 145–6, 152 n.34, 155 n.66
Cogley, Richard 110 n.71
Cohen, Hermann 103
Columbus, Christopher 33, 51 n.51
Comestor, Petrus 32
Commager, Henry Steele 275
Cooper, Frederick 38
Copland, Patrick 35

Davis, Christian S. 7, 157
de Biberstein, Albin 100
de Blois, Francis 94
de Gobineau, Arthur 44
de Gurowski, Adam G. 43
Delany, Martin Robinson 14, 194–201
Dernburg, Bernhard 8, 14, 20 n.27, 141, 156–79, 180 n.15, 182 n.47, 183 n.59, 184 n.80, 184 n.94, 234, 243–4, 251 n.55, 251 n.57
Dernburg, Friedrich 20 n.27

Index of Names

Din, Adolf Ngoso 124, 126
Din, J. 127
Diner, Dan 8–9, 21 n.35
Dohm, Christian Wilhelm 13, 56–60,
    62–6, 67 n.2, 67 n.6, 68 n.23,
    69 n.25, 79–83, 91
Dubnow, Simon 219
Du Bois, W. E. B. 6, 25, 114–15, 117–18,
    127, 130 n.14, 201

Efron, John M. 158
Eickhoff, Richard 173
Ekwe, John 127
Emin Pasha 14–15, 232–48, *see also*
    Schnitzer, Eduard
Erlewine, Robert 110 n.71
Etoa, H. 127
Eusebius 31

Fanon, Frantz 25
Feiwel, Berthold 217
Fichte, Johann Gottlieb 212
Flake, Otto 246
Förster, Emil Theodor 154 n.51
Forster, Georg 71
Foß, Max W. L. 237
Frank, Walter 15, 232–5, 240–2, 245–8
Frederick the Great 58, 62–3, 66
Freißler, Ernst W. 236–7, 241
Frenkel-Brunswik, Else 133 n.43
Friedlaender, Israel 104
Fritsch, Theodor 139, 155 n.54
Frobenius, Leo 36
Funke, Alfred 243

Gabriel 101
Gandhi, Mahatma 264, 273, 279 n.32
Garvey, Marcus 201
Gastfreund, Isaac 100
Geiger, Abraham 94–6, 98–101–5,
    107 n.28
Genghis Khan 50 n.37
Gerstenhauer, Max Robert 137, 139, 142
Goldstein, Evan 102, 110 n.71
Grady, Tim 247
Graetz, Heinrich 99–103
Grossmann, Erika 259–62, 270, 274
Grossmann, Hans 259, 261–2, 264–7,
    272, 274

Grossmann, Walter 259, 262
Grühl, Max 235–6, 249 n.12
Guggenheimer, Walter Maria 276 n.9
Gulbransson, Olaf 171–3

Halpert, Bodo 122
Ham 38–40, 42–3, 53 n.93, 53 n.97
Hamann, Ulrike 8
Hanke, Christine 75
Harand, Irene 247–8
Harden, Maximilian 156–7, 232
Hasse, Ernst 138–40, 143–6, 152 n.30,
    152 n.36, 155 n.54
Hegel, Georg Wilhelm Friedrich 92
Heine, Heinrich 100
Heine, Thomas Theodor 173–4
Herder, Johann Gottfried 212
Herf, Jeffrey 26
Herzl, Theodor 143, 155 n.53, 187–90,
    194–201, 206 n.41, 212, 221
Heschel, Abraham Joshua 105
Hess, Jonathan M. 7, 43
Hieronymus 31
Hirschfeld, Hartwig 100
Holz, Klaus 122
Honig, Camille 273
Hornius, Georgius 42
Horovitz, Josef 104
Hugenberg, Alfred 150 n.13
Hume, David 36

Israel, Alfred 151 n.26

Jandorf, Adolf 162
Jansen, Sarah 121
Japheth 38–40, 42
Jentzsch, Hans Gabriel 167–8
Jerome 53 n.93
Jersch-Wenzel, Steffi 2
Jesus 37, 93–6, 99, 101–2, 104–5, 225
Johach, Eva 120
Johnson, Arthur 170, 174, 183 n.59
Jones Nelson, Alissa 55
Joseph II 59
Jost, Issac Markus 98
Jungmann, Max 177–8
Jüttner, Franz 161, 164–5

Kafka, Franz 212

Index of Names

Kampling, Rainer 55
Katz, Ethan B. 5, 8, 17 n.8, 38, 55 n.114
Kaul, Pragya 276 n.4
Kayser, Paul 8, 182 n.47, 234–5, 243–5, 247, 251 n.63
Keim, Theodor 104
Kga. (monogrammist) 170
Kimchi, David 31
King David 29
King George VI 267
Klinkhardt, Theodor 240–1
Koch, Max 151 n.26
Kohn, Hans 14, 209–20, 222, 225–7, 229 n.30, 230 n.33
Kolb, Peter 35
Kopp, Kristin 92
Kopsch, Julius 173
Köstlin, Karl Reinhard 93
Kreth, Hermann 169, 176

Landauer, Gustav 212
Lange, Friedrich 155 n.54
Lattmann, Wilhelm 139, 161, 165, 169, 176
Leff, Lisa Moses 5, 8, 17 n.8
Leppmann, Marianne 255–7, 260, 262, 276 n.9
Leschnitzer, Adolf 16 n.1
Levinson, Daniel, L. 133 n.42
Levy, Lital 91, 102
Lewis, Sinclair 279 n.35
Liberles, Robert 91
Libson, Gideon 105
Liebermann von Sonnenberg, Max 139, 176–8
Lloyd, Harold 257
Ludewig, Anna-Dorothea 110 n.71
Luther, Martin 38, 52 n.86

MacMaster, Neil 45
Major, John 33
Maksymiak, Malgorzata 110 n.71
Mandel, Maud S. 5, 8, 17 n.8
Mandeville, John 32
Mandola von Groß Batanga 127
Manga, Eb. 127
Maor, Zohar 216, 229 n.30
Marmion, Simon 40–1
Marr, Wilhelm 43, 91

Marrāsh, Francis b. Fatḥ Allāh 89
Mary 96
Masuzawa, Tomoko 110 n.71
Mauch, Karl 36
May, Karl 233, 243, 246
Mbembe, Achille 48 n.12
Meiners, Christoph 12, 57, 70–84, 85 n.23, 87 n.46, 87 n.59
Mendelssohn, Moses 62, 69 n.25
Messiah ben Yoseph 31
Meyer, Michael 100, 110 n.71
Meyer Leviné, Rosa 276 n.6
Michaelis, Johann David 13, 56–9, 62, 66, 67 n.8, 68 n.17
Mittwoch, Eugen 100
Moeurs, Josef Lafitous 34
Moses 56, 156, 169–73, 178–9, 183 n.59, 193, 199
Mosse, George L. 226
Moyal, Shimon 102
Mufti, Aamir 21 n.38, 91
Muhammad 36, 94, 98–102
Mulobi, M. 127
Münkler, Marina 30
Musch, Sebastian 110 n.71

Nehru, Jawaharlal 273, 279 n.32
Neuwirth, Angelika 104
Nevins, Allan 275
Nietzsche, Friedrich 102, 212
Noah 36, 38–40, 42, 44, 99
Nordau, Max 143–4, 154 n.53

Paget, James Carleton 94
Pahlavi, Mohammad Reza 262
Pahlavi, Reza Shah 256–7, 261–4
Parfitt, Tudor 34
Paul 99, 101
Peters, Carl 36, 135–6, 233–5, 238–41, 243–7
Philippson, Ludwig 100
Polaschegg, Andrea 97

Rashi (Rabbi Shlomo Yitzhaki) 31
Rathenau, Walther 173, 232
Reckendorff, Hermann 100
Rhenius, C. T. E. 51 n.57
Richarz, Monika 2
Riemer, Jeremiah 110 n.71

Index of Names

Ritschl, Albrecht 94
Roeren, Hermann 157
Rohde, Achim 78
Rohling, August 184 n.80
Römer, Nils 98
Roosevelt, Franklin D. 263
Rosenfeld, A. W. 272
Rosenhagen, Hans 160
Rosenzweig, Franz 100
Rosman, Moshe 105
Rothberg, Michael 21 n.35, 255
Rürup, Reinhard 2, 79, 129 n.5

Samassa, Paul 139
Samba, Martin-Paul 127
Sanford, R. Nevitt 133 n.42
Sassoon, Victor 270
Schäfer, Julia 121
Schapiro, Israel 100
Schedel, Hartmann 39–40, 42
Schelling, Friedrich Wilhelm 92
Schemann, Ludwig 71
Schenkel, Daniel 104
Schliemann, Adolph 94
Schnee, Heinrich 273
Schnitzer, Eduard 15, 232, 237, *see also* Emin Pasha
Schnitzer, Melanie 235, 249 n.12
Schoeps, Hans-Joachim 94
Schwarzkopf Sr., Norman 263
Schwegler, Albert 93
Schweitzer, Georg 237
Seifert, Hermann Erich 242
Selzer, Herman 279 n.28
Shem 36, 38–40, 42–4
al-Shidyāq, Aḥmad Fāris 89, 102
Shohat, Ella 33
Silverman, Sydney 273
Simon, Ernst 215
Singer, Paul 163, 169, 175
Slevogt, Max 158–61, 174
Solf, Wilhelm 119–25
Sombart, Werner 91
Speyer, Heinrich 100, 104
Spinoza, Baruch 160
Stahl, Luise 20 n.27
Stanley, Henry Morton 233, 238
Stern, Ernst 164
Stoler, Ann Laura 38

Strauss, David Friedrich 92
Stutz, Ludwig 165–6, 172–3, 176
Sweeney, Dennis 137

al-Ṭahṭāwī, Rifāʿa Rāfiʿ 89, 102
Tal, Uriel 104
Thiersfeld, Samuel 183 n.59
Thompson, Edward 264, 272, 279 n.29
Thompson, Edward P. 279 n.29
Tokozo, A. 127
Tyson, Joseph B. 110 n.71

Ullmann, Ludwig 100

Venerabilis, Peter 37
Verheyen, Nina 76–7
Vohsen, Ernst 141–2, 154 n.51
Volkmar, Gustav 96
Volkov, Shulamit 2
Voltaire 35, 43
von Arnim-Muskau, Traugott-Herrman 139
von Bethmann-Hollweg, Theobald 176
von Bismarck, Otto 90, 120–1, 238
von Braun, Christina 110 n.71, 121, 123, 125
von Bülow, Bernhard 156, 176–7, 190
von der Heydt, Karl 136
von Gökingk, Leopold Friedrich Günther 60
von Harnack, Adolf 94–5
von Hase, Karl 104
von Hippel, Theodor 91
von Liebert, Eduard 139
von Moltke, Helmuth 143, 155 n.54
von Ranke, Leopold 44, 98
von Repgow, Eike 32
von Tirpitz, Alfred 174–5
von Treitschke, Heinrich 91, 98, 144–5
von Wissmann, Hermann 234, 239
Voß, Rebekka 32

Waldseemüller, Martin 33
Wallerstein, Immanuel 77
Warburg, Otto 21 n.37, 189, 204 n.12
Washington, Booker T. 142, 154 n.50
Wavell, Archibald 267
Weber, Max 138, 151 n.25
Wehler, Hans-Ulrich 120

Weil, Gustav 100, 103
Weiss, Leopold 264, *see also* Asad,
    Muhammad
Weizman, Chaim 197
Welk, Ehm 236–7, 242, 246
Weltsch, Felix 14, 212
Weltsch, Robert 209–16, 218–26,
    228 n.6
Wendland, H. 140
Wichterich, Richard 239, 244
Wiemer, Otto 173
Wilhelm I 183 n.59
Wilhelm II 189–90, 233

Wirth, Albrecht 237
Wisnovsky, Robert 105
Woermann, Carl 162
Wolffsohn, David 190

Yuval, Israel 97, 105

Zantop, Susanne 71, 90
Ziege, Eva-Maria 123
Zimmerer, Jürgen 6, 26
zu Eulenburg, Philipp 190
zu Klampen, Erich 240, 244–5
Zunz, Leopold 95, 98, 103

Printed in the USA
CPSIA information can be obtained
at www.ICGtesting.com
LVHW022001260424
778553LV00001B/50